Studies in
Matthew

Studies in
Matthew

INTERPRETATION PAST AND PRESENT

DALE C. ALLISON JR.

Baker Academic
Grand Rapids, Michigan

Published by Baker Academic
a division of Baker Publishing Group
P.O. Box 6287, Grand Rapids, MI 49516-6287
www.bakeracademic.com

Printed in the United States of America

An earlier version of chapter 7 appeared as "Matthew: Structure, Biographical Impulse, and the *Imitatio Christi*," pages 1202–21 of *The Four Gospels 1992: Festschrift Frans Neirynck,* © 1992 by Leuven University Press. Used by permission.

An earlier version of chapter 9 appeared as "Divorce, Celibacy and Joseph (Matthew 1:18–25 and 19:1–12)," *JSNT* 49 (1993): 3–10, © 1993 by JSOT Press. Used by permission of Sage Publications.

An earlier version of chapter 10 appeared as "The Structure of the Sermon on the Mount," *JBL* 106/3 (1987): 423–45, © 1987 by The Society of Biblical Literature. Used by permission.

An earlier version of chapter 11 appeared as "Anticipating the Passion: The Literary Reach of Matthew 26:47–27:56," *CBQ* 56 (1994): 701–14, © 1994 by The Catholic Biblical Society of America.

Library of Congress Cataloging-in-Publication Data
Allison, Dale C.
   Studies in Matthew : interpretation past and present / Dale C. Allison.
      p.   cm.
   Includes bibliographical references and index.
   ISBN 0-8010-2791-8 (hardcover)
   1. Bible. N.T. Matthew—Criticism, interpretation, etc. I. Title.
BS2575.52.A45 2005
226.2′06—dc22

2005018430

To my mentors

† Clifford Allison
† Richard Burson
† Art Boyer
† W. D. Davies
† Jim Naylor

Ad astra per aspera

Contents

Preface

Many years ago, after completing the first draft of a commentary on Matt. 1–7, I decided, for no reason that I can remember, to look at nineteenth-century German commentaries, which I had theretofore ignored. I quickly learned that the twentieth-century literature I had immersed myself in was, far more often than I had anticipated, rehearsing questions and answers from an earlier era. I also, at about the same time, began to read patristic literature in earnest and soon discovered that the Fathers are not just rhetorically interesting and theologically rewarding but also from time to time offer valid exegetical insights that the secondary literature, to its detriment, has forgotten. Subsequent study over two decades has only further persuaded me of just how profoundly the exegetical present is indebted to the exegetical past, of just how valuable exhuming that past can be, and of just how unfortunate it is that so many in the guild make so little use of older commentators, whether from one hundred or three hundred or sixteen hundred years ago.

The present collection serves in part as a sort of apology for my convictions in this matter, especially part I, which offers six studies reflecting my ever-increasing interest in the history of interpretation. Of these six chapters, all appear for the first time, although the first grows out of a much shorter article, "What Was the Star That Guided the Magi?" *Bible Review* 9/6 (1993), pp. 20–24, 63. Returning to the subject has allowed me to supply full documentation for claims initially made in the earlier piece and to offer some much-needed corrections.

The seven chapters in part II rely far less upon distant exegetical history than the chapters in part I. Four take up earlier work. Chapter 7 revises my contribution to *The Four Gospels 1992: Festschrift Frans Neirynck* (BETL 100; ed. F. Van Segbroeck et al.; Leuven: Leuven University Press/

Peeters), pp. 1203–21, and earlier editions of chapters 9, 10, and 11 appeared in the *Journal for the Study of the New Testament* 49 (1993), pp. 3–10, the *Journal of Biblical Literature* 106/3 (1987), pp. 423–45, and the *Catholic Biblical Quarterly* 56 (1994), pp. 701–14, respectively. The present versions of these pieces are thorough rewrites that reflect changes of mind, introduce new observations, and take account of recent scholarship. Because they are so different from the earlier publications, I ask those wishing to engage my views to cite the essays in their current form.

I gratefully acknowledge my debt to my wife, Kristine Allison, and to my secretary, Kathy Anderson, for reading through the entire manuscript and catching numerous errors; to the late W. D. Davies, for many engaging conversations about Matthew and for his comments on earlier versions of several chapters; to Joel Marcus, for his constant willingness to offer honest criticism of my work; to Anita Johnson and the staff of the Barbour Library at Pittsburgh Theological Seminary, for their continuing assistance; to the editors of *CBQ, JBL, JSNT,* and Leuven University Press, for permission to reuse material published previously; and to James Ernest of Baker Academic, for his interest and encouragement; without him I would not have undertaken this project.

DALE ALLISON
Epiphany 2005

Abbreviations

The following abbreviations are used in the footnotes for journals, series, and modern reference works. Abbreviations for ancient and medieval writings are as found in standard lexicons, *The SBL Handbook of Style,* or *The Chicago Manual of Style.*

AASF	Annales Academiae Scientiarum Fennicae
AB	Anchor Bible
ACNT	Augsburg Commentaries on the New Testament
AnBib	Analecta biblica
ANRW	*Aufstieg und Niedergang der römischen Welt: Geschichte und Kultur Roms im Spiegel der neueren Forschung.* Edited by H. Temporini and W. Haase. Berlin: De Gruyter, 1972–.
ANTC	Abingdon New Testament Commentaries
ANTJ	Arbeiten zum Neuen Testament und Judentum
AR	*Archiv für Religionswissenschaft*
ARN	*ʾAbot de Rabbi Nathan*
ASNU	Acta Seminarii Neotestamentici Upsaliensis
AUSS	*Andrews University Seminary Studies*
BAR	*Biblical Archaeology Review*
BBB	Bonner biblische Beiträge
BDAG	F. W. Danker, ed. *A Greek-English Lexicon of the New Testament and Other Early Christian Literature.* 3d ed. Chicago: University of Chicago Press, 1999.
BDF	F. Blass, A. Debrunner, and R. W. Funk. *A Greek Grammar of the New Testament and Other Early Christian Literature.* Chicago: University of Chicago Press, 1961.
BETL	Bibliotheca Ephemeridum Theologicarum Lovaniensium

BGBE	Beiträge zur Geschichte der biblischen Exegese
Bib	*Biblica*
CBQ	*Catholic Biblical Quarterly*
CBQMS	Catholic Biblical Quarterly Monograph Series
CCCM	Corpus Christianorum: Continuatio Mediaevalis
CCSL	Corpus Christianorum: Series Latina
CIJ	*Corpus Inscriptionum Iudaicarum.* Edited by J. B. Frey. 2 vols. Rome: Pontificio Istituto di Archeologia Christiana, 1936–1952.
CNT	Commentaire du Nouveau Testament
ConBNT	Coniectanea Neotestamentica or Coniectanea Biblica: New Testament Series
ConBOT	Coniectanea Biblica: Old Testament Series
CSCO	Corpus Scriptorum Christianorum Orientalium
CSEL	Corpus Scriptorum Ecclesiasticorum Latinorum
DDD	*Dictionary of Deities and Demons in the Bible.* Edited by K. van der Toorn, B. Becking, and P. W. van der Horst. Leiden: Brill, 1995.
EDNT	*Exegetical Dictionary of the New Testament.* Edited by H. Balz and G. Schneider. ET. Grand Rapids: Eerdmans, 1990–1993.
EKKNT	Evangelisch-katholischer Kommentar zum Neuen Testament
EstBib	*Estudios bíblicos*
ExpTim	*Expository Times*
ETL	*Ephemerides Theologicae Lovanienses*
FBBS	Facet Books, Biblical Series
FB	Forschung zur Bibel
FC	Fontes Christiani
FRLANT	Forschungen zur Religion und Literatur des Alten und Neuen Testaments
FZPhTh	Freiburger Zeitschrift für Philosophie und Theologie
GCS	Die griechische christliche Schriftsteller der ersten [drei] Jahrhunderte
HDR	Harvard Dissertations in Religion
HNT	Handbuch zum Neuen Testament
HNTC	Harper's New Testament Commentaries
HO	Handbuch der Orientalistik
HSem	Horae Semiticae
HSM	Harvard Semitic Monographs
HTR	*Harvard Theological Review*
HUCA	*Hebrew Union College Annual*
IBS	*Irish Biblical Studies*
IBC	Interpretation: A Bible Commentary for Teaching and Preaching
ICC	International Critical Commentary

IDB	*The Interpreter's Dictionary of the Bible.* Edited by G. A. Buttrick. 4 vols. Nashville: Abingdon, 1962.
IJO	*Inscriptiones Judaicae Orientis.* Edited by David Noy et al. 3 vols. Tübingen: Mohr Siebeck, 2004.
JBL	*Journal of Biblical Literature*
JJS	*Journal of Jewish Studies*
JSJ	*Journal for the Study of Judaism in the Persian, Hellenistic, and Roman Periods*
JSNT	*Journal for the Study of the New Testament*
JSNTSup	Journal for the Study of the New Testament: Supplement Series
JTS	*Journal of Theological Studies*
KEK	Kritisch-exegetischer Kommentar über das Neue Testament (Meyer-Kommentar)
NCB	New Century Bible
NICNT	New International Commentary on the New Testament
NovT	*Novum Testamentum*
NovTSup	Novum Testamentum Supplements
NTA	*New Testament Apocrypha.* English translation edited by R. Mcl. Wilson. Rev. ed. 2 vols. Louisville: Westminster John Knox, 1991–1992.
NTAbh	Neutestamentliche Abhandlungen
NTM	New Testament Message
NTOA	Novum Testamentum et Orbis Antiquus
NTS	*New Testament Studies*
OECT	Oxford Early Christian Texts
OS	Oudtestamentische Studiën
OSJCB	Osnabrücker Studien zur Jüdischen und Christlichen Bibel
OTL	Old Testament Library
OTP	*Old Testament Pseudepigrapha.* Edited by J. H. Charlesworth. 2 vols. New York: Doubleday, 1983.
PAAJR	*Proceedings of the American Academy of Jewish Research*
PG	Patrologia Graeca [= Patrologiae cursus completus: Series graeca]. Edited by J.-P. Migne. 162 vols. Paris, 1857–1886.
PGM	*Papyri Graecae Magicae: Die griechischen Zauberpapyri.* Edited by K. Preisendanz. Leipzig, etc.: B. G. Teubner, 1928–1931.
PL	Patrologia Latina [= Patrologiae cursus completus: Series latina]. Edited by J.-P. Migne. 217 vols., Paris. 1844–1864.
PTS	Patristische Texte und Studien
RAC	*Reallexikon für Antike und Christentum.* Edited by T. Kluser et al. Stuttgart: A. Hiersemann, 1950–.
RB	*Revue biblique*
RevQ	*Revue de Qumran*

RHPR	*Revue d'histoire et de philosophie religieuses*
RNT	Regensburger Neues Testament
SAQ	Sammlung ausgewählter Kirchen- und dogmengeschichtlicher Quellenschriften
SB	H. L. Strack and P. Billerbeck. *Kommentar zum Neuen Testament aus Talmud und Midrasch.* 6 vols. Munich, 1922–1961.
SBLDS	Society of Biblical Literature Dissertation Series
SBS	Stuttgarter Bibelstudien
SBT	Studies in Biblical Theology
SC	Sources Chrétiennes
SCHNT	Studia ad Corpus Hellenisticum Novi Testamenti
SD	Studies and Documents
SEÅ	*Svensk exegetisk årsbok*
SHR	Studies in the History of Religions (supplement to *Numen*)
SJLA	Studies in Judaism in Late Antiquity
SNTSMS	Society for New Testament Studies Monograph Series
SPB	Studia Post-Biblica
SuppJSJ	Supplements to the Journal for the Study of Judaism
SVTP	Studia in Veteris Testamenti Pseudepigrapha
TDNT	*Theological Dictionary of the New Testament.* Edited by G. Kittel and G. Friedrich. Translated by G. W. Bromiley. 10 vols. Grand Rapids: Eerdmans, 1964–1976.
THKNT	Theologische Handkommentar zum Neuen Testament
ThTo	*Theology Today*
TNTC	Tyndale New Testament Commentaries
TSAJ	Texte und Studien zum antike Judentum
TU	Texte und Untersuchungen
TynBul	*Tyndale Bulletin*
TzF	Texte zur Forschung
VC	*Vigiliae Christianae*
WBC	Word Biblical Commentary
WUNT	Wissenschaftliche Untersuchungen zum Neuen Testament
ZBK	Zürcher Bibelkommentare
ZNW	*Zeitschrift für die neutestamentliche Wissenschaft und die Kunde der älteren Kirche*
ZKT	*Zeitschrift für Theologie und Kirche*

PART I

The
Exegetical
Past

I

The Magi's Angel

(MATT. 2:2, 9–10)

In Matthew's second chapter, "magi from the East" appear in Jerusalem and ask, "Where is the child who has been born king of the Jews?" They immediately add as explanation, "For we observed his star in the East, and have come to pay him homage" (2:1–2). What exactly they mean by "his star" goes unsaid. Commentators have tried, as is their duty, to fill in the blank. Modern exegetes in particular have often affirmed that Matthew's star must have been one of three things: a planetary conjunction, a comet, or a supernova, that is, a new star.[1]

---

1. Review of discussion in Raymond E. Brown, *The Birth of the Messiah* (new updated ed.; New York: Doubleday, 1993), pp. 170–73; also Ernest L. Martin, *The Birth of Christ Recalculated* (Pasadena: Foundation for Biblical Research, 1980), pp. 4–25. Recent arguments for a planetary conjunction appear in Mark Kidger, *The Star of Bethlehem: An Astronomer's View* (Princeton: Princeton University Press, 1999), and Michael R. Molnar, *The Star of Bethlehem: The Legacy of the Magi* (New Brunswick, N.J.: Rutgers University Press, 1999). For a helpful critique of Molnar see J. Neville Birdsall's substantive review in *ExpT* 114 (2002), pp. 96–98. Robert S. McIvor, "The Star of Messiah," *IBS* 24 (2002), pp. 175–83, thinks rather of a supernova while Colin J. Humphreys, "The Star of Bethlehem, a Comet in 5 BC and the Date of Christ's Birth," *TynBul* 43 (1992), pp. 31–56, argues for a comet.

Traditional Exegesis and Stars in Antiquity

Insuperable difficulties beset each of these well-known albeit ill-grounded proposals. Matthew tells us quite plainly that the star "went before" (προῆγεν) the magi,[2] and likewise that "it stopped over the place where the child was" (2:9: ἕως ἐλθὼν ἐστάθη ἐπάνω οὗ ἦν τὸ παιδίον). These assertions make no sense if the so-called "star" (ἀστήρ) was astronomical. Comets of course traverse the sky; and supernovas and conjunctions, because of the earth's motion, do at least appear to move. But that a lighted object high in the sky above could guide someone on the earth below to a precise location just does not compute. Chrysostom observed the truth of this long ago:

> Bethlehem's star did not, remaining on high, point out the place, for it was not possible for them [the magi] in this way to ascertain it. Instead it came down (κάτω καταβάς) and did this thing. For you know that a spot of such small dimensions, being only as much as a shed would occupy, or rather as much as the body of a little infant would take up, could not possibly be marked out by a star. For by reasons of its immense height, it could not sufficiently distinguish so confined a spot and reveal it to those who were desiring to see it. . . . How then, tell me, did the star point out a spot so confined, just the space of a manger and shed, unless it left that height and came down (κάτω κατέβη), and stood over the very head of the child (ὑπὲρ αὐτῆς ἔστη τῆς κεφαλῆς τοῦ παιδίου)?[3]

Theophylact, several centuries later, said much the same thing:

> The star descended (κατέβη) from the heights and came closer to the earth (προσγειότερος) to show the place to them [the magi]. For if it had appeared to them in the heights, how would they have been able to perceive the particular spot where Christ was? For the stars are visible over a great area. You may accordingly behold the moon over your house while it appears to me that it is over my house only. In short, the moon or a star appears to one and all to stand over them alone. So this star could not have indicated where Christ was unless it descended and stood over the head of the child (ἐπάνω τῆς κεφαλῆς τοῦ παιδίου ἔστη).[4]

Because Theophylact knew Chrysostom's writings well, indeed sometimes more or less copied them, one might regard his take on Matthew's star as nothing more than repetition of his revered predecessor. One

2. The evangelist uses προάγω + personal pronoun elsewhere, and its meaning is always clear: 14:22; 21:9, 31; 26:32; 28:7.

3. Chrysostom, *Hom. Matt.* 6.2(3) (PG 57.64–65). Cf. Bede, *VIII quaest.* 1 (ed. Gorman in *RBén* 109 [1999], pp. 63–64).

4. Theophylact, *Comm. Matt.* ad 2:9 (PG 123.165B–C).

cannot, however, think this of the *Protevangelium of James*, which was written in the (early?) second century, many decades before Chrysostom.[5] Here too we run across the notion that the star was unattached to the firmament, so that it could descend and travel to the infant Jesus, until it took its place over his head: "And the magi went forth. And behold, the star which they had seen in the East went before (προῆγεν) them, until they came to the cave. And it stood over the head of the child (ἔστη ἐπὶ τὴν κεφαλὴν τοῦ παιδίου). And the magi saw the young child with Mary his mother" (21:3).[6]

The interpretation common to Chrysostom, Theophylact, and the *Protevangelium of James*, according to which Matthew's star actually left the heavens, came down to earth, and led the magi to a particular house, perhaps even to the infant Jesus himself, was common among the church fathers. Here are three more examples:

And at his birth the star appeared to the magi who dwelt in the East, and through this they learned that Christ was born. And they came to Judea, led by the star, until the star came to Bethlehem where Christ was born and entered the house wherein the child was laid, wrapped in swaddling clothes; and it stood over his head, declaring to the magi the Son of God, the Christ. (Irenaeus, *Dem.* 58 [SC 406, ed. Rousseau, p. 168])

[The star] came down to the very place where the infant was [and it remained] on the Christ [just as, when later he submitted to John's baptism, the Holy Spirit in the form of a dove descended and] remained on him. (Origen, *Hom. Num.* 18.3[4])[7]

This star was in control of its course. It ascended and descended as though there were no link holding it, because it had power over the spaces in the air, as though not fixed in the firmament. When it hid itself, this [was] lest [the magi] come directly to Bethlehem. . . . After the star had brought them to the Son, it stood over its appointed place and disclosed him, and [thus] completed its journey. (Ephraem, *Comm. Diat.* 20–21)[8]

5. For the date see George T. Zervos, "Seeking the Source of the Marian Myth: Have We Found the Missing Link?" in *Which Mary? The Marys of Early Christian Tradition* (ed. F. Stanley Jones; Atlanta: Society of Biblical Literature, 2002), pp. 107–20.

6. There are textual variants. τὴν κεφαλὴν τοῦ σπηλαίου (the head of the cave) is attested as well as τὴν κεφαλὴν τοῦ παιδίου (the head of the child) and οὗ ἦν τὸ παιδίον (where the child was). See C. Tischendorf, *Evangelia Apocrypha* (Leipzig: Avenarius et Mendelssohn, 1853), p. 40. Translation adapted from *NTA* 1:436.

7. SC 29, ed. Méhat, p. 370. Contrast the rather different account in *C. Cels.* 1.58 (ed. Marcovich, pp. 59–60).

8. SC 121, ed. Leloir, pp. 76–77. Cf. *Hymn. nat.* 24.8–9 (CSCO 186, Scriptores Syri 82, ed. Beck, p. 123).

That the star of Bethlehem was "strange,"[9] that it was a guiding light independent of the heavens,[10] that it was more like Tinker Bell in *Peter Pan* than anything known to astronomical science, is the dominant opinion for much of exegetical history.[11] It even seems to show up in a textual

9. So Clement of Alexandria, *Exc.* 74 (SD 1, ed. Casey, p. 86).

10. There are other examples of guiding lights in ancient literature; see, e.g., Virgil, *Aen.* 2.690–704 (a blazing "star" that leaves in its wake a long furrow of light as it guides Aeneas to the west); Diodorus Siculus 16.66.3 (a comet goes before Timoleon of Corinth as he travels to Sicily; cf. Plutarch, *Tim.* 8.2–3[239D]); Clement of Alexandria, *Strom.* 1.24 (GCS 15, ed. Stählin, p. 102: a pillar of fire led Thrasybulas and the exiles from Phyla to safety); *Tg. Ps.-J.* on Gen. 22:4 (a pillar of cloud shows Abraham Mount Moriah; cf. *Tanh.* B *Wayyera* 4:46; *Gen. Rab.* 56:1; *Lev. Rab.* 20:2; *PRK* 26:3). *Acts of Paul* 10, if rightly reconstructed in the edition of Schubart and Schmidt (p. 54), refers to Jesus walking on the sea and "going before" (προῆγεν) and showing the way "as a star" (φωστὴρ ἀπεδίκνυεν)—but this may well reflect the influence of Matthew 2.

11. In addition to the *Protevangelium of James*, Irenaeus, Origen, Chrysostom, Ephraem, and Theophylact, see Theodore of Heraclea, *Comm. Matt.* frag. 10 ad 2:9–10 (TU 61, ed. Reuss, p. 59); Ps.-Eusebius of Caesarea, *Concerning the Star* (Syriac text printed in W. Wright, *Journal of Sacred Literature* 4th series 9 [1866], pp. 17–36; Eng. trans. in vol. 10 [1867], pp. 150–64); *Hymn of the Virgin Mary*, folio 3 recto–folio 4 verso (ed. Roca-Puig, p. 58); Basil the Great, *Hom. in sanct. Christi gen.* 6 (PG 31.1472B–C); Ps.-Caesarius of Nazianzus, *Dial.* 2, q. 107 (PG 38.973–75); Gregory of Nyssa, *Nativ.* (PG 46.1133D); Augustine, *C. Faust.* 2.5 (CSEL 25, ed. Zyca, pp. 259–60); Ps.-Theodotus of Ancyra, *Hom. 1* (PG 77.1364D–1365A); Peter Chrysologus, *Serm.* 156 (CCSL 24B, ed. Olivar, pp. 973–74); Isidore of Pelusion, *Ep.* 1.378 (PG 78.396C: the star pointed like a finger); Fulgentius, *Hom. 4, De epiph.* 8 (PL 65.756A); *Opus Imperfectum in Matthaeum* (PG 56.637–42: in this, as in Origen, *Hom. Num.* 18.3[4] [SC 29, ed. Méhat, p. 370], the star becomes a nimbus around Jesus' head; also, when it initially descends to the magi to instruct them, it takes the form of a little boy and there is a cross above him; Isho'dad of Merv, *Comm. Matt.* ad loc. (HSem 6, ed. Gibson, pp. 26–27); *Glossa Ordinaria* (PL 114.74D); Dionysius bar Salibi, *Expl. Evang.* ad Matt. 2:9 (CSCO 77, Scriptores Syri 33, ed. Sedlaeck and Chabot, p. 105); Ps.-Anselm = Geoffrey Babion, *En. Matt.* ad loc. (PL 162.1256C); Albertus Magnus, *Super Mt. cap. I–XIV* ad 2:2 (Opera Omnia 21/1, ed. B. Schmidt, p. 48); Aquinas, *ST* 3 q. 36 a. 7 (who in large part summarizes Chrysostom's observations); Solomon of Khilât, *Book of the Bee* 38 (ed. Budge, pp. 91–92: "It had no fixed path. It did not remain always in the height of heaven, but sometimes it came down, and sometimes it mounted up"); Gregory Abu'l Faraj = Bar-Hebraeus, *Commentary on the Gospels from the Horreum Mysterium* (trans. and ed. Wilmot Eardley W. Carr; London; SPCK, 1925), p. 10; John of Hildesheim, *Historia Trium Regum* 20 (ed. Horstmann, pp. 68–69: before entering the house the star actually sits on the ground); Martin Luther, *Sermons II* (Luther's Works 52; ed. Hillerbrand; Philadelphia: Fortress, 1974), p. 193 ("The Gospel for the Festival of Epiphany": "This star differed from the stars in the heaven in nature, orbit, and position, and was not a fixed star, as the astronomers call them, but a movable star able to rise and descend and turn in any direction"). Cornelius à Lapide, *The Great Commentary of Cornelius à Lapide* (6 vols.; 2nd ed.; London: John Hodges, 1874–87), 1:56, reports the old legend, attributed to Gregory of Tours, that the star eventually descended into a well! (Cf. John Trapp, *A Commentary upon the Old and New Testaments* [ed. W. Webster; 5 vols.; 2nd ed.; London: Richard D. Dickinson, 1865], 5:11: "They still show at Bethlehem a little hole over the place where our Saviour was born, through which the star fell down to the ground.") On pp. 58–59, Lapide himself argues that the star literally accompanied the magi, and he regards this as "the common opinion of

variant to Matt. 2:9: "until it [the star] stopped over the child."[12] That this
should be so is no mystery: the old interpretation takes the wording of the
text at face value. Matthew 2 speaks of a light appearing, disappearing,
and reappearing, of it going before the magi, and of it eventually stopping over the place where Jesus is. One understands Calvin's comment:
"We do . . . infer from Matthew's words that it was not a natural star,
but extra-ordinary, for it was not of the order of nature to disappear at
certain times, and afterwards suddenly to shine again. Further, that it led
in a straight path to Bethlehem, and at length stood fixed over the place
where Christ was. None of this accords with natural stars."[13] Perhaps
the traditional fourth stanza of "The First Nowell," the well-known
Christmas carol from eighteenth-century England, assumes what Calvin
asserts: "O'er Bethlehem it took its rest, / And there it did both stop and
stay, / Right over the place where Jesus lay."

In the last few centuries, however, a large number of expositors, either
unacquainted with or desirous of avoiding the traditional speculations
on this subject, have shied away from a literal reading of Matthew's text
and instead substituted modern science. They have assumed that if Matt.
2 speaks of a "star" (ἀστήρ), then current astronomical knowledge can
tell us what that means. Yet aside from meteors, which hardly stand still,
heavenly objects do not leave their distant locales and descend to earth.
Were a true star indeed to approach our planet, we would all soon perish
in an inferno. We may be grateful that the stars are so far away and keep
to their courses. But what then do we make of Bethlehem's star, which in
no way behaves like a comet, supernova, or conjunction?

The resolution to the question lies, I submit, in an all-important distinction between ancient and modern conceptions of the heavenly bodies.
Quite simply, Matthew's idea of a star was not our idea of a star. He never
imagined heavenly lights to be immense, inanimate, energetic masses mil-
lions of light-years away from, and thousands of times larger than, our
planet. Why on earth would he or any other ancient Jew or Christian
have thought such a thing? We should not read ourselves into the past.
Heraclitus thought that the sun is the breadth of a person's foot (frag. 57).
Anaximenes believed that the heavenly orbs, including sun and moon,

---

believers." Contrast Cyril of Alexandria, *Comm. Matt.* frag. 13 (TU 61, ed. Reuss, p. 157):
Cyril contends that the star stayed in the heavens (an argument that implies knowledge of people
who thought otherwise).

12. ἐστάθη ἐπάνω τὸ παιδίον (so D it) instead of the majority reading, ἐστάθη ἐπάνω οὗ ἦν
τὸ παιδίον.

13. John Calvin, *A Harmony of the Gospels Matthew, Mark, and Luke* (vol. 1; Grand Rapids:
Eerdmans, 1972), p. 83. He continues: "It is more probable that it was like a comet, seen in the
atmosphere rather than in the heaven. There is nothing strange in Matthew using the everyday
word and speaking, improperly, of a star."

are flat and two-dimensional (Achilles Tatius, *Isag.* 12; Hippolytus, *Ref.* 1.7.4 [PTS 25, ed. Marcovich, p. 66]). Cosmas Indicopleustes argued that the sun sets when the higher parts of the earth cover it (*Top.* 2.34 [SC 141, ed. Wolska-Conus, pp. 339–41]). Now the astronomical opinions of those who were not philosophers, including Matthew, can hardly have been more sophisticated than the imaginings of such prominent thinkers. More simply: the evangelist knew nothing of modern scientific knowledge. He rather was a citizen of antiquity; and, in antiquity, stars were widely thought to be alive.[14] "When people looked into the sky, they thought they saw living creatures, who looked back at them, who planned their lives, and who communicated with them. The 'laws' of astrology were the habits of the gods from this point of view."[15] This fact, I shall now argue, is an important clue for interpreting Matthew's text aright.

The belief that the heavens are alive, that there is "a spirit in the stars" (Tatian, *Or. ad Graec.* 12 [ed. Otto, p. 54]), belongs to worldwide folklore and in fact lies behind the common phenomenon of star-worship and the notion of astral immortality. There are Greek myths that depict divinities (Venus, for example) and heroes (such as Hercules and Andromeda) as stars. The Zoroastrian Pahlavi texts equate the Fravashis (the eternal spirits of humanity) with heavenly bodies (*Mēnōg-i-Xrat* 49.22–23). Egyptian belief identifies the dead Pharaoh with the Pole Star. Oceanic mythology holds that the stars are the children of the sun (female) and the moon (male). One could easily go on and on in this vein. The sources that speak of the stars as animate are abundant.

What counts most for us, however, is that matters were much the same in the Jewish tradition. Philo, for one, took it for granted, as did Plato and the Stoics, that the stars are living beings.[16] Consider these four texts:

---

14. As a general rule, it is unwise to read our own distinction between animate and inanimate objects into premodern texts; see Dale C. Allison Jr., "4 Q 403 fragm. 1, col. I, 38–46 and the Revelation to John," *RevQ* 47 (1986), pp. 409–14.

15. Lester J. Ness, "Astrology and Judaism in Late Antiquity" (PhD diss., Miami University, Oxford, Ohio, 1999); I quote from the online version at http://www.smoe.org/arcana/diss0.html, accessed Aug. 30, 2004. On the relationship between the star and astrology in the early church see Nicola Denzey, "A New Star on the Horizon: Astral Christologies and Stellar Debates in Early Christian Discourse," in *Prayer, Magic, and the Stars in the Ancient and Late Antique World* (ed. Scott Noegel, Joel Walker, and Brannon Wheeler; University Park, Pa.: Pennsylvania State University Press, 2003), pp. 207–21.

16. Plato, in fact, contended that the entire cosmos is a living creature: *Timaeus* 30B; cf. also 38E–39A. So too the Stoics. Aristotle's thinking on the subject of stars is inconsistent from text to text. "On the question of whether the stars themselves are *empsucha* ['ensouled'] he seems to have found it difficult to make up his mind"; so W. K. C. Guthrie, *A History of Greek Philosophy*, vol. 6, *Aristotle: An Encounter* (Cambridge: University Press, 1981), p. 256, n. 1. See further Alan Scott, *Origen and the Life of the Stars: A History of an Idea* (Oxford: Clarendon, 1991), pp. 24–38.

The stars found their place in heaven. Those who have made philosophy their study tell us that these too are living creatures, but of a kind composed entirely of mind. (*Plant.* 12)

Heaven has the stars. For the stars are souls divine and without blemish throughout, and therefore as each of them is mind in its purest form, they move in the line most akin to mind—the circle. (*Gig.* 8)

The air is the abode of incorporeal souls, since it seemed good to their Maker to fill all parts of the universe with living beings. He set land-animals on the earth, aquatic creatures in the seas and rivers, and in heaven the stars, each of which is said to be not a living creature only but mind of the purest kind through and through; and therefore in air also, the remaining section of the universe, living creatures exist. (*Somn.* 1.135)

Among existences, some partake neither of virtue nor vice, like plants and animals. . . . Others have partnership with virtue only, and have no part or lot in vice. Such are the heavenly bodies; for these are said to be not only living creatures but living creatures endowed with mind, or rather each of them a mind in itself, excellent through and through and unsusceptible of any evil. (*Opif.* 73)[17]

Philo represents a rather refined, philosophical Judaism. Yet his conviction about the stars was not just due to his immersion in Hellenistic thought; it also stood in continuity with his Jewish tradition. From very olden times, Jews thought of the heavens as alive.[18] Already Judg. 5:20 has this: "From heaven fought the stars, from their courses they fought against Sisera." This is more than oriental poetry and rhetoric.[19] The text envisages the involvement of the stars, the cosmic forces of heaven, in Israel's great victory.[20]

That premodern readers of the Bible could understand Judg. 5:20 quite literally, in a way that would never occur to us today, appears from *LAB* 31:1–2:

17. See further *Spec.* 1.12–20 and contrast Philo's agnosticism on the question in *Som.* 1.22–24. Philo translations throughout the present volume are from F. H. Colson, G. H. Whitaker, J. W. Earp, and Ralph Marcus, *Philo* (12 vols.; LCL; Cambridge: Harvard University Press, 1929–1953).

18. For the ancient Near Eastern background and for astral deities among Israel's neighbors see J. W. McKay, *Religion in Judah under the Assyrians* (SBT 2.26; London: SCM, 1973), pp. 45–59.

19. On the subject of mistakenly giving figurative meaning to texts that ancients understood literally see Dale C. Allison, *Jesus of Nazareth: Millenarian Prophet* (Minneapolis: Fortress, 1998), pp. 152–60.

20. Cf. Frank Moore Cross, *Canaanite Myth and Hebrew Epic* (Cambridge: Harvard University Press, 1973), p. 70; E. Theodore Mullen Jr., *The Divine Council in Canaanite and Early Hebrew Literature* (HSM 24; Chico, Calif.: Scholars Press, 1980), pp. 194–95.

And Deborah sent and summoned Barak, and she said to him, "Rise and gird your loins like a man, and go down and attack Sisera, because I see the stars moved from their course and readying for battle on your side." . . . And when Deborah and the people and Barak went down to meet the enemies, immediately the Lord disturbed the movement of his stars. And he said to them, "Hurry and go, for your enemies fall upon you; and confound their arms and crush the power of their heart, because I have come that my people may prevail. For even if my people have sinned, nevertheless I will have mercy on them." And when these words had been said, the stars went forth as had been commanded them and burned up their enemies. And the number of those gathered together in one hour and slain was 90 times 97,000 men; but they did not destroy Sisera, because so it had been commanded them.[21]

In *b. Pesaḥ.* 118b we find yet another very literal—and to us preposterous—take on Judg. 5:20:

When Sisera came he advanced against them [the Israelites] with iron staves. Thereupon the Holy One, blessed be he, brought forth the stars out of the orbits against them [the army of Sisera], as it is written, "The stars in their courses fought against Sisera." As soon as the stars of heaven descended upon them, they [the stars] heated those staves; so they went down to cool them and to refresh themselves in the brook of Kishon. Said the Holy One, blessed be he, to the brook of Kishon, "Go and deliver your pledge." Straightway the brook of Kishon swept them out and cast them into the sea.

Without modern scientific knowledge, people who regularly saw what we even today call "falling stars" had no reason to doubt that the lights in the night sky could descend from heaven to earth and do things we would never imagine.

Job 38:7 also reflects a way of thinking about the heavenly lights now utterly foreign to us. Here we read of a time "when the morning stars sang together, and all the sons of God shouted together." These two lines are in synonymous parallelism, which "suggests that they [the angelic Sons of God] are considered one with the stars."[22] In line with this, and as a glance at the Hebrew dictionaries attests, the heavenly hosts (צבאות) are in some biblical texts the angels, in others the heavenly bodies.[23]

21. Trans. D. J. Harrington, *OTP* 2:344. Cf. 32:15 ("the stars fought for them"), 17 ("he has diverted the stars from their positions and attacked our enemies").

22. Norman C. Habel, *The Book of Job* (OTL; Philadelphia: Westminster, 1985), p. 538. Cf. Robert Gordis, *The Book of Job: Commentary, New Translation, and Special Studies* (New York: Jewish Theological Seminary, 1978), p. 443. Note also Job 15:15; 25:5.

23. See further Bernhard W. Anderson, "Host, Host of Heaven," *IDB* 2:654–56. Note also that צבאות can be translated by στρατία (army), ἀστέρες (stars), and ἄστρα (stars, constellation): LXX 1 Kings 22:19; Neh. 9:6; Dan. 8:10; and Eusebius, *Comm. Isa.* 2:7 ad 34:4 (GCS 53a, ed. Ziegler, p. 221).

The preceding paragraphs only begin to introduce the evidence. Many Jewish and Christian texts speak of stars as though they are animate while others conceptualize them as angels. To leave no doubt about the subject, I append to the present chapter a large sampling of the relevant material. Angels and stars go together.[24]

Pertinent Motifs in Jewish and Christian Literature

Before returning to Matthew's star, we should note several recurrent themes in Matthew's literary environment.

Angels as guides. The depiction of angels as guides was a standard motif. Exodus 14:19, in recounting how the children of Israel were led out of Egypt, says this: "The angel of God who was going before the Israelite army moved and went behind them; and the pillar of cloud moved from in front of them and took its place behind them."[25] Whether we have here the mixing of two different traditions—the Israelites were led by an angel versus the Israelites were led by a cloud[26]—or whether the text implies simply that the pillar was an angel or had within it an angel (so Philo, *Mos.* 1.166),[27] the idea that an angel led the way is clearly set

24. See further Wilhelm Bousset and Hugo Gressmann, *Die Religion des Judentums im späthellenistischen Zeitalter* (HNT 21; Tübingen: Mohr Siebeck, 1926), pp. 322–23 (suggesting that the designation of angels as "watchers" was borrowed from the stars); Cornelis Houtman, *Der Himmel im Alten Testament: Israels Weltbild und Weltanschauung* (OS 30; Leiden: Brill, 1993), pp. 194–204; F. Lelli, "Stars," in *Dictionary of Deities and Demons in the Bible* (ed. Karl van der Toorn, Bob Becking, and Pieter W. van der Horst; 2nd rev. ed.; Leiden: Brill, 1999), pp. 809–15; and Michael Mach, *Entwicklungsstadien des jüdischen Engelglaubens in vorrabbinischer Zeit* (TSAJ 34; Tübingen: Mohr-Siebeck, 1992), pp. 173–84. Oddly enough, the belief may not be wholly defunct in certain quarters. The famous twentieth-century evangelist William Marrion Branham told of a vision in which a ball of light, described as a "great star," transferred itself into an angelic messenger. See David Edwin Harrell Jr., *All Things Are Possible: The Healing and Charismatic Revivals in Modern America* (Bloomington, Ind.: Indiana University Press, 1975), pp. 27–28.
Angels were also often thought to move and guide the stars and sun and moon; see, e.g., *1 En.* 80:1; 82:11–12; 1QH 1:6–13; *Asc. Isa.* 4:18; *2 En.* 4:1–2; *T. Adam* 4:4—a belief that lived on among Christian thinkers; note, e.g., Clement of Alexandria, *Strom.* 5.37.2; Theodore of Mopsuestia, *Comm. Col.* ad 1:16 (ed. Swete, pp. 270–71); Cosmas Indicopleustes, *Top.* 2.83–84 (SC 141, ed. Wolska-Conus, pp. 401–3); Aquinas, *In II Sent. dist.* 14, art. 3c. Even someone as late as Kepler could deem angels to be the inner movers of stars; see Harry A. Wolfson, "The Problem of the Souls of the Spheres: From the Byzantine Commentaries on Aristotle through the Arabs and St. Thomas to Kepler," *Dumbarton Oaks Papers* 16 (1962), pp. 92–93, and cf. Marsilio Ficino, *Opera Omnia* (repr., Turin, 1959–1961), 1:489–90.
25. Cf. Exod. 13:21; 14:19; 23:20, 23; 40:38; Num. 9:15–23; Neh. 9:19; Ps. 78:14; 105:39; Wisd. 10:17; 18:1–4.
26. Scholars have commonly assigned the angel to E, the pillar to J.
27. This judgment was probably not confined to Philo. *Sepher Ha-Razim* Firmament 1.225–32 (ed. Margalioth, pp. 79–80), speaks of an angel who appears as a pillar of fire. Furthermore,

forth. As Exod. 23:20 explains: "I am going to send an angel in front of you, to guard you on the way and to bring you to the place that I have prepared." This declaration, that Israel had an angelic guide, reappears in 23:23; 32:34; and 33:2. It is no surprise, then, that something similar shows up in other ancient texts.

One of these texts is the very strange *History of the Rechabites*, of uncertain date and origin. At the beginning of this document, which is Christian in its present form (although it could take up Jewish materials), God sends an angel to the pious Zosimus to guide him on his trek to find the island of the blessed Rechabites. The angel initially addresses the monk with these words: "Zosimus, O man of God, I have been sent to you from the height (of heaven) to guide you and to show you the way so that you may journey and see these Blessed Ones as you petitioned the Lord" (1:3).[28] As the island turns out to be much like heaven, one is reminded of how often angels, in the apocalyptic literature, appear as tour guides: they conduct seers to otherworldly places and reveal divine secrets.[29]

Another illustration comes from the *Apocalypse of Elijah*, a Christian work of the third or late second century. Its depiction of the latter days includes this:

> On that day the Christ will take pity on those who are his own. And he will send from heaven his sixty-four thousand angels, each of whom has six wings. The sound will move heaven and earth when they give praise and glorify. Now those upon whose forehead the name of Christ is written and upon whose hand is the seal, both the small and the great, will be taken up upon their wings and lifted up before his wrath. Then Gabriel and Uriel will become a pillar of light leading them into the holy land. (5:2–5)[30]

Here, as in Philo, *Mos.* 1.166, where the pillar of cloud that led Israel through the wilderness is an angel, Gabriel and Uriel become guides by taking the form of "a pillar of light."[31]

(i) "The angel of God who was going before the Israelite army" (Exod. 14:19) has no anteced-ent, unless it be 13:21–22, where the pillar of cloud by day and fire by night goes before Israel, and (ii) if the angel moves and goes behind the Israelite army, the cloud does exactly the same thing (14:19): the two are either one or they act in tandem. For some relevant later Christian texts see n. 34.

28. Trans. J. H. Charlesworth, *OTP* 2:450.

29. *1 En.* 1–36; *T. Levi* 2–5; Revelation; *T. Ab.* 10–15; *3 Baruch*; *2 Enoch*; *Mart. Ascen. Isa.* 6–11; etc.

30. Trans. O. S. Wintermute, *OTP* 1:750.

31. Other texts in which angels serve as guides: Gen. 24:7, 40; Exod. 32:34; 33:2; Tob. 5:1–7:8.

The brightness of angels. Consistent with their sometime identity as stars, angels are often bright.[32] To cite five examples, the first four of which come from the first century CE: (1) the angel at Jesus' tomb in the Gospel of Matthew has the appearance of lightning (28:3); (2) Paul could write that Satan disguises himself as "an angel of light" (2 Cor. 11:14); (3) *Life of Adam and Eve* 29:15 (Greek) explains that Satan, in order to deceive Eve, made himself appear as an angel, and specifically like "the brightness of angels"; (4) the *Testament of Job* tells us that a "very bright light" conversed with Job and explains that this light was an angel (3:1; 4:1; 5:2); (5) the Dead Sea Scrolls refer to the archangel Michael as "the Prince of Lights" (1QS 3:20; 1QM 13:9–10; cf. 4Q405 46: אלוהי אורים—"Elohim of the Lights"). The meaning of Acts 6:15, when it states that Stephen's face "was like the face of an angel," is patent: it shone (cf. *Acts Paul. Thec.* 3; *Hist. monach. Aeg.* 2 [ed. Festugière, p. 35]).

Angels descending. In the Judeo-Christian tradition, angels, like "falling stars," regularly descend from heaven to earth. The story of Jacob's ladder in Gen. 28 comes immediately to mind (cf. John 1:51), as does the passage in 3 Macc. 6:16–29 where God opens "heaven's gates" to send forth two angels of glorious appearance who thereupon confound the persecutors of the righteous Jews. The author of Revelation twice declares, "And I saw an angel come down from heaven" (18:1; 20:1).

Perhaps most interesting for our purposes is the fourteenth chapter of *Joseph and Aseneth*. This seems to tell of a star in heaven that, come to earth, turns into an angel:

> And when Aseneth had ceased making confession to the Lord, behold, the morning star rose out of heaven in the east. And Aseneth saw it and rejoiced and said, "So the Lord God listened to my prayer, because this star rose as a messenger [ἄγγελος] and herald of the light of the great day." And Aseneth kept looking, and behold, close to the morning star, the heaven was torn apart and great and unutterable light appeared. And Aseneth saw (it) and fell on (her) face on the ashes. And a man came to her from heaven and stood by Aseneth's head. And he called her and said, "Aseneth, Aseneth." And she said, "Who is he that calls me, because the door of my chamber is closed, and the tower is high, and how then did he come into my chamber?" And the man called her a second time and said, "Aseneth, Aseneth." And she said, "Behold, (here) I (am), Lord. Who are you, tell me." And the man said, "I am the chief of the

32. Cf. the idea that angels are fiery: 4Q405 20–21–22 10; *1 En.* 14:11; *2 Bar.* 21:6; *Apoc. Abr.* 19:6; *2 En.* 29:1–3; 39:5; Tertullian, *Adv. Marc.* 3.9 (OECT, ed. Evans, 1:196). The rabbis, partly on the basis of Ps. 104:4, thought angels to be made of fire; cf. *b. Hag.* 13b–14a; *Gen. Rab.* 78:1; *Deut. Rab.* 11.4; *Pirq. R. El.* 22; *Rev. Mos.* A 3. שרף means both "seraph" and "burning." *Tg. Job* 25:2 says plainly that Michael is "of fire." So too Michael Psellus, *Orat. hag.* (ed. Fischer, pp. 238–39).

house of the Lord and commander of the whole host of the Most High." (*Jos. Asen.* 14:1–7)[33]

We should further keep in mind that the legend of Satan and his angels was commonly represented as the falling of stars from heaven. As Rev. 12:4 has it, the devil "swept down a third of the stars of heaven and threw them to the earth." *First Enoch* 86:1–6 offers the same picture. It is no wonder that Isa. 14:12 ("How you are fallen from heaven, O Day Star [= Latin *Lucifer*], son of Dawn! How you are cut down to the ground") has so often been read as an account of the fall of Satan (so already *LAB* 15:3, from the first century CE).

The Magi's Angel

We are now finally in a position to make an informed judgment on Bethlehem's star. Stars do not leave the sky and come down to earth. Nor can the astronomical objects of modern science go before people to guide them on their way. Nor can they come to rest over a person, a city, or a house. In old Jewish and Christian tradition, however, angels, who are identified with stars, can do these things and in fact often do do them. Near to hand is the inference that the star of Matt. 2 should be identified with an angel. In other words, the star that goes before the magi is like the pillar and cloud that went before Israel as the people fled Pharaoh's armies (and which Philo, *Mos.* 1.166, identified with an angel).[34] It is like

---

33. Trans. C. Burchard, *OTP* 2:224–25. Cf. *PGM* 1:74–77, quoted below.

34. Exod. 13:21; 14:19; 23:20; 40:38; Neh. 9:19; Ps. 78:14; 105:39. Exegetes have often noticed this parallel; indeed, we may speak here of an exegetical tradition. See, e.g., Chrysostom, *Hom. Matt.* 6:2(3) (PG 557.64); *Book of the Bee* 38 (ed. Budge, p. 92: "when they [the magi] halted, it [the star] also halted; like the pillar of cloud which stopped and went forward when it was convenient for the camp of Israel"); Aquinas, *ST* 3 q. 36 a. 7 ("when the magi had to continue their journey, the star moved on; when they had to stop the star stood still, as happened to the pillar of cloud in the desert"); Lapide, *Commentary*, p. 56 ("that pillar was a type of this star"; cf. p. 59); John Guyse, *A Practical Exposition of the Four Evangelists*, vol. 1 (2nd ed.; London: Edward Dilly, 1761), p. 212; Matthew Henry, *Commentary on the Whole Bible*, vol. 5, *Matthew to John* (New York: Fleming H. Revell, n.d.), ad 2:9; Thomas Scott, *The Holy Bible: Containing the Old and New Testaments, according to the Authorized Version, with Explanatory Notes, Practical Observations, and Copious Marginal References* (6 vols.; Boston: Crocker and Brewster, 1844), vol. 5 ad 2:9; Joseph Knabenbauer, *Commentarius in quatuor S. Evangelia Domini N. Jesu Christi. I, Evangelium secundum S. Matthaeum* (Paris: P. Lethielleux, 1892), p. 85; Joachim Gnilka, *Das Matthäusevangelium* (2 vols.; HTKNT I/1, 2; Freiburg: Herder, 1986, 1988), 1:40; George M. Soares Prabhu, *The Formula Quotations in the Infancy Narrative of Matthew* (AnBib 63; Rome: Biblical Institute, 1976), pp. 280–81; and Leopold Sabourin, *The Gospel according to St. Matthew* (2 vols.; Bombay: St. Paul's Press, 1982), 1:219. According to *The History of the Blessed Virgin Mary* (ed. Budge, 1:33), the angelic

the angel that conducted Zosimus to the island of the Rechabites (*Hist. Rech.* 1:3). It is like the angels who will, according to the prophecy in *Apoc. El.* 5:2–5, become a pillar of light and lead Israel into Palestine.

I can cite, as support for my reading of Matt. 2.1–12, an old and little-studied apocryphal gospel, the so-called *Arabic Gospel of the Savior.*[35] This relates, in chapter 7, the following story:

> And it came to pass, when the Lord Jesus was born at Bethlehem of Judea, in the time of King Herod, behold, magi came from the east. . . . And there were with them gifts of gold, frankincense, and myrrh. And they adored him [Jesus], and presented to Him their gifts. . . . In the same hour there appeared to them an angel in the form of that star which had before guided them on their journey; and they went away, following the guidance of its light, until they arrived in their own country. (trans. ANF 8:406)

This, I believe, only makes explicit what is implicit in Matthew, namely, that the guiding star was a guiding angel.

The author of this legend was scarcely alone. The apocryphal *History of the Blessed Virgin Mary*, an old Syriac text, tells us that "a watcher[36] was sent into Persia, and he showed himself to the Persians in the form of an exceedingly brilliant star, which lit up the whole region of the country." It was this watcher that the magi followed.[37] One also finds the angelic interpretation of Matthew's star, or acknowledgement of its possibility, in, among others, Ps.-Caesarius of Nazianzus, Ps.-Theodotus of Ancyra, Chrysostom,[38] Remigius of Auxerre, Theodore the Studite, Isho'dad of

---

star that led the magi to Bethlehem became "a pillar a light" (עמודא דנוהרא), which is surely an allusion to the exodus (Exod.13:22 MT: עמוד האש). Cf. the *Chronicle of Zuqnin* (CSCO 91, Scriptores Syri 43, ed. Chabot, p. 67: עמודא דנוהרא), and note *Apoc. El.* 5:2–5 (quoted above, on p. 26), where Gabriel and Uriel are transfigured into a guiding pillar of light. Benedict T. Viviano, "The Movement of the Star, Matt. 2:9 and Num. 9:17," *RB* 103 (1996), pp. 58–64, plausibly argues that Matthew's text itself reflects a midrashic understanding of the cloud and fire tradition. Particularly interesting is his observation that Wisd. 10:17 and 18:3 make the pillar of fire a "starry flame" and a "harmless sun" respectively.

35. For a brief introduction and a list of secondary literature see J. K. Elliott, *The Apocryphal New Testament: A Collection of Apocryphal Christian Literature in an English Translation* (Oxford: Clarendon, 1993), pp. 100–102. Elliott conjectures a Syrian archetype perhaps as early as the fifth century.

36. "Watcher" designates an angelic being, as in Dan. 4:13, 17, 23 (the LXX here translates the Hebrew עיר with ἄγγελος); *1 En.* 1:5; 10:9, 15; 12:2, 4; 13:10; 14:1, 3; 20:1 (here the watchers are the four archangels); 93:2 Aramaic; *Jub.* 4:15, 22; 7:21; 8:3; 1QapGen 2:1, 16; CD 2:17–18; *T. Reub.* 5:6; *T. Naph.* 3:5; *2 En.* 18:1–9; Clement of Alexandria, *Paed.* 2.9.79.3 (SC 108, ed. Mondésert and Marroua, p. 158); etc.

37. *The History of the Blessed Virgin Mary* (ed. Budge, 1:30). The text goes on to identify this angel with other angels from sacred history.

38. Chrysostom, *Hom. Matt.* 6.2(3) (PG 57.63), uses the term δύναμις ἀόρατος (invisible power), instead of ἄγγελος. Cf. Ps.-Caesarius of Nazianzus, *Dial.* 2, q. 107 (PG 38.973–75:

Merv, Theophylact, Solomon of Khilât, Bar-Hebraeus, Thomas Aquinas, and Maldonatus.[39] It is no surprise, then, that Christian artistic depictions of the nativity sometimes replace Bethlehem's star with an angel or show both an angel and a star.[40]

Detours in the History of Exegesis

Before concluding, I must confess that the angelic interpretation of Matthew's star is not, despite its far-flung attestation and popular character, the only interpretation in Christian exegetical history. As already observed, many commentators, especially since the Renaissance, have argued or assumed that the star was an inanimate celestial phenomenon or event. There are, I should now like to suggest, at least two reasons for alternative readings of Matt. 2.

The fate of Origen. Like most Greek philosophers, Origen believed that the heavenly bodies are alive and have rational souls. Indeed this great

---

νοερά τις καὶ λογικὴ δύναμις: "a certain rational and intellectual power"), and Diodore of Tarsus in Photius, *Bib.* 223 (PG 103.877A: the magi saw not a star in the heavens but δύναμίν τινα θειοτέραν, "a certain holy power," that was in the form of a star).

39. Ps.-Caesarius of Nazianzus, *Dial.* 2, q. 107 (PG 38.973–75); Ps.-Theodotus of Ancyra, *Hom. 1* (PG 77.1364D-1365A: δύναμιν ἀγγελική . . . δύναμιν ἐν ἄστρου σχήματι φαινομένην, "an angelic power . . . a power appearing in the form of a star"); Remigius of Auxerre apud Aquinas, *Catena Aurea* (trans. Newman, 1:67); Theodore the Studite, *Orat. 6—In sanct. angel.* 10 (PG 99.744A) ("an angel as a light of heaven, having transformed itself into the form of a star, led the magi on the way"); Isho'dad of Merv, *Comm. Matt.* ad loc. (HSem 6, ed. Gibson, pp. 26–27); Theophylact, *Comm. Matt.* ad loc. (PG 123.161C); Solomon of Khilât, *Book of the Bee* 38 (ed. Budge, pp. 91–92: "a rational power"); cf. the anonymous comment in *Catenae in Evangelia S. Matthaei et S. Marci ad fidem codd. mss.* (ed. J. A. Cramer; Hildesheim: Georg Olms, 1967 [reprint of 1842 ed.]), p. 16: λογικωτάτη τις φύσις; *Book of the Bee* 38 (ed. Budge, p. 92: "a rational power"); Gregory Abu'l Faraj = Bar-Hebraeus, *Commentary on the Gospels from the Horreum Mysterium* (trans. Carr), p. 10; Thomas Aquinas, *Super Ev. S. Matt.* ad cap. 2, lectio 1; cf. idem, *ST* 3 q. 36 a. 7; John Maldonatus, *S. Matthew's Gospel* (London: John Hodges, 1888), p. 56 (omitted from the 1853 Latin edition). Although Lapide, *Commentary* 1:54–56, does not identify the star with an angel, he says that angels formed it to guide the magi and that an angel moved it.

40. Franco Cardini, *La stella e i re: Mito e storia dei magi* (Firenze: Edifir: 1993), pp. 47–48, with plates 3 (the star with a face), 6, 12, 19, 21; T. Klauser, "Engel X (in der Kunst)," *RAC* 5 (1962), p. 299; Louis Réau, *Iconographie de l'art chrétien*, tome second, *Iconographie de la Bible II: Nouveau Testament* (Paris: Presses Universitaires, 1957), p. 249; Gertrud Schiller, *Iconography of Christian Art*, vol. 1, *Christ's Incarnation—Childhood—Baptism—Temptation—Transfiguration—Works and Miracles* (Greenwich, Conn.: New York Graphic Society, 1971), pp. 101–2, with plates 262, 269, 270, 272, 275. Note also that the star is directly above the manger and in the house in the relevant illumination in the 10th-century Codex Egberti. Already the earliest artistic depiction of our scene, in the Priscilla Catacomb at 430 Via Salaria, Rome, seems to depict the star as immediately over the heads of Mary and Jesus.

and controversial figure of the early church spent some time discoursing on the subject.[41] But, for a complex of reasons I need not review here, his theology, which allowed both for universalism and for the transmigration of souls, aroused much opposition in the fourth, fifth, and sixth centuries. Eventually the orthodox officially deemed Origen's teaching heretical. This condemnation of Origenist teaching, combined with a desire to obliterate all traces of polytheism and astronomy from the Christian world, led Jerome and other prominent Christians to argue that the stars are not alive.[42] They prevailed with many. As the Second Council of Constantinople (553 CE) put it: "If anyone shall say that the sun, the moon, and the stars are also reasonable beings . . . let him be anathema."[43] With this decree, the idea that the heavenly bodies are animate ceased to be an option for many Christian theologians.[44] This cannot but have discouraged some from adopting the popular identification of Bethlehem's star with an angel.

Despite the denunciation of Origen's theology and the authoritative censure of his opinions about the heavenly bodies, some commentators nonetheless continued to think of Matthew's ἀστήρ as animate. Theophylact, whose orthodoxy was impeccable, indeed thought it angelic:

> When you hear "star," do not think that it was a star such as we see, but a divine and angelic power that appeared in the form of a star. The magi were astrologers, and so the Lord used what was familiar to them to draw them to himself. . . . That the star was an angelic power is apparent from the fact that it shone even by day, and that it moved as they moved, and stood still as they rested; also, that it moved from Persia in the north to Jerusalem in the south. For a star never moves from north to south.[45]

41. See especially *Prin.* 1.7 (TzF 24, ed. Görgemanns and Karpp, pp. 232–47, with additional patristic testimony to Origen's beliefs on pp. 248–51); cf. *Cels.* 5.11 (ed. Marcovich, pp. 328–29); Scott, *Origen*, pp. 113–67.

42. Jerome, *Contra Joan. Hier. ad Pam.* 17 (PL 23.369A–B). Cf. Basil the Great, *Hex.* 3.9 (SC 26, ed. Giet, pp. 236, 238). In all this, Christian thinkers were in continuity with a critical stream of the Greek philosophical tradition; see Scott, *Origen*, pp. 3–23, and recall the complaint against Socrates, in Plato, *Apol.* 26D, that he thought the sun and moon to be nothing more than rocks (cf. the opinion of Anaxagoras in Diogenes Laertius 2.12). Augustine could not make up his mind on the issue; see *Ench.* 58 (SAQ 2.4, ed. Scheel, p. 37).

43. This belongs to the third of the fifteen canons against Origen; see *Concilium Universale Constantinopolitanum sub Iustiniano Habitum* (ed. Johannes Straub; Berlin: W. de Gruyter: 1971), p. 248.

44. Cf. John Philoponus, *Opif.* 6.2 (FC 23/3, ed. Scholten, pp. 500–508); John of Damascus, *Dialect.* 68 (PTS 7, ed. Kotter, p. 141). Notwithstanding this decree, which was heeded less in the West than in the East, many Christian intellectuals continued to discuss, in dialogue with Aristotle, the issue of the rational nature of stars; see Wolfson, "Souls of the Spheres," pp. 67–93.

45. Theophylact, *Comm. Matt.* ad loc. (PG 123.161C).

Bar Hebraeus, without censorship, or fear of the same, wrote: "Some say that it was an angel that appeared to them like a star."[46] Remigius in like fashion observed: "Others say it was an angel, the same who appeared to the shepherds."[47] John of Hildesheim similarly says that, in some book of "the East," the magi's star talks to them, and its voice is the same as that of the angel that speaks to the shepherds in Luke 2.[48]

As Theophylact attests, orthodox Christians could continue, even after the condemnation of Origen's teaching, to identify Bethlehem's star with an angel because they understood it to belong to a class by itself, that is, to have been specially created for the occasion and so unlike the other stars.[49] For them, Matthew's "star" was not really a star. Chrysostom, who reckoned the star to be "some invisible power" (δύναμίς τις ἀόρατος) that had been "transformed" (μετασχηματισθεῖσα) into the appearance of a star, was already of this opinion;[50] so too later Isho'dad of Merv, whose detailed argumentation that the star was not really a star but rather an angel merits quotation:

It is evident from many things that it was not a real star, nor an imagination, nor a fantasy, nor an automaton, but an angel who shone like a star from Persia to Bethlehem; first, because it shone equally by night and by day; second, that it was seen only by the magi and not by others; third, that it shone alone, without

46. Gregory Abu'l Faraj = Bar-Hebraeus, *Commentary on the Gospels from the Horreum Mysterium* (trans. Carr), p. 10.

47. Remigius of Auxerre apud Aquinas, *Catena Aurea* (trans. Newman, 1:67). Cf. Ps.-Augustine, *De mirab. sacr. script.* 3.4 (PL 35.2194) = Sedulius Scotus, *Comm. Matt.* ad 2:2 (ed. Löfstedt, pp. 65–66). The link with the shepherds, which appears from time to time in the commentaries, comes because of the angelic "glory" in Luke 2:9. But against M. L. W. Laistner, "The Western Church and Astrology during the Early Middle Ages," *HTR* 34 (1941), pp. 260–61, the traditional identification of Matthew's star with an angel is scarcely due to influence from Luke 2:9–10.

48. John of Hildesheim, *Historia Trium Regum* 19 (ed. Horstmann, pp. 64–65).

49. That the star was "new" or created not at the beginning of the world but only later, for the sole purpose of leading the magi, appears in Ignatius, *Eph.* 19.2; *Sib. Or.* 8.476; Clement of Alexandria, *Exc. Theod.* 74 (SC 23, ed. Sagnard, p. 196); Eusebius, *Dem. ev.* 9.1 (GCS, ed. Heikel, p. 405); Gregory of Nazianzus, *Poem. arc.* 5.53–63 (ed. Moreschini, Sykes, and Holford-Strevens, pp. 24, 26) = *Carm. dog.* 1.1.5 (PG 37.428A–429A); Augustine, *C. Faust.* 2.5 (CSEL 25, ed. Zyca, p. 259); Christian Druthmar (Stablo), *Exp. in Matt.* ad loc. (PL 106.1282A); John of Damascus, *Exp. fid.* 21(2.7) (PTS 12, ed. Kotter, p. 60); Rabanus Maurus, *Comm. Matt.* ad loc. (PL 107.759A); *Glossa Ordinaria* (PL 114.75C); Jacobus de Voragine, *Legenda aurea* 14 (ed. Graesse, pp. 91–92); Luther, *Sermons II*, p. 169; William Burkitt, *Expository Notes, with Practical Observations upon the New Testament of Our Lord and Savior* (New Haven: Abel Morse, 1794), p. 10; etc. Lapide (*Great Commentary*, 1:54), while he does not regard the star as alive, thinks it wholly different from other stars and gives, among other reasons, that it was created not on the fourth day of creation but at Christ's nativity.

50. Chrysostom, *Hom. Matt.* 6.2(3) (PG 57.63). Cf. Ps.-Chrysostom, *Ecl. i–xlviii ex div. hom.* 34 (PG 63.831).

burning, although it came down so low from the region of the ether, to show
the way, as if by a finger, to the magi, even to the house; fourth, it shone so
much at midday that it surpassed the rays of the sun in their eyes; fifth, because
all the lights of the zodiac move, as fixed, from east to west, but according
to astronomers and astrologers, seven of them which are called planets move
from west to east; but of the rest all the signs of the zodiac, fixed in the body
of the firmament, move from east to west with the revolution of the heavens.
This moved in the opposite way, that is to say, from south-east to north and
from this to west; for thus is the road from Persia to Palestine; sixth, because it
did not shine continuously but when they had gone into each of the cities and
villages by the way, until they came out, it was hid, in order that by question
and answer the birth of King Messiah should be made known to everyone;
as it was hid from them in their entering Jerusalem; and when that cunning
fox Herod sent spies after them many times, the star was not seen until they
knew that it was the finger of God; and Herod planned to destroy the child in
another way. So it is clear from all these things, that *it was not a natural star,
but a starry likeness.*[51]

Clearly it was possible to identify Matthew's "star" with an angel and
yet not fall into the heresy of identifying the heavenly lights in their entirety with the angelic host. For the old equation, stars = angels, could be
reduced to a less comprehensive equation: the star of Bethlehem = an angel.
Despite the condemnation of Origenism, then, the old exegetical tradition
persisted: even the orthodox who accepted the verdict of the Second Council
of Constantinople could regard Matthew's star as an angel.

The advent of modern astronomy. A second blow, however, eventually befell the traditional reading. Beginning in the twelfth century and
continuing through the Renaissance, Western thinkers, for a number of
convergent reasons, finally abandoned every vestige of the old notion
of an animate heaven.[52] This prepared the way for Copernicus, Galileo,
and Kepler to create the modern science of astronomy, and their startling
discoveries became authoritative. The result was inevitable. Christian
commentators felt moved to read their old texts in the light of the new
astronomical knowledge. Although Kepler himself wisely confessed that
Matthew's star could not have been "of the ordinary run of comets or
new stars," that it must rather have been "a special miracle [that] moved
in the lower layer of the atmosphere,"[53] many failed to heed his acknowl-
edgment of the obvious.

51. Isho'dad of Merv, *Comm. Matt.* ad loc. (HSem 6, ed. Gibson, pp. 26–27).

52. See esp. Richard C. Dales, "The De-animation of the Heavens in the Middle Ages,"
Journal of the History of Ideas 41 (1980), pp. 531–50. The old ecclesiastical condemnation of
astral animation (see p. 31) clearly had not been fully effective; see, e.g., Isidore of Seville, *De
nat. rer.* 27 (PL 83.1000C–1001A).

53. Johannes Kepler, *Omnia Opera* 4.346, as quoted in Molnar, *Star*, p. 24.

After the Renaissance, fewer and fewer exegetes seriously entertained identifying Matthew's star with an angel. Maldonatus (1534–1583) could still write: "Some suppose it [Matthew's star] to have been the Holy Spirit, as he appeared after the baptism in the form of a dove, so now he descended in the appearance of a star to point to Christ. Others think that it was an angel who assumed the form of a star; for angels are called stars. Many others suppose it to have been a comet. I have said that it was either a comet or an angel."[54] But Maldonatus appears to be near the end of the line for the old interpretation. Others, if aware of the tradition, typically mention it only to dismiss it without argument. John Gill (1697–1771), for instance, concedes that the star "was indeed a very unusual one; its being seen in the daytime, its motion and standing still, its situation, which must be very low, and its use to point out the very house where Christ was, show it to be so." Gill nonetheless discards the notion, sponsored by some he fails to name, that the star was an angel; and he feels no need to offer any justification for his negative verdict.[55]

Not long after Gill, memory of the ancient interpretation rapidly dissipates, to the point now that it has barely put in an appearance in the literature of the last one hundred years.[56] The Enlightenment not only inherited and furthered the Renaissance's thoroughly materialistic understanding of the skies, but it also bestowed a widespread unease with the miraculous. In recent decades even orthodox commentators have often favored a rationalistic explanation of the star rather than the massive

---

54. John Maldonatus, *S. Matthew's Gospel*, p. 56.

55. John Gill, *Gill's Commentary* (6 vols.; Grand Rapids: Baker, 1980), 5:9. 12; cf. H. Elsley, *Annotations on the Four Gospels and the Acts of the Apostles* (Oxford: J. Vincent, 1844), p. 68.

56. I know of very few exceptions: W. D. Davies and Dale C. Allison Jr., *A Critical and Exegetical Commentary on the Gospel according to Saint Matthew* (3 vols.; ICC; Edinburgh: T&T Clark, 1988, 1991, 1998), 1:246–47; George Wesley Buchanan, *The Gospel of Matthew* (2 vols.; Lewiston, N.Y.: Edwin Mellen, 1996), 1:90 ("The assumption of the author was that every star represented an angel in heaven, and angels could move about as they were sent"; Buchanan may here be borrowing from my own commentary, which he otherwise often cites); and Wolfgang Wiefel, *Das Evangelium nach Matthäus* (THNT 1; Leipzig: Evangelische Verlagsanstalt, 1998), p. 41. More vaguely, Walter Grundmann, *Das Evangelium nach Matthäus* (THKNT 1; Berlin: Evangelische Verlagsanstalt, 1968), pp. 78–79, observes that angels were in charge of stars, and Martin Hengel and Helmut Merklein, "Die Magier aus dem Osten und die Flucht nach Ägypten (Mt 2) im Rahmen der antiken Religionsgeschichte und der Theologie des Matthäus," in *Orientierung an Jesus: Zur Theologie der Synoptiker: Für Josef Schmid* (ed. Paul Hoffmann, Norbert Brox, and Wilhelm Pesch; Freiburg: Herder, 1973), p. 154, n. 65, mention the close link between angels and stars in ancient Judaism and cite the *Arabic Gospel of the Savior*. Molnar, *Star*, pp. 15–16, cites my earlier work, but as an astronomer he pursues an astronomical resolution. Popular literature occasionally retains traces of the old tradition; see, e.g., the work of the Seventh Day Adventist E. G. H. White, *The Desire of Ages* (Mountain View, Calif.: Pacific Press, 1898), p. 61: the magi's star "was not a fixed star nor a planet. . . . The star was a distant company of shining angels, but of this the wise men were ignorant."

supernaturalism that Matthew clearly entails.[57] Although J. Gresham Machen defended at great length the literal historicity of the canonical infancy narratives, he persuaded himself that Matthew's language about the star must be a "poetical, oriental way of describing events that we should describe in very different terms."[58] Contemporary exegetes, citizens of the modern, scientific world, have regularly tended either to dismiss Matthew's star as pure fiction or, like Machen, have read the text with their own presuppositions and so tried to understand it in modern scientific categories: surely it must have been a conjunction, or maybe a comet, or perhaps a supernova. Furthermore, even when exegetes have recognized that the magi's guiding light precludes any scientific explanation, they have still failed to note that ancient readers, unlike modern readers, might readily have identified it with an angel.[59]

It may well be that all the sincere investigative effort mustered to discover what modern astronomy might tell us about Bethlehem's star amounts to a search for what was never there. It is always hazardous to read ancient texts with modern minds, and in the present instance many of us have unwittingly supposed that, because Matthew speaks of a "star," he must refer to an inanimate heavenly phenomenon, to something that fits comfortably into our modern view of the universe. But, to reiterate, modern notions of stars are modern notions, not ancient notions. The yet ongoing search for a heavenly body or conjunction that will explain Matt. 2:1–12 is, one suspects, wholly misconceived. We cannot look for an angel that has come and gone.

Nothing said herein prejudices one's answer to the inevitable question, What, if anything, really happened? Did magi from the East follow a light to Bethlehem and so discover Jesus? Or, as I myself am strongly inclined

57. David Friedrich Strauss, *The Life of Jesus Critically Examined* (Philadelphia: Fortress, 1972), p. 166, in connection with Matthew's star, already speaks of the "transplantation of rationalistic artifice into the soil of orthodox exegesis."

58. J. Gresham Machen, *The Virgin Birth of Christ* (New York: Harper, 1930), pp. 223–26.

59. Cf. F. Boll, "Der Stern des Weisen," *ZNW* 18 (1917/18), pp. 40–48; Larry Chouinard, *The College Press NIV Commentary: Matthew* (Joplin, Mo.: College Press, 1997), p. 59; David Hill, *The Gospel of Matthew* (NCB; London: Oliphants, 1975), p. 83; Daniel Whitby, *A Paraphrase and Commentary on the New Testament* (2 vols.; 10th ed.; London: James Moyes, 1808), vol. 1, pp. 10, 12; Franz Zinniker, *Probleme der sogenannten Kindheitsgeschichte bei Mattäus* (Freiburg: Paulusverlag, 1972), pp. 118–19. J. Dwight Pentecost, *The Words and Works of Jesus Christ: A Study of the Life of Christ* (Grand Rapids: Zondervan, 1981), p. 67, perceiving the difficulties of any conventional explanation, cryptically identifies Matthew's "star" with "the shining glory of God that He reveals to those who are recipients of revelation."

to believe, is Matthew's story to be reckoned a haggadic-type legend whose meaning is to be found elsewhere than in its correspondence to the historical facts? Those heretofore disinclined to believe that distant foreigners trailed a heavenly portent to Judea will, obviously, be no more inclined to credit the report of an angelic guide. It is equally true that those accustomed to believing that the Creator arranged a conjunction, supernova, or comet to coincide with Jesus' birth will surely have little trouble accepting that the same Creator directed the magi to the Messiah through the instrument of an angel. Which is to say: the issue of interpretation is not the issue of historicity. This last is a separate subject for a separate occasion.[60]

Appendix: Texts Identifying or Closely Associating Stars and Angels

- Neh. 9:6: "You are the LORD, you alone; you have made heaven, the heaven of heavens, with all their host, the earth and all that is on it, the seas and all that is in them. To all of them you give life, and the host of heaven worships you." The catalogue of creation—heaven, the heaven of heavens, earth, seas—encourages us to identify "the hosts of heaven" with the stars, and their act of worship shows that they are conceptualized as personal beings.

- Job 25:4–6: "How then can a mortal be righteous before God? How can one born of woman be pure? If even the moon is not bright and the stars are not pure in his sight, how much less a mortal, who is a maggot, and a human being, who is a worm!" Read in the light of 4:17–19 and 15:14–16, the meaning of vv. 4–6 is that "even in God's heavenly court God's holy ones are found guilty (Ps 82:1)."[61]

- Ps. 148:1–4: "Praise the Lord! Praise the Lord from the heavens; praise him in the heights! Praise him, all his angels; praise him, all his host! Praise him, sun and moon; praise him, all you shining stars! Praise him, you highest heavens, and you waters above the heavens!" (cf. Dan. 3:57–60 LXX). Here the heavenly "host" consists of "his angels" as well as the sun, moon, and stars. Older exegetes, who did not believe in an animate heaven, recognized nevertheless that such a belief could be discovered in this passage, which is why

60. I do note, however, that continued attempts to defend the historicity of Matthew's account by establishing a relationship to known astronomical phenomena are, ironically, self-defeating; for as nothing in the sky behaves like Matthew's star, the proper conclusion, were one to decide, let us say, that memory of a conjunction lies behind our story, would be that memory of some unusual sight grew into a myth.

61. Habel, *Job*, p. 369.

they sought to dismiss it in their commentaries; see, e.g., Theodoret, *Comm. Ps.* on 148:3 (PG 80.1987B–C).

- Isa. 24:21–23: "On that day the Lord will punish the host of heaven in heaven, and on earth the kings of the earth. They will be gathered together like prisoners in a pit. . . . Then the moon will be abashed, and the sun ashamed." "The moon" and "the sun" are clearly members of "the host of heaven," which must then be personified objects in the heavens.

- Jer. 19:13: The prophet attacks the astral religion of those who make offerings from their roofs and pour out libations to "the whole host of heaven" and "other gods"; cf. 8:2; Deut. 4:19; 2 Kings 21:5; 23:4–5; Zeph. 1:5.

- Dan. 8:10: "It [the 'horn' of v. 9] grew as high as the host of heaven. It threw down to the earth some of the host and some of the stars, and trampled on them." To judge from the context, the stars are celestial beings, either gods or angels.[62]

- *1 En.* 18:11–14: "And I saw a deep pit with heavenly fire on its pillars. . . . And on top of that pit I saw a place without the heavenly firmament above it or earthly foundation under it or water. There was nothing on it—not even birds—but it was a desolate and terrible place. And I saw there the seven stars (which) were like great, burning mountains. (Then) the angel said (to me), 'This place is the (ultimate) end of heaven and earth; it is a prison house for the stars and the powers of heaven. And the stars which roll over upon the fire, they are the ones which have transgressed the commandments of God from the beginning of their rising because they did not arrive punctually'";[63] cf. 21:3–6; 80:6; Jude 13; *Apoc. El.* 4:11.

- *1 En.* 43:1–2: "And I saw other lightnings and the stars of heaven. And I saw how he called them each by their (respective) names, and they obeyed him. And . . . in number they are (as many as) the angels; they keep their faith each one according to their names";[64] cf. 41:5; Sir. 43:8–10.

- *1 En.* 86:1–6: In this retelling of Gen. 6:1–4, the giants are spoken of as stars that descend from heaven, and one of those stars is Asael, the first angelic rebel; cf. *1 En.* 10:4–8; 88:1–3; 90:24.

- Ezekiel the Tragedian, *Exag.* 77–81: An enthroned Moses relates, "I gazed upon the whole earth round about; / things under it, and high

---

62. So John J. Collins, *Daniel: A Commentary on the Book of Daniel* (Hermeneia; Minneapolis: Fortress, 1993), p. 331.

63. Trans. E. Isaac, *OTP* 1:23.

64. Trans. E. Isaac, *OTP* 1:33.

above the skies. / Then at my feet a multitude of stars / fell down, and I their number reckoned up. / They passed by me like armed ranks of men."[65]

- 1QH 9(1):9–12: "You have stretched out the heavens for your glory. Everything [which it contains] you have [es]tablished according to your will, and powerful spirits, according to their laws, before they became h[oly] angels [. . .] eternal spirits in their realms: luminaries according to their mysteries, stars according to [their] circuits."

- 1QS 3:20 and CD 5:18: The "prince of lights" is an angelic figure who should probably be identified with Michael, and the use of the plural "lights" makes one think of the heavenly orbs.[66]

- Bar. 3:34: "The stars shone in their watches, and were glad; he called them, and they said, 'Here we are!' They shone with gladness for him who made them."

- *Jos. Asen.* 14:1–7: A star descends from heaven and transforms itself into an angel.[67]

- 1 Cor. 15:39–42: "Not all flesh is alike, but there is one flesh for human beings, another for animals, another for birds, and another for fish. There are both heavenly bodies and earthly bodies, but the glory of the heavenly is one thing, and that of the earthly is another. There is one glory of the sun, and another glory of the moon, and another glory of the stars; indeed, star differs from star in glory. So it is with the resurrection of the dead." The context has led many exegetes to suppose that, for Paul, the stars are "living beings equipped with bodies emitting light."[68]

- Mark 13:25: "And the stars will be falling from heaven, and the powers in the heavens will be shaken." "The stars" (οἱ ἀστέρες) and "the powers" (αἱ δυνάμεις) are in poetic parallelism, and the latter are either the heavenly armies (so BDAG, s.v. δύναμις 4) or unspecified heavenly beings (cf. Rom. 8:38; Eph. 1:21; 1 Pet. 3:22);

---

65. Trans. R. G. Robertson, *OTP* 2:812. Note Larry W. Hurtado, *One God, One Lord: Early Christian Devotion and Ancient Jewish Monotheism* (Philadelphia: Fortress, 1988), p. 59: "The stars could be taken as symbolic of the people over whom Moses is to be placed as leader and judge. . . . Or, more likely in my judgment, they may represent the acceptance by the heavenly host of Moses' appointed place as God's chief agent."

66. Cf. P. Guilbert, "Le règle de la communauté," in J. Carmignac and P. Guilbert, *Les textes de Qumran: Traduits et annotés* (Paris: Letouzey et Ané, 1961), p. 33.

67. See above, pp. 27–28.

68. C. K. Barrett, *A Commentary on the First Epistle to the Corinthians* (HNTC; New York: Harper & Row, 1968), p. 371; cf. Wolfgang Schrage, *Der erste Brief an die Korinther*, vol. 4, *1 Kor 15,1–16,24* (EKKNT 7/4; Düsseldorf: Benziger, 2001), p. 292.

cf. the parallelism between "stars" (τοῖς ἄστροις) and "powers" (ταῖς δυνάμεσιν) in the Greek *1 En.* 18:14, quoted above.[69]

- *LAE* (Latin) 19:3: Eve "said to herself, 'Who will give the news to my lord Adam? I beg you, O lights of heaven [*luminaria celi*], when you return to the East, tell my lord Adam."[70] This is a request to the heavenly lights to act as personal messengers on Eve's behalf and speak to Adam of what has happened.

- *Ps.-Phoc.* 71–75: "The heavenly ones [Οὐρανίδαι] also are without envy toward each other. The moon does not envy the much stronger beams of the sun. . . . For if there were strife among the blessed ones [μάκαρες], heaven would not stand firm."[71]

- Jas. 1:17: God is "the Father of lights" (to my knowledge an unparalleled expression in Jewish and early Christian literature). The use of the personal "Father" may betray belief in the animate nature of the heavenly lights.[72]

- Rev. 1:20: "The seven stars [seen in John's vision of Jesus] are the angels of the seven churches"; cf. 3:1.

- Rev. 9:1–2: The star that falls from heaven and is then given the key to the bottomless pit is clearly an angel: "And the fifth angel blew his trumpet, and I saw a star that had fallen from heaven to earth, and he was given the key to the shaft of the bottomless pit; he opened the shaft of the bottomless pit, and from the shaft rose smoke like the smoke of a great furnace."

- Rev. 12:3–4: The primordial rebellion of angels in heaven under the leadership of Satan is described as a fall of stars: the tail of "a great red dragon . . . swept down a third of the stars of heaven and threw them to the earth"; cf. vv. 7–9.

---

69. Eusebius, *Praep. ev.* 7.15 (GCS 43,1, ed. Mras, p. 393), is explicit about the equation of the "powers" with the heavenly lights: "After those first luminaries [sun and moon] which are reckoned among the incorporeal powers, and excel in power and essence of intellectual light, there are countless tribes and families of stars. . . ."; cf. idem, *Comm. Isa.* 2.7 ad 34:4 (GCS 53a, ed. Ziegler, pp. 221–22), and Origen, *Apoc. 1–27* scholion 38 (TU 38.3, ed. Diobouniotis and Harnack, p. 41). Jerome, *Comm. Matt.* ad loc. (SC 259, ed. Bonnard, p. 200), and Theophylact, *Comm. Matt.* ad loc. (PG 123.413D), explicitly equate "the powers" with angelic hosts.

70. Trans. M. D. Johnson, *OTP* 2:264.

71. Trans. P. W. van der Horst, *OTP* 2:576. On this see the commentary of Pieter W. van der Horst, *The Sentences of Pseudo-Phocylides* (SVTP 4; Leiden: Brill, 1978), pp. 163–64. Van der Horst recognizes that here, as in Philo, the stars are animate beings, and that Greek terminology for the gods is applied to them.

72. Cf. Philo, *Decal.* 64: "Let us . . . refrain from worshipping those who by nature are our brothers [the heavenly bodies], even though they have been given a substance purer and more immortal than ours, for created things, in so far as they are created, are brothers, since they have all one father, the maker of the universe."

- *2 Bar.* 51:10: "They will live in the heights of that world and they will be like the angels and be equal to the stars."[73] The synonymous parallelism in this sentence seemingly combines astral immortality with the notion that the saints will become like angels in the eschatological future.[74]

- *Apoc. Abr.* 19:9: The hosts of stars belong to the angelic hosts in the fifth firmament.

- *2 En.* 29:3 A: "From the fire I [God] created all the armies of the bodiless ones, and all the armies of the stars and cherubim and seraphim and ophanim."[75] That the stars are spoken of as "armies" implies their living character, and their close association with the cherubim and other celestial beings confirms the inference.

- *T. Sol.* 6:7: Solomon asks Beelzebul, "Tell me in which star you reside." Beelzebul answers, "The one called by men the Evening Star."[76]

- *T. Sol.* 20:14–17: Whereas the stars of heaven have their foundation laid in the firmament, the lights that fall to earth ("falling stars" in our jargon) are demons.

- Tertullian, *Carn. Chr.* 6, opposes the view of some who teach that angels "derived their flesh from the stars."

- *3 En.* 46: Stars have spirits and wings and sing God's praises: "Metatron said to me: [Come and I will show you] the spirits of the stars, which stand in the Raqiaᶜ every night in fear of the Omnipresent One—where they go and where they stand. . . . They were standing like fiery sparks around the chariots of the Omnipresent One. . . . They flew up on wings of flame and fled to the four sides of the throne of the chariot, and he told me the name of each of them. . . .

---

73. Trans. A. F. J. Klijn, *OTP* 1:638.

74. For astral immortality in Judaism (which was no doubt sometimes encouraged by tendentious readings of Gen. 15:5 and 22:17, where Abraham is told that his descendants will be as the stars of heaven) see Pieter W. van der Horst, *Ancient Jewish Epitaphs: An Introductory Survey of a Millennium of Jewish Funerary Epigraphy (300 BCE—700 CE)* (Kampen: Kok Pharos, 1991), pp. 123–24; note esp. Dan. 12:3; *1 En.* 104:2; *T. Mos.* 10:9; 4 Macc. 17:4–5; *LAB* 33:5; *4 Ezra* 7:97 (cf. 125); CIJ 2.788 = Ameling, *IJO* 2.236. Astral immortality was the dominant conception of the afterlife in the post-classical world. It was held by, among others, Pythagoreans, Platonists, and Stoics. See Franz Cumont, *After Life in Roman Paganism* (New Haven: Yale University Press, 1922), pp. 91–109, and idem, *Lux Perpetua* (Paris: Librairie Orientaliste Paul Geuthner, 1949), pp. 142–88. For the saints becoming angelic see Wisd. 5:5 (assuming that "sons of God" = angels); 4QSb 4:25; 4Q511 fr. 35; *1 En.* 104:1–6; Mark 12:25; *2 Bar.* 51:5, 10; Acts 6:15; *T. Isaac* 4:43–8; etc.

75. Trans. F. I. Andersen, *OTP* 1:149.

76. Trans. D. C. Duling, *OTP* 1:968. It is characteristic of the *Testament of Solomon* that the stars are evil spirits or demons; see 2:2 and esp. chapters 8 and 18.

They . . . go and glorify the Holy One, blessed be he, with songs and praises."[77]

- *b. ʾAbod. Zar.* 43b: The sun, moon, stars, and planets are attendants who serve before God in the heights; cf. *Lev. Rab.* 31.9, where they are reluctant to go forth lest people worship them.
- *Sepher Ha-Razim* Firmament 2.147: Instructions for a magical spell include this: "I beseech you, O great angel who is called 'Sun.'" Firmament 4 contains petitions directly addressed to the sun.
- *PGM* 1.74–77: "At once there will be a sign for you like this: [A blazing star] will descend and come to a stop in the middle of the housetop, and when the star [has dissolved] before your eyes, you will behold an angel whom you have summoned and who has been sent [to you], and you will quickly learn the decisions of the god."[78]

77. Trans. P. Alexander, *OTP* 1:299.
78. Cf. *PGM* 7.829, where the angel Zizaubio is "from the company of the Pleiades."

2

Seeing God

(MATT. 5:8)

Matthew 5:8 promises "the pure in heart" that "they will see God." Recent commentaries typically focus upon the first half of this verse; that is, they concern themselves with clarifying the meaning of "pure in heart." They usually have much less to say about the second half, αὐτοὶ τὸν θεὸν ὄψονται. One guesses that this common neglect is due partly to the conviction that there is a consensus, and when there is a consensus, what is the point of discussion? Perhaps the Protestant "tyranny of the word," its privileging of hearing over seeing, has also played some role in the apparent lack of interest.[1] Be that as it may, David Hill represents a majority when he writes, with scant argument: "To 'see God' is a pictorial expression indicating the bliss of fellowship with God in the Kingdom (cf. Ps. 17:15; 42:2; 4 Ezra 7:98—'for they hasten to behold the face of him whom they served in life and from whom they are to receive their reward when glorified')."[2] Donald Hagner, who agrees that we have here an eschatological promise,[3] offers a similar comment: "The reference to

---

1. Calvin, in his commentary on Matt. 5:8, explicates "they will see God" with nothing more than "they shall enjoy the sight of God in heaven": John Calvin, *Commentary on a Harmony of the Evangelists, Matthew, Mark, and Luke* (3 vols.; Grand Rapids: Eerdmans, 1949), 1:171–72. The distance from the medieval commentaries at this junction is remarkable.

2. David Hill, *The Gospel of Matthew* (NCB; London: Oliphants, 1972), p. 113.

3. This was also obvious to many of the ancients; cf. Irenaeus, *Adv. haer.* 4.9.2 (SC 100, ed. Rousseau, p. 483); Theophilus of Antioch, *Autol.* 1.7 (OECT, ed. Grant, p. 10); Clement

seeing God in the present passage is . . . eschatological in tone. In contrast to the strong O.T. statement that no one can see the face of God and live (e.g., Exod. 33:20), the righteous in the eschatological age will experience the beatific vision; they will see the face of God (cf. too Rev. 22:4). . . . Matthew describes the greatest possible eschatological reward, one that by its nature includes all else."[4]

Once Hill and Hagner inform us, correctly I believe, that "they will see God" is an eschatological hope,[5] they quickly move on to the next subject. In this they are representative of modern interpreters.[6] One does occasionally find exegetes who wonder, if only in passing, about the tension between sources that make seeing God impossible and those that make it either a blessed eschatological goal or an experience a few have already known.[7] But what the recent commentators consistently neglect to tell us is that exegetical history offers a number of different and rather interesting ways of resolving the contradiction and so of imagining what it might mean for human beings to "see God." Even

---

of Alexandria, *Strom.* 5.1.7.7 (GCS 15, ed. Stählin, p. 330); *Ps.-Clem. Rec.* 3.30 (GCS 42, ed. Rehm, p. 118); Hilary of Poitiers, *Comm. Matt.* ad loc. (SC 254, ed. Doignon, p. 126); Ambrose, *Exp. Luke* 1.27 (SC 45, ed. Tissot, p. 60); Augustine, *Ep.* 147 23 (CSEL 44, ed. Goldbacher, p. 297); Cassiodorus, *Exp. Ps.* 30:27; 109:3 (PL 70.215B–C, 795D); John Philoponus, *Opif.* 6.9 (FC 23/3, ed. Scholten, p. 529); etc. Cf. *Corpus Hermeticum* 10:6 (ed. Nock and Festugière, 1:116): "It is not possible for a soul to be deified while it yet remains in a human body; but it is necessary that it be changed and then it will behold the beauty of the Good and thus become deified." Medieval Catholic Christians debated whether the beatific vision would come at death or only after the general resurrection, even though Augustine implied that it is also possible to see God in this life; see Roland J. Teske, "St. Augustine and the Vision of God," in *Augustine: Mystic and Mystagogue* (ed. Frederick Van Fleteren, Joseph C. Schnaubelt, and Joseph Reino; Collectanea Augustiniana; New York: Peter Lang, 1994), pp. 207–308. Augustine's apparent openness on this matter aligns him with many Eastern theologians, such as Symeon the New Theologian; see Hilarion Alfeyev, *St. Symeon the New Theologian and Orthodox Tradition* (Oxford: Oxford University Press, 2000), p. 224.

4. Donald A. Hagner, *Matthew 1–13* (WBC 33A; Dallas: Word, 1993), p. 94.

5. Cf. Wolf Wilhelm Grafen Baudissin, "'Gott schauen' in der alttestamentlichen Religion," *AR* 18 (1915), p. 173: Matt. 5:8 "undoubtedly has in view the fulfilled messianic reign, because all the other Beatitudes refer to this and because the future, 'will see God,' would not be justified if it had to do with a divine presence or knowledge of God promised already for the present life."

6. See, e.g., Joachim Gnilka, *Das Matthäusevangelium* (2 vols.; HTKNT 1/1–2; Freiburg: Herder, 1986–88), 1:125–26; Walter Grundmann, *Das Evangelium nach Matthäus* (THKNT 1; Berlin: Evangelische Verlagsanstalt, 1968), p. 130; Douglas R. A. Hare, *Matthew* (IBC; Louisville: John Knox, 1993), p. 41; John P. Meier, *Matthew* (NTM 3; Wilmington, Del.: Michael Glazier, 1980), p. 41. Not every recent commentator, however, offers an eschatological interpretation. David E. Garland, *Reading Matthew: A Literary and Theological Commentary on the First Gospel* (London: SPCK, 1993), p. 57, for instance, speaks without elaboration of "communion with God."

7. Cf. Hagner, *Matthew 1–13*, p. 94 (quoted above); Francis Wright Beare, *The Gospel according to Matthew: Translation, Introduction, and Commentary* (San Francisco: Harper &

Ulrich Luz, in his magnificent commentary on Matthew, which pays so much attention to the history of interpretation, fails us on this score.[8] I should like in this chapter, then, to review what some readers have thought when pondering the second half of Matthew's sixth beatitude. After a survey of opinion, which I shall sort into seven categories, I shall offer some closing remarks on the theological value of knowing the neglected exegetical history.

Options from the History of Exegesis

An embodied deity. An interpretation of Matt. 5:8b that modern exegetes, inevitably informed by their own theological presuppositions, never mention, perhaps because it does not occur to them, is that the text assumes an embodied deity. Augustine discussed, if only to reject, this idea.[9] Up through the fourth and fifth centuries, however, Christian belief in a corporeal God was quite widespread: it was scarcely confined to Tertullian and the Egyptian Anthropomorphites.[10] Just such a belief

---

Row, 1981), pp. 132–33; and Robert A. Guelich, *The Sermon on the Mount: A Foundation for Understanding* (Waco, Tex.: Word, 1982), pp. 90–91. Exod.33:20; *1 En.* 14:21; *Sib. Or.* 3:17; 4:12; John 1:18; 1 Tim. 6:16; 1 John 4:12; Ps.-Orpheus 22–24; and *Tg.* Ezek. 1:17 teach that God cannot be seen; cf. Deut. 4:12; Ps. 77:19; 97:2. For the vision of God, however understood, seemingly being, on the contrary, a possibility here or hereafter see Gen. 12:7; 17:1; 18:1; 32:30 (cf. 4Q158 frags. 1–2 10); 35:9; 48:3; Exod. 4:5; 24:10–11 (cf. *Mek.* on Exod.19:11 and *b. Ber.* 17a; but contrast the LXX and MT at Deut 4:12); 33:11; Lev 9:4; 16:2; Num. 12:8; Deut. 31:15; 34:10; Judg. 13:22; 1 Sam. 3:21; 2 Sam. 22:11; 1 Kings 3:5; 9:2; 11:9; 22:19; 2 Chron. 1:7; 3:1; 7:12; Job 19:26–27; Ps. 11:7; 17:15; 24:3–6; 27:4; 42:2; Ps. 63:2; 84:7; 102:16; Isa. 6:1; Ezek. 1:26–28; Amos 9:1; *Jub.* 1:28; *1 En.* 47:3; Philo, *Mut.* 81–82; *Abr.* 58; *Contempl.* 12; *QE* 2.51 ("the beginning and end of happiness is to see God," which God grants to those "purified"); 1 Cor. 13:12; Heb. 12:14; 1 John 3:2; 3 John 11; Rev. 22:4; Josephus, *Ant.* 3.88; *4 Ezra* 7:98; *T. Levi* 5:1; *Asc. Isa* 3:8–9; *2 En.* 20:3; 39:3–6; *Prayer of Joseph* apud Origen, *Comm. John* 2.188–90 (SC 120, ed. Blanc, pp. 334–35). For additional texts and discussion see Arthur Marmorstein, *The Old Rabbinic Doctrine of God*, vol. 2, *Essays in Anthropomorphism* (London: Oxford University Press, 1937), esp. pp. 94–106; Friedrich Nötscher, *"Das Angesicht Gottes schauen" nach biblischer und babylonischer Auffassung* (Darmstadt: Wissenschaftliche Buchgesellschaft, 1969); and SB 1:206–15. For a typology of patristic attempts to harmonize the conflicting scriptural texts see Alfeyev, *Symeon*, pp. 215–18.

8. Ulrich Luz, *Das Evangelium nach Matthäus* (4 vols.; EKK 1/1–4; Düsseldorf: Benziger, 1990–2002), 1:286–87. Although he refers to interpreters who make the vision of God a present possibility, he nowhere hints at the various ways of understanding the beatific vision.

9. See David L. Paulsen, "Early Christian Belief in a Corporeal Deity: Origen and Augustine as Reluctant Witnesses," *HTR* 83 (1990), pp. 105–16; cf. Augustine, *Ep. 147* 49 (CSEL 44, ed. Goldbacher, p. 324): "There are some who assume that God himself is wholly corporeal."

10. See Paulsen, "Corporeal Deity"; Carl W. Griffin and David L. Paulsen, "Augustine and the Corporeality of God," *HTR* 95 (2002), pp. 97–118; also John Cassian, *Conf.* 10 (SC 54, ed. Pichery, pp. 74–99). For Tertullian see *Adv. Prax.* 7.8–9 (FC 34, ed. Sieben, p. 128), and for the

appears, moreover, in *Ps.-Clem. Hom.* 17.7, which contains one of the
earliest comments on our verse: God "has shape, and he has every limb
primarily and solely for beauty's sake, and not for use. For he has not
eyes that he may see with them, for he sees on every side."[11] The author
goes on to state that God "has the most beautiful shape on account of
humanity, that the pure in heart may be able to see him."[12]

What should we make of this interpretation? Can it correspond to the
evangelist's intention? Nothing to my knowledge speaks against the possibility that Matthew and his first readers believed God to be embodied.
We can hardly take for granted that he or they shared something like
our conventional take on John's declaration that "God is spirit" (John
4:24).[13] Quite a few Old Testament passages assume an anthropomorphic
God,[14] including probably Gen. 1:26–27, where the deity announces the

---

Audians, Epiphanius, *Haer.* 70.2 (GCS 37, ed. Holl, p. 234), and H.-Ch. Puech, "Audianer,"
RAC 1 (1950), pp. 910–15. Note also *Pass. Perp. et Fel.* 12 (ed. Musurillo, p. 120), where
martyrs "see an aged man with white hair and a youthful face": he is clearly God. Perhaps the
Messalians of Syro-Mesopotamia belong here too; see Theodoret of Cyrrhus, *HE* 4.11 (GCS 19,
ed. Parmentier, pp. 229–31; they claim to see "with the eyes the divine Trinity"); idem, *Haer.*
4.11 (PG 83.429–32, "they claim haughtily to see the Father and the Son and the all-Holy Spirit
with the eyes of the body"); Timothy of Constantinople, *Haer.* (PG 86.48–49, "the all-holy and
life-giving and blessed Trinity, which is by nature invisible to every creature, can be seen with
the eyes of the flesh by those who have come into what they call *apatheia*; and to such people
alone occurs the vision seen by them bodily"). Discussion in Klaus Fitschen, *Messalianismus und
Antimessalianismus: Ein Beispiel ostkirchlicher Ketzergeschichte* (Forschungen zur Kirchen- und
Dogmengeschichte 71; Göttingen: Vandenhoeck & Ruprecht, 1998), pp. 60–88. Although one
cannot without further ado move from the present to the past, I nonetheless find it suggestive
that, to judge from my conversations with contemporary Christians and seminary students over
the years, some even now think of God as a sort of large human being.

11. GCS 42, ed. Rehm, p. 232: μορφὴν γάρ ἔχει—διὰ πρῶτον καὶ μόνον κάλλος—καὶ πάντα
μέλη, οὐ διὰ χρῆσιν· οὐ γὰρ διὰ τοῦτο ὀφθαλμοὺς ἔχει, ἵνα ἐκεῖθεν βλέπῃ, πανταχόθεν γὰρ ὁρᾷ. For
the possibility that this depends upon a tradition also reflected in *Eccles. Rab.* 8.2 see David H.
Aaron, "Shedding Light on God's Body in Rabbinic Midrashim: Reflections on the Theory of
a Luminous Adam," *HTR* 90 (1997), pp. 299–314.

12. GCS 42, ed. Rehm, p. 232: τὴν δὲ καλλίστην μορφὴν ἔχει δι᾽ ἄνθρωπον, ἵνα οἱ καθαροὶ τῇ
καρδίᾳ αὐτὸν ἰδεῖν δυνηθῶσιν. Cf. 17.10 (GCS 42, ed. Rehm, p. 235): in order to be seen, God
must have a form. Contrast the judgment in *Ps.-Clem. Rec.* 3.30 (GCS 51, ed. Rehm, p. 118):
"God is seen by the mind, not by the body, by the spirit, not by the flesh. And so angels, who
are spirits, see God; and so people, as long as they are people, are unable to see him. But after
the resurrection of the dead, when they will have been made like the angels, they will be able
to see God. . . . A time will come when people will be made angels, who in the spirit of their
mind will see God."

13. It is instructive to recall that, according to Origen, *Prin.* 1.1 (TzF 24, ed. Görgemanns
and Karpp, pp. 98, 100), some Christians (presumably under Stoic influence) took John 4:24
to imply that God must have a body!

14. E.g., Gen. 3:8 (God walks in the garden of Eden); 32:30 (Jacob sees God "face to face");
Exod. 33:23 (Moses sees God's "back"); Deut. 34:10 (Moses knew God "face to face"); Isa.
6:1 ("I saw the Lord sitting upon a throne"); Dan. 7:9–13 ("the Ancient of Days" is seated
upon a throne).

intention of creating human beings "in our image" (MT: בצלמנו; LXX: κατ᾽ εἰκόνα ἡμετέραν) and "in our likeness" (MT: כדמותנו; LXX: καθ᾽ ὁμοίωσιν).[15] Rabbinic thinkers, it is no surprise, often understood "the image of God" literally.[16] The Merkabah mystics later on made the same assumption when they recounted their visions of a somatic deity.[17] Some of them even discussed the details of God's body.[18]

As for Matthew, his world paid some heed to seers who wrote apocalypses in which God is seen;[19] and the evangelist (who in my judgment was probably familiar with parts of *1 Enoch*)[20] might well have believed that what in this world is possible for only a privileged few will be, in the world to come, possible for many. A literal reading of Matt. 5:8b

15. Cf. Gen. 5:1–3; 9:6 and see J. Maxwell Miller, "In the 'Image' and 'Likeness' of God," *JBL* 91 (1972), pp. 289–304. Note also Ps.-Justin, *Res.* 7.1–8 (PTS 54, ed. Heimgartner), p. 118 (this vindicates the resurrection of the flesh by reference to the divine image of the human body) and *Ps.-Clem. Hom.* 11.4 (GCS 42, ed. Rehm, p. 155: the human body bears the divine image).

16. Pertinent texts include *Mek.* on Exod. 20:16; *ARN* A 2; *ARN* B 30 (33b); *Exod. Rab.* 30:12; *Lev. Rab.* 34:3; *Deut. Rab.* 2:21; Justin, *Dial.* 114 (PTS 47, ed. Marcovich, p. 266); Basil the Great, *Hex.* 10 1.5 (SC 160, ed. Smets and Van Esbroeck, p. 176); Arnobius, *Adv. nat.* 3.12 (PL 5.952); *Dialogue of Athanasius and Zacchaeus* 10 (ed. Conybeare, p. 7). See further Alon Goshen-Gottstein, "The Body as Image of God in Rabbinic Literature," *HTR* 87 (1994), pp. 171–95; Marmorstein, *Anthropomorphism*; and Morton Smith, "On the Shape of God and the Humanity of Gentiles," in *Religions in Antiquity: Essays in Memory of Erwin Randall Goodenough* (ed. Jacob Neusner; SHR 14; Leiden: Brill, 1968), pp. 315–26. That God was invisible—so Philo, *Mos.* 1.158; Rom. 1:20; Col. 1:15; 1 Tim. 1:17; Heb. 11:27; Josephus, *Ant.* 6.189; *Sib. Or.* 3:12, 17; *2 En.* 48:5; *Apoc. Abr.* 19:4; etc.—did not entail that God lacked a body but rather that God was hidden from view; invisibility was simply "a matter of tactics" for the biblical God; so Edmond La Beaume Cherbonnier, "The Logic of Biblical Anthropomorphism," *HTR* 55 (1962), p. 199.

17. See esp. Ira Chernus, "Visions of God in Merkabah Mysticism," *JSJ* 13 (1982), pp. 123–46.

18. See Martin Samuel Cohen, *The Shi'ur Qomah: Texts and Recensions* (TSAJ 9; Tübingen: Mohr Siebeck, 1985); also idem, *The Shi'ur Qomah: Liturgy and Theurgy in Pre-Kabbalistic Jewish Mysticism* (Lanham, Md.: University Press of America, 1983). It is common to suppose that the *Shi'ur Qomah* literature was used to induce "a hallucinogenic state in the mystic . . . so that in the end he attained the desired vision of God's body"; so Pieter W. van der Horst, "The Measurement of the Body: A Chapter in the History of Ancient Jewish Mysticism," in *Essays on the Jewish World of Early Christianity* (NTOA 14; Freiburg: Universitätsverlag, 1990), p. 124. Against J. Dan, "The Concept of Knowledge in the Shi'ur Qomah," in *Studies in Jewish Religious and Intellectual History Presented to Alexander Altmann on the Occasion of His Seventieth Birthday* (ed. Siegfried Stein and Raphael Loewe; N.P.: University of Alabama, 1979), pp. 67–73, who argues for figurative readings of the *Shi'ur Qomah*, see Naomi Janowitz, "God's Body: Theological and Ritual Roles of *Shi'ur Komah*," in *People of the Body: Jews and Judaism from an Embodied Perspective* (ed. Howard Eilberg-Schwartz; Albany, N.Y.: State University of New York Press, 1992), pp. 183–201.

19. Overview in Christopher Rowland, "The Visions of God in Apocalyptic Literature," *JSJ* 10 (1970), pp. 137–54.

20. Cf. David W. Suter, *Tradition and Composition in the Parables of Enoch* (SBLDS 47; Missoula, Mont.: 1979), pp. 25–29.

can, moreover, summon strong support from 18:10: "Take care that you do not despise one of these little ones; for, I tell you, in heaven their angels continually see the face of my Father (τὸ πρόσωπον τοῦ πατρός) in heaven." The quoted words presuppose a particular category of heavenly being, the "angels of the face" (מלאכי פנים; ἄγγελοι τοῦ προσώπου).[21] These angels were imagined to have privileged access to the deity. In Tob. 12:15, for instance, Raphael declares: "I am . . . one of the seven holy angels who stand ready and enter before the glory of the Lord." The angels "of the face" are those heavenly beings who have direct dealings with God and so see the divinity face to face. When Matthew, then, refers to the angels "of the little ones" who "see the face of my Father who is in heaven," he is adopting not only the traditional belief in guardian angels[22] but also the conventional idea that there are angels "of the face"; and there is no reason to imagine that the evangelist or other Jews understood the latter notion any less literally than the former. One can understand Matt. 5:8 accordingly. The beatific vision, which the angels enjoy even now, will be bestowed upon the saints in the world to come, just as in other ways the redeemed will become like the angels in heaven (22:30).[23] Which is to say: a literal interpretation of Matt. 5:8b is a plausible historical reading.

   A christological interpretation. Clement of Alexandria, Origen, the Cappadocians, Augustine, and others, following Philo's claim that God

---

21. Isa. 63:9 MT; 1QH 14(6).13; 1QSb 4:25–26; *Jub.* 1:27, 29; 2:1–2, 18; 15:27; 31:14; *T. Levi* 3:5, 7; *T. Jud.* 25:2; *Prayer of Joseph* apud Origen, *Comm. John* 2.189 (SC 120, ed. Blanc, p. 334). Cf. those texts in which angels stand before or in the presence of God: Job 1:6; 2:1; Dan. 7:16; *1 En.* 40:1; 4QShirShabb[a] 1 i 4; Luke 1:19; Rev. 8:2; *T. Abr.* Rec. Lng. 7:11; Eustathius *Encom. on Michael*, ed. Budge, p. 132. Presumably the idiom was modeled on the expression "to see the face of the king"; cf. 2 Sam. 14:24, 28, 32; Esther 1:14. I leave aside here the question of the relationship of these texts to those that (influenced perhaps by Isa. 6:2, where the seraphs hide their faces from God) declare that even the angels cannot behold the Supreme Being: *1 En.* 14:21; *Sifra* 2:3 on Lev. 1:1; *Sifre* 53:4 on Num. 12.8; *Tg. Ps.-J., Tg. Neof.* 1, and *Frg. Tg.* on Gen. 28:12; *Hekalot Zutarti* (Schäfer, *Synopse* 421: "God, who is hidden from the eyes of all creatures and concealed from the ministering angels"). For awareness of the two conflicting traditions and an attempt to harmonize them see Augustine, *Ep. 148* 7 (CSEL 44, ed. Goldbacher, pp. 337–38).

22. Ps. 34:7; 91:11; 1QH 5:20; *1 En.* 100:5; *Jub.* 35:17; *T. Levi* 5:3; Philo, *Gig.* 12; *T. Job* 43:10; *LAB* 33:1; 59:4; Heb. 1:14; *3 Bar.* 12–13; *T. Adam* 4:1; *T. Jacob* 2:5; *b. Taʿan.* 11a; etc.

23. Theological literature often brings Matt. 5:8 and 18:10 together and identifies the eschatological vision of God with the blessedness angels possess even now; see, e.g., Clement of Alexandria, *Exc.* 11 (SD 1, ed. Casey, p. 48); *Ps.-Clem. Rec.* 3.30 (GCS 51, ed. Rehm, p. 118); *Ps.-Clem. Hom.* 17.7 (GCS 42, ed. Rehm, p. 232); Augustine, *Ep. 147* 37 (CSEL 44, ed. Goldbacher, pp. 310–11); idem, *Civ. dei* 22.29 (CCSL 48, ed. Hoffmann, p. 857); Ps.-Dionysius, *Div. nom.* 1.4 (PTS 33, ed. Suchla, p. 115); cf. Aquinas, *ST* 1, q. 12, aa 4–5; q. 62, a. 1, who writes of the redeemed human intellect becoming like the angelic intellect. For Jewish parallels see *ARN* A 1.

49

is immaterial (e.g., *Opif.* 69; *Mos.* 1.158) and that the image of God is the soul or its rational nature (e.g., *Opif.* 69; *Det.* 86),[24] eventually succeeded in persuading the church at large that God does not have a body. Thereafter nonliteral interpretations of Matt. 5:8 proliferated. It remained possible, however, to offer a literal interpretation that was still orthodox. For one could think that, although the saints will never be able to see God the Father, they will someday behold the resurrected and glorified body of God the Son. The New Testament, including Matthew, promises that people will someday see the returning Jesus,[25] and it depicts this event in language borrowed from Old Testament prophecies about the coming of God and the Day of the Lord.[26] So given the Christian confession of his true divinity, might this not be reckoned the beatific vision of Matt. 5:8b? Colossians 1:15 reckons Jesus to be "the [visible] image of the invisible God," and Jesus says in John 14:9, "Whoever has seen me has seen the Father." So if one were persuaded, as is Robert Gundry in his commentary, that Matthew presents Jesus as divine, one could entertain the possibility that Matt. 5:8 is a prophecy of Jesus' *parousia*. Gundry himself is inclined to this option: "Since Matthew has identified Jesus as 'God with us' (1:23), he may intend his readers to understand the blessed vision of God in the future as the sight of Jesus returning in glory (24:30; 26:64; cf. 28:7, 10)."[27]

The christological interpretation of Matt. 5:8b, although never a favorite of the commentaries, has a long history. An early instance of it occurs in the *Acts of Thomas*. Chapter 94 of this third-century text contains a string of ten beatitudes. The eighth of these, which combines Matt. 5:5 with 5:8, says this: "Blessed are you meek, because you will see the face of the Lord."[28] Although the identity of "the Lord" (τοῦ κυρίου) is not here

24. See further J. Giblet, "L'homme image de Dieu dans les commentaires littéraires de Philon d'Alexandrie," *Studia Hellenistica* 5 (1948), pp. 93–118. In this, of course, Philo follows the Greek philosophical tradition. Xenophanes, frag. 23 (= Clement of Alexandria, *Strom.* 5.109.1 [GCS 15, ed. Stählin, p. 399]), e.g., asserted that God is "in no way similar to mortals either in body or in mind."

25. Matt. 16:28; 23:39; 24:30; 26:64; Mark 13:26; 14:62; Luke 13:35; 21:27; Acts 1:11; Heb. 12:14; 1 John 3:2; Rev. 1:7.

26. T. Francis Glasson, *The Second Advent: The Origin of the New Testament Doctrine* (2nd ed.; London: Epworth, 1947).

27. Robert H. Gundry, *Matthew: A Commentary on His Handbook for a Mixed Church under Persecution* (2nd ed.; Grand Rapids: Eerdmans, 1994), p. 71. So too David P. Scaer, *The Sermon on the Mount* (St. Louis: Concordia, 2000), p. 88; cf. Adolf Schlatter, *Der Evangelist Matthäus: Seine Sprache, sein Ziel, seine Selbständigkeit* (Stuttgart: Calwer, 1948), p. 139, who in commenting on 5:8 observes that Jesus makes his own *parousia* the center of eschatological expectation.

28. *Acts Thom.* 94 (ed. Bonnet, p. 208): μακάριοί ἐστε οἱ πραεῖς, ὅτι ὑμεῖς ὄψεσθε τὸ πρόσωπον τοῦ κυρίου.

specified, the "Lord" in the very next line is Jesus,[29] and throughout the *Acts* the title ὁ κύριος, with one possible exception, refers to him.[30] So in this book Matt. 5:8 becomes a promise that the pure in heart will see Jesus. With this we may compare the *Passion of Bartholomew*: "The true God and man (= Jesus Christ) has not given himself out to be known, except to those who are pure in heart, and who serve him by good works."[31] Here purity of heart issues in knowing the divine Jesus.[32]

What are the chances that a first-century Christian such as Matthew might have equated the τὸν θεόν of Matt. 5:8b with Jesus and so thought of a vision of the resurrected or returning Jesus as the vision of God? Even when one doubts that Matthew's Gospel ever calls Jesus θεός—it is not clear to me that it does—we do know that some Christians thought of

29. *Acts Thom.* 94 (ed. Bonnet, p. 208): μακάριοί ἐστε οἱ πεινῶντες ἕνεκεν κυρίου, ὅτι ὑμῖν τετήρηται ἡ ἀνάπαυσις· ὧν καὶ αἱ ψυχαὶ ἀπὸ νῦν ἀγαλλιῶνται. This is largely a pastiche of Matt. 5 and Luke 6, as one can see at a glance: μακάριοί ἐστε (cf. Matt. 5:11/Luke: 6:22: μακάριοί ἐστε) οἱ πεινῶντες (cf. Matt. 5:6/Luke 6:21: οἱ πεινῶντες) ἕνεκεν κυρίου (cf. Matt. 5:11/Luke 6:22: ἕνεκεν ἐμοῦ/τοῦ υἱοῦ τοῦ ἀνθρώπου) νῦν (cf. Luke 6:21, 25: νῦν) ἀγαλλιῶνται (cf. Matt. 5:11: ἀγαλλιᾶσθε). "On account of the Lord" in *Acts Thom.* 94 is a transformation of the christological expression in Matt. 5:11 and Luke 6:22, "on account of me/the Son of Man."

30. The exception is in chapter 67: "And when they had prayed with them, remaining a long time in prayer and supplication, he commended them to the Lord and said, 'Lord, who rules over every soul that is in a body; Lord, father of the souls that have their hope in you and await your mercies." And yet 143 calls Jesus "father of the height," so he could likewise be the "father" of 67.

31. *Pass. Barth.* 5(11) (ed. Bonnet, pp. 137–38).

32. For additional christological interpretations of Matt. 5:8b—something impossible for Arians and Homoians who did not equate Jesus with God (cf. Palladius, frag. 106 [SC 267, ed. Gryson, p. 290])—see Clement of Alexandria, *Exc.* 11–12 (SD 1, ed. Casey, pp. 48, 50); Eusebius, *E. Th.* 3.21 (GCS 13, ed. Klostermann, p. 181); Athanasius, *Gent.* 2 (OECT, ed. Thomson, p. 6); *Liber Graduum* 12.7; 18.3 (Patrologia Syriaca 3, ed. Kmosko, pp. 303, 440); Cassiodorus, *Exp. Ps.* on 76:15 (CSEL 98, ed. Adriaen, p. 705); Martyrius, *Perf.* 2.8.47 (CSCO 252 Scriptores Syri 110, p. 15). According to Raymond E. Brown, *The Epistles of John* (AB 30; Garden City, N.Y.: Doubleday, 1982), p. 395, Latin exegetes traditionally referred 1 John 3:2 ("we will see him as he is")—a verse the Cappadocians seemingly never cite—to Jesus Christ. For Augustine's christological reading of Matt. 5:8, where the emphasis is upon spiritual understanding as opposed to physical sight, see *Trin.* 1.8(16), 13 (28, 30) (CCSL 50, ed. Mountain, pp. 51, 70, 74), and Michel René Barnes, "The Visible Christ and the Invisible Trinity: Mt. 5:8 in Augustine's Trinitarian Theology of 400," *Modern Theology* (2003), pp. 329–55. For the possibility that the Egyptian Anthropomorphites were misunderstood and that they equated the form and glory of God with Jesus Christ and so would have understood the vision of God to be the vision of Christ, see Alexander Golitzin, "The Vision of God and the Form of Glory: More Reflections on the Anthropomorphite Controversy of AD 399," in *Abba: The Tradition of Orthodoxy in the West: Festschrift for Bishop Kallistos (Ware) of Diokleia* (ed. John Behr, Andrew Louth, and Dimitri Conomos; Crestwood, N.Y.: St. Vladimir's Seminary Press, 2003), pp. 273–97, and Graham Gould, "The Image of God and the Anthropomorphite Controversy in Fourth Century Monasticism," in *Origeniana Quinta: Historica—Text and Method—Biblica—Philosophica—Theologica—Origenism and Later Developments* (ed. Robert J. Daly; Leuven: Peeters, 1992), pp. 549–57.

Jesus as "the image of God" (e.g., 2 Cor. 4:4; Col. 1:15) and "the glory of God" (2 Cor. 4:6; Rev. 21:23; Origen, *Comm. John* 32.28 [GCS 4, ed. Preuschen, p. 474]); and there are intriguing links between early christological doctrine and Jewish speculations about the exalted angel who bears God's name and can be seen.[33] Furthermore, Justin Martyr and others could identify the figure of biblical theophanies with the pre-incarnate Son.[34] So we can entertain the possibility that some early Christians might well have identified seeing the returning Jesus with the beatific vision. One recalls that, in the famous fifth-century image of the returning Christ at the Latomou monastery in Thessalonica, Christ holds in his left hand a scroll with the words "Behold our God" (from Isa. 25:9).[35]

On balance, however, one should probably cast a vote against the christological interpretation of Matt. 5:8, at least if one is thinking of the intended sense of the evangelist. This is not only because Matthew never clearly calls Jesus θεός but also because the one other verse in Matthew that speaks of the beatific vision makes it plain that God the Father is in view. In 18:10 Jesus says, "in heaven their angels continually see the face of my Father in heaven." Here the *visio dei* is a vision of the Father, not the Son. Beyond this, the objection of Novatian seems to the point: in Matt. 5:8 Jesus "promises the contemplation and vision of the Father. It follows that he had not yet bestowed such (sight); for why should he promise it if he had already bestowed it? For if he (Jesus) were the Father, he had (already) bestowed it, for he was being seen and being touched."[36] Perhaps an observation of Augustine is also worth noting: the promise that the pure in heart will see God implies that the impure in heart will not see God; but, according to Matthew, when people see Jesus at the *parousia*, the wicked as well as the righteous will see him (cf. Matt. 24:30; 25:32; 26:64).[37]

A mystical encounter. If Christian theology eventually ended up with an asomatic God the Father, later reflection also moved many to believe

33. Jarl Fossum, "Jewish-Christian Christology and Jewish Mysticism," *VC* 37 (1983), pp. 260–87; Golitzin, "Vision of God"; Christopher Rowland, *The Open Heaven: A Study of Apocalyptic in Judaism and Early Christianity* (New York: Crossroad, 1982), pp. 94–112; D. Steenburg, "The Worship of Adam and Christ as the Image of God," *JSNT* 39 (1990), pp. 95–109; Gedaliahu G. Stroumsa, "Form(s) of God: Some Notes on Metatron and Christ," *HTR* 76 (1983), pp. 269–88.

34. Justin, *Dial.* 59–62 (PTS 47, ed. Marcovich, pp. 172–78); cf. *Liber Graduum* 28:10–11 (Patrologia Syriaca 3, ed. Kmosko, p. 802). Augustine famously rejected this thesis; see *Trin.* 1–3 (CCSL 50, ed. Mountain, pp. 27–158).

35. Wayne A. Meeks, "Vision of God and Scripture: Interpretation in a Fifth-Century Mosaic," in *In Search of the Early Christians: Selected Essays* (ed. Allen R. Hilton and H. Gregory Snyder; New Haven: Yale University Press, 2002), pp. 230–53.

36. Novatian, *Trin.* 28(161) (Fuentes Patrísticas 8, ed. Granado, p. 244). For Novatian this functions as an argument against the Modalists: the Son is not the Father.

37. Augustine, *Ep.* 92 4 (CSEL 34.2, ed. Goldbacher, pp. 440–41).

that it was likewise impossible to perceive Jesus in his divinity.[38] For this reason, it may be, the christological interpretation of Matt. 5:8b has remained at the margin of exegetical history. Other possibilities, in any case, have come to the fore.

Perhaps the earliest comment on Matt. 5:8 is in a fragment from Valentinus: "When the father, who alone is good, visits the heart, he makes it holy and fills it with light. And so a person who has such a heart is called blessed, for that person will see God."[39] These words equate seeing God with having a heart full of light. Elaboration is lacking. Perhaps some sort of mystical experience, interpreted as an encounter with the divinity, is in view.

Whatever the case with Valentinus, the Byzantine Hesychasts had just such a view of Matt. 5:8b. They believed, or rather were persuaded by their experience, that the pure in heart can even now see the uncreated light of Christ once manifested at the transfiguration, and that this is the promise of Matthew's beatitude. Gregory of Palamas wrote: "He who participates in the divine energy . . . becomes himself, in a sense, Light; he is united to the Light and with the Light he sees in full consciousness all that remains hidden for those who have not this grace; he thus surpasses not only the corporeal senses, but also all that can be known [by the mind] . . . for the pure in heart see God . . . who, being the Light, abides in them and reveals Himself to those who love Him."[40]

Although it would be anachronistic to read the elaborated theology of Hesychasm, with its distinction between God's (super)essence and God's

---

38. Cf. Clement of Alexandria, *Exc.* 10.5 (SD 1, ed. Casey, p. 48); Cyril of Jerusalem on John 1:18, in *Catenae in Evangelia S. Lucae et S. Joannis ad fidem codd. mss.* (ed. J. A. Cramer; Hildesheim: Georg Olms, 1967 [reprint of 1842 ed.]), p. 189; Jerome, *Comm. Isa.* on 6:1 (ed. Gryson, 1:310–11); Chrysostom, *Hom. John* 15.1 (PG 59.98); Augustine, *Ep.* 148 6 (CSEL 44, ed. Goldbacher, p. 337); Nicetas of Remesiana, *Rat. fid.* 7 (PL 52.852 A–C). Already Origen had famously spoken of Jesus not as "the visible image of the invisible God" but as "the invisible image of the invisible God": *Prin.* 1.2.6 (TzF 24, ed. Görgemanns and Karpp, p. 132). For this theme in Theodoret see J. L. Stewardson, "Vision of God according to Theodoret of Cyrus," in *Studia Patristica* 32 (1995), pp. 371–75.

39. Preserved in Clement of Alexandria, *Strom.* 2.20.114.6 (GCS 15, ed. Stählin, p. 175).

40. Gregory Palamas, "Sermon for the Feast of the Presentation of the Blessed Virgin in the Temple," as quoted by Vladimir Lossky, *In the Image and Likeness of God* (Crestwood, N.Y.: St. Vladimir's Seminary Press, 1974), p. 61. For the sort of experience that may lie behind these words see Archbishop Basil Krivocheine, *St. Symeon the New Theologian: Life—Spirituality—Doctrine* (Crestwood, N.Y.: St. Vladimir's Seminary Press, 1986), esp. pp. 163–238; also Alfeyev, *Symeon*, pp. 226–41. For similar experience outside of Hesychast circles see Guigues du Pont, *De contemplatione* 3.9 (Analecta Cartusiana 72, ed. Dupont, pp. 308–12), and for anticipations of Hesychast ideas see Alexander Golitzin, "'The Demons Suggest an Illusion of God's Glory in a Form': Controversy over the Divine Body and Vision of Glory in Some Late Fourth, Early Fifth Century Monastic Literature," *Studia Monastica* 44 (2002), pp. 13–43.

energies, back into Matthew's time and place,[41] the notion that one might encounter God through some kind of mystical experience or through a created instrument of God's presence would not have been foreign to our evangelist. In the Greco-Roman world, "epiphanies of the gods were no longer their personal appearances but manifestations of their power";[42] and, within the Jewish tradition, there were old stories about God's "glory" (כבוד, δόξα), which manifested the presence of the deity while at the same time concealing him. It seems to have been conceived of as something like a glowing or fiery cloud.[43] Further, Exodus tells a story in which God meets the law-giver through the medium of a burning bush that is not consumed. Moses, to use later terminology, here encounters the divine reality or presence even if he does not directly perceive God.[44] Exodus also famously tells of Moses seeing God's "back," which some exegetes have understood as a way of saying that, although he truly met God, Moses could see God only indirectly.[45] Maybe Ephraem the Syrian was thinking along these lines when he wrote that "those whose hearts are pure will see God, like Moses."[46] One hesitates, however, to surmise the same of Matthew. This is because, in Matt. 18:10, the *visio dei* is characterized

41. But see Gershom G. Scholem, *Major Trends in Jewish Mysticism* (New York: Schocken, 1961), pp. 63–67, for an analogous distinction between the divine substance and the divine appearance in the *Shiur Komah*; also the works cited in n. 33 and Gilles Quispel, "Ezekiel 1:26 in Jewish Mysticism and Gnosis," *VC* 34 (1980), pp. 1–13. According to Alan F. Segal, *Rebecca's Children: Judaism and Christianity in the Roman World* (Cambridge, Mass.: Harvard University Press, 1986), p. 14, already the vision of the divine throne in Ezek. 1, like later Kabbalistic texts, may "distinguish the essential personhood of God from the human figure, the form in which He manifests himself. It was God's glory, not He himself, who has a human form." Whatever the case about Ezekiel, this thought would probably have been at home in the first century; see Jarl E. Fossum, *The Image of the Invisible God: Essays on the Influence of Jewish Mysticism on Early Christology* (NTOA 30; Freiburg: Universitätsverlag, 1995), pp. 13–39. Christian theologians, when discussing the vision of God, have often had recourse to a distinction between form and essence or nature and revelation; see, e.g., Augustine, *Ep. 147* 19–20 (CSEL 44, ed. Goldbacher, pp. 292–94; here following Ambrose), and Chrysostom, *Hom. John* 15 (PG 59.98).

42. Martin P. Nilsson, "The High God and the Mediator," *HTR* 56 (1963), p. 107.

43. Cf. Exod. 16:10; 24:16–17; 40:34–35; Num. 16:42; Deut. 5:24; 1 Kings 8:11; 2 Chron. 5:14; 7:3; Isa. 4:5; Ezek. 10:4; 2 Macc. 2:8; and see further A. Joseph Everson, "Ezekiel and the Glory of the Lord tradition," in *Sin, Salvation, and the Spirit: Commemorating the Fiftieth Year of The Liturgical Press* (ed. Daniel Durken; Collegeville, Minn.: Liturgical Press, 1979), pp. 163–74.

44. According to Philo, *Mos.* 1.66–67, there was an image in the fire, not as one might suppose of the divinity, but of an angel or herald, "a symbol of God's providence." Cf. Ps.-Dionysius, *CH* 4.3 (PTS 36, ed. Heil and Ritter, p. 22), where an OT theophany is defined as a vision in which "the formless God is *represented* in forms." Note also the use of ὁράματι as a way of communicating indirectness in Symm. Exod. 24:10: "saw the God of Israel" becomes "saw the God of Israel in a vision."

45. Philo even argued that Moses' prayer to know God was not really answered: Philo, *Post.* 13; *Spec.* 1.42–43; *Fug.* 164–65; *Mut.* 7–10; cf. John 1:18.

46. Ephraem, *Comm. Diat.* 6.1 (SC 121, ed. Leloir, p. 122).

as unmediated: the angels see the *face* of the heavenly Father (οἱ ἄγγελοι
. . . βλέπουσι τὸ πρόσωπον τοῦ πατρός).

A metaphor for insight. Origen, influenced by Plato's equation of vision
with knowledge, by the LXX's cautious treatment of theophanies,[47] and
by Philo's philosophical theology, urged a metaphorical interpretation of
Matt. 5:8b: the sixth beatitude refers not to physical sight but to spiritual
and intellectual apprehension. When we say, "I see the point," we are
rarely talking about dots. "They will see God," according to Origen, is
similar. "The names of the organs of sense are often applied to the soul,
so that we speak of seeing with the eyes of the heart, that is, of drawing
some intellectual conclusions by means of the faculty of intelligence."
There are within us, says Origen, "two kinds of senses, the one being
mortal, corruptible and human, and the other immortal and intellectual,
which here he [Solomon in Proverbs] calls 'divine.' By this divine sense,
therefore, not of the eyes but of a pure heart, that is, the mind, God can
be seen by those who are worthy."[48]

Origen's comments on Matt. 5:8b put him at the head of a long interpretive tradition. The official Roman Catholic understanding of the
beatific vision is that it will be a supernaturally bestowed, unmediated,
and imageless intuition or perception (without full comprehension) of
the divine essence.[49] From the Protestant side, Schleiermacher wrote that
the eschatological vision of God is simply the "unimpeded knowledge of
God in all and along with all."[50]

47. See Anthony Hanson, "The Treatment in the LXX of the Theme of Seeing God," in
*Septuagint, Scrolls and Cognate Writings: Papers Presented to the International Symposium
on the Septuagint and Its Relations to the Dead Sea Scrolls and Other Writings* (ed. George J.
Brooke and Barnabas Lindars; Atlanta: Scholars Press, 1992), pp. 557–68, with this conclusion:
"Within the LXX itself we can trace the beginning of the exegetical tradition, which, no doubt
under the influence of Greek rationalism, softened down anthropomorphisms and modified
cruder notions of how human beings may know God" (p. 566).

48. Origen, *Prin.* 1.1.9 (TzF 24, ed. Görgemanns and Karpp, p. 121); cf. Origen, *Cels.* 6.4;
7.33 (ed. Marcovich, pp. 381, 487) and see further Gedaliahu Stroumsa, "The Incorporeality
of God: Context and Implications of Origen's Position," *Religion* 15 (1983), pp. 345–58. For
Philo see, e.g., *Det.* 86 and *Somn.* 1 79.

49. Cf. Gregory the Great, *Mor.* 2.3 (SC 32bis, ed. Gillet and Gaudemaris, pp. 256–60);
Albertus Magnus, *Super Mt. cap. I–XIV* ad loc. (Opera Omnia 21/1, ed. B. Schmidt, p. 113);
Thomas Aquinas, *ST* ii, 2 q. 173, a. 2. For the very complex debates from the Middle Ages see
the comprehensive survey of Christian Trottmann, *La vision béatifique des disputes scholas-
tiques à sa définition par Benoît XII* (Paris: École Française de Rome, 1995). Eastern Orthodox
theology, by contrast, came to identify the object of the beatific vision with something other
than the divine essence.

50. Friedrich Schleiermacher, *The Christian Faith* (2 vols.; New York: Harper & Row, 1963),
2:719. Cf. Didymus of Alexandria, *Gen.* 248 ad 16:12–14 (SC 244, ed. Nautin, p. 232); Ambrose, *Exp. Luke* 1.24–27 (SC 45, ed. Tissot, pp. 58–61); Chrysostom, *Hom. John* 15.2; 73.6
(PG 59.99, 398); Augustine, *Ep.* 147 28 (CSEL 44, ed. Goldbacher, pp. 302–3); Anonymous,

A variant of this view finds in Matt. 5:8b a statement not about an eschatological knowledge but about present insight into the world as it really is. According to A. B. Bruce, our beatitude "states a self-acting law of the moral world." Matthew's Jesus does not promise us that we will literally see the face of God, whether in this life or the life to come, but that we will have "clear vision." It was Jesus' wont, according to Bruce, "to insist on the connection between clear vision and moral simplicity; to teach that it is the single eye that is full of light (Matt. vi.22). It is true that the pure shall have access to God's presence, but *the* truth to be insisted on in connection with this beatitude is that through purity, singleness of mind, they are qualified for seeing, knowing, truly conceiving God and all that relates to the moral universe." The pure in heart grasp the truth and know that "God is good," and they can "rightly interpret the whole phenomena of life in relation to Providence."[51] So Bruce does not find eschatology in Matt. 5:8 but rather information about how things work in this world. If one has the proper moral disposition, one will gain insight into the way things really are.[52]

A thousand years before Bruce, Isho'dad of Merv seems to have said much the same thing:

> Sight, although it is said to be of seven kinds, may be summed up under three kinds: in the senses, in the mind, and in faith. God is seen only by faith. Faith, it is said, is the persuasion about those things that are in hope, as if they were really possessed, and the revelation of things not seen; he (God) is seen also in his works; let them be enquiring about God, and they will find him from his creatures; but the organ of this vision is a pure heart that is not attached to earthly things. Again, he calls sight here the light and revelation which the soul receives inwardly by knowledge about him, and about these spiritual things: like this, "Uncover my eyes so that I may behold wondrous things."[53]

Expositio Evang. sec. Luc. 1.1 (CCSL, ed. Gryson, p. 199); John Philoponus, *Opif.* 1.22 (FC 23/1, ed. Scholten, pp. 176, 178); John of Dalyatha (= "Greek Isaac"), *Hom.* 43 (ed. Theotokis, pp. 177–78); Paschasius Radbertus, *Exp. Matt. Libri XII* ad loc. (CCCM 56, ed. Paulus, pp. 293–94); *Glossa Ordinaria* (1545 Lyon ed.), p. 19. I cannot here discuss how theologians have defined and understood the different sorts of intellectual and spiritual senses; for some aspects of the problem see Columba Stewart, *"Working the Earth of the Heart": The Messalian Controversy in History, Texts, and Language to AD 431* (Oxford: Clarendon, 1991), pp. 116–38.

51. Alexander Balmain Bruce, "The Synoptic Gospels," in *The Expositor's Greek Testament* (5 vols.; ed. W. Robertson Nicoll; New York: George H. Doran, 1912), 1:99.

52. Cf. David Dickson, *A Brief Exposition of the Evangel of Jesus Christ according to Matthew* (Carlisle, Pa.: Banner of Truth, 1981), p. 47. Although Alfred Plummer, *An Exegetical Commentary on the Gospel according to Matthew* (New York: Scribner, 1909), p. 67, gives the standard eschatological reading to Matt. 5:8, he also sounds much like Bruce.

53. Isho'dad of Merv, *Comm. Matt.* 3 ad 5:8 (HSem 6, ed. Gibson, p. 56). Almost identical words appear in Dionysius bar Salibi, *Expl. Evang.* ad loc. (CSCO 77, Scriptores Syri 33, ed. Sedlaeck and Chabot, pp. 205–6).

Such a metaphorical interpretation of Matt. 5:8b has in its favor this, that ὁράω can refer to mental perception (BDAG, ὁράω 4). Further, Matthew himself does not consistently give ὁράω its literal sense; for instance, he often uses it to mean "pay attention" (8:4; 9:30; 16:6; 18:10; 24:6). Even more significantly, another first-century text, John 1:18 ("No one has ever seen God; it is God the only Son, who is close to the Father's heart, who has made him known"), passes from the vision of God to the knowledge of God as though the two are identical. The same equation is implicit in 3 John 11, which declares that "whoever does evil has not seen God." This must mean something like: "whoever does not believe in Jesus is alienated from God."[54] First John 3:6 confirms this: "No one who abides in him sins; no one who sins has either seen him or known him." Paul similarly, in 1 Cor. 13:12, seems to equate seeing God with knowing God: "For now we see in a mirror, dimly, but then we will see face to face. Now I know only in part; then I will know fully, even as I have been fully known."[55]

Having said all this, neither Matt. 5:8 nor Matthew's Gospel as a whole does much to prod readers to find a metaphorical meaning in "they will see God." As we have already observed, 18:10, which speaks of angels who behold the face of the Father in heaven, rather encourages us to entertain a more literal understanding of Matt. 5:8b.

God in perfected creation. Augustine offers several different interpretations of "they will see God." But in *The City of God* he contends, with appropriate modesty (for it is hard, he says, to talk about what one has not yet experienced), that in the new world the perfected saints will be able to perceive God directly through a perfected creation. People often perceive things indirectly, through their effects. As Paul says in Rom. 1:20, God's invisible attributes are seen through the things God has made; and, according to Augustine,

we will then see the physical bodies of the new heaven and the new earth in such a fashion as to observe God in utter clarity and distinctness, seeing him present everywhere and governing the whole material scheme of things by means of the bodies we will then inhabit and the bodies we will see wherever we turn our eyes. It will not be as it is now, when the invisible realities of God are apprehended and observed through the material things of his creation, and are partially apprehended by means of a puzzling reflection in a mirror. Rather in that new age the faith, by which we believe, will have a

54. Cf. Rudolf Schnackenburg, *The Johannine Epistles: Introduction and Commentary* (New York: Crossroad, 1992), p. 300.

55. It is possible that Job 42:5 belongs here: "I had heard of you by the hearing of the ear, but now my eye sees you." This may refer primarily to Job's new understanding, not to a literal, visual theophany.

greater reality for us than the appearance of material things which we see with our bodily eyes. Now in this present life we are in contact with fellow beings who are alive and display the motions of life; and as soon as we see them we do not believe them to be alive, we observe the fact. We could not observe their life without their bodies; but we see it in them, without any possibility of doubt, through their bodies. Similarly, in the future life, wherever we turn the spiritual eyes of our bodies we will discern, by means of our bodies, the incorporeal God directing the whole universe. God then will be seen by those eyes in virtue of their possession (in this transformed condition) of something of an intellectual quality, a power to discern things of an immaterial nature.[56]

There is little chance that Augustine's sophisticated interpretation of the eschatological vision of God, which is not unparalleled,[57] preserves the evangelist's own view. Yet Augustine's speculations about perceiving God through the re-created universe bring to mind some words of C. H. Dodd, who thought that the realism of the parables of Jesus

arises from a conviction that there is no mere analogy, but an inward affinity, between the natural order and the spiritual order; or as we might put in the language of the parables themselves, the Kingdom of God is intrinsically *like* the processes of nature and of the daily life of men. Jesus therefore did not feel the need of making up artificial illustrations for the truths He wished to teach. He found them ready-made by the Maker of man and nature. . . . Since nature and super-nature are one order, you can take any part of that order and find in it illumination for other parts. Thus the falling of rain is a religious thing, for it is God who makes the rain to fall on the just and the unjust. . . . This sense of the divineness of the natural order is the major premise of all the parables.[58]

One could, if so inclined, regard Augustine's understanding of the beatific vision as an intensification or bringing to perfection of the perception of God in nature that Jesus' parables, on Dodd's reading, seem to reflect.

God in perfected self and neighbor. In his beautiful commentary on the Beatitudes, Gregory of Nyssa at one point construes Matt. 5:8b very much as does Augustine in *The City of God*: God, "who is by nature invisible, becomes visible in his operations, being seen in certain cases by

56. Augustine, *Civ. dei* 22.29 (CCSL 48, ed. Hoffmann, p. 861).

57. Note, e.g., Apollinarius of Laodicea, *Comm. Matt.* frag. 13 ad loc. (TU 61, ed. Reuss, p. 5; although Apollinarius writes about a perception of God in the present), and Nicodemus of the Holy Mountain, *Handbook of Spiritual Counsel* (trans. Chamberas, p. 215). The notion that God cannot be perceived directly but only through "effects" is already well developed in Philo; see, e.g., *Spec.* 1.41–50, and *QE* 2.51. As with so much else, the thought ultimately goes back to Plato.

58. C. H. Dodd, *The Parables of the Kingdom* (rev. ed.; New York: Scribner, 1961), p. 10.

the properties he possesses."[59] Gregory goes on, however, to stress another point that Augustine for his part makes only in passing.[60] According to Gregory, we will, in the world to come, see God in ourselves and in our neighbor. In the eschatological paradise the likeness to God originally given to Adam and Eve but then obscured through sin will be perfectly regained, which will enable us to see God in the restored human being. Furthermore, the same thing happens, so Gregory argues, in the here and now, when the saints gain purity of heart. While we cannot look directly at the sun but can see it only indirectly, in a mirror, so too is it with God. Our perception can never encompass more than a reflection:

> Just as happens in the case of iron, when it is stripped of rust by a whetstone, and what once was dull gleams of its own accord as it faces the sun and gives forth beams and shafts of light, so also the inner man, which is what the Lord calls "the heart," once it has wiped off the rusty filth which has spread by evil corrosion over its form, will once again recover its likeness to its archetype and be good. . . . Therefore the one who looks at himself sees in himself what he desires, and so the pure in heart becomes blessed, because by looking at his own purity he perceives the archetype in the copy.[61]

Maybe the same thought appears in the *Opus Imperfectum* ad loc. (PG 56.682): "To the degree that one removes himself from evils and does good things, to that degree he also sees God." The author goes on to say such sight will characterize the age to come.

Centuries after Gregory and the *Opus Imperfectum* and, I presume, independently of them, John Trapp, when expounding Matt. 5:8, offered a very similar exegesis. Citing John 1:18, where God shines in human hearts, Trapp argued that God "shines through" the pure in heart, and "as the pearl by the beams of the sun becomes bright and radiant as the sun itself, so 'we all with open face beholding the glory of the Lord, are transformed into the same image from glory to glory, as by the Spirit of the Lord'" (2 Cor. 3:18).[62] For Trapp, as for Gregory, the vision of God is

59. Gregory of Nyssa, *Orat. dom. de beat.* 6.3 (Gregorii Nysseni Opera 7.2, ed. Callahan, p. 141). For general reflections on the vision of God in Gregory see Edward Baert, "Le thème de la vision de Dieu chez S. Justin, Clément d'Alexandrie, et S. Grégoire de Nysse," *FZPhTh* 12 (1965), pp. 481–97.

60. Augustine, *Civ. dei* 29.30 (CCSL 48, ed. Hoffmann, pp. 861–62): "Perhaps God will be known to us and visible to us in the sense that he will be spiritually perceived by each one of us in each one of us, perceived in one another, perceived by each in himself."

61. Gregory of Nyssa, *Orat. dom. de beat.* 6.4 (Gregorii Nysseni Opera 7.2, ed. Callahan, p. 143). Cf. Evagrius's teaching that the mind in pure prayer "sees" the divine light that illumines it; on this see William Harmless, *Desert Christians: An Introduction to the Literature of Early Monasticism* (Oxford: Oxford University Press, 2004), pp. 353–54.

62. Cf. John Trapp, *A Commentary or Exposition upon All the Books of the New Testament* (ed. W. Webster; London: Richard D. Dickinson, 1865), p. 49.

the perception of the divine light that shines through the redeemed, and he even managed to cite one of Gregory's favorite verses, 2 Cor. 3:18.

Present and future experience. A final suggestion is perhaps the simplest of all. Sometimes—although never in Matthew, if one leaves 5:8 to the side—the idiom "to see" can mean "to experience" (cf. BDAG, ὁράω 3; cf. the English: "I hope to see that day"). This appears to be the likely meaning in those psalms in which people go up to the Jerusalem temple to see God:

> The upright shall behold his face. (Ps. 11:7)

> I shall behold your face in righteousness; when I awake I shall be satisfied, beholding your likeness. (Ps. 17:15)

> Who shall ascend the hill of the Lord? And who shall stand in his holy place? Those who have clean hands and pure hearts. . . . Such is the company of those who seek him, who seek the face of the God of Jacob. (Ps. 24:3–6)

> One thing I asked of the Lord, that will I seek after: to live in the house of the Lord all the days of my life, to behold the beauty of the Lord, and to inquire in his temple. (Ps. 27:4)

> My soul thirsts for God, for the living God. When shall I come and behold the face of God? (Ps. 42:2)

> I have looked upon you in the sanctuary, beholding your power and glory. (Ps. 63:2)[63]

One might deem it significant that 5:8 has often been understood to allude to Ps. 24:3–6 (quoted in part above)[64] and then find in this a reason for taking Matt. 5:8b to mean "will experience God."

---

63. See Nötscher, *Angesicht*, pp. 147–55, and Mark S. Smith, "'Seeing God' in the Psalms: The Background to the Beatific Vision in the Hebrew Bible," *CBQ* 50 (1988), pp. 171–83. (Although some of the verses in Psalms may have referred in their original settings to experiences at sunrise, this does not dictate how people later read them.) Note also *CIJ* 1.634 (ed. Frey, p. 452), where "find the face of God" must be general and metaphorical.

64. The commentators on Matt. 5:8 regularly cite it: Chromatius, *Tract. Matt.* 3.6 (CCSL 9, ed. Hoste, p. 399); Albertus Magnus, *Super Mt. cap. I–XIV* ad loc. (Opera Omnia 21/1, ed. B. Schmidt, p. 113); Dickson, *Matthew*, p. 47; A. H. McNeile, *The Gospel according to St. Matthew* (London: Macmillan, 1915), p. 52; Hans Dieter Betz, *The Sermon on the Mount: A Commentary on the Sermon on the Mount, Including the Sermon on the Plain (Matthew 5:3–7:27 and Luke 6:20–49)* (Hermeneia; Minneapolis: Fortress, 1995), pp. 134–35; Wolfgang Wiefel, *Das Evangelium nach Matthäus* (THNT 1; Leipzig: Evangelische Verlagsanstalt, 1998), p. 88; etc. Contrast Julius Wellhausen, *Das Evangelium Matthaei übersetzt und erklärt* (2nd ed.; Berlin: Georg Reimer, 1914), p. 14, who finds the background of Matt. 5:8 in Ps. 11:7.

However that may be, the equation of "to see" with "to experience" does show up in the secondary literature on Matthew. In recent commentaries, there is a tendency to think of such experience as eschatological experience: Jesus here promises experiencing the fullness of salvation.[65] Earlier commentators tended to want to say something about the present also. John Gill, giving a rather wide meaning to Matthew's beatitude, indicates that we experience the vision of God

> in this life, enjoying communion with him, both in private and public, in the several duties of religion, in the house and ordinances of God; where they often behold his beauty, see his power and his glory, and taste, and know, that he is good and gracious: and in the other world, where they shall see God in Christ, with the eyes of their understanding; and God incarnate, with the eyes of their bodies, after the resurrection; which sight of Christ, and God in Christ, will be unspeakably glorious, desirable, delightful, and satisfying; it will be free from all darkness and error, and from all interruption; it will be an appropriate and transforming one, and will last forever.[66]

John Wesley, commenting on "they will see God," said the same thing as Gill, but with considerable more economy: "In all things here; hereafter in glory."[67]

The Theological Value of Exegetical History

What is the value of the preceding survey? What can we learn from the various interpretations of "they will see God"? Some might respond that, while the exercise is intrinsically interesting, it really has little exegetical or theological value, for while Matthew's Gospel may move us to ask the meaning of "they will see God," it nowhere returns an answer; and surely most of the proposed interpretations are unlikely to correspond to the intentions of a first-century Christian Jew.

Such a response would be, from a theological point of view, a shortsighted prejudice, a sort of textual fundamentalism. Despite Matthew's silence, the odds are good that he and his early readers understood Matt.

65. E.g., Wiefel, *Matthäus*, p. 89.

66. John Gill, *Gill's Commentary* (6 vols.; Grand Rapids: Baker, 1980), 5:31. Cf. Adam Clarke, *The Holy Bible, Containing the Old and New Testaments: The New Testament*, vol. 1, *Matthew to Romans* (London: Thomas Tegg & Son, 1836), p. 69 (aptly citing Ps. 16:10 and urging that "You will not suffer your Holy One to see corruption" means "You will not suffer your Holy One to experience corruption").

67. John Wesley, *Explanatory Notes upon the New Testament* (London: Epworth, 1950), p. 29. Cf. Matthew Poole, *Annotations on the Holy Bible* (3 vols.; London: Henry G. Bohn, 1846), 3:21.

5:8b rather literally. They probably hoped one day to share the experience of the angels in heaven and to see a somatic God face to face. This, however, creates a problem. Ecclesiastical theologians eventually decided that an anthropomorphic God is a fiction, and today most of us would agree with them, so what should we do with a biblical passage whose author may well have thought otherwise? How do we appropriate a text when the probable pristine sense leaves us unsympathetic? If one tries to avoid the question by insisting that the author's intention remains unspoken and so unknown or irrelevant, and that we may simply remain silent where the Bible is silent, then the question becomes, How can "they will see God" mean anything if it does not have some specific content? We cannot, I believe, so easily bypass the traditional exegetical speculations that have attached themselves to Matt. 5:8b. Further, we should not want to, because it is precisely the history of interpretation that can help us with a text whose original meaning, if I have figured the facts rightly, has become problematic. I offer four brief suggestions.

Texts in transition. Any given biblical text is a point on a line of developing tradition and so cannot be well understood in isolation. In the present case, Matt. 5:8b has a pre-history, that being Jewish speculation about the nature of God and the vision of God, and it has a post-history, that being Christian speculation about the nature of God and the vision of God. The verse itself, from one point of view, is only a station on the way, and so its full meaning can only be pondered by retracing the paths that led to it and by uncovering the paths that have gone out from it. It is those multiple paths running to and from our verse that raise the relevant historical, exegetical, and theological questions we must ask and that also supply us with a gamut of possible answers, all of which can send our thoughts in useful directions. To interpret the part while neglecting the whole is to constrict and distort meaning. It is like looking at a single frame while ignoring the rest of the motion picture.

Readers in context. The history of interpretation shows us how readings always change because readers are always changing. Granted the once-common assumption of a somatic deity, some early readers of Matt. 5:8b naturally thought of literally seeing God; and granted the church's formal deification of Jesus as the second person of the Trinity, others understandably came to suppose that "will see God" refers to seeing God's Son; and granted the eventual victory of a Hellenistic, asomatic understanding of God, metaphorical readings—"to see" = "to know" or "to experience"—inevitably became self-evident to many; and granted that some mystics had visions that they construed as encounters with the deity, they readily interpreted their experience in terms of Matt. 5:8b and vice versa. And so it goes. Doctrinal developments, religious experience, and cultural changes inexorably generate new interpretations.

Just as water takes the shape of the container it fills, so textual meaning necessarily adapts itself to the theological worlds of those deciphering it: readers and their contexts sculpt the content they discover. It follows that contemporary attempts to adhere solely to the original content are futile, for the original context is long gone: we are somewhere else. Instead of vainly defying this inescapable fact we should instead embrace it. Although we may be grateful that the plain sense of a text usually guarantees some stability of meaning across the centuries, we may be equally grateful that such stability does not prevent the ceaseless and creative reapplication of the Scriptures, from which we can bring forth treasures new as well as old.[68]

Multiple meanings. Regarding the interpretation of Matt. 5:8b in particular, the various interpretations happily need not, for the most part, be mutually exclusive. Christians can conceive of the eschatological vision of God as being several things at once—as fully encountering God in Jesus Christ (the second option described above), as a transforming religious experience (the third), as knowing as we have been known (the fourth), as perceiving the Creator through a redeemed cosmos (the fifth), and as beholding God in human beings restored to the divine likeness (the sixth). The last interpretation introduced ("to see" = "to experience") can, furthermore, legitimately be construed as comprehensive, holding within itself all the other interpretations. One can indeed urge that anything less than all of these together would be less than the *summum bonum* and so not the *visio dei.*

If we allow ourselves to think thoughts that were not yet born in the first-century—we cannot really do otherwise—and if we interpret Matt. 5:8b not just within its Matthean context but within the context of the entirety of Christian tradition, then the unspecified nature of "they will see God" opens itself up to a number of possible interpretations; and surely informed readers will find it theologically profitable to ponder them all, even those that have little chance of preserving the author's intention. It is altogether fitting that Origen, Eusebius, and other commentators have entertained and endorsed more than one way of understanding "they will see God."[69] Augustine's hefty corpus of writings even manages to endorse at least once every option canvassed herein save the literal seeing of a divine body (interpretation 1). Jeremiah Burroughs, in his mammoth

---

68. Helpful here, in different ways, are Ulrich Luz, "Reflections on the Appropriate Interpretation of New Testament Texts," in *Studies in Matthew* (Grand Rapids: Eerdmans, 2005), pp. 265–89, and David C. Steinmetz, "The Superiority of Pre-critical Exegesis," *ThTo* 37 (1980), pp. 27–38.

69. Cf. the words of Gill quoted on p. 60 above.

commentary on the Beatitudes, *The Saints' Happiness*, does exactly the same thing in about a dozen pages.[70]

Revelation in process. If texts cannot be divorced from the traditions that birthed them or from the traditions they in turn begat, and if new readers inevitably make for new readings, and if multiple meanings need not always be contradictory meanings, then it makes little sense to confine revelation to the words on a biblical page. Exegetical history in its entirety rather confronts us with an ongoing, evolving divine disclosure. Denial of this is a sort of practical deism, an implicit assertion that God created the biblical texts *ex nihilo* and then just let them go, thereafter abdicating further responsibility and doing nothing about them. To identify the beginning and end of the canon with the beginning and end of revelation is not only to sunder unpersuasively the Bible from its antecedent and attendant traditions but also to relegate divine speaking to a bygone age. The Bible itself, however, as so many recent studies have established, is an intramural conversation that continually rewrites, enlarges, and contradicts itself. Thus the divine dialogue comes to us not as a homogeneous product once and for all delivered to the saints but as an intertextual wonderland full of revisions and reinterpretations. And neither revision nor reinterpretation has ever stopped because neither activity can stop this side of the world to come.[71]

70. Jeremiah Burroughs, *The Saints' Happiness, together with the Several Steps Leading thereunto: Delivered in Divers Lectures on the Beatitudes: Being Part of Christ's Sermon on the Mount, Contained in the Fifth of Matthew* (Edinburgh: James Nichol, 1867), pp. 162–75.

71. See further the significant work of David Brown, *Tradition and Imagination: Revelation and Change* (Oxford: Oxford University Press, 1999).

3

Murder and Anger, Cain and Abel

(MATT. 5:21-25)

I mmediately after telling his hearers that their righteousness must surpass the righteousness of the scribes and Pharisees (5:20), Jesus begins to clarify what he means with these words:

> You have heard that it was said to those of old, "You will not murder," and "whoever murders will be liable to judgment." But I say to you that everyone who is angry with his brother will be liable to judgment; and whoever says to his brother, "Raka," will be liable to the sanhedrin; and whoever says, "Fool," will be liable to the Gehenna of fire. If then you are offering your gift upon the altar and there remember that your brother has something against you, leave your gift there before the altar and go. First be reconciled to your brother, and then come and offer your gift. (Matt. 5:21–24 my trans.)

This passage overflows with difficulties. Does Jesus here prohibit all anger, so that it is never justified?[1] What exactly does "raka" (ῥακά) mean, and from whence does the word derive?[2] Do the punishments become more severe as the paragraph moves forward—liable to judgment,

---

1. For this vexed issue see Dale C. Allison Jr., *The Sermon on the Mount: Inspiring the Moral Imagination* (New York: Crossroad, 1999), pp. 63–71, and chapter 12 below. The famous textual variant, "without cause" (εἰκῇ), is probably secondary, as John Cassian, *Inst.* 8.21 (SC 109, ed. Guy, p. 365), already recognized. But for a different view see David Alan Black, "Jesus on Anger: The Text of Matthew 5:22a Revisited," *NovT* 30 (1988), pp. 1–8.

2. Our best guess is that the Greek ῥακά represents the Aramaic ריקה/ריקא, a word of insult meaning "empty-head," "good for nothing," "fool"; cf. Neh. 5:13; SB 1:278–79; Chrysostom, *Hom. Matt.* 16.10(7) (PG 57.248).

liable to the sanhedrin, liable to the Gehenna of fire? And if there is an ascending order of punishments, does this match an ascending order of crimes?[3] Is saying "raka" worse than being angry? And is saying "fool" (μωρέ) worse than saying "raka"? There is also the question of whether vv. 23–24 demand that the offender or the offended make reconciliation. To all these traditional exegetical questions modern scholarship has added its own. What is the extent of Matthew's redaction? Does 5:21–26 contain two or three originally isolated pieces? And what if anything could go back to the historical Jesus?

Although these are all interesting issues, in the present chapter I should like to direct attention to a matter that modern commentators have failed to consider, namely, whether or not Matt. 5:21–24 is designed to send informed readers back to Gen. 4, to the story of Cain and Abel.

I begin with two quotations from Cyprian, the third-century bishop of Carthage. In his book *The Unity of the Catholic Church*, he wrote as follows:

> And so, if a person comes to the sacrifice with strife in his heart, he [Jesus] calls him back from the altar and bids him to be reconciled to his brother first, and then in peace of soul to return and to make his offering to God. For the very gifts of Cain did not win God's regard. Such a person could not have God at peace with him when he was torn with jealousy towards his brother and was at war with him. What sort of peace then do the enemies of the brethren promise themselves? What sort of sacrifice do they think they offer in competition with the priests? Do they think that Christ is with them in their gatherings, when those gatherings are outside the church of Christ?[4]

In discussing strife among Christians, Cyprian naturally enough turned to Matt. 5:23–24. The latter verses in turn moved the bishop to think of Cain, who offered his gift at the altar and yet remained unreconciled to his brother.

Cyprian forged the same intertextual link between Matt. 5:23–24 and Gen. 4:1–16 in a second treatise. In his work on *The Lord's Prayer*, we find this:

> God does not receive the sacrifice of a person who is in disagreement but commands him to go back from the altar and first be reconciled to his brother, so that God also may be appeased by the prayers of a peacemaker. Our peace and brotherly agreement is the greater sacrifice to God—and a people united in one in the unity of the Father, Son, and Holy Spirit. For even in the sacrifices that

---

3. Cf. David Smith, *The Days of His Flesh: The Earthly Life of Our Lord and Saviour Jesus Christ* (8th ed.; New York/London: Hodder & Stoughton, 1910), p. 97.

4. Cyprian, *De eccl. cath. unit.* 13 (OECT, ed. Bévenot, p. 78).

Abel and Cain first offered, God looked not at their gifts, but at their hearts, so that he was acceptable in his gift who was acceptable in his heart. Abel, peaceable and righteous in sacrificing in innocence to God, taught others also, when they bring their gift to the altar, thus to come with the fear of God, with a simple heart, with the law of righteousness, with the peace of concord. . . . The quarrelsome and disunited and he who has not peace with his brothers . . . will not be able to escape the crime of fraternal dissension, because, as it is written, "He who hates his brother is a murderer" (1 John 3:15), and no murderer attains to the kingdom of heaven nor does he live with God.[5]

In these two passages Cyprian is, in my judgment, making the imaginative contribution that the First Gospel wants its readers to make, and it is my goal in this brief chapter to support the Father's intertextual intuition. For an informed audience, Matt. 5:21–24 interacts with authoritative parental texts in several ways. Not only does the passage quote the Decalogue ("You will not murder," Exod. 20:13 = Deut. 5:17) and summarize the legislation in Gen. 9:6; Exod. 21:12 = Lev. 24:17; Num. 35:12; and Deut. 17:8–13 (murder merits the death penalty), but it also expands its meaning and lends force to its argument by tacit recall of Genesis and its famous story of fratricide.

History of interpretation. If one text has regularly reminded readers of another text, then the odds that we are dealing with deliberate design go up. Conversely, if commentators have uniformly missed an allusion, a good dose of doubt is surely in order. How do things stand with Matt. 5:21–24 and Gen. 4:1–16?

Modern exegetes, I freely confess, do not sanction the proposal that our New Testament text quietly alludes to the Old Testament text; for, to the extent of my research and memory, only one of them—Hans Dieter Betz[6]—says anything at all about Gen. 4:1–16 when commenting on Matt. 5:21–24.[7] If, however, we close the covers of recent volumes and instead

---

5. Cyprian, *De dom. orat.* 23–24 (CSEL 3, ed. Hartel, p. 285). Cf. also Cyprian, *De zel. et liv.* 17–18 (CCSL 3A, ed. Simonetti, p. 85).

6. Hans Dieter Betz, *The Sermon on the Mount: A Commentary on the Sermon on the Mount, Including the Sermon on the Plain (Matt. 5:3–7:27 and Luke 6:20–49)* (Hermeneia; Minneapolis: Fortress, 1995) ad loc. In n. 163 on p. 219, Betz writes that "the great example" in the biblical tradition of anger leading to murder "is the brothers Cain and Abel: Gen 4:5." In n. 205 on p. 224, he says, with reference to Jesus' demand to make reconciliation, that if "1 Sam. 29:4 [sic] shows David taking the initiative in getting reconciled with the angry Saul," then "the opposite is Cain in Gen. 4:5–8." Finally, on p. 230 he summarizes the content of 5:21–26 with this: "Simply stated, the source of murder is a broken relationship with the brother. The famous case of Cain's murder of his brother Abel (Gen. 4:8–16) comes to everyone's mind [sic!], although it is not mentioned in the text."

7. I do note, however, that P. B. Overland, "Abel," in *Dictionary of the Old Testament: Pentateuch* (ed. T. Desmond Alexander and David W. Baker; Downers Grove, Ill.: InterVarsity, 2003), p. 6, refers to Matt. 5:23–24 when summarizing the meaning of the story of Cain and Abel.

open some old books, the story is very different. Cyprian's mind, we have already seen, moved from Matt. 5:21–24 to Gen. 4:1–6, and he was far from being the only reader to have made this connection. Before him, the scripturally saturated Tertullian also seems to have done so.[8] Later on, Chrysostom, Chromatius, and Geoffrey Babion likewise thought of Cain when expounding the teaching on anger in Matt. 5:21–24.[9] So too did Paschasius Radbertus, Rupert of Deutz, Hugh of St. Cher, and Albert the Great.[10] To these names we can also add, from less distant days, Hugo Grotius and Matthew Henry.[11]

One might reduce the force of all this testimony by observing that most of these authors were surely familiar with Cyprian's famed *De ecclesiae unitate*, as perhaps also with his *De dominica oratione*. So it is possible to query their value as independent witnesses. Yet this is not a weighty objection. There is, for one thing, no reason to believe that any of the commentators I have cited had Cyprian open before him as he composed his own work. For another, what matters in the end is that a number of writers found the parallel illuminating and worthy of remark: drawing a connection from Matt. 5 back to Gen. 4 made excellent sense to them. We can, then, give some weight to the testimony of our eleven older authorities and our one contemporary scholar. At the least, their united voices on this particular encourage us to inquire further.

8. Tertullian, *Orat.* 11 (CSEL 20, ed. Reifferscheid and Wissowa, pp. 187–88): the chief precept is "not to go up to God's altar before composing whatever of discord or offence we have contracted with our brothers. For what sort of deed is it to approach the peace of God without peace, the remission of debts while you retain them? How will he appease his Father who is angry with his brother, when from the beginning all anger is forbidden us." "From the beginning" (*ab initio*) is hard to explain unless it alludes to the primeval murder and its root cause; cf. the function of John 8:44 and n. 17. Note also the sequence in *Pat.* 5.15–6.5 (SC 310, ed. Fredouille, pp. 76–82): Tertullian discusses Cain's impatience (5.15–17), then, perhaps alluding to Matt. 5:21–24 (especially as he immediately equates lust with adultery, as in Matt. 5:27–28), the church father roots murder in anger (5.19–25), after which he clearly cites Matt. 5:21–24 (6.5).

9. Chrysostom, *Hom. Matt.* 16:11(8) (PG 57.250); Chromatius, *Tract.* 7.3 (CCSL 9, ed. Hoste, p. 413); Ps.-Anselm = Geoffrey Babion, *En. Matt.* ad loc. (PL 162.1296A).

10. Paschasius Radbertus, *Exp. Matt. Libri XII* ad loc. (CCCM 56, ed. Paulus, p. 321); Rupert of Deutz, *Comm. Matt.* ad loc. (PL 168.1405C); Hugh of St. Cher, *In Evangelia secundum Matthaeum, Lucam, Marcum, & Joannem* ad loc. (Opera Omnia 6 [Venice: Nicolaus Pezzana, 1732], p. 19); Albertus Magnus, *Super Mt. cap. I–XIV* ad loc. (Opera Omnia 21/1, ed. B. Schmidt, p. 135).

11. Hugo Grotius, *Opera omnia theologica*, vol. 2, part 1 (Amsterdam: Joannis Blaeu, 1679), p. 46; Matthew Henry, *Commentary on the Whole Bible*, vol. 5: *Matthew to John* (New York: Fleming H. Revell, n.d.), p. 58. Note also that Irenaeus, *Adv. haer.* 4.18.1–3 (SC 100, ed. Rousseau, pp. 596–600), moves from Matt. 5:23–24 to the story of Cain and Abel; here, however, there is some material in between.

Thematic connection. Matthew 5:21–24 and Gen. 4:1–16 share several thematic and verbal links. If the former opens by raising the subject of murder, the latter recounts the sacred history's very first murder. If Matt. 5:21–24 makes the Decalogue's prohibition of homicide the occasion to discuss anger, Gen. 4:5 says that "Cain was very angry" (MT: יִחַר לְקַיִן מְאֹד) at Abel or on his account, and it implies that this wrath is what led to his atrocious act of murder.[12] If Matt. 5:21–24 addresses the relationship between two brothers, the same is true of Gen. 4:1–16. In both places ἀδελφός is a key word, occurring as it does four times in Matt. 5:21–24 and seven times in Gen. 4:2–11 LXX; and in Jewish and Christian references to the story of Cain and Abel, "brother," which adds so much pathos, is almost always prominent.[13] If, moreover, the situation in Matt. 5:23–24 is that of an individual offering a sacrificial gift on an altar (v. 23: προσφέρῃς τὸ δῶρόν σου ἐπὶ τὸ θυσιαστήριον; cf. v. 24), in Gen. 4 the offering of sacrificial gifts is the proximate cause for Cain murdering his brother: "Cain brought . . . an offering (LXX: ἤνεγκεν . . . θυσίαν)[14] of the fruit of the ground, and Abel . . . brought of the firstlings of his flock, their fat portions. And the LORD had regard for Abel and his offering (LXX: δώροις), but for Cain and his offering (LXX: θυσίαις) he had no regard" (Gen. 4:3–5).[15] In short, Matt. 5:21–24 concerns the

---

12. Even though the LXX translates the Hebrew with καὶ ἐλύπησεν τὸν Κάϊν λίαν (and Cain grieved much), readers have nonetheless, in line with the MT, almost unavoidably thought of Cain's murder of Abel as activated by anger or hatred; see, e.g., *Jub.* 4:5 ("Cursed is the one who strikes his fellow with malice"); Wisd. 10:3 ("But when an unrighteous man departed from her [wisdom] in anger [ὀργῇ], he perished because in rage he slew his brother"); Josephus, *Ant.* 1:55 ("Cain, incensed at God's preference for Abel"); *T. Benj.* 7:5 ("Until eternity those who are like Cain in their moral corruption and hatred of brother [μισαδελφίαν] will be punished with a similar judgment"); *LAE* (Gk.) (Cain is "a son of anger" [ὀργῆς]); Tertullian, *Pat.* 5.15–19 (SC 310, ed. Fredouille, pp. 76–78; Cain acted out of a wrath born of impatience); Origen, *Comm. Rom.* ad 4:14–15 (ed. Scherer, p. 204; human nature "worked anger [ὀργήν] in Cain"); *LAE* (Georgian) 23:3 ("let us [Adam and Eve] be with them, so as to provide no room for anger"; "he [Cain] became angry"); Theodoret of Cyrrhus, *Quaest. in Oct.* 1.42 (ed. Marcos and Sáenz-Badillos, p. 43; "The Lord said to Cain, 'Why are you inclined to anger [ὀργίλον]?'"); etc. Note also that Aquila read ὀργίλον in Gen. 4:5 and 6 and that Symmachus had in these two verses ὠργίσθη and ὠργίσθης respectively.

13. E.g., *Jub.* 4:4; *1 En.* 22:7; Philo, *Det.* 96; *LAB* 2:1; Josephus, *Ant.* 1.52–57; *LAE* (Gk.) 40:4; 1 John 3:12; *T. Benj.* 7:4–5; *T. Adam* 3:5; *Const. ap.* 8.12.21 (ed. Funk, p. 502); *Pesiq. Rab. Qah.* 16:5; etc. Cain was known as "fratricidal," ἀδελφοκτόνος; cf. Wisd. 10:3; *T. Abr.* Rec. Lng. 13:2; *Const. ap.* 8:12:21 (ed. Funk, p. 502); Chrysostom, *Hom. Rom.* 23.4 (PG 60.620). The related ἀδελφοκτονία is used of him in Gk. frag. *Jub.* 4:15; Philo, *Agric.* 21; Josephus, *Ant.* 1.65; *1 Clem.* 4:7; Epiphanius, *Haer.* 1.1.3 (GCS 25, ed. Holl, p. 172); Chrysostom, *Hom. Rom.* 12.8 (PG 60.505). For ἀδελφοκτονέω of Cain see Theophilus of Antioch, *Autol.* 2.30 (PTS 44, ed. Marcovich, p. 80).

14. Cf. Philo, *QG* 1.64: τοὺς τὰ δῶρα προσφέροντας.

15. Some of the older philological commentaries cite Gen. 4:4 LXX when explaining the meaning of δῶρον in Matt. 5:23–24; see, e.g., Johann Georg Rosenmüller, *Scholia in Novum*

affiliation of murder and anger,[16] and it depicts a circumstance in which someone, while offering a gift on an altar, is upset with his brother—all of which is strongly reminiscent of the story in Gen. 4, where Cain offers his gift, becomes angry, and attempts no reconciliation with his brother, whereupon murder ensues.

Prominence of the Genesis text. The plausibility that text A implicitly recalls text B unquestionably increases if the latter is prominent in the tradition of the former, and especially when other, related texts cite or allude to text B. A proposed allusion to a central theme of the exodus is, for example, much more credible than a proposed allusion to some lesser-known line or story from Nehemiah. On this account, Cyprian's intertextual reading of Matt. 5:21–24 has an initial plausibility, for the story of Cain murdering Abel has never been obscure. It belongs to the beginning of the foundational, primeval history, and ancient Jews and Christians knew the stories in that portion of Scripture as well as any part of the Bible. A good index of this is that writers felt free to refer to the tragedy of Adam's two sons without elaboration. Clearly they assumed that their audiences would know the details. Wisd. 10:3, for instance, has this: "But when an unrighteous man departed from her [wisdom] in his anger, he perished because in rage he killed his brother." The text does not even name either Cain or Abel.[17]

Perhaps we should also remember that Philo found the story of Cain and Abel sufficiently important to write four separate treatises on it (*On the Cherubim, and the Flaming Sword, and Cain the First Man Created out of Man; The Sacrifices of Cain and Abel; The Worse Attacks the Better;* and *On the Posterity of Cain*); that both *Targum Pseudo-Jonathan* and *Targum Neofiti* 1 on Gen. 4 greatly expand Genesis' short story by adding the account of a quarrel between the brothers; and that there are retellings in Josephus (*Ant.* 1:52–59) as well as in *Jubilees* (4:1–6), the *Life*

Testamentum (5 vols.; Nuremberg: In Officina Felseckeriana, 1815–1831), 1:114, and Christian Gottlieb Kuinoel, *Commentarius in libros Novi Testamenti historicos* (4 vols.; Leipzig: I. A. Barth, 1823–1827), 1:147.

16. *Did.* 3:2 offers the correct interpretation: "Be not inclined to anger, for anger leads to murder."

17. Other relevant texts include *LAB* 2:1; 4 Macc. 18:11; *T. Benj.* 7:3–5; Heb 11:4; 12:24; Matt. 23:35 (cf. Luke 11:51); John 8:44 (on this as a subtle allusion to Cain and the legend of his being literally the son of the devil see 1 John 3:10–12; Tertullian, *Pat.* 5:15 [SC 310, ed. Fredouille, p. 76]; *Carn.* 17.5–6 [SC 217, ed. Mahe, p. 282]; *Gos. Philip* 61:5–10; Epiphanius, *Haer.* 40.5.3 [GCS 31, ed. Holl, p. 85]; *Tg. Ps.-J.* Gen. 4:1; *Pirq. R. El.* 21; A. Goldberg, "Kain: Sohn des Menschen oder Sohn der Schlange?" *Judaica* 25 [1969] 203–21; Günter Reim, "Joh. 8.44—Gotteskinder/Teufelskinder: Wie antijudaistisch ist 'Die wohl antijudaistischste Äußerung des NT'?" *NTS* 30 [1984], pp. 619–24); Jude 11; *Apoc. Abr.* 24:5; *Mart. Isa.* 9:8; *T. Isaac* 4:37; *Hellenistic Synagogal Prayer* in *Ap. Const.* 8.12.21.

of Adam and Eve (Latin 23:1–5), and *1 Clem.* 4:1–7. The prominence of the story in Jewish and Christian memory cannot be gainsaid.[18]

Genesis elsewhere in Matthew. Beyond the generality that Gen. 4:1–16 was a popular passage among Jews and Christians, we also know that Matthew wrote for an audience whose members were familiar with the book of Genesis. We shall see in a later chapter that the evangelist's very first words, βίβλος γενέσεως (1:1), hearken back to a phrase in the primeval history (Gen. 2:4 and 5:1). He thereafter evokes Genesis on a number of occasions. One need only recall the several mentions of Abraham (1:1–2; 3:9; 8:11; 22:32), the naming of Sodom in 10:15, the use of Gen. 1:27; 2:24; and 5:2 in support of monogamy in Matt. 19:4–5, and the reference to "the days of Noah" in 24:37. All of these verses assume that readers have some real acquaintance with Genesis.

What matters even more for our purposes, however, is that Matthew draws upon the story of Cain and Abel in particular. In 18:21–22, Peter asks Jesus, "If my brother sins against me, how often should I forgive? As many as seven times?" Jesus responds, "I say to you, not seven times, but seventy-seven times." The Greek ἑβδομηκοντάκις ἑπτά, translated here as "seventy-seven times,"[19] occurs also in Gen. 4:24 LXX: "If Cain is avenged sevenfold (cf. Gen. 4:15), truly Lamech ἑβδομηκοντάκις ἑπτά" (for the MT's שבעים ושבעה). Matthew is plainly alluding to one of the classic texts about vengeance. As T. W. Manson remarked, Gen. 4:24 refers to a blood-feud "carried on without mercy and without limit. The reply of Jesus in verse 22 says: Just as in those old days there was no limit to hatred and vengeance, so among Christians there is to be no limit to mercy and forgiveness."[20] Naturally the commentators on Matt. 18:21–22 have, through the centuries, seen the point and cited Gen. 4:24 as well as 4:15 ("Whoever kills Cain will suffer a sevenfold vengeance").[21]

---

18. It is also one of the biblical tales that the Qur'an retells; see 5:27–31.

19. This is probably the meaning, rather than "seventy times seven"; see Robert H. Gundry, *The Use of the Old Testament in St. Matthew's Gospel, with Special Reference to the Messianic Hope* (NovTSup 18; Leiden: Brill, 1967), p. 140.

20. T. W. Manson, *The Sayings of Jesus* (London: SCM, 1949), p. 212.

21. See, e.g., Tertullian, *Orat.* 7.3 (CCSL 1, p. 262); Origen, *Comm. Matt.* 14.5 (GCS 40, ed. E. Klostermann, p. 282 [= PG 13.1192B-C]); Hilary of Poitiers, *Comm. Matt.* ad loc. (SC 258, ed. Doignon, p. 84); Bede, *Quaest. super Gen.* (PL 93.288A–B); Chromatius of Aquileia, *Tract. Matt.* 59.3 (CCSL 9a, ed. Étaix and Lemarié, p. 494); Paschasius Radbertus, *Exp. Matt. Libri XII* ad loc. (CCCM 56A, ed. Paulus, p. 899); Juan Maldonatus, *Comentarii in Quatuor Evangelistas* (2 vols.; Mainz: F. Kirchhemius, 1853–1854), 1:250; Cornelius à Lapide, *The Great Commentary of Cornelius à Lapide* (6 vols.; 2nd ed.; London: John Hodges, 1874–1887), 2:310; Adolf Schlatter, *Der Evangelist Matthäus: Seine Sprache, sein Ziel, seine Selbständigkeit* (Stuttgart: Calwer, 1948), p. 559; Gundry, *Old Testament*, p. 140; Ulrich Luz, *Das Evangelium nach Matthäus* (4 vols.; EKK 1/1–4; Düsseldorf: Benziger, 1990–2002), 3:62; cf. Philoxenus, *Comm. Lk.* frag. 56 (CSCO 392, Scriptores Syri 171, ed. Watt, p. 84).

In addition to this one obvious allusion, there is also an explicit reference to Gen. 4:1–16. In 23:34–36, Matthew's Jesus warns the scribes and Pharisees with words that speak of "the blood of Abel the just." The text does not elaborate any further. Cain is not mentioned, and how or why Abel's blood was spilled goes unsaid. Obviously a familiarity with Gen. 4—and probably legends about it[22]—is taken for granted. In other words, Matthew's Gospel assumes an audience whose members carry in their memories the story of Cain murdering his brother Abel.

Cain in Matthew's environment. Finding an allusion to Gen. 4 in Matt. 5:21–25 means that Cain implicitly serves to illustrate the wrath that can lead to murder. It accords with this not only that there was a tendency in both Jewish and Christian works to make Cain a negative role model[23] but that two other sources from the first century, one Jewish and one Christian, also turn Cain, the prototype of the wicked individual, into a warning of murderous anger. The first source is Wisd. 10:3, which relates the story of Cain this way: "But when an unrighteous man departed from her [Wisdom] in his anger (ὀργῇ), he perished because in rage he killed his brother." Here the tragedy in Gen. 4:1–16 becomes an exhortation to shun anger because its presence is the absence of wisdom. Related is the discussion of love in 1 John 3:11–17. After characterizing Cain as being "from the evil one" (= the devil) and as the murderer of his (unnamed) brother (v. 12), the author goes on to say that "everyone who hates his brother is a murderer." Here hatred is equated with murder, just as, in Matt. 5:21–22, anger is equated with murder. Furthermore, for the author of 1 John, Cain, illustrating what hatred can lead to, is the exact opposite of those who, living by the gospel, love one another. It is no surprise that the commentaries on 1 John 3:11–17 have regularly appealed to Matt. 5:21–24 for illustration.[24] The upshot is that the intertextual reading of

22. See Dale C. Allison Jr., *The Intertextual Jesus: Scripture in Q* (Harrisburg, Pa.: Trinity Press International, 2000), pp. 84–87.

23. See Raymond E. Brown, *The Epistles of John* (AB 30; Garden City, N.Y.: Doubleday, 1982), p. 443.

24. Johann Albrecht Bengel, *Gnomon Novi Testamenti* (2 vols.; Tübingen: Ludov. Frid. Fues, 1850), 1:49; A. E. Brooke, *The Johannine Epistles* (ICC; New York: Charles Scribner's Sons, 1912), p. 94; Brown, *Epistles*, p. 447; C. H. Dodd, *The Johannine Epistles* (London: Hodder & Stoughton, 1946), p. 83; Hans-Josef Klauck, *Der erste Johannesbrief* (EKKNT 23/1; Zürich: Benziger, 1991), p. 210; I. Howard Marshall, *The Epistles of John* (NICNT; Grand Rapids: Eerdmans, 1978), p. 190; Georg Strecker, *The Johannine Letters: A Commentary on 1, 2, and 3 John* (Hermeneia; Minneapolis: Fortress, 1996), p. 113, n. 36. See further below. Commentators on Matt. 5:21–24 have also cited 1 John 3:15; see, e.g., Bruno of Segni, *Comm. Matt.* ad loc. (PL 165.104D–105A); Ps.-Anselm = Geoffrey Babion, *En. Matt.* ad loc. (PL 162.1295B–1296A); Rupert of Deutz, *Comm. Matt.* ad loc. (PL 168.1405B–C); Matthew Poole, *Annotations on the Holy Bible* (3 vols.; London: Henry G. Bohn, 1846), 3:23; Alfred Plummer, *An Exegetical Commentary on the Gospel according to Matthew* (New York: Scribner, 1909), p. 78; Theodor

Matt. 5:21–24 posits an application of Gen. 4:1–16 that is otherwise attested in Matthew's Jewish and Christian worlds.

Why "at the altar"? There is a peculiarity in Matt. 5:23–24 that Cyprian's reading may help us resolve. These verses speak of an individual offering a gift "at the altar": προσφέρῃς τὸ δῶρόν σου ἐπὶ τὸ θυσιαστήριον. One might expect the simpler προσφέρῃς τὴν θυσίαν or προσφέρῃς τὸ δῶρον. The problem is that the addition of ἐπὶ τὸ θυσιαστήριον encourages the mind's eye to see someone actually at an altar (cf. James 2:21; Rev. 8:3).[25] Modern commentators typically think of the great altar at the temple in Jerusalem.[26] But unless our text, unlike anything else in Matthew, addresses itself to priests, it is hard to see what could be meant, for only priests were allowed at the altar. Eduard Schweizer saw the problem: "The situation depicted in fact corresponds more closely to [that of] the Old Testament [before the building of the temple in Jerusalem] than to the time of Jesus, when only the priest offered the sacrifice at the altar."[27] Josephus, *Ant.* 3:226–27, does, admittedly, say, in accord with Lev. 1:5 (although against Philo, *Spec.* 1.198–99), that a man presenting an animal sacrifice actually did the slaughter himself, that is, he pulled back the head and slit the throat while the priest held the animal. But presumably the individual making the sacrifice leaned over the low wall separating the court of the priests from the court of the Israelites.[28] He certainly did not sprinkle the blood around the circuit of the altar or otherwise perform ritual actions at the site of the altar itself. Why then does Matthew mention the altar?

Zahn, *Das Evangelium des Matthäus* (4th ed.; Leipzig: A. Deichert, 1922), 225, n. 93; Betz, *Sermon*, p. 230, n. 267. Tertullian, *Idol.* 2 (CSEL 20, ed. Reifferscheid and Wissowa, pp. 31–32), already brings the two texts together.

25. See further Joachim Jeremias, "'Laß allda deine Gabe' (Mt. 5,23f.)," in *Abba: Studien zur neutestamentlichen Theologie und Zeitgeschichte* (Göttingen: Vandenhoeck & Ruprecht, 1966), pp. 103–4; he recognizes the plain meaning of the Greek but then posits an Aramaic original with slightly different sense.

26. E.g., Jacques Dupont, *Les Béatitudes*, vol. 1 (2nd ed.; Paris: J. Gabalda, 1969), p. 149; Robert A. Guelich, *The Sermon on the Mount: A Foundation for Understanding* (Waco, Tex.: Word, 1982), p. 189; Donald A. Hagner, *Matthew 1–13* (WBC 33A; Dallas: Word, 1993), p. 117; Julius Wellhausen, *Das Evangelium Matthaei übersetzt und erklärt* (2nd ed.; Berlin: Georg Reimer, 1914), pp. 19–20.

27. Eduard Schweizer, *According to Matthew* (Atlanta: John Knox, 1975), p. 115. Zahn, *Matthäus*, p. 230, also observes the difficulty, but he dismisses it as of negligible import. Betz, *Sermon*, pp. 222–23, notes, "Remarkably, this sequence does not presuppose a priest functioning as an intermediary who receives the gift and places it on the altar." Many earlier commentators had no problem here because they thought of the Christian sacrifice of the Eucharist. *Did.* 14:2 already makes an application to the Lord's Supper; cf. Cyril of Jerusalem, *Myst. Cat.* 5.3 (FC 7, ed. Röwekamp, pp. 146–48), and Palladius, *V. Chrys.* 14 (PG 47.48).

28. So E. P. Sanders, *Judaism: Practice and Belief, 63 BCE–66 CE* (Philadelphia: SCM, 1992), p. 107.

One might discount the problem as taking Matthew's language too literally, of failing to see the absurdity in a hyperbole. Augustine, observing the additional problem that a person could hardly leave a gift at an altar and depart to traverse land and sea in search of an unreconciled brother, decided that "we must embrace an inward, spiritual sense of the whole, if we would understand it without involving any absurdity."[29] But recognizing the background in Gen. 4:1–16 permits us to think something else, to judge instead that the text means exactly what it says because it really does want us to envisage an individual offering a gift at an altar, an individual whose brother is nearby. The image, that is, is not of someone in the Jerusalem temple but of Cain, acting as priest for himself and offering his own sacrifice with his sibling to hand. It is true that Gen. 4 does not refer to the altars of Cain and Abel; but readers, knowing that there can be no sacrifice without some sort of altar, have always, we can be sure, envisaged the brothers acting just like Noah, Abraham, and Jacob, who are said to have built their own altars for their sacrifices: Gen. 8:20; 12:7–8; 13:18; 22:9; 35:1–7. Art history is instructive in this matter: artists have typically supplied an altar or altars for Cain and Abel when depicting their sacrificial acts.[30] Jewish haggadah tells the same story. *Targum Pseudo-Jonathan* on Gen. 8:20 reads: "Then Noah built an altar before the Lord—it is the altar which Adam built at the time he was banished from the Garden of Eden and on which he offered an offering, and upon which Cain and Abel offered their offerings. But when the waters of the flood came down it was destroyed. Noah rebuilt it." This tradition recurs in *Pirq. R. El.* 23; 31.

Influence on 1 John 3? We have already remarked upon the similarities between 1 John 3:11–17 and Matt. 5:21–24. One might suppose that the intertextual link I am defending arose from the circumstance that Christians read Cain into the latter because he is present in the former; that is, their thoughts moved from Matt. 5:21–24, which does not name Cain, to the similar 1 John 3:11–17, which does name him; returning then to Mat-

29. Augustine apud Aquinas, *Catena Aurea* ad loc. Cf. David E. Garland, *Reading Matthew: A Literary and Theological Commentary on the First Gospel* (London: SPCK, 1993), p. 65: "It would be inconceivable for Galileans . . . to halt sacrificial proceedings, to return to Galilee, to search out the offended person and do whatever is necessary to bring about reconciliation, and then to return to the temple in Jerusalem and pick up the sacrifice where they had left off."

30. Examples: the painting in the North Chapel at Kelmscott, Oxfordshire (ca. 1280; Cain and Abel on either side of a high stack of firewood); Petrus Christus, "The Offerings of Cain and Abel" (ca. 1445–50, National Gallery of Art, Washington, D.C.; Cain and Abel on their knees before a raised platform); Gustav Doré, "Cain and Abel Offering Their Sacrifices" (1865; fire on top of a stone platform). According to the *Lexicon der christlichen Ikonographie* (8 vols.; ed. Engelbert Kirschbaum; Rome: Herder, 1968–1976), 1:7–8, s.v. "Abel und Kain," the most common artistic type has Cain and Abel on either side of the same altar.

thew, they brought Cain along and planted him where he was not. Cyprian himself quotes 1 John 3:15 when enlarging upon Matt. 5:21–24.[31]

There are, however, two difficulties with such a scenario. The first is that most of the commentators who remark upon Cain when expounding Matt. 5:21–24 fail to cite 1 John 3:11–17, so it seems gratuitous to maintain that the latter passage must have influenced their exegesis of the former passage.[32] The second difficulty is that 1 John 3:11–17 itself may very well reflect a knowledge of Matt. 5:21–24 or the tradition behind it. Several commentators on 1 John 3:11–17 have thought this more or less obvious. Stephen Smalley has remarked on 1 John 3:12: "In asking the question (why did Cain butcher Abel?) the writer draws out the teaching of Jesus on the subject of murder (see Matt. 5:21–26). Jesus had indicated that the penalty for anger with one's brother (as in the case of Cain!) was the same as that for murder (vv. 21–22). John not only picks up the implied notion that 'all hatred is embryonic murder'[33] . . . he also probes the ultimate motivation for murder itself."[34]

One understands why so many commentators on 1 John have cited

31. Cyprian, *De dom. orat.* 23–24 (CSEL 3, ed. Hartel, p. 285). See further above, pp. 66–67.

32. See Tertullian, *Orat.* 11 (CSEL 20, ed. Reifferscheid and Wissowa, pp. 187–88; although note that, in *Idol.* 2 [CSEL 20, pp. 31–32], Tertullian does closely associate the two passages); Chrysostom, *Hom. Matt.* 16.7–14(5–11) (PG 57.245–54); Chromatius, *Tract. Matt.* 7.1–3 (CCSL 9, ed. Hoste, pp. 411–14); Paschasius Radbertus, *Exp. Matt. Libri XII* ad loc. (CCCM 56, ed. Paulus, p. 321); Hugh of St. Cher, *In Evangelia secundum Matthaeum, Lucam, Marcum, et Joannem* 6:19; Albertus Magnus, *Super Mt. cap. I–XIV* ad loc. (Opera Omnia 21/1, ed. B. Schmidt, pp. 130–39); Hugo Grotius, *Opera omnia theologica*, vol. 2, part 1, p. 46; Henry, *Matthew to John*, p. 58.

33. The citation is from Marshall, *Epistles*, p. 190.

34. Stephen S. Smalley, *1, 2, 3 John* (SBC 51; Waco, Tex.: Word, 1984), p. 185. On p. 191 he writes: "Clearly the example of Cain who 'butchered his brother' (v. 12), and John's earlier description of the hatred encountered by the Church from the world (v. 13), have prompted the association in this v[erse] between *murder* and hatred. Developing the teaching of Jesus recorded in Matt. 5:21–22 (cf. 5:27–28), John explicitly states that hatred and murder are synonymous." Cf. Marshall, *Epistles*, pp. 190 (Jesus "indicated that the penalty for hatred was the same as that for murder [Matt. 5:21–28]. John is simply bringing out the implications of his teaching") and 191 ("John takes up the thought implied in Matthew 5:21f. and states quite bluntly that hatred is tantamount to murder"); David Smith, "The Epistles of John," in *The Expositor's Greek Testament* (5 vols.; ed. W. Robertson Nicoll; New York: George H. Doran, 1912), 5:186 ("An echo of the teaching of Jesus. See Matt. v. 21–22"). Note also John Painter, *1, 2, and 3 John* (Sacra Pagina 18; Collegeville, Minn.: Liturgical Press, 2002), p. 241 ("That the one who hates is identified as a murderer seems noncontroversial, perhaps because this is a variation of the theme of Matt. 5:21–22, which notes the relation of anger and contempt to the command 'Do not murder'"); David Rensberger, *1 John, 2 John, 3 John* (Nashville: Abingdon, 1997), p. 99 ("It is also strikingly reminiscent of Matt. 5:21–27. Whether or not the author was aware of that . . ."); and Rudolf Schnackenburg, *The Johannine Epistles: Introduction and Commentary* (New York: Crossroad, 1992), p. 181 ("which reminds us of the judgment of Jesus in the Sermon on the Mount").

Matt. 5:21–24 and indeed why Smalley and others have affirmed that
the author of 1 John knew the Matthean tradition about anger. The
parallels between the gospel text and 1 John 3:11–17 are certainly
intriguing:

1 John 3:11–17	Matt. 5:21–24
Hatred = murder	Anger = murder
Repetition of ἀδελφός (7×)	Repetition of ἀδελφός (5×)
Reference to Cain	Apparent allusion to Cain
Eschatological punishment for hatred	Eschatological punishment for anger
Theme: love	Theme: reconciliation

What would follow if 1 John 3:11–16 does indeed reflect the tradition
in Matt. 5:21–24? The circumstance would establish that, long before
Tertullian and Cyprian, the words about murder and reconciliation moved
someone to recollect Gen. 4:1–16, for 1 John 3:12 is explicit: "We must not
be like Cain who was from the evil one and murdered his brother."[35]

The significance of the Cain allusion. Allusions, which give us more
to do and so heighten our attention, invite informed imaginations to
make their own contributions. Meaning is infolded not to obscure but to
improve communication. The implicit allows the pleasure of discovery,
and readers who are invited to fill gaps appreciate authors who respect
them enough not to shout. But what exactly beyond that is the payoff in
the present case? What happens when we divine an allusion to Cain and
Abel in Matt. 5:21–24? I have three suggestions.

1. The first rhetorical plus is additional support for the argument. Jesus
enlarges the penalty for anger so that it becomes the penalty for murder.
One might query the wisdom of this equation. Surely anger is much the
lesser sin? But remembering Gen. 4:1–16 establishes not only how dan-
gerous anger can be but that it in fact can lead to murder, even murder of
a brother. So Cain's anger and consequent sin add both plausibility and
solemnity to Jesus' seemingly hyperbolic equation.

2. Jewish and Christian tradition exalted Abel and debased Cain. The
one was sanctified and so became an object of imitation. The other was
demonized and so became an example to be shunned.[36] So associating Gen.

---

35. It also follows either that the author of 1 John knew the First Gospel or (more likely) that
the tradition in Matt. 5:22–24 was united to the material in 5:21–22 before Matthew.

36. See Philo, *QG* 1.59; Josephus, *Ant.* 1.53; Heb 11:4; *T. Abr.* Rec. Lng. 13:2; *T. Benj.*
7:4; *Mart. Isa.* 9:8, 28; *Const. ap.* 8.12.21 (ed. Funk, p. 502); Augustine, *Civ. dei* 15.7 (CCSL
48, ed. Hoffmann, pp. 459–60); *Tg. Neof.* 1 on Gen. 4:8; Ps.-Bede, *Exp. in prim. lib. Mosi* (PL
91.217A); etc. The targums, however, reveal a later tendency to have Cain repent: *Tg. Ps.-J.*
Gen. 4:13, 24; *Tg. Neof.* 1 on Gen. 4:13. On this motif see Ruth Mellinkoff, *The Mark of Cain*

4:1–16 with Matt. 5:21–24 implies that failure to heed Jesus' injunctions is to take the side of Cain: harboring anger against a brother will make one like the archetypal murderer. But no pious reader of Scripture would want to identify with the wretched man who wandered the earth with God's curse upon him (Gen. 4:12–16). In this way then one's revulsion for Cain spills over into an aversion for what Jesus condemns. First John 3:12 is once again pertinent: "We must not be like Cain, who was from the evil one and murdered his brother."

3. As observed earlier, there has been some discussion regarding the implication of the phrase "your brother has something against you" (v. 23: ὁ ἀδελφός σου ἔχει τι κατὰ σοῦ). Probably most exegetes have thought of the one who leaves the gift at the altar as the guilty party,[37] although one could also surmise that his brother has done something wrong (cf. 6:11–12; 18:15–18). Other exegetes ignore the question or regard it as beside the point.[38] Now even without discerning the background in Gen. 4:1–16 it is likely that the majority is here right. The context itself (vv. 21–22) moves us to imagine "some degree of anger in the person offering the sacrifice."[39] But to this observation we can now add another. I have contended in this chapter that the main actor in verses 23–24 is implicitly likened to Cain. Let us then recall the obvious: Cain was in the wrong, not Abel. It was Cain who needed to leave his gift at the altar and seek reconciliation with his brother Abel, who according to tradition had done Cain no injustice. So those who read Matt. 5:23–24 with Gen. 4 in mind will naturally think of the brother at the altar as the unjust offender, not the unjustly offended.

Having argued in favor of Cyprian's intertextual reading of Matt. 5:21–24, I should like to end by observing that the foregoing discussion leads to an interesting question about contemporary Bible translations. Here are two modern editions of our passage:

(Berkeley: University of California Press, 1981), pp. 5–13, and cf. *Gen. Rab.* 22:13. There is a wealth of relevant material on ancient perceptions of the characters of Cain and Abel in Johannes Bartholdy Glenthøj, *Cain and Abel in Syriac and Greek Writers (4th–6th Centuries)* (CSCO 567, Subsidia 95; Louvain: Peeters, 1997).

37. Cf. vv. 25–26 and Jeremias, "'Laß allda deine Gabe,'" p. 104.

38. So Betz, *Sermon*, p. 223: "What specifically is the grudge that the sacrificer remembers? We do not know, and it is not important." Cf. Cassian, *Conf.* 16.16 (SC 54, ed. Pichery, pp. 235–36).

39. Hagner, *Matthew 1–13*, p. 117.

Revised Standard Version	New Revised Standard Version
So if you are offering your gift 　at the altar,	So when you are offering your gift 　at the altar,
and there remember that 　your brother 　　has something against you,	if you remember that 　your brother or sister 　　has something against you,
leave your gift there before the altar 　and go;	leave your gift there before the altar 　and go;
first be reconciled 　to your brother,	first be reconciled 　to your brother or sister,
and then come and offer your gift.	and then come and offer your gift.

The most notable difference between these two renderings of the Greek has to do with the underlying ἀδελφός. In the older translation, "brother," naturally enough, does duty for the masculine noun. In the newer translation, the one Greek word becomes two English nouns joined by a conjunction: "brother or sister."

Although I in no way wish to argue against inclusive translation where it is appropriate, I do wonder whether it is appropriate here. The problem is that the laudable wish to have the text speak today directly to women as well as to men interferes with the latent intertextuality. A biblically literate reader of the Revised Standard Version might be able to put together "anger," "murder," "brother," and "offering your gift at the altar" and come up with the old story of Cain and Abel. But could that same person, reading the New Revised Standard Version, work the same result with "brother or sister" in verses 23–24? This seems most unlikely. Admittedly, the latter version stays honest with a footnote that says, "G[ree]k *your brother*." Most readers, however, probably do not ponder footnotes overmuch, which means that the potential allusion to Cain and Abel will never be realized in their reading. Surely the elimination of such potential is not an aid toward a better understanding of Matthew.

4

Darkness at Noon

(MATT. 27:45)

After Jesus, in Matt. 27:45, is hung upon a cross, darkness reigns from the sixth hour to the ninth: ἀπὸ δὲ ἕκτης ὥρας σκότος ἐγένετο ἐπὶ πᾶσαν τὴν γῆν ἕως ὥρας ἐνάτης. Like his fellow evangelists, Matthew offers no explanation and no interpretation (cf. Mark 15:33; Luke 23:44). His silence, which enhances the aura of mystery, has become opportunity for the commentators, who have done their best to fill in the blanks; and it is my goal, in the following pages, to catalogue and evaluate some of their efforts. Four topics will pass under review. First, I shall consider which Old Testament passages interpreters have thought might be in the background (intertextuality). Then, second, I shall highlight the ways in which readers have related 27:45 to other portions of Matthew (intratextuality). Third, I shall review the traditional issues surrounding the historicity of the darkness and its possible cause(s) (apologetics). Finally, I shall furnish some account of the chief theological and literary meanings that exegetes have uncovered (interpretation). Such a survey will allow us to see to what extent the modern discussions of Matt. 27:45 are innovative and to what extent they largely replay earlier exegetical performances.[1]

1. In addition to what follows see Rufino María Grández, "Las tinieblas en la muerte de Jesús: Historia de la exégesis de Lc 23,44–54a (Mt 27,45; Mc 15,33)," *EstBib* 47 (1989), pp. 177–224. Grández offers a chronological rather than thematic review and discusses all three Synoptics. I shall, as much as possible, confine myself to Matthew's text.

Intertextuality

Recent interpreters regularly affirm that Matt. 27:45 alludes to a prophecy in Amos 8:9–10: "On that day, says the Lord GOD, I will make the sun go down at noon, and darken [LXX: συσκοτάσει] the earth in broad daylight. I will turn your feasts into mourning, and all your songs into lamentation. . . . I will make it like the mourning for an only son [LXX: ἀγαπητοῦ]."[2] Their judgment commends itself. (1) The history of interpretation, as we shall see directly, reveals that Matthew's words have, ever since the second century, habitually sent readers back to Amos 8:9–10. (2) Matthew constantly alludes to the Bible in subtle ways,[3] and the passion narrative especially is full of implicit claims to prophetic fulfillment.[4] (3) If the death of Jesus is an eschatological event in Matthew,[5] Amos 8:9–10 has to do with "the day of the LORD." (4) The parallel between Amos 8:9–10 and Matt. 27:45 is substantial: darkness falls in both; in both that darkness is at noon; and whereas there is mourning as for "an only son" or "a beloved one" in Amos, Jesus is, in Matthew, God's beloved Son (cf.

2. See Raymond E. Brown, *The Death of the Messiah: From Gethsemane to the Grave: A Commentary on the Passion Narratives* (2 vols.; New York: Doubleday, 1994), 2:1035; J. C. Fenton, *Saint Matthew* (Pelican Gospel Commentaries; Harmondsworth: Penguin, 1963), p. 442; Walter Grundmann, *Das Evangelium nach Matthäus* (THKNT 1; Berlin: Evangelische Verlagsanstalt, 1968), p. 560; Daniel J. Harrington, *The Gospel of Matthew* (Sacra Pagina 1; Collegeville, Minn.: Liturgical Press, 1991), p. 402 ("probably"); John Paul Heil, *The Death and Resurrection of Jesus: A Narrative-Critical Reading of Matthew 26–28* (Minneapolis: Fortress, 1991), p. 83; David Hill, *The Gospel of Matthew* (New Century Bible; London: Oliphants, 1972), p. 354 ("may well be"); Ernst Lohmeyer, *Das Evangelium nach Matthäus* (ed. Werner Schmauch; KEK; Göttingen: Vandenhoeck & Ruprecht, 1958), p. 394; Julius Schniewind, *Das Evangelium nach Matthäus* (Göttingen: Vandenhoeck & Ruprecht, 1962), p. 270; Eduard Schweizer, *The Good News according to Matthew* (Atlanta: John Knox, 1975), p. 525 ("probably . . . literal fulfillment"). Amos 8:9 may itself draw upon the curse in Deut. 28:29 ("you will grope about at noon as blind people grope in darkness, but you will be unable to find your way").

3. Some of the data are helpfully presented in Robert Horton Gundry, *The Use of the Old Testament in St. Matthew's Gospel, with Special Reference to the Messianic Hope* (NovTSup 18; Leiden: Brill, 1967).

4. Note W. D. Davies and Dale C. Allison Jr., *A Critical and Exegetical Commentary on the Gospel according to Saint Matthew* (3 vols.; ICC; Edinburgh: T&T Clark, 1988, 1991, 1998), 3:608–9.

5. Dale C. Allison Jr., *The End of the Ages Has Come: An Early Interpretation of the Passion and Resurrection of Jesus* (Philadelphia: Fortress, 1985), pp. 40–50; Hans-Werner Bartsch, "Die Passions- und Ostergeschichten bei Matthäus," in *Entmythologisierende Auslegung: Aufsätze aus den Jahren 1940 bis 1960* (Hamburg: Herbert Reich, 1962), pp. 80–92; Jeffrey A. Gibbs, *Jerusalem and Parousia: Jesus' Eschatological Discourse in Matthew's Gospel* (St. Louis: Concordia, 2000), pp. 139–66; and John P. Meier, *Law and History in Matthew's Gospel* (AnBib 71; Rome: Biblical Institute, 1976), pp. 30–35.

3:17; 12:18; 17:5), and he is confessed to be God's Son precisely at the crucifixion itself (27:54).[6]

Discerning an implicit reference to Amos 8:9–10 in Matt. 27:45 is, as already indicated, nothing new. Tertullian, Cyprian, Cyril of Alexandria, Jerome, Cyril of Jerusalem, Lactantius, Rabanus Maurus, Paschasius Radbertus, Geoffrey Babion, Dionysius bar Salibi, Sedulius Scotus, and Albert the Great, among others, did so long before the moderns.[7] So too did Irenaeus, already in the second century: "Those [sic] who said, 'In that day, says the Lord, the sun will go down at noon, and there will be darkness over the earth in the clear day; and I will turn your feast days into mourning, and all your songs into lamentation,' plainly announced that obscuration of the sun which at the time of his crucifixion took place from the sixth hour onward."[8] An even earlier witness to forging a link between Amos 8:9 and the darkness of Jesus' crucifixion is *Gos. Pet.* 5:15 (which probably shows a knowledge of Matthew):[9] "Now it was midday, and darkness covered all of Judea. And they became anxious and distressed lest the sun had already set since he was still alive."[10] These sentences speak of the "sun" (ἥλιος) and of "midday" (μεσημβρία), both of which appear also in Amos 8:9 LXX.[11]

6. Ps.-Chrysostom, *In sanc. pascha* 46 (SC 48, ed. Floëri and Nautin, pp. 157–59), makes much of this last similarity. Perhaps it is also worth observing, given the nearby rending of the veil (27:51), that, only a few verses later in Amos, the temple is shaken (9:1: "I saw the Lord standing beside the altar, and he said, 'Strike the capitals until the thresholds shake, and shatter them on the heads of the people'").

7. Tertullian, *Adv. Marc.* 4.42 (OECT, ed. Evans, 2:500); Cyprian, *Test.* 2.23 (CSEL 3, ed. Hartel, p. 91); Cyril of Alexandria, *Os.–Mal.* ad Amos 8:9–10 (ed. Pusey, 1:520); Jerome, *Comm. Matt.* ad loc. (SC 259, ed. Bonnard, p. 296); Ps.-Chrysostom, *In sanc. pascha* 45 (SC 48, ed. Floëri and Nautin, p. 157); Cyril of Jerusalem, *Cat.* 13.25 (PG 33.804A); Lactantius, *Div. inst.* 4.19.3 (SC 377, ed. Monat, pp. 174–76); Rabanus Maurus, *Comm. Matt.* ad loc. (PL 107.1141A); Paschasius Radbertus, *Exp. Matt. Libri XII* ad loc. (CCCM 56B, ed. Paulus, p. 1380); Ps.-Anselm = Geoffrey Babion, *En. Matt.* ad loc. (PL 162.1488A); Dionysius bar Salibi, *Expl. Evang.* ad loc. (CSCO 77, Scriptores Syri 33, ed. Sedlaeck and Chabot, p. 131; mistakenly attributing the prophecy to Zechariah); Sedulius Scotus, *Comm. Matt.* ad loc. (ed. Löfstedt, p. 613); Albertus Magnus, *Super Mt. cap. XV–XXVIII* ad loc. (Opera Omnia 21/2, ed. B. Schmidt, p. 647). Note also Ps.-Epiphanius, *Test.* 60 (ed. Hotchkiss, p. 54), and Juan Maldonatus, *Comentarii in Quatuor Evangelistas* (2 vols.; Mainz: F. Kirchhemius, 1853–1854), 1:468–69.

8. Irenaeus, *Adv. haer.* 4.33.12 (SC 100, ed. Rousseau, p. 836).

9. For a survey of opinion see John Dominic Crossan, "The Gospel of Peter and the Canonical Gospels: Independence, Dependence, or Both?" *Forum* n.s. 1 (1998), pp. 7–51. My own view is that, at least in the passage to hand, dependence upon Mark or Luke is likely. See further Raymond E. Brown, "The Gospel of Peter and Canonical Gospel Priority," *NTS* 33 (1987), pp. 321–43, and Alan Kirk, "Examining Priorities: Another Look at the *Gospel of Peter*'s Relationship to the New Testament Gospels," *NTS* 40 (1994), pp. 572–95.

10. *Gos. Pet.* 5:15: ἦν δὲ μεσημβρία, καὶ σκότος κατέσχε πᾶσαν τὴν Ἰουδαίαν. καὶ ἐθορυβοῦντο καὶ ἠγωνίων μήποτε ὁ ἥλιος ἔδυ ἐπειδὴ ἔτι ἔζη. The text goes on to refer to Deut. 21:22–23.

11. The use of "midday" (ἤματι μέσσῳ) in the *ex eventu* prophecies of Jesus' passion in *Sib. Or.* 1:374–75 ("for three hours there will be monstrous dark night in midday") and 8:305–306

If binding Amos 8:9–10 to Matt. 27:45 is the most common intertextual tie in the commentaries, it has been almost as common to juxtapose 27:45 and Exod. 10:22: "So Moses stretched out his hand toward heaven, and there was dense darkness in all the land of Egypt for three days." According to John Fenton, "Mark had *over the whole world* . . . and Matthew changes this to *over all the land* . . . this apparently unimportant alteration may be due to his recollection of Exodus 10:22, *there was thick darkness in all the land* . . . of Egypt before the death of the first born: Jesus' death is parallel to the last plague, so it may be that Matthew saw this three-hour darkness as the fulfillment of the three-day darkness in Egypt."[12] This typological reading, which occurs fairly frequently in the modern commentaries,[13] was already known to Chrysostom, who had this to say about our verse: when Jesus died, the sign from heaven, which an evil and adulterous generation had asked for, was given, "and it was over all the world, which had never before happened, but in Egypt only, when the passover was to be fulfilled. For indeed those events were a type of these."[14] Other premoderns whose thoughts went back to Exod. 10:22 when commenting on Matt. 27:45 include Origen—who appears to be the source of this exegetical tradition—Cyril of Alexandria, Paschasius Radbertus, Dionysius bar Salibi, Albert the Great, and Matthew Henry.[15]

("in midday there will be dark monstrous night for three hours") does not so obviously reflect the influence of Amos.

12. J. C. Fenton, *Saint Matthew*, p. 442.

13. Cf. Brown, *Death of the Messiah*, 2:1035; Larry Chouinard, *The College Press NIV Commentary: Matthew* (Joplin, Mo.: College Press, 1997), p. 494; John Fleetwood, *The Life of Our Lord and Saviour Jesus Christ* (Philadelphia: W. A. Leary & Co., 1849), p. 394; R. T. France, *The Gospel according to Matthew: An Introduction and Commentary* (TNTC; Leicester: InterVarsity, 1985), p. 398; Robert H. Gundry, *Matthew: A Commentary on His Handbook for a Mixed Church under Persecution* (2nd ed.; Grand Rapids: Eerdmans, 1994), p. 572; Craig S. Keener, *Commentary on the Gospel of Matthew* (Grand Rapids: Eerdmans, 1999), p. 685 (citing, like Albertus Magnus, *Super Mt. cap. I–XIV* ad loc. [Opera Omnia 21/2, ed. B. Schmidt, p. 647], Wisd. 17 as well as Exod. 10:21–23); John P. Meier, *Matthew* (New Testament Message 3; Wilmington, Del.: Michael Glazier, 1980), p. 349; Philip A. Micklem, *St Matthew* (London: Methuen & Co., 1917), p. 274; A. Plummer, *An Exegetical Commentary on the Gospel according to St. Matthew* (London: Macmillan, 1910), p. 398 ("perhaps"); Donald P. Senior, *The Passion Narrative according to Matthew: A Redactional Study* (BETL 39; Leuven: Leuven University Press, 1975), pp. 293–94.

14. Chrysostom, *Hom. on Matt.* 88.1 (PG 58.775). Cf. the allegorical equation of Jerusalem with Egypt in Rev. 11:8.

15. Origen, *Comm. Matt.* frag. 134 (GCS 38, ed. Klostermann, pp. 276–77; cf. PG 13.1784A); idem, *Scholia Matt.* (PG 17.308D–309A); Cyril of Alexandria, *Comm. Matt.* frag. 311 (TU 61, ed. Reuss, p. 265); Paschasius Radbertus, *Exp. Matt. Libri XII* ad loc. (CCCM 56B, ed. Paulus, p. 1379); Dionysius bar Salibi, *Expl. Evang.* ad loc. (CSCO 77, Scriptores Syri 33, ed. Sedlaeck and Chabot, p. 131); Albertus Magnus, *Super Mt. cap. I–XIV* ad loc. (Opera Omnia 21/2, ed. B. Schmidt, p. 647); Matthew Henry, *Commentary on the Whole Bible*, vol. 5, *Matthew to John* (New York: Fleming H. Revell, n.d.), ad Matt. 27:45.

This reading is understandable, for multiple observations suggest that the evangelist Matthew himself may well have had Exod. 10:22 in mind as he wrote about Jesus' crucifixion. (1) If the formal quotation in Matt. 2:6 can juxtapose Mic. 5:2, 4 with 2 Sam. 5:2 = 1 Chron. 11:2, so that readers are sent to two parental scriptures at once, and if 3:17 can recall both Ps. 2:7 and Isa. 42:1,[16] then nothing prohibits the possibility that Matt. 27:45 simultaneously alludes to Exod. 10:22 as well as to Amos 8:9–10. (2) Matthew's penchant for drawing parallels between the story of Jesus and the story of the exodus is well known, and it is unfailing; it begins in chapter 1 and it continues until the very last pericope.[17] (3) The proposed typological correlation between three hours (in Matthew) and three days (in Exodus) has a parallel in chapter 4, in the temptation narrative, where the forty days of Jesus' temptation in the wilderness are the typological correlative of the forty years of Israel's sojourn in the desert: it is the number, not the unit of measurement, that matters for typology.[18] (4) If Jesus' crucifixion belongs to Passover week, Exod. 10:22 recounts the story of the very first Passover. (5) As Fenton observed, Matthew has, on the theory of Markan priority, slightly rewritten his source, and the result brings him a bit nearer to Exod. 10:22:[19]

σκότος ἐγένετο	ἐφ᾽ ὅλην	τὴν γῆν	(Mark 10:33)
ἐγένετο σκότος . . .	ἐπὶ πᾶσαν	γῆν Αἰγύπτου	(Exod. 10:22)
σκότος ἐγένετο	ἐπὶ πᾶσαν	τὴν γῆν	(Matt. 27:45)

The case for Exod. 10:22 is as strong as that for Amos 8:9–10.

Although most commentators looking for a biblical intertext for Matt. 27:45 have justifiably thought either of the prophecy in Amos 8 or of the famous event in Exod. 10, we should perhaps note, before passing on to the next section, that three additional passages appear in more than one commentary in connection with Matthew's darkness at noon: Gen. 1:2; Jer. 15:9; and Zech. 14:6–7. W. D. Davies offered that Jesus' death, in a way reminiscent of the βίβλος γενέσεως of 1:1[20] and the dove of 3:16,[21] might recall Gen. 1 and so "suggest . . . the return of that darkness which was at creation, the earth having, symbolically, returned to the first be-

16. Davies and Allison, *Matthew*, 1:336–39.
17. Dale C. Allison Jr., *The New Moses: A Matthean Typology* (Minneapolis: Fortress, 1993).
18. Birger Gerhardsson, *The Testing of God's Son (Matt. 4:1–11 and Par): An Analysis of an Early Christian Midrash* (ConBNT 2; Lund: G. W. K. Gleerup, 1966), pp. 41–43.
19. See further Senior, *Passion*, pp. 293–94.
20. See chapter 8 of the present book.
21. See my article "The Baptism of Jesus and a New Dead Sea Scroll," *BAR* 18 (1992), pp. 58–60.

ginning" (cf. Gen. 1:2).[22] Isho'dad of Merv had the same thought: the darkness of the crucifixion made it "just like it was in the beginning of creation before the light was created."[23] But Irenaeus, Cyprian, Jerome, Lactantius, and Sedulius Scotus recalled rather Jer. 15:9. This, like Amos 8:9–10—which all of the authorities just cited also thought fulfilled by Matt. 27:45—has a daytime darkness: "She who bore seven has languished; she has swooned away; her sun went down while it was yet day [LXX: μεσούσης τῆς ἡμέρας]; she has been shamed and disgraced."[24]

Eusebius and Cyril of Jerusalem, however, were rather put in mind of yet another text, Zech. 14:6–7 LXX: "And it will come to pass in that day that there will be no light. And there will be one day of cold and frost, and that day will be known to the Lord, and it will not be day or night; but it will become light toward evening."[25] This prophecy, according to Eusebius and Cyril, was literally fulfilled because, in addition to the darkness that fell at the crucifixion, John 18:18 tells us it was cold at the time: "The slaves and police had made a charcoal fire because it was cold, and they were standing around it and warming themselves. Peter also was standing with them and warming himself."[26]

Intratextuality

Commentators, both ancient and modern, have been more inclined to draw lines between Matt. 27:45 and the Old Testament than between 27:45 and other verses in the First Gospel. Only a few, for instance, have remarked upon some of the striking contrasts between the transfiguration, the private epiphany in which Jesus gives off light, and the crucifixion, the public spectacle when all goes dark.[27] Also few and far between are

22. W. D. Davies, *The Setting of the Sermon on the Mount* (Cambridge: Cambridge University Press, 1966), p. 84. Cf. Brown, *Death of the Messiah*, 2:1035, and Davies and Allison, *Matthew*, 3:621. For other returns to the primeval darkness see Jer. 4:23 and *Liv. Pro. Hab.* 13 ("darkness as from the beginning").

23. Isho'dad of Merv, *Comm. Matt.* 7 (HSem 6, ed. Gibson, p. 189).

24. Irenaeus, *Adv. haer.* 4.33.12; Cyprian, *Test.* 2.23 (CSEL 3, ed. Hartel, p. 91); Jerome, *Comm. Matt.* ad loc. (SC 259, ed. Bonnard, p. 296); Lactantius, *Div. inst.* 4.19.4 (SC 377, ed. Monat, p. 176); Sedulius Scotus, *Comm. Matt.* ad loc. (ed. Löfstedt, p. 613). Lactantius further cites *Sib. Or.* 8:305–306 ("in midday there will be dark monstrous night for three hours," cf. *Sib. Or.* 1.375) as fulfilled in the death of Jesus.

25. Eusebius, *Dem. ev.* 10.7 (GCS 23, ed. Heikel, pp 469–70), and Cyril of Jerusalem, *Cat.* 13.24 (PG 33.801B–C). Cf. Origen, *Scholia Matt.* (PG 17.308C); *Const. Ap.* 5:14:16 (ed. Funk, p. 277); and Ps.-Chrysostom, *In sanc. pascha* 45 (SC 48, ed. Floëri and Nautin, p. 157). I have translated the Greek the way Eusebius and Cyril seem to have read it, which does not agree with the punctuation of Rahlfs' LXX.

26. So also Ps.-Epiphanius, *Test.* 59–60 ed. Hotchkiss, p. 54.

27. See pp. 226–30 of chapter 11 below.

contrasts between Matt. 27:45 and the star of Bethlehem, although F. C. Cook did write that "the birth and the death of the Savior have . . . analogous accompaniments; the star announcing life, the darkness prefiguring death, alike bear witness to the Lord of Nature."[28] Perhaps Cook had read Matthew Henry, who said much the same thing: "An extraordinary light gave intelligence of the birth of Christ (ch. ii. 2), and therefore it was proper that an extraordinary darkness should notify his death, for he is the Light of the world."[29]

Others have gone to 24:29 when expounding 27:45: "The sun will be darkened, and the moon will not give its light" (cf. Isa. 13:10; 34:4).[30] This move has a good chance of being faithful to Matthew's theology. For it is common, at least in the modern commentaries, to urge that Matt. 26–28 is a sort of mini-apocalypse, or that it marks "the beginning of the end-time."[31] The reason for this appears when one lists the parallels between Jesus' eschatological prophecies, especially as found in the great eschatological discourse, which prefaces the passion narrative (24–25), and what happens in the immediately subsequent chapters (26–28):

Eschatological exhortations and prophecies	The fate of Jesus
"Keep awake (γρηγορεῖτε), then, for you do not know in what day your Lord is coming (ἔρχεται)," 24:42; "all of them became drowsy and slept" (ἐκάθευδον), 25:5	Jesus tells his disciples to stay awake (γρηγορεῖτε) and then comes (ἔρχεται) and finds them sleeping (καθεύδοντας), 26:38–40
Disciples will be handed over, 10:17, 19, 21; 24:9–10 (all with forms of παραδίδωμι)	Jesus is handed over, 26:2, 15, 16, etc. (all with forms of παραδίδωμι)
"Brother will betray brother to death," 10:21	Jesus is betrayed by Judas, "one of the twelve," 26:15–16, 24–25, 46–48
"Then many will fall away" (σκανδαλισθήσονται), 24:10	The disciples fall away, 26:31 (σκανδαλισθήσεσθε), 33 (σκανδαλισθήσονται)

28. F. C. Cook, "St. Matthew," in *The Holy Bible according to the Authorized Version A.D. (1611), with an Explanatory and Critical Commentary: New Testament*, vol. 1, *St. Matthew—St. Mark—St. Luke* (ed. F. C. Cook; New York: Scribner, 1878), p. 183.

29. Henry, *Matthew to John*, ad loc.

30. Note, e.g., Hendrikus Berkhof, *Christ: The Meaning of History* (London: SCM, 1966), p. 63; Warren Carter, *Matthew and the Margins: A Sociopolitical and Religous Reading* (Maryknoll, N.Y.: Orbis, 2000), p. 534; Davies and Allison, *Matthew*, 3:622; Heil, *Death*, p. 83.

31. So Daniel Patte, *The Gospel according to Matthew: A Structural Commentary on Matthew's Faith* (Philadelphia: Fortress, 1987), p. 390. Cf. Douglas J. Moo, *The Old Testament in the Gospel Passion Narratives* (Sheffield: Almond, 1983), p. 343: "'Darkness' as a phenomenon appropriate to the eschaton is the general background conception."

Eschatological exhortations and prophecies	The fate of Jesus
Disciples will flee, 10:23 (φεύγετε); 24:16 (φευγέτωσαν)	The disciples flee (ἔφυγον), 26:56
Disciples will be delivered up to sanhedrins (συνέδρια), 10:17	Jesus appears before a sanhedrin (συνέδριον) of Jewish elders, 26:59
Disciples will be led (ἀχθήσεσθε) before "governors" (ἡγεμόνας), 10:18	Jesus is led (ἀπήγαγον) away to the "governor" (ἡγεμόνι) Pilate, 27:2; cf. 11–26
The disciples will be flogged (μαστιγώσουσιν), 10:17	Jesus is flogged (μαστιγῶσαι), 20:19; 27:26
Jesus will reign upon his throne, 19:28; 25:31	Jesus suffers a mock enthronement, 27:27–31
The sky will go dark, 24:29	There is a supernatural darkness, 27:45
The temple will be destroyed, 24:1–2	The veil of the temple splits, symbolically destroying the institution, 27:51[32]
There will be earthquakes (σεισμοί), 24:7	There is an earthquake (ἡ γῆ ἐσείσθη), 27:51
The disciples will be killed, 10:21 (θάνατον, θανατώσουσιν), 28 (ἀποκτεινόντων); 24:9 (ἀποκτενοῦσιν)	Jesus is killed, 26:4 (ἀποκτείνωσιν), 59 (θανατώσωσιν); 27:1 (θανατῶσαι)
The dead will rise, 12:41 (ἀναστήσονται), 42 (ἐγερθήσεται); 22:23–33 (ἀνάστασιν, ἀναστάσει, ἀναστάσεως)	Jesus and others rise from the dead, 17:9 (ἀναστῇ), 23 (ἀναστήσεται); 20:19 (ἀναστήσεται); 26:32 (ἐγερθῆναι); 27:52–53 (ἠγέρθησαν), 64 (ἠγέρθη); 28:6–7 (ἠγέρθη)
Jesus will return as the Son of Man, 24:27, 30, 37, 39, 44; 25:31; etc.	Jesus is vindicated as the Son of Man, 28:18[33]

In Matthew, even more than in Mark,[34] the crucifixion and resurrection and the events leading up to them have an eschatological character. The passion narrates the initial or partial realization of eschatological

32. According to Josephus, *Bell.* 5.4, a Babylonian curtain, embroidered with blue, scarlet, linen thread, and purple hung before the main entrance of the sanctuary, at the back of the vestibule, and "worked into the tapestry was the whole vista of the heavens (excepting the signs of the Zodiac)." If Matt. 27:45 pertains to this particular curtain (an unresolved problem), then the picture conjured up by the verse would be of a panorama of the heavens splitting. (Note that Ps. 104:2; Isa. 40:22; and *b. B. Mes.* 59a liken the sky to a curtain or tent.) It may, then, not be coincidence that the rending or dissolution of the heavenly firmament occurs in the Old Testament and later came to be a fixed item of the eschatological scenario: Job 14:12 LXX; Ps. 102:26; Isa. 34:4; Hag. 2:6, 21; *Sib. Or.* 3:82; 8:233, 413; Matt. 24:29; Rev. 6:14; 2 Pet. 3:10.

33. On the allusion to the eschatological vision of Dan. 7:13–14 in Matt. 28:18 see Davies and Allison, *Matthew*, 3:682–83. Matt. 24:30 also alludes to Dan. 7:13–14.

34. Here the foundational work is R. H. Lightfoot, *The Gospel Message of St. Mark* (Cambridge: Cambridge University Press, 1950), pp. 48–59.

expectations, and the darkness common to Jesus' end and the end of the age is part of the pattern of prophecy and fulfillment.

The correlation of Jesus' end with eschatology is, from what I have been able to discover, found, not in older commentaries, but rather in modern academic commentaries, which have, since Johannes Weiss and Albert Schweitzer, been so conscious of early Christian eschatology. I can observe, however, that the *Dialogue of Timothy and Aquila* (ed. Conybeare, p. 100) says that, at the death of Jesus, a prophecy of Isaiah was fulfilled, and that this apocryphon quotes not Isaiah but rather mingles Matt. 24:29 (ὁ ἥλιος σκοτισθήσεται), which foretells the *parousia*, and Amos 8:9–10 (see above): "When he was crucified, the sun was darkened, and there was a darkness on all the earth, from the sixth hour to the ninth. And again there was light, as it has been written in Isaiah, that 'The sun will be darkened (σκοτισθήσεται ὁ ἥλιος) at midday, and the sun will darken in the middle of the day.'" This may be unconscious assimilation of Matt. 27:45 to Matt. 24:29, but it is also possible that the author of the *Dialogue* saw a more thematic connection, as have some recent interpreters: the crucifixion is an eschatological event.

The odds that this is so are raised because the assimilation of the darkness at noon to the language about the *parousia* in Matt. 24:29 par. appears elsewhere in antiquity. For example, in the *Evangelium Jerosolymitanum*, a Syriac lectionary of the Gospels, Luke 23:44 (Luke's account of the darkness at Jesus' death) is expanded so that the moon goes dark and the stars fall from the sky, as Matt. 24:29 = Mark 13:24 prophesies.[35] Again, Ps.-Chrysostom, *Pasch.* 6 55 (SC 27, ed. Nautin, p. 182), recounts the darkness of the crucifixion in the same way, by speaking of the stars falling from heaven and the moon being darkened. It is also relevant, in this connection, that Cyril of Alexandria, the *Anaphora Pilati*, and Isho'dad of Merv speak of the moon turning to blood at the crucifixion, which brings to mind the eschatological prophecy in Joel 2:31 = Acts 2:20 (cf. Rev. 6:12).[36] One may of course regard all this as the poetry of devotion, but the point stands nonetheless: some thought it fitting to move the language of the *parousia* and the Day of the Lord to the story of the crucifixion. An

35. Paul de Lagarde, *Bibliothecae Syriacae* (Göttingen: Lüder Horstmann, 1892), p. 356; Agnes Smith Lewis and Margaret Dunlop Gibson, *The Palestinian Syriac Lectionary of the Gospels* (London: K. Paul, Trench, Trübner, 1899), pp. li, 205.

36. Cyril of Alexandria, *Os.–Mal.* ad Joel 2:30–31 (ed. Pusey, 1:342); *Anaphora Pilati* (ed. Tischendorf, p. 417); and Isho'dad of Merv, *Comm. Matt.* 7 (HSem 6, ed. Gibson, p. 189). Although commentators on Matt. 27:45 never go to Acts 2:20, where Peter at Pentecost quotes as fulfilled the prophecy that "the sun will be turned to darkness and the moon to blood," commentators on Acts 2:20 have sometimes gone to Matt. 27:45 par.; cf. Bede, *Comm. Acts* ad 2:20 (CCSL 121, ed. Laistner, p. 19); F. F. Bruce, *Commentary on the Book of the Acts* (NICNT; Grand Rapids: Eerdmans, 1954), p. 69; and Colin J. Humphreys and W. G. Waddington, "The Jewish Calendar, A Lunar Eclipse, and the Date of Christ's Crucifixion," *TynBul* 43 (1992), p. 341.

eschatological interpretation of the passion, in continuity with primitive Christian theology, is perhaps thereby suggested, even though it finds no clear statement in the ancient commentaries I have read.[37]

Before quitting this review of intratextual associations, I should like to take note of three additional readings that, although they are idiosyncratic and have scant chance of catching the evangelist's intention, are nonetheless memorable. The first comes from Bruno of Segni, whose thoughts moved from Matt. 27:45 back to 4:16, to wit: whereas Jesus lighted the world, so that we read, in chapter 4, "the people who sat in darkness have seen a great light," those very people, by hardening their hearts—Bruno cites Romans 11:25—extinguished that light. The upshot was the outer darkness of chapter 27, which mirrored the people's inner darkness.[38] A second novel but arresting association comes from Matthew Henry, who went from 27:45 back to 5:45: "This darkness signified that dark cloud which the human soul of Jesus was now under. God makes his sun to shine upon the just and the unjust; but even the light of the sun was withheld from our Savior, when he was made sin for us."[39] Finally, we may note that Chrysostom judged the supernatural darkness of 27:45 to be precisely the sort of sign from heaven that the scribes and Pharisees demanded of Jesus in 12:38 and 16:1, and which they, when they finally saw it, understood not.[40]

Apologetics

Much labor has gone into vain efforts to defend the historicity of the darkness at the crucifixion and to understand its nature. Most of the issues are already to the fore in Origen. In one place, in response to Celsus's accusation that Jesus did nothing truly remarkable, Origen says that a certain Phlegon, "in the thirteenth or fourteenth book of his Chronicles," spoke of "the eclipse (ἐκλείψεως) in the time of Tiberius Caesar, in whose reign Jesus appears to have been crucified."[41] This is a reference to a lost book of Phlegon of Tralles, a pagan historian of the second century CE.[42] Origen is claiming that the gospel miracle is credible because it is documented by a non-Christian.

37. See further below, pp. 100–101. On the passion and resurrection as properly eschatological events in several early Christian writings see Allison, *End*, esp. pp. 26–82.

38. Bruno of Segni, *Comm. Matt.* ad loc. (PL 165.305B).

39. Matthew Henry, *Matthew to John* ad loc.

40. Chrysostom, *Hom. Matt.* 85.1 (PG 58.775). Cf. Origen, *Scholia Matt.* (PG 17.308D–309A).

41. Origen, *Cels.* 2.33 (ed. Marcovich, pp. 108–9). Cf. the more general appeal to Phlegon in 2.14 (ed. Marcovich, p. 93); also Origen, *Scholia Matt.* (PG 17.309B).

42. For a convenient introduction to Phlegon see William Hansen, *Phlegon of Tralles' Book of Marvels* (Exeter: University of Exeter, 1996).

Origen answered Celsus in the last decade of his life. During that very same decade he also wrote his mammoth commentary on Matthew; yet in this he takes a different approach to Matt. 27:45 and its parallels. Here he confronts two objections. First, how can it be that an eclipse of three hours is unknown to historians: *nulla refert historia?* "No Greek or barbarian recorded such a wonder at the time, especially those who have written chronicles and noted novel occurrences." Only Christians know the story. Origen's hypothetical opponent—he does not here name Celsus—goes on to concede that Phlegon recorded a striking darkness, but he asserts that Phlegon was not writing about Jesus' crucifixion. Origen does not demur. Second, the opposition holds that the darkness surrounding Jesus could have been due to an eclipse, so there is no need to invoke divine intervention.[43]

Origen's apologetical rejoinder develops in several steps. He initially establishes that the darkness was not an eclipse because sun and moon do not meet together at the time of Passover (midmonth), an argument repeated after him in commentary after commentary. He next observes that neither Matthew nor Mark says anything about the sun; they only mention darkness, so we need not take them to claim that an eclipse occurred. As for Luke, Origen (like our modern critical editions) knows that there are two different readings at 23:45, and while one uses the language of eclipse (τοῦ ἡλίου ἐκλιπόντος), the other asserts only that "the sun was darkened" (καὶ ἐσκοτίσθη ὁ ἥλιος). This second text is ambiguous regarding the cause, and Origen prefers it. He even implausibly raises the possibility that the verse "was altered by people plotting against the church of Christ, to make it easier to attack the gospel."

Having established that Matt. 27:45 and its parallels do not plainly say that there was an eclipse, Origen contends that the other miracles surrounding the crucifixion were local, not universal. The earthquake of Matt. 27:51–53 was felt only in and about Jerusalem, where the veil of the temple was rent, and only the saints buried near the holy city left their tombs, not the saints scattered abroad. In like manner, Origen urges, the darkness was not worldwide but confined.[44] This neatly accounts for the lacuna in secular histories, which Origen here (but not in

---

43. Origen, *Comm. Matt.* frag. 134 (GCS 38, ed. Klostermann, p. 271–78; cf. PG 13.1781D–82A). Cf. *Acts of Pilate* 11:2, where the Roman soldiers report to Pilate that "there was an eclipse of the sun in the usual way." It is likely that Porphyry, in his attack on Christianity, also explained away the darkness as a natural eclipse; see John Granger Cook, *The Interpretation of the New Testament in Greco-Roman Paganism* (Peabody, Mass.: Hendrickson, 2000), pp. 146–47.

44. Cf. *Gos. Pet.* 5:15: "Now it was midday, and darkness covered all of Judea. And they became anxious and distressed lest the sun had already set since he was still alive." Contrast Julius Africanus apud George Syncellus, *Ecl. chron.* (ed. Mosshammer, p. 391), and the *Second Treatise of the Great Seth* 58:17–22 (7.2): in these the phenomenon is global.

Contra Celsum) admits. It also allows one to imagine that a gathering of very dark clouds was responsible for obscuring the sun. In making this suggestion, Origen—anticipating Hollywood lives of Christ—adds that this may also have been what happened when, in biblical times, darkness fell upon Egypt for three days; certainly an eclipse cannot account for a darkness of such duration.

Origen's understanding of the extent of the darkness neatly dovetails with his theological interpretation. He takes the lack of light to be a divine judgment against the Jewish people for their rejection of Jesus. The rest of the world, however, was about to welcome the gospel, so whereas "darkness came upon all the land of Judea three hours . . . in all the rest of the earth there was light, which everywhere lightens all the church of God in Christ."

Origen's defense of the historicity of the darkness at Jesus' crucifixion and his understanding of its cause (clouds) failed to find much subsequent endorsement. Christians by and large did not, for one thing, concede that the event in question was unattested outside the Gospels.[45] Phlegon's doubtful testimony has been dragged up again and again over the centuries as vindication of the historicity of the darkness at the crucifixion. Commentaries written as recently as a hundred years ago still mention him with satisfaction.[46]

Perhaps the first to claim Phlegon for the Christian cause was Sextus Julius Africanus. (As Origen and Africanus were acquainted,[47] maybe one

45. One sometimes runs into unspecified appeal to pagan witnesses; note, e.g., Tertullian, *Apol.* 21.19 (ed. Becker, p. 134: "you yourselves have the account of the world-portent still in your archives"), and Paulus Orosius, *Hist. lib. sept.* 7.4 (PL 31.1069A: "some books of the Greeks").

46. For additional citations of Phlegon's alleged testimony to the evangelical darkness see Jerome's version of Eusebius, *Chron.* Olympiad 202 (GCS 47, ed. Helm, pp. 174–75; cf. PG 19.535); Apollonarius of Laodicea, *Comm. Matt.* frag. 143 (TU 61, ed. Reuss, p. 50); Theodore of Heraclea, *Comm. Matt.* frag. 131 (TU 61, ed. Reuss, p. 94); John Philoponus, *Opif.* 2.21; 3.9 (FC 23/2–3, ed. Scholten, pp. 254–56, 312); Paschasius Radbertus, *Exp. Matt. Libri XII* ad loc. (CCCM 56B, ed. Paulus, pp. 1381); *Chronicon Paschale* (PG 92.536A, 541A); John Malalas, *Chron.* (PG 97.369A); Nicephorus, *Chron. brev.* (PG 108.1193D); anonymous comment in *Catenae in Evangelia S. Lucae et S. Joannis ad fidem codd. mss.* (ed. J. A. Cramer; Hildesheim: Georg Olms, 1967 [reprint of 1842 ed.]), p. 237; Hugo Grotius, *Opera omnia theologica*, vol. 2, part 1 (Amsterdam: Joannis Blaeu, 1679), p. 272; Juan Maldonatus, *Comentarii,* 1:470; Augustin Calmet, *Commentarium literale in omnes ac singulos tum Veteris cum Novi Testamenti* (8 vols.; Augsburg/Graz: Sumptibus Philippi, ac Martini Veith, et Joannis Fratris Haeredum, 1734–1735), 7:332–33; John Gill, *Gill's Commentary* (6 vols.; Grand Rapids: Baker, 1980), 5:295; and Cook, "Matthew," p. 183 (also appealing to Tertullian's statement about Roman archives; see n. 45). I have not had access to William Whiston, *The Testimony of Phlegon Vindicated, or, An Account of the Great Darkness and Earthquake at Our Savior's Passion Described by Phlegon* (London: Fletcher Gyles, 1732).

47. A letter from Julius Africanus to Origen survives; see *Die Briefe des Sextus Julius Africanus an Aristides und Origenes* (ed. W. Reichardt; TU 34.3; Leipzig: J. C. Hinrichs, 1909), pp. 63–80.

of them learned from the other of the relevant passage in Phlegon.) In his lost history, Africanus, as preserved in George Syncellus, the ninth-century Byzantine historian, wrote this: "Phlegon relates that a total eclipse of the sun took place under Tiberius Caesar at full moon, from the sixth hour to the ninth hour. It was clearly this one," that is, the darkness at the crucifixion.[48] In order to substantiate that the dimness in the Synoptics was something other than a normal eclipse, Africanus went on to insist that naturalistic explanations for the other events surrounding the crucifixion—the rending of rocks and the resurrection of dead saints (Matt. 27:51–53)—are impossible: clearly everything involved divine intervention. The argument does not work for us. Although Phlegon's work survived for centuries, many Christians familiar with it failed to cite him as support for the gospel miracle. With the exception of Africanus, moreover, those who did cite his notice of an eclipse under Tiberius reported him saying neither that it lasted from the sixth to the ninth hour nor that it was seen in Judea, so one very much doubts Phlegon's relevance to the Christian story—all the more when it is added that, whereas Phlegon speaks of an eclipse, daytime eclipses do not occur at Passover. There is really no reason to associate his eclipse with Jewish history, much less with Jesus. Phlegon's name has rightly dropped out of the commentaries.[49]

Africanus was not content to cite Phlegon alone. He also appealed to the testimony of Thallus, a pagan historian who wrote, in Greek, a history of the eastern Mediterranean world from before the Trojan War to the middle or latter part of the first century CE, Thallus's own time.[50] This history, composed in Greek, has perished. We know it only through references in later writers. Among them is George Syncellus. In the same place that he quotes Africanus on Phlegon, he also quotes Africanus on Thallus. To judge by this, Julius Africanus said that Thallus wrote about the darkness that accompanied the death of Jesus and attributed that darkness to an eclipse.[51]

48. George Syncellus, *Ecl. chron.* 610 (ed. Mosshammer, p. 391); cf. p. 394, where it is added that the stars shone during the day.

49. See further George Ogg, *The Chronology of the Public Ministry of Jesus* (Cambridge: Cambridge University Press, 1940), pp. 244–46. Kepler, for what it is worth, calculated that Phlegon's eclipse occurred in 29 CE, which dissociates it from the two most likely years for Jesus' death, 30 and 33 CE.

50. For what we know about Thallus see Horace A. Rigg Jr., "Thallus: The Samaritan?" *HTR* 34 (1941), pp. 111–19.

51. Julius Africanus, *Chron.* apud George Syncellus, *Ecl. chron.* 610 (ed. Mosshammer, p. 391): "There fell upon the whole world (κόσμου) a most fearful darkness, and, with an earthquake, the rocks were rent, and many places in Judea and the rest of the earth were thrown down. This darkness, Thallus, in the third book of his *Histories*, calls an eclipse of the sun. This is unreasonable. For the Hebrews celebrate the Passover on the fourteenth day of the moon, and what happened to our savior happened one day before Passover. Yet an eclipse of the sun

We unfortunately do not have Thallus's own words about the matter, only Julius Africanus's summary of their import. Yet that the latter seemingly disputes Thallus's interpretation—"This, it seems to me, is contrary to reason"—implies that Thallus was offering a mundane explanation for what had happened when Jesus died.[52] If so, and if Thallus, as so many have thought, wrote in the 50s of the first century,[53] then he would indeed be a pagan witness, not necessarily to a darkness at the crucifixion, but at least to a Christian tradition about such. Oddly enough, however, Thallus's supposed testimony to the darkness at noon, unlike that of Phlegon, fails, to the extent of my knowledge, to show up in patristic or medieval commentaries, and it is not until post-Reformation times that he once again becomes a topic of conversation in connection with the gospel miracle.[54]

Another extrabiblical source that has sometimes been thought to add its testimony to the synoptic record is the seventh epistle of Pseudo-Dionysius. This rebuts the unbelief of a certain Apollophanes by appealing to several preternatural signs, such as the stasis of the sun in Josh. 10:2–14. The clincher is the darkness at Jesus' crucifixion, which Pseudo-Dionysius claims he and Apollophanes witnessed together:

> But ask him, "What do you say about the eclipse at the time of the crucifixion?" For we both were present and standing together at Heliopolis at the time we saw the moon paradoxically going over the sun (it not being the right time for a conjunction), and then from the ninth hour until evening the moon miraculously stood in place of the sun's diameter. Remind him also of this other thing. For he knows that we saw the adumbration itself begin from the east and proceed to the edge of the sun, and then it proceeded back, and the adumbration and reclearing happened not in a single direction but in a diametrically opposite direction. So great were the marvels of that time, possible only to Christ the Cause of all, the maker of great and marvelous things, of which there is not number.[55]

---

happens only when the moon comes under the sun [that is, when the moon is not full]." Cf. the Greek text and translation printed in Carl R. Holladay, *Fragments from Hellenistic Jewish Authors,* vol. 1, *Historians* (Chico, Cal.: Scholars Press, 1983), pp. 354–55.

52. So also Maurice Goguel, *The Life of Jesus* (New York: Macmillan, 1933), p. 92.

53. He has often been identified with the individual in Josephus, *Ant.* 18.167, on the assumption that ἄλλος should be emended to Θάλλος; see Goguel, *Jesus,* p. 93, n. 1. But it is not clear that the text should be altered; see Rigg, "Thallus."

54. See, e.g., Grotius, *Opera omnia theologica,* vol. 2, part 1, p. 272; Pierre-Daniel Huet, *Demonstratio evangelica ad serenissimum delphinum* (Frankfurt: Sumptibus Thomae Fritschii, 1722), p. 28; Calmet, *Commentarium,* 7:333; and, more recently, F. F. Bruce, *Jesus and Christian Origins outside the New Testament* (Grand Rapids: Eerdmans, 1974), pp. 29–30; Robert Eisler, *The Messiah Jesus and John the Baptist* (New York: Dial, 1931), pp. 297–99; Goguel, *Jesus,* pp. 91–93; Gerd Theissen and Annette Merz, *The Historical Jesus: A Comprehensive Guide* (Minneapolis: Fortress, 1998), pp. 84–85.

55. Translation of Ronald F. Hathaway, *Hierarchy and the Definition of Order in the Letters of Pseudo-Dionysius: A Study in the Form and Meaning of the Pseudo-Dionysian Writings* (The

A later embellishment of this oft-quoted fiction is that Apollophanes cried out at the time that God or the gods were suffering.[56] Although John Wesley still quoted this as though it were rock solid history, the recognition, increasingly common from the sixteenth century, that the epistles attributed to Dionysius are pseudepigraphic, and that they come from ca. 500, not ca. 50, gradually erased from the literature appeals to the famous seventh epistle.[57]

If, until relatively recent times, Origen was pretty much alone in admitting that there was no persuasive extrabiblical testimony to the darkness at the crucifixion, he was also pretty much alone in guessing that the cause of that darkness was a gathering of dark clouds. Later apologists did concur with him (and with Julius Africanus) that a normal eclipse could not have been the cause of the sun's failure, for they observed that eclipses do not take place at the time of Passover, in midmonth, and further that, whereas the darkness in the Gospels lasts three hours, eclipses are shorter lived.[58] Against Origen, however, almost everyone, at least before Erasmus, was persuaded that the

Hague: Martinus Nijhoff, 1969), p. 139. For the Greek text see PTS 36 (Corpus Dionysiacum 2), ed. Heil and Ritter, pp. 168–68. Subsequent references to this include John Philoponus, *Opif.* 2.21 (FC 23/2, ed. Scholten, p. 256); Hilduino, *Dionys. Vit.* 14 (PL 106.33C–D); Paschasius Radbertus, *Exp. Matt. Libri XII* ad loc. (CCCM 56B, ed. Paulus, pp. 1382); Albertus Magnus, *Super Mt. cap. I–XIV* ad 2:2 (Opera Omnia 21/1, ed. B. Schmidt, p. 646); Nicolas de Gorran, *In quatuor Evangelia Commentarius* (Antwerp: Ioannes Keerbergius, 1617), p. 253; Juan Maldonatus, *Comentarii*, 1:468–70; Matthew Poole, *Annotations on the Holy Bible* (3 vols.; London: Henry G. Bohn, 1846), 3:141; Calmet, *Commentarium*, 7:333; John Trapp, *A Commentary or Exposition upon All the Books of the New Testament* (ed. W. Webster; London: Richard D. Dickinson, 1865), p. 275; Fred W. Krummacher, *The Suffering Saviour; or Meditations on the Last Days of Christ* (Boston: Gould & Lincoln, 1860), p. 412. Dante, *Paradiso* 29.85–126, also echoes Dionysius: "Everyone strains his wits to make a display and show his inventiveness. . . . One says that the moon reversed when Christ suffered, and blocked the sun's light from shining below."

56. Cf. Isho'dad of Merv, *Comm. Matt.* 6 (HSem 6, ed. Gibson, p. 188), who is followed by Dionysius bar Salibi, *Expl. Evang.* ad loc. (CSCO 77, Scriptores Syri 33, ed. Sedlaeck and Chabot, p. 132); also Suidas, s.v. Ἀνέκαθεν, ed. Bernhardy 1/1:399; s.v. Διονύσιος ὁ Ἀρεωπαγίτης, 1/1:1387–88; Cornelius à Lapide, *The Great Commentary of Cornelius à Lapide* (6 vols.; 2nd ed.; London: John Hodges, 1874–1887), 3:300; Henry, *Matthew to John* ad loc. (he quotes a Latin version: *Aut Deus naturae patitur, aut mundi machina dissolvitur*); John Wesley, *Explanatory Notes upon the New Testament* (London: Epworth, 1950), p. 134. Trapp, *Commentary*, p. 275, attributes the quotation to Ptolemy.

57. Note the dismissal of Dionysius's testimony and recognition that his epistle is a pseudepigraphon in Erasmus, *Annot. in Matt.* ad 27:45 (Opera Omnia 6/5, ed. Hovingh, p. 342).

58. See, e.g., Apollonarius of Laodicea, *Comm. Matt.* frag. 143 (TU 61, ed. Reuss, pp. 50–51); Theodore of Heraclea, *Comm. Matt.* frag. 131 (TU 61, ed. Reuss, p. 94); Jerome, *Comm. Matt.* ad loc. (SC 259, ed. Bonnard, pp. 294–96); Augustine, *Civ. dei* 3.15 (CCSL 47, ed. Hoffmann, p. 78); Paulus Orosius, *Hist. lib. sept.* 7.4 (PL 31.1069A, rejecting both clouds and an eclipse as explanation); John Philoponus, *Opif.* 3.9 (FC 23/3, ed. Scholten, p. 312); Ps.-Anselm = Geoffrey Babion, *En. Matt.* ad loc. (PL 162.1487D–88A); Isho'dad of Merv, *Comm. Matt.* 7 (HSem 6, ed. Gibson, pp. 188–89); Poole, *Annotations*, 3:141; Adam Clarke, *The Holy Bible, Contain-*

darkness was a worldwide miracle.[59] The upshot was that the sign could not be explained in any normal fashion, as the quotation from Pseudo-Dionysius, which has the moon moving backwards, nicely illustrates.

Having, through the ages, played its minor role as confirmation of the gospel message, by the seventeenth and eighteenth centuries, the darkness at Jesus' crucifixion began to lose its apologetical function.[60] Not only did the powerful deistic critique of biblical prophecy make appeal to Amos 8:9–10 as a fulfilled oracle seem less and less persuasive, but the Enlightenment raised difficult questions about the biblical miracles. (It is no coincidence that more and more even of the orthodox commentators had begun, by then, to contract the size of the miracle, from the entirety of the globe to Judea.) There was further the progress of historical knowledge, which brought the realization that Phlegon's testimony might well be ambiguous and that the seventh epistle attributed to Dionysius was a pseudepigraphon. The detailed review, in the eighteenth century, of pagan witnesses to the crucifixion by Nathaniel Lardner (1684–1768) shows us where things then stood.[61] A Christian apologist, Lardner nonetheless determined that the alleged extrabiblical witnesses—Phlegon, Thallus, Dionysius—were nothing substantial; he swept them into the dustbin of history. While Lardner himself believed that the sky went dark when Jesus was crucified, he did not think that there was any evidence for this,

---

ing the Old and New Testaments: The New Testament, vol. 1, *Matthew to Romans* (London: Thomas Tegg & Son, 1836), p. 290; Henry Alford, *The Greek Testament*, vol. 1, *The Four Gospels* (Chicago: Moody, 1958), p. 294; etc.

59. Cf. *Acts John* 1:97 and Paschasius Radbertus, *Exp. Matt. Libri XII* ad loc. (CCCM 56B, ed. Paulus, pp. 1379–80), and those cited in the previous note. Contrast Erasmus, *Annot. in Matt.* ad 27:45 (Opera Omnia 6/5, ed. Hovingh, p. 342), and John Calvin, *Commentary on a Harmony of the Evangelists, Matthew, Mark, and Luke* (Grand Rapids: Eerdmans, 1972), 3:207: "When some extend this eclipse of the sun to every corner of the globe, I doubt if they are correct. Even if it has been recorded by one or two writers, the history of those times was too widespread for such a remarkable miracle to have been overlooked by so many others, who have given accurate accounts of things far less worth remembering." Erasmus and Calvin have effectively returned to Origen, whose position becomes common in the eighteenth and nineteenth centuries. Grotius, *Opera omnia theologica*, vol. 2, part 1, p. 272, however, argued for an eclipse over the Roman world, while others, such as August Nebe, *Die Leidensgeschichte unsers Herrn Jesu Christi nach den vier Evangelien* (Wiesbaden: J. Niedner, 1881), p. 298, claimed that the darkness was broad but of unspecified extent. More recently, those deeming the darkness mythological have typically understood Matthew's ἐπὶ πᾶσαν τὴν γῆν to cover the whole world. Maldonatus, *Comentarii*, 1:470, was perhaps the first to observe that a truly worldwide darkness was impossible because when it was noon in Israel, it would have been dark already on the other side of the world!

60. But not without a dying gasp; see the list in Grández, "Tinieblas," pp. 194–97, of seventeen books and tractates on our subject published between 1661 and 1734.

61. Nathaniel Lardner, "Phlegon, Thallus, and Dionysius the Areopagite," in *The Works of Nathaniel Lardner* (10 vols.; London: William Ball, 1838), 7:105–24. Cf. the reference to Lardner in Clarke, *Bible*, p. 290.

beyond that in the Gospels. It was not long before the sky's purported occlusion ceased to be a piece of evidence for Christianity and became rather a controversial assertion itself in need of defense.

Writing shortly after Lardner, whom he had read, Edward Gibbon (1737–1794) could summon the darkness at noon as a reason to suppose the Gospels unhistorical. His argument, in his delightful if overblown rhetoric, was that "this miraculous event, which ought to have excited the wonder, the curiosity, and the devotion of mankind, passed without notice in an age of science and history. It happened during the lifetime of Seneca and the elder Pliny, who must have experienced the immediate effects, or received the earliest intelligence, of the prodigy. Each of these philosophers, in a laborious work, has recorded all the great phenomena of Nature, earthquakes, meteors, comets, and eclipses, which his indefatigable curiosity could collect. Both the one and the other have omitted to mention the greatest phenomenon to which the mortal eye has been witness since the creation of the globe."[62]

The final setback for the old apologetical use of Matt. 27:45 par. came from the post-Renaissance penchant for compiling Greco-Roman and Jewish parallels to the gospel materials. Particularly important here was the work of Johann Jakob Wettstein (1693–1754). His influential edition of the Greek New Testament gathered numerous texts of the sky going dark at the deaths of important people or kingdoms, to which other scholars have since added.[63] Such parallels became testimonies against finding

---

62. Edward Gibbon, *The Decline and Fall of the Roman Empire* (6 vols.; new ed.; New York: Peter Fenelon Collier & Son, 1899–1901), 1:599. He goes on: "A distinct chapter of Pliny (*Hist. Natur.* ii.30) is designed for eclipses of an extraordinary nature and unusual duration; but he contents himself with describing the singular defect of light which followed the murder of Caesar, when, during the greater part of the year, the orb of the sun appeared pale and without splendor. This season of obscurity, which cannot surely be compared with the preternatural darkness of the Passion, had been already celebrated by most of the poets and historians of that memorable age." In making his point, Gibbon observes that most of the church fathers believed that the darkness covered the whole earth; he also dismisses the testimony of both Phlegon and Tertullian (see n. 45).

63. Johann Jakob Wettstein, Η ΚΑΙΝΗ ΔΙΑΘΗΚΗ: *Novum Testamentum graecum editionis receptae cum lectionibus variantibus codicum mss., editionum aliarum, versionum et patrum nec non commentario pleniore ex scriptoribus veteribus hebraeis, graecis* (2 vols.; Amsterdam: Ex Officina Dommeriana, 1751–1752), pp. 537–39. The wealth of comparative materials includes the following: Cicero, *Rep.* 2.10; 6.21–22 (darkness at the death of Romulus); Virgil, *Georg.* 1.466–67, 480 (darkness at the death of Julius Caesar); Dionysius Halicarnassus, *Ant. rom.* 2.56 (Romulus); Livy 1.16 (Romulus); Ovid, *Met.* 2.330 (a day without sun because of the death of Phaëthon); 15.779–86 (darkness as a portent of woe); *Fast.* 485–98 (Romulus); Valerius Maximus, *Mem.* 8.11 ext. 1 (an eclipse of the sun portends the destruction of Athens); Pliny, *Nat.* 2.30 (Julius Caesar); Petronius, *Satyr.* 122 (the gods darken the sky because of crimes); Plutarch, *Caes.* 69 (Julius Caesar); *Rom.* 27 (Romulus); *Pelop.* 31 (an eclipse as "a great sign from heaven"; cf. Diodorus Siculus 15.80); Florus, *Epit.* 1.1 (Romulus); Valerius Flaccus, *Arg.* 6.621–23 (Colaxes, son of Jove, makes the heavens gloomy with his mourning); Dio Cassius 56.29.3 (darkness at the death of Augustus); Diogenes Laertius 4.64 (eclipse of moon at death

history in the Gospels. In the words of Strauss, "these parallels, instead of being supports to the credibility of the evangelical narrative, are so many premises to the conclusion, that we have here also nothing more than the mythical offspring of universally prevalent ideas,—a Christian legend, which would make all nature put on the weeds of mourning to solemnize the tragic death of the Messiah."[64]

This view has become, since Strauss, more and more common, especially among Protestant commentators.[65] The situation at present is such that many simply assume, without further ado, that we have here a literary or mythological motif.[66] Those defending the historicity of the darkness have become increasingly few, and their positions have often become rationalistic; that is, they have, even when professing a belief in miracles, appealed to clouds or sand storms or volcanic dust.[67] No one any longer wants to urge that maybe the moon reversed its course.[68]

---

of Carneades); Claudian, *De bello Gild.* 399–40 ("a deed . . . that put the sun to rout and turned back the day"); Philo apud Eusebius, *Praep. ev.* 8.14 (395d; eclipses "are indications either of the death of kings or of the destruction of cities"); *LAE* 46:1 (the death of Adam); Josephus, *Ant.* 14.309 (Julius Caesar; *2 En.* 67.1–2 (darkness at the death of Enoch); *T. Adam* 3.6 (Adam); Marinus, *Proc.* 37 (the death of Proclus); Ambrose, *Obitu Theod.* 1 (CSEL 73, ed. Faller, p. 371: the death of Theodosius I). For wonders associated with the deaths of rabbis, see Paul Fiebig, *Jüdische Wundergeschichten des neutestamentlichen Zeitalters* (Tübingen: J. C. B. Mohr [Paul Siebeck], 1911), pp. 38–49, 57–61; also SB 1:1040–41. Note that Calvin's Renaissance education made him aware that "the ancient poets in their tragedies describe the sun's light being withdrawn from the earth when any foul crime is committed, and so aim to show a portent of divine wrath: this was a fiction that drew from the common feelings of nature" (*Harmony*, 3:206).

64. David Friedrich Strauss, *The Life of Jesus Critically Examined* (Philadelphia: Fortress, 1972), p. 692.

65. For the situation among Catholic scholars, who until recently have been much slower to adopt a skeptical view, see Grández, "Tinieblas," pp. 212–15.

66. E.g., Rudolf Bultmann, *History of the Synoptic Tradition* (rev. ed.; New York: Harper & Row, 1963), p. 282.

67. E.g., Pierre Benoit, *The Passion and Resurrection of Jesus Christ* (New York: Herder & Herder, 1969), p. 201 ("the black sirocco"); Cook, "Matthew," p. 183 (darkness sometimes precedes earthquakes); Gustaf Dalman, *Jesus-Jeshua: Studies in the Gospels* (New York: Macmillan, 1929), p. 204 ("a sirocco vapour"); G. R. Driver, "Two Problems in the New Testament," *JTS* 16 (1965), pp. 327–37 (a sirocco); Keener, *Matthew*, p. 685 (clouds are a possibility); H. E. G. Paulus, *Das Leben Jesu als Grundlage einer reinen Geschichte des Urchristentums* (Heidelberg: F. C. Winter, 1928), p. 242 (darkness can be associated with earthquakes); and U. Holzmeister, "Die Finsternis beim Tode Iesu," *Bib* 22 (1941), pp. 404–11 (volcanic dust, a sirocco, and clouds are all possibilities). Although I am unaware of any ancient writer who thought of a volcano, the proposal that the darkness was due to clouds is ancient (so Origen); and if one were to regard *Sib. Or.* 3:800–802 as Christian (an uncertain issue), then it might reflect a tradition that a dust storm caused the darkness at the crucifixion: "again dust is brought forth from heaven upon the earth and all the light of the sun is eclipsed from the middle of heaven."

68. Some now refuse to offer any explanation and simply stick with the silence of the text. Cf. Alexander Balmain Bruce, "The Synoptic Gospels," in *The Expositor's Greek Testament* (ed. W. Robertson Nicoll; New York: George H. Doran, n.d.), 1:331, and David A. Carson,

Interpretation

Many and sundry interpretations have attached themselves to the darkness at noon, this because Matt. 27:45 stands naked, without interpretive gloss. In the following few pages, I should like to catalogue the most popular of these interpretations. I shall review them in the order of their popularity, the most common coming first.[69]

Judgment. Numerous passages in the Old Testament associate darkness with God's judgment. In Isa. 13:9–16, the prophet introduces his announcement of the coming judgment of God by proclaiming that the stars "and their constellations will not give their light," that "the sun will be dark at its rising," and that the moon will hide its face. In Amos 5:18 and 20, because the Day of the Lord is a day of judgment, it is darkness, not light. In Jer. 13:16, the addressees are implored to give glory to God before God brings darkness and renders fitting judgment.[70] Given these and kindred scriptures, one understands why the commentators have been so much inclined to suppose that Matt. 27:45 is a sign of God's wrath and so a symbol of judgment, specifically judgment upon the Jews who reject Jesus: the light has been taken from them.[71] Calvin is representative: "They were shown a sight full of terror, to make them tremble at God's judgment. It was certainly an incomparable proof of God's anger that he did not spare his only-begotten Son and was only placated by this price of expiation."[72] The Reformer goes on to rail against the Jewish

---

"Matthew," in *The Expositor's Bible Commentary* (ed. Frank E. Gaebelein; Grand Rapids: Zondervan, 1984), 8:578 ("we do not know how it happened").

69. Whether a survey of interpretations of Mark 15:33 or Luke 23:44 would produce a list with the same order is an interesting question to which I do not have an answer.

70. See further Isa. 5:30; 8:22; Jer. 15:9; Amos 8:9–10; Joel 2:2; 3:15; Zeph. 1:15; *Sib. Or.* 4:56–58 (darkness at midday will presage the destruction of the Medes); 11:45; Rev. 16:10; 2 *En.* 7:1–2 J (angels are punished in darkness); *t. Suk.* 2.5–6 (an eclipse is a bad omen; cf. *b. Suk.* 29a); *Gen. Rab.* 28:1 ("Once the Holy One, blessed be he, turns day into night and lulls them into a false sense of security before the punishment, he then exacts punishment from them"). One may compare the notion that an eclipse is a bad omen: Diodorus Siculus 20.5.5; Plutarch, *Aemilius Paulus* 17.5.

71. Cf. esp. Theophylact, *Comm. Matt.* ad 27:45 (PG 123.469C: "light had been taken from the Jews"); Lapide, *Commentary*, 3:300; and Clarke, *Bible*, p. 290 ("because they did not walk" in the light of the world "it was now taken away from them"). In this connection it may be relevant that darkness is consistently pejorative in Matthew; cf. 4:16; 6:23; 8:12; 22:13; 25:30.

72. Calvin, *Commentary*, 3:207. Cf. Chrysostom, *Hom. on Matt.* 89.1 (PG 58.775: "that darkness was a token of his anger"; the same words appear in Apollinarius of Laodicea, *Comm. Matt.* frag. 142 ad loc. [TU 61, ed. Reuss, p. 51]; Origen, *Scholia Matt.* [PG 17.309]; and Cramer, *Catenae*, p. 237); Cyril of Alexandria, *Comm. Matt.* frag. 13 (TU 61, ed. Reuss, p. 157); Leo the Great, *Tract.* 61.5 (CCSL 138A, ed. Chavasse, p. 374); Maldonatus, *Comentarii*, 1:469; Wesley, *Explanatory Notes*, p. 134; Garland, *Matthew*, p. 260; Gundry, *Matthew*, p. 572 (he speaks of "God's displeasure").

leaders: "That the scribes and priests and a great part of the people care-
lessly overlooked this darkening of the sun, and passed through it with
eyes closed, should strike us with horror, for their formidable degree of
stupidity. They must have been more foolish than dumb beasts to have
continued their mockery with such a portent of force of heavenly judgment, and with open warning."[73] While this expression of anti-Judaism
is, lamentably, all too typical, Calvin's words at least condemn only "a
great part of the people," not all the people. He does, furthermore, finally
turn the tables and use the darkness to warn Christians themselves: "As
the warning was general, it should be useful for our understanding today,
that the sacrifice by which we were redeemed was of no less importance
than if the sun fell out of heaven, or the whole structure of the world
collapsed. So we shall abhor our sins the more."[74]

Although Calvin does not make the connection explicit, others have
clearly associated the darkness of judgment at the crucifixion with the
destruction of the Jewish capital in 70 CE. Ephraem wrote, "It was because
the natural sun was darkened that this darkness revealed the imminence
of the destruction of their city."[75] Irenaeus was already thinking along
the same lines when he linked Matt. 27:45 par. to the circumstance that
the Jewish nation was "handed over to the Gentiles." He then cited Jer.
15:9, which has Jerusalem being given to the sword.[76]

Mourning. Amos 8:9–10, which, as we have seen, appears to stand
behind Matt. 27:45, is a text of judgment and so supports the interpretation just introduced. Amos also, however, speaks of mourning: "I will
make it like the mourning for an only son, and the end of it like a bitter
day." Mourning is, furthermore, conjoined with darkness in several additional Jewish texts, including Jer. 4:27–28: "For thus says the LORD:
The whole land shall be a desolation; yet I will not make a full end. Because of this the earth shall mourn, and the heavens above grow black;
for I have spoken, I have purposed; I have not relented nor will I turn
back." Darkness seems to function similarly in *2 Bar.* 10:12: "And you,
sun, keep the light of your rays within you. And you, moon, extinguish

73. Calvin, *Commentary*, 3:207. Cf. Cyril of Alexandria, *Os.–Mal.* ad Amos 8:9–10 (ed.
Pusey, 1:520).

74. Calvin, *Commentary*, 3:207. Sadly, this is not a very common exegetical move.

75. Ephraem, *Comm. Diat.* 20.28 (SC 121, ed. Leloir, p. 363). Cf. Herodotus 7.37, where
a daytime darkness is interpreted (wrongly as it turns out) to foretell the destruction of the
Greek cities.

76. Irenaeus, *Adv. haer.* 4.33.12. Cf. Origen, *Comm. Matt.* frag. 134 (GCS 38, ed. Klostermann, pp. 277–78; cf. PG 13.1785A); Apollinarius of Laodicea, *Comm. Matt.* frag. 142 ad
loc. (TU 61, ed. Reuss, p. 51: the darkness was a "token of what was about to overtake the
murderers"); Theodore of Heraclea, *Comm. Matt.* frag. 131 (TU 61, ed. Reuss, p. 94); Ps.-
Chrysostom, *In sanc. pascha* 47 (SC 48, ed. Floëri and Nautin, p. 159). A recent twist on this
appears in Carter, *Matthew*, p. 534, who thinks of divine judgment falling upon the Romans.

the multitude of your light; for why should the light rise again, where the light of Zion is darkened?"[77] One recalls further *b. Sukk.* 29a, where we read that, on account of four things, the sun is in eclipse, the first being the *Ab Beth din* who dies and was not properly mourned. The thought seems to be that the sun mourns for the man if people do not. Also to the point is the memorable passage in *Lam. Rab.* 3:9 on 3:28:

> R. Samuel b. Nahman said, "The Holy One, blessed be he, summoned the ministering angels and said to them, 'If a human king [is in mourning], what does he do?' They answered, 'He dons black garments and covers his head with sackcloth.' He said to them, 'I will do likewise.' That is what is written, 'I clothe the heavens with blackness and I make sackcloth their covering' [Isa. 50:3]. He further inquired of them, 'What else does he do?' They replied, 'He extinguishes the lamps.' He said to them, 'I will do likewise.' That is what is stated, 'The sun and the moon become black, and the stars withdraw their shining' [Joel 3:15]."[78]

Given the silence of Matthew's darkness,[79] it is interesting that the rabbinic text goes on to speak of God sitting in silence.

These texts help us appreciate why, next to finding judgment in our text, commentators have regularly—and often at the same time—thought the darkness to betoken mourning. Sometimes they assert that it is God who mourns, as in the quotation ascribed variously to Dionysius, Ptolemy, or unnamed pagan philosophers.[80] Other times it is human beings who mourn. Cyril of Jerusalem, citing Amos 8:9–10, glossed the prophecy thus: "What sort of season is this, O Prophet, and what sort of day? And I will turn your feasts into mourning; for this was done in the days of unleavened bread, and at the feast of the Passover; then afterwards he says, And I will make Him as the mourning of an Only Son, and those with Him as a day of anguish; for in the day of unleavened bread, and at the feast, their women were wailing and weeping, and the Apostles had hidden themselves and were in anguish."[81] Most often, however, it is nature that is said to mourn, as in *Ps.-Clem. Rec.* 1:41 ("While he [Jesus] was suffering, all the world suffered with Him; for the sun was darkened"); Ephraem (the sun "retracted its light so as to die with him"); and Theophylact ("all creation mourned").[82] Isho'dad of Merv

---

77. Trans. A. F. J. Klijn, *OTP* 1:624.

78. Trans. A. Cohen (London: Soncino, 1939), pp. 203–4.

79. See p. 103 below.

80. See above, p. 93; cf. Joachim Gnilka, *Das Matthäusevangelium* (2 vols.; HTKNT 1/1–2; Freiburg: Herder, 1986–1988), 2:474.

81. Cyril of Jerusalem, *Cat.* 13.25 (PG 33.804A–B).

82. *Ps.-Clem. Rec.* 1.41 (GCS 42, ed. Rehm, p. 32); Ephraem, *Comm. Diat.* 21.5 (SC 121, ed. Leloir, p. 377); and Theophylact, *Comm. Matt.* ad loc. (PG 123.469C). Cf. Tertullian,

is eloquent: "The whole creation was like a maidservant weaving a lamentation for her Lord, when the Sun, the lantern of the world, wore the color of pitch, and the moon reddened and became like blood; and when it was not the time of its newness, suddenly it was seen in the east and ran with an impetus towards the west, and it adhered to the sun, and they both sat in mourning like good servants, who suffer in the sufferings of their Lord."[83]

Eschatology. If Matthew's allusion to Amos 8:9–10 connotes both judgment and mourning, it also takes one into the realm of eschatology, for Amos 8:9–10 is a prophecy about "the day of the LORD," and if it is fulfilled in the passion of Jesus, that passion must have an eschatological character or dimension.[84] The same inference lies near to hand for those who trace an intratextual line back to 24:29, where the scene of the Son of Man's *parousia* is set against a cosmic darkness. More generally, an obscuration of heavenly lights belongs to the eschatological expectations of Judaism.[85] One can then, and as already observed, construe the darkness of the crucifixion as the darkness of the latter days or somehow analogous to it.[86]

This is a characteristically modern take on our text. It is not, however, without precedent.[87] It has a clear forerunner in Martin Luther, who

De ieiunio 10 (CSEL 20, ed. Reifferscheid and Wissowa, p. 287); Origen, *Scholia Matt.* (PG 17.309B); Apollinarius of Laodicea, *Comm. Matt.* frag. 142 ad loc. (TU 61, ed. Reuss, p. 50: "creation mourned"); Lapide, *Commentary*, 3:299–30; William Burkitt, *Expository Notes, with Practical Observations upon the New Testament of Our Lord and Savior* (New Haven: Abel Morse, 1794), p. 114 ("The sun in the firmament becomes a close mourner at our Lord's death, and the whole frame of nature puts itself into a funeral habit"); Henry Alford, *The Greek Testament*, vol. 1, *The Four Gospels* (Chicago: Moody, 1958), p. 294 ("Those whose belief leads them to reflect WHO was then suffering, will have no difficulty in accounting for these signs of sympathy in nature").

83. Isho'dad of Merv, *Comm. Matt.* 7 (HSem 6, ed. Gibson, p. 189); cf. *LAB* 40:3 ("the trees of the field shall bewail me and the beasts of the field shall lament for me"); Leo the Great, *Tract.* 57.4 (CCSL 138A, ed. Chavasse, p. 336: Leo's "all creation groaned" echoes Rom. 8:22); and Zwingli, *De vera et falsa religione* 6, at end (trans. Jackson, p. 117). The idea of creation rebelling against a crime is common in Christian martyrologies, wherein nature sometimes refuses to cooperate in evil deeds; cf. *Mart. Polyc.* 15–16; Eusebius, *Mart. Pal.* 4.12 (SC 55, ed. Bardy, pp. 133–34).

84. Cf. W. Hackenburg, "σκότος," *EDNT* 3 (1993), p. 256: "This darkness is considered an apocalyptic sign anticipating the day of God (cf. Amos 8:9)."

85. *As. Mos.* 10:5; *Sib. Or.* 3.801–2; 5:344–50; *T. Levi* 4:1; *2 Bar.* 10:12; 18:2; 46:2; 77:14; *Liv. Pro. Hab.* 14; *2 En.* 34:3; *b. Sanh.* 99a; etc.

86. In addition to the discussion above, on pp. 85–88, see Brown, *Death of the Messiah*, 2:1036; Carter, *Matthew*, p. 534; Fenton, *Matthew*, p. 442; Grundmann, *Matthäus*, p. 560; Hagner, *Matthew*, 2:844; Meier, *Matthew*, p. 349; Moo, *Old Testament*, pp. 341–46; Alexander Sand, *Das Evangelium nach Matthäus* (RNT; Regensburg: Friedrich Pustet, 1986), p. 564.

87. In addition to what follows, recall that some older sources do use eschatological language in describing the darkness of Matt. 27:45 par.; see above, pp. 87–88.

believed that the darkness at the crucifixion marked the beginning of a new age.[88] More than a millennium before that, the Gnostic author of *The Conception of Our Great Power*, an apocalyptic treatise from Nag Hammadi (VI.4), interpreted the night that fell during the day of Jesus' death with these words: "The archons searched after that which had come to pass. They did not know that this is the sign of their dissolution, and that it is the change of the aeon. The sun sets during the day; the day became dark" (42:12–17).

Shame. A fourth interpretation one often runs across in the commentaries is that the sky went dark when Jesus suffered because the sun could not bear to look upon what was happening. Melito of Sardis put it this way: "O unprecedented murder! Unprecedented crime! The Sovereign has been made unrecognizable by his naked body, and is not even allowed a garment to keep him from view. This is why the luminaries turned away, and the day was darkened, that he might hide the one stripped bare upon the tree, darkening not the body of the Lord but the eyes of men."[89] The same notion reappears in Cyprian, Ephraem, and Jerome;[90] and, centuries after those church fathers, John Gill wrote that the sun hid its light because it was "ashamed to behold those base indignities done to the Son of righteousness by the sons of men."[91]

Miscellaneous. Advocates of the four interpretations just introduced are easy to find. Other views, however, also show up in the commentaries, and these may, if only briefly, and for the sake of completeness, be listed here:

- Some have urged that, when light forsakes the tormented Jesus, this connotes the cosmic dimensions of the crucifixion or simply its signal consequences. Exodus 20:21 (the giving of the Torah on Sinai) and 2 Sam. 22:10 (the descent of Yahweh for battle) emphasize the importance or cosmic significance of some particular matter by making reference to an unnatural darkness.[92]

88. See Grández, "Tinieblas," p. 190. (Grández does not name the particular sermon of Luther he quotes from, and I have been unable to find it.)

89. Melito of Sardis, *Pasch.* 97 (OECT, ed. Hall, p. 54).

90. Cyprian, *De bono pat.* 7 (CSEL 3, ed. Hartel, p. 402); Ephraem, *Comm. Diat.* 21.5 (SC 121, ed. Leloir, p. 377); and Jerome, *Comm. Matt.* ad loc. (SC 259, ed. Bonnard, p. 296); cf. Ps.-Chrysostom, *In sanc. pascha* 47 (SC 48, ed. Floëri and Nautin, p. 159), and Sedulius Scotus, *Comm. Matt.* ad loc. (ed. Löfstedt, p. 613).

91. Gill, *Commentary*, 5:275. Cf. David Dickson, *A Brief Exposition of the Evangel of Jesus Christ according to Matthew* (Carlisle, Pa.: Banner of Truth, 1981), p. 396; David Smith, *The Days of His Flesh: The Earthly Life of Our Lord and Saviour Jesus Christ* (New York: Hodder & Stoughton, 1910), p. 500; and Bernhard Weiss, *A Commentary on the New Testament*, vol. 1, *Matthew–Mark* (New York: Funk & Wagnells, 1906), p. 244.

92. Cf. Hans Conzelmann, "σκότος," *TDNT* 7 (1971), p. 439.

- Those who have moved from Matt. 27:45 to Gen. 1:2, where darkness covers the face of the deep, have thought of a return to the primeval chaos. Just as the primordial darkness preceded the creation of the world, so does the darkness at noon preface his resurrection and the new age it introduces.[93]

- Matthew Henry and John Wesley associated the darkness of the crucifixion with the powers of darkness: this especially was the time of conflict with them. In Henry's splendid words, "Now the prince of this world, and his forces, the rulers of the darkness of this world, were to be cast out, to be spoiled and vanquished; and to make his victory all the more illustrious, he fights them on their own ground; gives them all the advantage they could have against him by this darkness, lets them take the wind and sun, and yet baffles them, and so becomes more than a conqueror."[94]

- The view of Broadus was that Matt. 27:45 offers "a sort of symbol of the Saviour's mental suffering."[95] That is, the eclipse of the sun manifests the eclipse of Jesus' soul; his interior darkness is mirrored in an external darkness.

- One correlative of divine judgment (see above for this theme) is fear, so it is no surprise that we find this in the Eastern Orthodox Matins for Holy Friday: "When Thou wast crucified, O Christ, all the creation saw and trembled. The foundations of the earth quaked in fear of Thy power. The lights of heaven hid themselves. . . . The whole creation was changed by fear."

- According to John Monro Gibson, the darkness was a necessary part of the atonement: "Alone with God, and the sin of the world is on Him. 'He bare our sins in His own body on the tree,' therefore is it that He must enter even into the very deepest darkness of the soul, the feeling of separation from God, the sense of forsakenness, which is so appalling to the awakened sinner, and which even the sinless One must taste, because of the burden laid upon Him."[96]

93. See the comment of Davies on p. 83 above. Creation and eschatological themes belong together; cf. *Liv. Pro. Hab.* 13 ("The Lord will be recognized at the end, for they will illuminate those who are being pursued by the serpent in darkness as from the beginning") and esp. *4 Ezra* 7:30: "And the world shall be turned back to primeval silence for seven days, as it was at the first beginnings."

94. Henry, *Matthew to John*, ad loc. Cf. Gill, *Commentary*, 5:295, and Wesley, *Expository Notes*, p. 134.

95. John A. Broadus, *Commentary on the Gospel of Matthew* (Philadelphia: American Baptist Publication Society, 1886), p. 574. Cf. Bruce, "Synoptic Gospels," p. 331.

96. John Monro Gibson, "The Gospel of St. Matthew," in *The Expositor's Bible*, vol. 4, *Jeremiah–St. Mark* (ed. W. Robertson Nicoll; Rahway, N.J.: Expositor Bible Company, n.d.), p. 804. Cf. Henry, *Matthew to John*. Contrast Melanchthon, *Euangelij secundum Mattheum*

- Arnobius urged that the subsidence of the sun betokened bewilderment: when Jesus died, "all the elements of the universe, bewildered by the strange events, were thrown into confusion. An earthquake shook the world, the sea was heaved up from its depths, the heaven was shrouded in darkness, the sun's fiery blaze was checked, and his heat became moderate; for what else could occur when He was discovered to be God who heretofore was reckoned one of us?"[97]
- In my own commentary on Matthew, I observed that nothing but darkness fills the time between noon and 3 PM—typically the brightest time of day—and further that the darkness is accompanied by silence; it is the speech of 27:46 that terminates the period. "So the darkness is silent, and although time advances, nothing happens: the narrative stops. Such narrative stillness is a common literary device, one which reappears in the apocryphal gospels (e.g., *Prot. Jas.* 18: the birth of Jesus). The effect is to isolate and so magnify a single circumstance: all attention is directed to one thing."[98] I then compared *LAB* 19:16, where the angels cease their singing when Moses dies, and further recalled Thomas de Quincey's famous essay, "The Knocking at the Gate in Macbeth," in which the author writes of the effect in narrative of an "awful parenthesis," when "ordinary life is suddenly arrested—laid asleep—tranced—racked into a dread armistice."[99]

Lessons from the Exegetical Past

In drawing this chapter to a close, I should like to suggest that the preceding sojourn among the commentaries on Matt. 27:45 holds at least four lessons.

Repetition in interpretation. Recent work adds only a little to earlier reflections upon 27:45. Although the eschatological interpretation is characteristically modern,[100] older exegetes, just like their recent counterparts, regularly discerned judgment and mourning in the darkness of the crucifixion (although, as expected, there is less animosity against Judaism or none at all in the contemporary literature). Our predecessors also detected

---

(Omnia opera 3; Wittenberg: Iohannes Crato, 1564), p. 583, who combines the darkness with the other miracles in Matthew 27 and sees them all as signs of God's presence.

97. Arnobius, *Adv. nat.* 1.53 (PL 5.792A).

98. Davies and Allison, *Matthew*, 3:622–23. Cf. now Luz, *Matthäus*, 4:334, citing my work and adding Rev. 8:1: "There was silence in heaven for about half an hour."

99. Thomas de Quincey, "The Knocking at the Gate in Macbeth," in *Literary Criticism* (New York: Hurd and Houghton, 1876), p. 539.

100. Although see above, pp. 85–88.

all of the intertextual and intratextual associations typically paraded in
the modern commentaries. One could scarcely expect otherwise. Because
the exegetical present confronts the selfsame text as the exegetical past,
repetition must be the rule, novelty the exception.

Abandonment of apologetics. The chief difference between commentaries
from earlier ages and those of the last two or three centuries is that 27:45
does apologetical duty in the former, not the latter. Before the Enlightenment, the historicity of the darkness at noon was roundly thought to be
established by pagan testimony, which supposedly supplied good reason
to believe that the death of Jesus really did coincide with a marvelous circumstance. Today such facticity is only baldly asserted or tepidly defended
or, in view of the many parallels in Greco-Roman and Jewish literature
that began to enter the literature during the Renaissance, dismissed as
a literary legend. To some extent, however, this abandonment of an old
argument marks a return to Origen, who, at least in his commentary on
Matthew, adopted a defensive posture vis-à-vis the historical question. He
recognized the difficulty of believing that a worldwide darkness descended
upon the scene of Jesus' martyrdom, so he turned the evangelical miracle
into a local affair and assigned its probable cause to clouds, as do a few yet
today. The relative modesty of Origen's claims corresponds to the modesty
of those who today confess belief in the historicity of Matt. 27:45 par. No
one any longer makes the text a prop for faith.

The complementarity of multiple meanings. The multiple meanings
pinned upon Matt. 27:45 are not antagonistic; they are rather complementary. An allusion to Amos 8:9–10 does not exclude an allusion to
Exod. 10:22 or vice versa, and the theme of judgment does not crowd
out the theme of mourning or vice versa. The evangelist himself refrained
from appending any interpretation, perhaps precisely because he wanted
to respect the richly symbolic connotations of the sun's failure. Be that
as it may, 27:45 should not be constricted so as to carry only a single
connotation. The commentaries themselves recognize this. Calvin atypi-
cally lists several options before giving his own view, apparently because
he finds them all sensible.[101] Douglas Moo wisely writes that the various
interpretive "options are not, of course, mutually exclusive," and that
"it is probably inadmissible to confine the OT background to any single
passage."[102] Luz similarly speaks of the *Vieldeutigkeit* or ambiguity of the
darkness and refrains from deciphering it to mean this or to mean that.[103]
Bengel rightly speaks of "three hours full of mystery,"[104] and surely an

101. Calvin, *Commentary*, p. 207.
102. Moo, *Old Testament*, p. 343.
103. Luz, *Matthäus*, 4:334.
104. Johann Albrecht Bengel, *Gnomon Novi Testamenti* (2 vols.; Tübingen: Ludov. Frid.
Fues, 1850), 1:188.

element of the mystery is the plenitude of meaning in the lack of light. Gill's commentary moves from one view to another without contradicting any: the sun was

> hiding its face, and refusing to afford its comforting light and heat to him [Jesus]; and yet [its act] might be in detestation of the heinousness of the sin the Jews were committing, and as expressive of the divine anger and resentment; for God's purposes and decrees, and the end he had in view, did not excuse, nor extenuate their wickedness. . . . It was an emblem of the judicial blindness and darkness of the Jewish nation; and signified, that now was the hour and power of darkness, or the time for the prince of darkness, with his principalities and powers to exert himself: and was a representation of that darkness that was now on the soul of Christ, expressed in the following verse; as well as of the eclipse of him, the Sun of righteousness, of the glory of his person, both by his incarnation and by his sufferings.[105]

We must, furthermore, recognize that the darkness has, within its context in Matthew's passion narrative, an affective component. Indeed, surely it—like many other biblical texts—is designed to make one feel as much as to make one think.

Finally, although we can set out to discover the likely meaning(s) of Matt. 27:45 in its original context, that is a rather narrow inquiry, and the fact remains that the book to which our verse belongs soon enough escaped that initial context. Matthew 27:45 has accordingly found a continual readership through the centuries and so has stimulated much reflection. Further, an acquaintance with some of that reflection is unavoidable if we have been raised in a Christian tradition or if, as scholars, we have become familiar with the relevant secondary literature. So we do not come to 27:45 as though for the first time. As with any well-known biblical text, when we hear it, we simultaneously hear the voices of an interpretive tradition. For myself, this is not a misfortune to be undone but a boon to be appreciated. To peel away the glosses of the centuries is to strip away what the text has, as a matter of historical fact, wrought—and to what good end? That centuries of readers have not only unfolded implicit meaning but infolded supplementary sense just means that their labors are for us doubly rewarding.[106]

---

105. Gill, *Commentary*, 5:295.
106. See further the discussion of Matt. 5:8 on pp. 60–63 above.

5

Touching Jesus' Feet

(MATT. 28:9)

I n Matthew's account of Easter, Mary Magdalene and "the other Mary" set out for the tomb of the crucified. Upon arriving, they witness an explosion of supernatural events. There is an earthquake (28:2). Then an angel, shining like lightning, descends from heaven (28:2–3). Then the governor's guards tremble and faint away as though dead (28:4). Then the two Marys, learning about the resurrection from the angel, and being commissioned to convey the good news to his disciples, depart immediately with fear and joy (28:5–8). Suddenly, they encounter Jesus himself, who hails them with a greeting (28:9). They then approach him, take hold of his feet, and worship him (28:9). He in turn repeats the angelic commission to let his disciples know what has happened (28:10).

In the following few pages I should like to focus on Matthew's passing notice that the women, after coming to Jesus, took hold of his feet: αἱ δὲ προσελθοῦσαι ἐκράτησαν αὐτοῦ τοὺς πόδας. Some commentators, to judge from their complete silence, have seemingly regarded these words as unimportant or without need of clarification. Others have fretted over them because of their apparent conflict with John 20:17, where Jesus tells Mary Magdalene not to handle him: "Do not touch me, for I have not yet ascended to the Father." This prohibition plus its notoriously cryptic explanation pose a riddle. If, according to John, the risen Jesus told Mary not to touch him, then how can it be that, according to Matthew, she did indeed touch him? Some interpreters have imagined that the women touched Jesus before he forbade them to do so.[1] This is perhaps the import of a textual variant in John 20:16 ("and she ran forward to touch him. Jesus said to her, 'Do not touch me'").[2] Other exegetes, although they have rightly regarded that variant as secondary, have nonetheless taken μή μου ἅπτου to mean, "Stop touching me," which results in the same picture.[3] More common among older writers was precisely the opposite suggestion—that whereas Jesus did not originally let Mary touch him (so John), he allowed her to do this after she came to authentic faith (so Matthew).[4]

Options from the History of Interpretation

What should we make of Matt. 28:9, however, if we set aside the canonical tension with John and contemplate the synoptic text by itself? A survey of the commentaries reveals at least four options.[5]

Joy and affection. For some readers, the two women grasping Jesus' feet is a sign of their joy and affection.[6] Mary Magdalene and the other Mary, learning what seems too good to be true, that they are no longer bereft of their dearest friend, who now lives again, cannot help spontaneously expressing their love in a physical way. One recalls immediately Luke

1. So already Hippolytus, *Comm. Cant.* 15 (TU 23, ed. Bonwetsch, p. 63). For a later example see F. C. Cook, "St. Matthew," in *The Holy Bible according to the Authorized Version (A.D. 1611), with an Explanatory and Critical Commentary: New Testament*, vol. 1, *St. Matthew—St. Mark—St. Luke* (ed. F. C. Cook; New York: Scribner, 1878), p. 194, and Pierre Benoit, *The Passion and Resurrection of Jesus Christ* (New York: Herder & Herder, 1969), p. 259.

2. καὶ προσέδραμεν ἅψασθαι αὐτοῦ; so ℵ¹ Θ Ψ (*f*¹³) *pc* vg^mss sy^(s).h.

3. See C. H. Dodd, *Historical Tradition in the Fourth Gospel* (Cambridge: Cambridge University Press, 1963), p. 147, and D. Moody Smith, *John* (ANTC; Nashville: Abingdon, 1999), p. 377. Cf. BDF § 336.3 and the interpretation of John Calvin, *Commentary on a Harmony of the Evangelists, Matthew, Mark, and Luke* (Grand Rapids: Eerdmans, 1972), 3:227. The NRSV translates the μή μου ἅπτου of John 20:17 with "Do not hold on to me."

4. Note Eusebius, *Quaest. ev. ad Marinum* 3 (PG 22.952A), and Paschasius Radbertus, *Exp. Matt. Libri XII* ad loc. (CCCM 56B, ed. Paulus, p. 1425).

5. I ignore idiosyncratic interpretations, such as the unfortunate take of Peter Chrysologus, *Serm.* 80.6 (CCSL 24A, ed. Olivar, p. 494), who asserts that the women being at Jesus' feet signals their gender's subordination to men. I also leave aside consideration of other traditions about the feet of Jesus; cf. Rev. 1:15 and the legend about Jesus' footprints at the church on the Mount of Olives: Adamnan, *De locis sanctis* 1.23 (ed. Meehan, p. 66).

6. E.g., Peter Chrysologus, *Serm.* 76.3 (CCSL 24A, ed. Olivar, p. 467); the anonymous exposition in *Catenae in Evangelia S. Matthaei et S. Marci ad fidem codd. mss.* (ed. J. A. Cramer; Hildesheim: Georg Olms, 1967 [reprint of 1842 ed.]), p. 241; Matthew Henry, *Commentary on the Whole Bible*, vol. 5, *Matthew to John* (New York: Fleming H. Revell, n.d.), p. 442; John Guyse, *A Practical Exposition of the Four Evangelists* (2nd ed.; London: Edward Dilly, 1761), 1:212.

7:38, where an unnamed woman bathes Jesus' feet with her tears and then dries them with her hair: "she continued kissing his feet and anointing them with ointment." Displaying affection by embracing another's feet is also prominent in *T. Abr.* Rec. Lng. 15:4, where Abraham's wife, full of gratitude that her husband has come back to her—she, like the two Marys in Matthew, has thought him dead—thanks the archangel Michael, who has escorted the patriarch home: "His wife Sarah came and embraced the feet of the incorporeal one . . . saying, 'I thank you, my lord, that you have brought lord Abraham. For behold, I thought he had been taken up from us.'" A similar scene also plays itself out in *b. Ketub.* 63a, where Akiba returns home after being away for many years. His wife goes out to meet him, falls upon her face, and kisses his feet.[7] Given texts such as these, one understands the interpretation that Hippolytus gave to Matt. 28:9: "They held him by the feet, saying, 'I will not leave you until I bring you into my heart.'"[8]

Submission. Grabbing the feet can also, however, be what an inferior does when supplicating a superior and so betoken submission. R. V. G. Tasker wrote, regarding Matt. 28:9: "By this action the women were showing their submission to their Lord in the manner in which subjects in the East were accustomed to render obeisance to a sovereign prince."[9] One may compare Dionysius Halicarnassus, *Ant. Rom.* 8.54, where Coriolanus's mother, in an act of petition, embraces his feet and kisses them, as well as 2 Kings 4:27, where the Shunammite woman pleads with Elisha for the life of her son by laying hold of the prophet's feet.

Worship. If taking hold of the feet can be an act of submission, it can equally be—and often is at the same time—an act of reverence, adoration, or even worship, and many commentators have understood Matt. 28:9 accordingly.[10] The reason is obvious. Matthew's remark that the women

---

7. For additional rabbinic examples see SB 1:996.

8. Hippolytus, *Comm. Cant.* 15 (TU 23, ed. Bonwetsch, p. 63). Cf. the Greek text printed in Marcel Richard, "Une paraphrase grecque résumée du commentaire d'Hippolyte sur le Cantique de cantiques," *Muséon* 77 (1964), p. 153.

9. R. V. G. Tasker, *Matthew: An Introduction and Commentary* (TNTC 1; Grand Rapids: Eerdmans, 1973), p. 272. Cf. Cook, "Matthew," p. 194: "an act of deep humility."

10. See, e.g., Jerome, *Comm. Matt.* ad loc. (SC 242, ed. Bonnard, p. 72); Bede, *Matt. Exp.* 4 (PL 92.129C); Albertus Magnus, *Super Mt. cap. I–XIV* ad loc. (Opera Omnia 21/1, ed. B. Schmidt, p. 658; he cites for comparison Ps. 132:7 ["let us worship at his footstool"] and Matt. 2:11 [the magi fall down and pay homage to Jesus]); Adam Clarke, *The Holy Bible, Containing the Old and New Testaments: The New Testament*, vol. 1, *Matthew to Romans* (London: Thomas Tegg & Son, 1836), p. 207; Philip Doddridge, *The Family Expositor* (6 vols.; Charlestown, Mass.: S. Etheridge, 1807), 2:588; John Peter Lange, *Commentary on the Holy Scripture: Critical, Doctrinal, and Homiletical: Matthew* (Grand Rapids: Zondervan, n.d.), p. 545; Paul Gaechter, *Das Matthäus Evangelium* (Innsbruck: Tyrolia, 1963), p. 957; Alexander Sand, *Das Evangelium nach Matthäus* (RNT; Regensburg: Friedrich Pustet, 1986), p. 591; Donald A.

laid hold of Jesus' feet is immediately followed by this: "and they worshiped him" (καὶ προσεκύνησαν αὐτῷ). So it is altogether natural to construe
ἐκράτησαν αὐτοῦ τοὺς πόδας καὶ προσεκύνησαν αὐτῷ as the near equivalent
of πίπτω + προσκύνεω, a combination that Matthew uses three times:

πεσόντες	προσεκύνησαν	(Matt. 2:11)
πεσών	προσεκυνήσῃς	(Matt. 4:9)
πεσών...	προσεκύνει	(Matt. 18:26)[11]

The ἐκράτησαν αὐτοῦ τοὺς πόδας of Matt. 28:9 tells us, in other words,
that the women assumed the proper posture for worship.

A real physical body. Despite the creditable nature of the three interpretations just introduced, none of them dominates the commentaries.
This honor goes rather to an apologetical reading, which emphasizes less
the nature of the women's action than the nature of Jesus himself. This
is Theophylact: "With much reverence and honor for him they grasped
his feet, in their piety not daring to touch any other part of his body, but
only the lowest extremities of his body. Some say that they grasped his
feet purposely to ascertain if he had truly risen, and was not only an apparition (φαντασίαν) or a spirit (πνεῦμα). For they suspected that he was
a spirit (πνεῦμα)."[12] The view here introduced by "Some say," but which
would be better introduced by "Many say," appears again and again in
the literature from Origen to the present day.[13] A recent commentator

---

Hagner, *Matthew 14–28* (WBC 33B; Dallas: Word, 1995), p. 875; Larry Chouinard, *The College
Press NIV Commentary: Matthew* (Joplin, Mo.: College Press, 1997), p. 506.

    11. Cf. 2 Chron. 20:18; Ps. 72:11; Dan. 3:5–7; Sir. 50:17; *LAE* (Gk.) 27:5; *Jos. Asen.* 15:11;
T. Abr. Rec. Lng. 18:10; 33:5; Josephus, *Ant.* 7.95; 9.11; 10.213; Acts 10:25; 1 Cor. 14:25;
Rev. 4:10; 7:11; 19:10; 22:8; etc.

    12. Theophylact, *Comm. Matt.* ad 28:9–10 (PG 123.480C–81A).

    13. E.g., Origen, *Comm. Matt.* frag. 568 (GCS 41, ed. Klostermann and Benz, p. 234);
Chrysostom, *Hom. on Matt.* 89.3 (PG 58.784); Rabanus Maurus apud Aquinas, *Catena* ad
loc.; Sedulius Scotus, *Comm. Matt.* ad loc. (ed. Löfstedt, pp. 636–37); Ps.-Anselm = Geoffrey
Babion, *En. Matt.* ad loc. (PL 162.1496A); *Glossa Ordinaria* (PL 114.177D); Dionysius bar
Salibi, *Expl. Evang.* ad loc. (CSCO 77, Scriptores Syri 33, ed. Sedlaeck and Chabot, p. 160);
Euthymius Zigabenus, *Comm. Matt.* ad loc. (PG 129.758A); Nicolas de Gorran, *In quatuor
Evangelia Commentarius* (Antwerp: Ioannes Keerbergius, 1617), p. 259; Anonymous in Cramer,
Catenae, p. 241; Hugo Grotius, *Opera omnia theologica*, vol. 2, part 1 (Amsterdam: Joannis
Blaeu, 1679), pp. 283–84; John Gill, *Gill's Commentary* (6 vols.; Grand Rapids: Baker, 1980),
5:303 (see below, p. 116); John Guyse, *A Practical Exposition of the Four Evangelists* (2nd ed.;
London: Edward Dilly, 1761), 1:212; John A. Broadus, *Commentary on the Gospel of Mat-
thew* (Philadelphia: American Baptist Publication Society, 1886), p. 587; Adolf Schlatter, *Der
Evangelist Matthäus: Seine Sprache, sein Ziel, seine Selbständigkeit* (Stuttgart: Calwer, 1948),
p. 559; Walter Grundmann, *Das Evangelium nach Matthäus* (THKNT 1; Berlin: Evangelische
Verlagsanstalt, 1968), p. 570; John P. Meier, *Matthew* (New Testament Message 3; Wilmington, Del.: Michael Glazier, 1980), p. 364; R. T. France, *The Gospel according to Matthew: An*

on Matthew has this to say: "The mention of Jesus' 'feet' (9) is an odd detail, but its homeliness underscores the corporeality of Jesus' resurrected body, and it is at variance with the theories of the resurrection as a series of 'mystical visions' or spiritual awakenings. It also opposes the Gnostic and docetist heresies that Jesus only *seemed* to be human."[14] That the women laid hold of Jesus' feet demonstrates, on this view, that he was truly resurrected from the dead, and further that his post-Easter body was not wholly dissimilar from his pre-Easter body. If the latter had feet (cf. Matt. 4:6; 15:30), so does the former.

In Support of the Dominant Tradition

In the remainder of this chapter I should like to urge that the prevailing patristic and medieval interpretation of Matt. 28:9, which survives in the modern commentaries, is probably the right one. My justification for this exercise is that, while the position is well known, it is nowhere well argued. Although the commentators often enough express their views on Matt. 28:9, they typically do so without giving a reason; and even when they do bother to marshal an argument, they do so much too quickly. The following few pages are, then, intended to fill a gap in the exegetical literature.

Parallel interests in Luke and John. Some initial support for the apologetical understanding of Matt. 28:9 derives from the fact that two of the other canonical evangelists were demonstrably interested in stories that endorse the corporeal nature of Jesus' risen body. Luke 24:37–43 contains the following:

> They were startled and terrified, and thought that they were seeing a ghost. He said to them, "Why are you frightened, and why do doubts arise in your hearts? Look at my hands and my feet; see that it is I myself. Touch me and see; for a ghost does not have flesh and bones as you see that I have." And when he had said this, he showed them his hands and his feet. While in their joy they were disbelieving and still wondering, he said to them, "Have you

---

Introduction and Commentary (TNTC; Leicester: Inter-Varsity, 1985), p. 409; Joachim Gnilka, *Das Matthäusevangelium* (2 vols.; HTKNT 1/1–2; Freiburg: Herder, 1986–1988), 2:495; Craig L. Blomberg, *The New American Commentary*, vol. 22, *Matthew* (Nashville, Tenn.: Broadman, 1992), p. 428; M. Eugene Boring, "The Gospel of Matthew," in *The New Interpreter's Bible* (Nashville: Abingdon, 1995), 8:500; Wolfgang Wiefel, *Das Evangelium nach Matthäus* (THNT 1; Leipzig: Evangelische Verlagsanstalt, 1998), p. 490; Warren Carter, *Matthew and the Margins: A Sociopolitical and Religious Reading* (Maryknoll, N.Y.: Orbis, 2000), p. 547.

14. Howard Clarke, *The Gospel of Matthew and Its Readers: A Historical Introduction to the First Gospel* (Bloomington and Indianapolis, Ind.: Indiana University Press, 2003), p. 247.

anything here to eat?" They gave him a piece of broiled fish, and he took it and ate in their presence.

Luke is, in this pericope, clearly offering evidence that the disciples saw not a ghost (πνεῦμα) but Jesus come back to life: he had hands, he had feet, he could eat. The same apologetical interest animates John 20:19–29, where the risen Jesus shows his disciples "his hands and his side" and then, on a second occasion, invites doubting Thomas to touch him with these words: "Put your finger here and see my hands. Reach out your hand and put it in my side. Do not doubt, but believe."[15]

Now we cannot know whether, as some earlier commentators alleged, Luke and John told their stories as they did because they wished to combat an advancing docetism. All that really matters for our purposes is the sure knowledge that, very close to Matthew's time and place, some Christians were indeed anxious to establish that the risen Jesus was not a ghost but a resurrected body. We know this further from Ignatius, *Smyrn.* 3:1–3, where the proof that Jesus "was in the flesh even after the resurrection" comes from the disciples' obedient response to the invitation, "Take, handle me, and see that I am not a bodiless phantom" (δαιμόνιον ἀσώματον).

Apologetic aims in Matthew. Although there is no real evidence that Matthew cared to counter docetists, we can discern in his Gospel a desire to oppose the slander that Jesus' resurrection was a fraud. This is apparent above all in 27:62–66; 28:2–4, and 11–15, which together tell the tale of the guard at Jesus' tomb, of how the soldiers, although they had rolled a stone before the entrance and sealed it, were unable to prevent the miracle of the resurrection; and of how they later spread abroad the lie that the disciples came by night and filched Jesus' body. Matthew 28:17 likewise seems to target doubt about the resurrection, although doubt among Christians themselves. Whether the relevant Greek (οἱ δὲ ἐδίστασαν) means "but some [of the twelve] doubted" or "but they [all the twelve] doubted" or "but they [others beside the twelve] doubted,"[16] the motif of disbelief is attested elsewhere in the traditions about Jesus' resurrection (Mark 16:11, 13–14; Luke 24:13–35; John 20:14; 21:4), and it everywhere lends itself to addressing second thoughts among Christian readers. If the disciples experienced doubt and then overcame it, others can do the same. As Jerome put it, "their doubt enlarges our faith."[17] So

---

15. These passages from Luke and John are, naturally, often brought together; see, e.g., Methodius of Olympus, *Res.* 3.12 (GCS 27, ed. Bonwetsch, p. 408); Ps.-Athanasius, *Apoll.* 1–2 (PG 26.1101–4A).

16. See esp. Pieter van der Horst, "Once More: the Translation of οἱ δέ in Matthew 28.17," *JSNT* 27 (1986), pp. 27–30.

17. Jerome, *Comm. Matt.* ad loc. (SC 259, ed. Bonnard, p. 314).

Matt. 28:17, just like 27:62–66; 28:2–4, and 11–15, is consistent with the proposal that, in 28:9, we may see Matthew's interest in defending the reality of Jesus' resurrection.

A Matthean idiom. As observed above, Matthew, when recounting that people paid homage to Jesus, three times uses the idiom πίπτω + προσκυνέω: 2:11; 4:9; 18:26. In this connection he nowhere mentions Jesus' feet. This is cause to wonder whether there may not be some special motive for mentioning them in 28:9. It accords with this that the different construction that Matthew uses here, κρατέω + πούς + προσκυνέω, cannot, according to my researches, be reckoned stereotypical: Matthew may even have minted it for the occasion.

The history of interpretation. The history of interpretation, although it also offers other possibilities, establishes that Matt. 28:9 has in fact moved numerous readers from sundry times and divers places to comment on the physicality or concrete reality of Jesus' resurrection. To judge from the secondary literature I have perused, and as already indicated, such readers would appear indeed to be in the majority. Surely this is a point not to be passed over lightly.

Ghosts and feet across cultures. Matthew may have had a very specific reason for mentioning Jesus' feet in particular. There is a body of folklore regarding the feet of otherworldly beings. According to later Jewish superstition, for example, demons can disguise themselves well enough (cf. 2 Cor. 11:14) except for their feet, which always remain ugly and so inescapably betray their evil identity. The relevant and intriguing fact for our purposes, however, is that, throughout worldwide ghost lore, the spirits of the dead often appear without feet or legs. The explanation for this appears to be the phenomenology of human experience.[18] For, however one explains or explains away first-hand reports of ghosts, they sometimes come with the claim that a phantom glided rather than walked or that it appeared to lack lower extremities. Here are three modern examples:

> At night I have seen her in my room, standing near my bed, or near the fireplace. She has also appeared to walk through the locked door. . . . I have not seen her feet; she seemed to just move along. . . . The last time I saw her, she was dressed in a red dress, which she often wore in life. I still did not see her feet.[19]

18. With what follows see David J. Hufford, "Beings without Bodies: An Experience-Centered Theory of the Belief in Spirits," in *Out of the Ordinary: Folklore and the Supernatural* (ed. Barbara Walker; Logan, Utah: Utah State University Press, 1995), pp. 11–45, and James McClenon, *Wondrous Events: Foundations of Religious Belief* (Philadelphia: University of Pennsylvania Press, 1994), esp. pp. 57–77.

19. N. Lukianowicz, "Hallucinations à Troix," *Archives of General Psychiatry* 1 (1959), p. 325.

He then saw a man and a woman who looked at him for a while before disappearing into the wall. The man was in his mid-thirties, with a longish face. His naked upper body was muscular, but he had no legs. The woman, of average height and build, wore a kimono, and had a round, expressionless face, her head held to one side. She, too, had no legs.[20]

N. E. was at first frightened and pulled the bed covers over her head. She then seemed to receive the word "Mother," and uncovered her head. Then she saw her mother, but not in full length; only the upper part of the body and the face were visible.[21]

For our immediate purposes it does not matter, I wish to repeat, what one makes of ghosts, or how one accounts for incomplete phantoms. What does matter is that belief in ghosts without feet is both widespread and ancient—and, furthermore, that this belief appears precisely in one of the very earliest defenses of Jesus' resurrection. The following account of a resurrection appearance is from the Coptic version of the *Epistle of the Apostles* 11:

He called out to us. But we thought it was a ghost, and we did not believe it was the Lord. Then he said to us, "Come, do not be afraid. I am your teacher whom you, Peter, denied three times; and now do you deny me again?" But we went to him, doubting in our hearts whether it was possibly he. Then he said to us, "Why do you still doubt and not believe? I am he who spoke to you concerning my flesh, my death, and my resurrection. That you may know that it is I, put your finger, Peter, in the nail-prints of my hands; and you, Thomas, put your finger in the spear-wounds of my side; but you, Andrew, look at my feet and

20. Catrien Ross, *Supernatural and Mysterious Japan: Spirits, Hauntings, and Paranormal Phenomena* (Tokyo: Yenbooks, 1996), p. 114. Regarding the Japanese ghosts known as *yurei*, Tim Screech, in *Mangajin* 40 (http://www.mangajin.com/mangajin/samplemj/ghosts/ghosts. htm; accessed 10/21/04), writes: "An interesting physical aspect of *yurei* is that they have no legs, trailing off instead into smoke-like wisps where a person's legs would normally be. The absence of legs fits with the general non-corporeality of the *yurei*, for their whole bodies are wraithlike and lacking in that outer boundary of skin or scale that holds other living things in shape. Legs serve to join creatures to the soil, they root being to the earth, and so to be legless is in a sense to be disengaged. This feature of the Japanese ghost is not dissimilar to the ability of the Western ghost to float slightly above the ground, or slightly beneath it, without using the legs it still theoretically has."

21. Ian Stevenson, "Six Modern Apparitional Experiences," *Journal of Scientific Exploration* 9 (1995), p. 353. For additional examples see Hilary Evans and Patrick Huyghe, *The Field Guide to Ghosts and Other Apparitions* (New York: Quill, 2000), pp. 52, 82, 86; and for gliding ghosts see further Andrew Mackenzie, *The Seen and Unseen* (London: Weidenfeld & Nicholson, 1987), pp. 144–45, and Harry Price, *The Most Haunted House in England* (London: Longmans, Green, 1940), pp. 24, 45. Even visions of the Virgin Mary can come without feet; see Randall Sullivan, *The Miracle Detective: An Investigation of Holy Visions* (New York: Atlantic Monthly Press, 2004), pp. 76, 84, 114.

see if they do not touch the ground. For it is written in the prophet, 'The foot of the apparition of a departed spirit does not join to the ground.'"[22] But we touched him that we might truly know whether he had risen in the flesh, and we fell on our faces confessing our sin, that we had been unbelieving.

Whatever the source of the quotation attributed to "the prophet,"[23] this apocryphal story is indisputable evidence that an ancient Christian could construe the feet of the risen Jesus as effective testimony to the reality of his resurrection.[24] Surely this ups the odds that Matthew and his original audience—who were certainly familiar with the concept of a ghost[25]—could have thought the same thing.

Complementary interpretations. According to Ulrich Luz, the women's act of grasping Jesus' feet is one of homage, and thus there is no emphasis upon the corporeality of Jesus' resurrection.[26] This objection seems to assume that the interpreter must choose between homage and apologetics: the text cannot serve the latter if it expresses the former. Eduard Schweizer betrays a similar antithesis when he writes that the women touching Jesus' feet "is not yet meant to counter false notions of the resurrection; it grows quite naturally out of the narrative"[27]—as though something that grows naturally out of the narrative could not simultaneously serve, or is less likely to serve, an apologetical purpose. I am, with due deference to both Luz and Schweizer, at a loss to understand their verdicts. Who passed the hermeneutical law that a text must, like a one-way street sign, send us in one direction only? Many of Matthew's sentences are, without a doubt, intertextually, intratextually, and theologically dense and so signify several things at once. Why must 28:9 be excluded from their company?

22. For this translation of ογφαντασια ⲛⲇⲁⲓⲙⲱⲛ ⲙⲁⲣⲉ ⲣⲉⲧ̄ϥ̄ ⲧⲟⲩⲙⲉ ϩⲓⲭⲛ̄ ⲡⲕⲁϩ see Julian Hills, *Tradition and Composition in the Epistula Apostolorum* (HDR 24; Minneapolis: Fortress, 1990), pp. 89–90. The Ethiopic is slightly different: "But a ghost, a demon, leaves no print on the ground." Cf. Commodian, *Carm. apol.* 560 (ed. Ludwig, p. 17): "A shadow does not make a mark." Likewise similar is the docetic *Acts of John* 93, where the earthly Jesus can walk without leaving footprints.

23. Among the proposals are 1 Sam. 28:7–25; Job 11:7 LXX; Bel 14:20; and Wisd. 18:17. One suspects, however, that the words are probably from a lost apocryphon.

24. Cf. the way in which Tertullian argues for the bodily reality of angels by reference to the footwashing in Gen. 18: Tertullian, *Res.* 62 (ed. Evans, p. 182); *Carn. Chr.* 3.6 (SC 216, ed. Mahé, p. 218).

25. Cf. 14:26: "But when the disciples saw him walking on the sea, they were terrified, saying, 'It is a ghost!'" (φάντασμα).

26. Ulrich Luz, *Das Evangelium nach Matthäus* (4 vols.; EKK 1/1–4; Düsseldorf: Benziger, 1990–2002), 4:418.

27. Eduard Schweizer, *The Good News according to Matthew* (Atlanta: John Knox, 1975), p. 525.

We need not, in my judgment, choose between the four interpretations of Matt. 28:9 introduced in this chapter. Affection, submission, and worship readily belong to one and the same act; and that the notice of people grasping Jesus' feet could additionally serve an apologetical end is scarcely far-fetched. That I am not alone in this conclusion follows from the history of interpretation, which offers repeated examples of exegetes who fail to opt for one interpretation rather than another but instead combine two or more of them. Let me end, then, with one such, John Gill, and his remarks upon Matt. 28:9, which seem to me just right: "They threw themselves prostrate at his feet, in token of reverence and humility; and they laid hold on his feet, that they might know, and be assured that he was really risen, and that it was not a spirit, or a mere phantom and appearance; and they held him in affection to him, and as desirous of his continuance with them."[28]

28. Gill, Commentary, 5:303. Cf. Sedulius Scotus, Comm. Matt. ad loc. (ed. Löfstedt, pp. 636–37); Dionysius bar Salibi, Expl. Evang. ad loc. (CSCO 77, Scriptores Syri 33, ed. Sedlaeck and Chabot, p. 160); Euthymius Zigabenus, Comm. Matt. ad loc. (PG 129.758A); H. N. Ridderbos, Matthew (Grand Rapids: Zondervan, 1987), p. 550; Carter, Matthew, p. 547.

6

Reading Matthew
through the Church Fathers

A s the literature in the field of biblical studies continues to grow at
a dismaying rate, we may be increasingly tempted to ignore old
writers. How can one keep up with what is going on now if one is still
catching up with what went on then—if one is spending time, let us say,
with books from the fourth or sixteenth centuries? The temptation is the
greater because of our uncritical faith that anything of real importance
said once will be said again and so not forgotten. Have not all the good
observations and plausible hypotheses been passed down from book to
book and from generation to generation and so on to us? We may also
be disinclined to pay the past keen attention because we are under the
illusion that exegesis progresses like the hard sciences. Who among us
would read a physics textbook from 1919? Surely today's work makes
yesterday's obsolete, so that we do not really have to bother much with
writers who have expired. Such a restricted vision, such a condescending
attitude toward the past, however, impoverishes exegesis, as I hope the

The following pages largely reproduce a lecture I gave in 1991, long before I read Ulrich Luz,
"The Significance of the Church Fathers for Biblical Interpretation in Western Protestant Perspective," in *Studies in Matthew* (Grand Rapids: Eerdmans, 2005), pp. 290–312. Luz's article,
among other things, documents and seeks to explain the decline of the church fathers in modern
Protestant biblical exegesis. There are some important convergences with my present chapter,
above all the continuing relevance of the patristic contribution to gospel studies.

preceding chapters have illustrated. In the present chapter, I should like to continue to make the case against ignoring our exegetical past by sharing how study of patristic sources has significantly influenced some of my work on Matthew. I shall group my observations under four headings: intertextuality, culture, theology, and rhetoric.

Intertextuality

Matthew has this apparent defect, that its author did not trumpet all his intentions. Although he made much clear, he also left much, even much of importance, unsaid. The careful reader knows this after only the first few verses, for the striking insertion of four women into the genealogy must mean something (1:3, 5, 6). But what? We are, to our frustration, never told. Matthew was in one respect akin to Clement of Alexandria, whose "preferred style of discourse" was "allusion and implication."[1] Perhaps our evangelist expected too much of his readers. Or—this is my own supposition—his first readers were better equipped than us, which is to say they had a knowledge we lack, a knowledge, that is, of the tradition behind the Gospel, which tradition has ceased to be.

In addition to not revealing all his intentions, Matthew also failed to instruct us about his literary methods. In this regard he was like most authors, who "seldom write about the essentials of their art. A true convention in any age is accepted without comment. In the main, we cannot expect our authors to tell us what their conventions were. We shall have to hunt for ourselves."[2]

What then do we find when we hunt in Matthew? The first discovery is that the Gospel is like a chapter in a book. The ubiquitous scriptural citations and allusions, which are anything but detachable ornamentation, direct the reader to other books and so teach that Matthew is not a self-contained entity: much is missing. The Gospel, in other words, stipulates that it be interpreted in the context of other texts. This means that it is, in a fundamental sense, an incomplete utterance, a book full of holes. Readers must make present what is absent; they must become actively engaged and bring to the Gospel knowledge of what it presupposes, that being a pre-existing collection of interacting texts, the Jewish Bible. The First Gospel is a mnemonic device, designed, to use the current

1. Raoul Mortley, "The Past in Clement of Alexandria," in *Jewish and Christian Self-Definition* (ed. E. P. Sanders; Philadelphia: Fortress, 1980), 1:194.

2. C. W. Jones, *Saints Lives and Chronicles in Early England* (Ithaca, N.Y.: Cornell University Press, 1948), p. 53.

jargon, to trigger intertextual exchanges which depend upon informed and imaginative reading.

But how does the contemporary reader of an ancient work come to perceive such exchanges? Or, more simply, when is an allusion an allusion?[3] Anyone familiar with the critical literature on the New Testament knows that the discovery of allusions is an uncertain enterprise. Surely John 1:51 ("you will see heaven opened, and the angels of God ascending and descending upon the Son of Man") adverts to Jacob's ladder and Gen. 28, but is Rom. 8:32 (God "did not withhold his own Son, but gave him up for all of us") a reminiscence of Gen. 32 and the *Akedah*, the sacrifice of Isaac? The text is silent, and scholars disagree. How then does one decide? All concur that the New Testament books, not unlike "The Waste Land" of T. S. Eliot, constantly elicit tradition through the device of allusion. Yet whereas Eliot condescended to footnote his poem, the New Testament writers did not add scholia. As modern readers of the Bible are we not in the position of the college student struggling to understand Dante or Milton in an old edition, one without annotations? Every phrase has something in it, much more than initially perceived; but how can we perceive it? Time removes us from all texts and subtexts and so cripples our ability to detect tacit references, which is why, as history marches on, annotated editions of the classics, including the Bible, become longer and longer. With time, once transparent allusions become, to quote William Empson, "delicate cross-references that are now the discoveries of the learned."[4]

It is here that the Fathers help us. For they were, in so many ways, closer to the first-century Christians than we are. Unlike most of us, they lived and moved and had their being in the Scriptures. It was their popular music. They still read aloud. They still had a small literary canon. And they still heard Scripture chanted. They were accordingly attuned to *hear* things that we no longer *hear*, things which we can only *see* after picking up concordances or doing word searches on our computers. I have come to believe that if we find in Matthew or another New Testament book an allusion to the Old Testament that the Fathers did not find, the burden of proof is on us; and if they detected an allusion which modern commentators have not detected, investigation is in order. The indices at the end of patristic volumes have become invaluable to me.

To offer an example: No modern commentary known to me refers to Moses in connection with Matt. 5:5, the third beatitude: "Blessed are

3. See further Dale C. Allison Jr., *The Intertextual Jesus: Scripture in Q* (Harrisburg, Pa.: Trinity Press International, 2000), pp. 1–24.

4. William Empson, *Seven Types of Ambiguity* (3rd ed.; Norfolk, Conn.: New Directions, 1953), p. 47.

the meek, for they will inherit the earth." But Eusebius and Theodoret of Cyrrhus both did. The latter cited Num. 12:3 (Moses was "very meek, more than all men that were on the face of the earth") as illustration of Matt. 5:5,[5] and Eusebius remarked that whereas Jesus promised the meek inheritance of the earth, Moses promised Israel inheritance of the land.[6] Perhaps we should follow the interpretive lead of Theodoret and Eusebius and set Matt. 5:5 against the Moses traditions. Moses was, in meekness, the exemplar.[7] He promised the Israelites inheritance of the land.[8] And he himself did not enter the land.[9] From this last fact, sufficiently unexpected to have engendered much rabbinic reflection, one might extract that the third beatitude pledges something Moses never gained. On such an interpretation, the members of the new covenant would be more blessed than the chief figure of the old. If, in the past, the meek one did not enter the land, now that the kingdom of God has come, "the meek shall inherit the earth." One thinks of Matt. 11:11: the least in the kingdom of heaven is greater than all those who came before, a statement which must include Moses.

I hesitate to pronounce whether or not the Mosaic interpretation of Matt. 5:5 should be endorsed. The arguments pro and con I must ignore here. I only wish to urge, first, that the proposed interpretation should be seriously considered; second, that at the very least it could be homiletically fruitful; and, third, that patristic texts tell us what Old Testament texts the Fathers heard echoed in the New Testament, and that what they heard may be our best guide to determining allusions the author intended.

Let me offer a second example. In the missionary account in Matt. 10, Jesus forbids his disciples to take several items: on their way (εἰς ὁδόν) they should not take gold (χρυσόν), silver (ἄργυρον), copper, wallet (for bread), two shirts, sandals (ὑποδήματα), or staff. Mark 6 allows the staff and sandals and says that the disciples should not take bread, wallet, copper, or two shirts. Luke 9 and 10 together disallow taking staff, wallet, bread, silver, or purse. Now it is intriguing that most of the items in Matt. 10 and its parallels famously appear in the exodus from

5. Theodoret of Cyrrhus, *Rel. hist.* 11:2 (SC 234, ed. Canivet and Leroy-Molinghen, p. 456). Cf. Robert H. Gundry, *Matthew: A Commentary on His Handbook for a Mixed Church under Persecution* (2nd ed.; Grand Rapids: Eerdmans, 1994), p. 69: "Jesus himself provides an example of meekness that corresponds to Moses, who was 'very meek, more than any man who was on the face of the earth' (Num. 12:3)."

6. Eusebius, *Dem. ev.* 3.2 (GCS 23, ed. Heikel, p. 97).

7. Cf. Num. 12:3; Sir. 45:4; Philo, *Mos.* 1.26; *Mek.* on Exod. 20:21; *b. Ned.* 38a; *Tanhuma* Bereshit 1; Origen, *Exod. hom.* 11.6 (SC 321, ed. Borret, p. 348); Jerome, *Ep.* 82.3 (CSEL 55, ed. Hilberg, p. 110); *Apophthegmata Patrum* Syncletica 11 (PG 65.425B).

8. Exod. 15:17; 23:30; 32:13; Num. 26:53–55; Deut. 1:38; 2:31; etc.

9. Deut. 1:37; 3:23–29; 31:2; 32:48–52; 34:4.

Egypt. Exodus 12 tells us that Moses commanded the Israelites to eat the Passover hurriedly, with sandals (12:11 LXX: ὑποδήματα) on their feet and staff in hand, and that they went forth on their way (12:39 LXX: εἰς τὴν ὁδόν) with bread, with silver (12:35 LXX: ἀργυρᾶ), with gold (12:35 LXX: χρυσᾶ), and with clothing (12:35–36). Deuteronomy 8:4 and 29:5, moreover, relate that the Israelites' garments were indestructible, so that they only needed one pair of sandals and one set of clothes. Is it just coincidence that Jesus' disciples are similarly in a hurry but still more so, and that they accordingly take even less than the fleeing Israelites? Maybe Matt. 10 and its parallels are drawing some sort of analogy or contrast. Certainly elsewhere the Synoptics draw analogies between the history of Jesus and the history of the exodus.

This, then, is a reading worth exploring. But it is, with only one exception known to me, not found in the modern literature on the Gospels. Joel Marcus has recently, in his commentary on Mark, observed the parallel and suggested that it is part of a new exodus typology.[10] Now Marcus may well be right, yet he has not espied anything new: his discovery is a rediscovery. If we go back to the patristic period, we learn that several theologians remarked upon the correlation. Tertullian, for one, saw it:

> When the children of Israel went out from Egypt, the creator brought them forth laden with their spoils of gold and silver vessels, and with loads besides of raiment and unleavened dough, whereas Christ commanded his disciples not to carry even a staff for their journey. . . . Consider the different purposes in the occasions and you will understand how it was one and the same power that arranged the mission of his people according to their poverty in the one case and their plenty in the other. . . . Even shoes he forbade them (the disciples) to carry, for he it was under whose protection the people wore out not even a shoe (Deut. 29:5), even in the wilderness for the space of so many years.[11]

Ambrose and Isho'dad of Merv said similar things.[12] And then there is the exegesis of the Megethius, a fourth-century (?) Marcionite who wanted to contrast the God of Jesus with the God of Moses:

> The God of Genesis commanded Moses in the going up from Egypt saying, "Make ready with loins girded, having sandals on feet, staffs in your hands, and traveler's bags upon you. Carry away the gold and silver and all the other things of the Egyptians." But our good Lord, sending his disciples out into the

10. Joel Marcus, *Mark 1–8* (AB; New York: Doubleday, 2000), pp. 388–90.
11. Tertullian, *Adv. Marc.* 4.24 (OECT, ed. Evans, 2:390).
12. Ambrose, *Exp. Luke* 7.57–60 (SC 52, ed. Tissot, pp. 27–29); Isho'dad of Merv, *Comm. Matt.* 7 (HSem 6, ed. Gibson, pp. 74–75). Cf. Dionysius bar Salibi, *Expl. Evang.* ad Matt. 10:10 (CSCO 77, Scriptores Syri 33, ed. Sedlaeck and Chabo, p. 281).

world, says, "Neither sandals on your feet, nor traveler's bag, nor two cloaks, nor money in your belts. See how clearly the good one opposes the teachings of that one."[13]

This is a very interesting comment. Yet observance of the correspondence, or maybe I should say the antithesis, is confined, to the extent of my knowledge, to the first millennium of exegesis, after which it goes away, until it turns up suddenly and independently in the new Anchor Bible on Mark.[14]

Chapter 3 herein, in which I have discussed the likely allusion to the story of Cain and Abel in Matt. 5:21–24, supplies yet another instance of an allusion the ancients caught much more often than we moderns do. At this juncture, however, I should like to turn from isolated allusions to a series of proposed allusions that, in the judgment of many, myself included, constitute an extended typology.

R. H. Fuller has written: "Matthew presents Jesus first and foremost as a Moseslike figure."[15] Ulrich Luz, on the other hand, has given it as his judgment that Matthew nowhere emphasizes "any personal correspondence between Jesus and Moses."[16] How is it that two first-rate scholars can look at the same book and come to such disparate conclusions?

The problem exists because those who claim to find a Moses typology in the First Gospel are making a claim about something allegedly implicit: not once is there an express comparison between Jesus and Moses. It is true that Matthew opens with circumstances quite reminiscent of Exodus. The life of the infant hero is threatened by a wicked king, after which the hero passes through the waters, after which he enters into the desert to fast (like Moses) for forty days and forty nights, during which time he is tempted with the desert temptations of Israel, after which he goes up on a mountain to deliver his commandments.[17] These and other possible parallels are, however, never spelled out by the text. Whence the debate.

One difficulty with attempts to pass judgment on the issue of a Moses typology in the First Gospel is that they have tended to be un-

13. *De recta in Deum fide* (GCS 4, ed. van de Sande Bakhuyzen, p. 22).

14. In conversation, Marcus has indicated that he came to his interpretation independently, not by reading any other commentators, ancient or modern.

15. R. H. Fuller, "Christology in Matthew and Luke," in *Who Is This Christ? Gospel Christology and Contemporary Faith* (with Pheme Perkins; Philadelphia: Fortress, 1983), p. 84.

16. Ulrich Luz, *Matthew 1–7: A Commentary* (Minneapolis: Augsburg, 1989), 1:186, n. 18. Note, however, the apparent change in opinion in the second German edition of Luz's commentary: *Das Evangelium nach Matthäus*, vol. 1, *Mt 1–7* (5th rev. ed.; EKKNT 1/1; Düsseldorf: Benziger, 2002), p. 225, n. 28.

17. See Dale C. Allison Jr., *The New Moses: A Matthean Typology* (Minneapolis: Fortress, 1993), pp. 140–207.

informed about a crucial fact, namely, the existence of extensive Moses typologies in other ancient texts, including patristic texts. In addition to numerous ancient Christian artifacts, several Fathers, including Pseudo-Macarius and Augustine, depicted Peter as a new Moses.[18] Basil the Great and Gregory of Nyssa both received and developed the tradition that likened Gregory the Wonderworker to the lawgiver.[19] Eusebius, as is well known, offered, in more than one book, extensive comparisons between Constantine and Moses.[20] Comparison with Moses was also part of the traditions about Ephraem the Syrian;[21] and Theodoret, in his *Life of the Monks of Syria*, presented many ascetics as in certain respects duplicates of Moses.[22] I also wonder—I do not assert, I just wonder—whether Athanasius's *Life of Anthony* does not have a bit of a Moses typology. In this book the hero is God's friend, the man of God, and the servant of God—all titles of Moses. He is born in Egypt and goes forth into the Egyptian desert. He spends vast amounts of time on a mountain, where, like Philo's Moses, he is initiated into divine mysteries and inspired by God. He is, again like Moses, meek, and he brings forth water in the desert. Finally, when he dies, his eyes remain undimmed, as Deut. 34:7 reports of Moses; and, to quote Athanasius, "to this day no one knows where it [Anthony's body] has been hidden," a sentence strikingly reminiscent of Deut. 34:6: "But no man knows the place of his burial to this day."[23]

What does all this mean for Matthew? It means first of all that it was commonplace in early Christianity to compare heroes to Moses and, further, that because we find some people likened to Moses in several different authors, likeness to Moses could be a characteristic of the tradition about certain saints—just as it became, from very early on, a characteristic of the tradition about Jesus. Second, the existence of various Moses typologies affords us the opportunity to compare propositions about what Matthew

18. Augustine, *C. Faust.* 22.70 (CSEL 25, ed. Zycha, p. 667); Ps.-Macarius, *Hom. 1–50* 26.23 (PTS 4, ed. Dörries, Klostermann, and Kroeger, p. 216). See further Allison, *New Moses*, pp. 106–9.

19. Basil, *Spir.* 29.74 (FT 12, ed. Sieben, p. 304); Gregory of Nyssa, *V. G. Thaum.* (Gregorii Nysseni Opera 10.1, ed. Heil, Cavarnos, and Lendle, pp. 14, 19, 49). See Allison, *New Moses*, pp. 112–14.

20. Eusebius, *HE* 9.9 (SC 55, ed. Bardy, pp. 65–67); idem, *V. Const.* 1.12, 19–20, 38–39 (GCS 7, ed. Heikel, pp. 13, 17–18, 24–26). See Allison, *New Moses*, pp. 118–21.

21. *Acta Martyrum et Sanctorum Syriace III* (ed. Paul Bedjan; Leipzig: Harrassowitz, 1892), pp. 668, 672; Ps.-Gregory of Nyssa, *V. Ephr.* (PG 46.837, 840, 844–45). See Allison, *New Moses*, pp. 121–23.

22. Theodoret of Cyrrhus, *Rel. hist.* 1.4, 11–12; 2.4, 7, 8, 13; 10.7; 26.2, 7 (SC 234, 257, ed. Canivet and Leroy-Molinghen, 1:166–68, 186–88, 202–4, 212–14, 222–24, 448; 2:161, 172). See Allison, *New Moses*, pp. 126–29.

23. Texts and discussion in Allison, *New Moses*, pp. 114–18.

allegedly did with what others did later. When people constructed Moses typologies, what events from the Pentateuch did they latch onto? What items were most frequently alluded to? To what extent were typologies implicit, to what extent explicit? In other words, the rhetorical techniques used to construct Moses typologies in patristic literature supply crucial comparative material. Third, we can ask whether those who themselves constructed typologies, and Moses typologies in particular, did in fact recognize such in Matthew, to which the answer is yes. Aphraates, who likened Peter to Moses,[24] found, just like many later commentators, a Moses typology in Matt. 2:

> Moses also was persecuted, as Jesus was persecuted. When Moses was born, they concealed him that he might not be slain by his persecutors. When Jesus was born they carried Him off in flight into Egypt that Herod, His persecutor, might not slay Him. In the days when Moses was born, children used to be drowned in the river; and at the birth of Jesus the children of Bethlehem and in its border were slain. To Moses God said: "The men are dead who were seeking your life;" and to Joseph the angel said in Egypt: "Arise, take up the child, and go into the land of Israel, for they are dead who were seeking the life of the child to take it away." Moses brought out his people from the service of Pharaoh; and Jesus delivered all nations from the service of Satan.[25]

Eusebius, who made Constantine the counterpart of Moses, also found a Moses typology in Matthew. Among other things, he compared Moses' fast of forty days and forty nights with Jesus' fast of forty days and forty nights; he compared the provision of manna in the wilderness with Jesus' miraculous feeding of the five thousand and four thousand; he compared Moses' driving back of the Red Sea with Jesus' calming of the Sea of Galilee; and he compared Moses' transfiguration into light on Sinai with Jesus' transfiguration.[26]

I do not contend that the patristic witness should, of itself, settle for us whether there really is an extensive Moses typology in Matthew. For one thing, one must also look at the many Moses typologies in Jewish literature.[27] Dozens of old texts contain implicit typologies likening Joshua and Samuel and Elijah and Josiah and Jeremiah and others to the lawgiver. The patristic sources do, however, suffice to provoke much thought; and they have certainly encouraged me in my conviction that Matthew does indeed contain an extensive and well-considered Moses

24. Aphraates, *Dem.* 21.10 (PS 1, ed. Parisot, p. 959).
25. Aphraates, *Dem.* 21.10 (PS 1, ed. Parisot, pp. 958–59).
26. Eusebius, *Dem. ev.* 3.2 (GCS 23, ed. Heikel, pp. 98–99).
27. See Allison, *New Moses*, pp. 11–95.

typology. Neglect of the Fathers in this particular has, I suggest, impoverished exegesis.

Culture

Sometimes our knowledge, not the lack thereof, gets in the way, and if we are to understand the past, we may need to unlearn some things. The point is beyond obvious. It amounts to little more than that exegetes should be historians, should think themselves back into the past. Although the lesson is learned in exegetical kindergarten, we must relearn it again and again because, if I may so put it, we take our assumptions for granted. Here again the Fathers can help us, by exposing the preconceptions of our own time and place. Here I need not elaborate with an example but only remind readers of the first chapter herein, which is proof enough. There we saw that contemporary exegetes, when writing about the so-called star that the magi follow in Matt. 2, often contemplate whether it might have been a comet, a conjunction, or a supernova. They are reading the old text in the light of their own, very modern astronomical knowledge. If, however, one instead examines the Fathers, who shared with Matthew a complete ignorance of post-Renaissance astronomy, one finds that they thought instead about a portable ball of light, independent of the heavens, a light that some could, in continuity with both Jewish and Hellenistic thought about the heavens, identify with an angel come down to earth. Here the Fathers remind us that Matthew was not a modern and so could not have been thinking in terms of modern astronomical objects, and that we are not ancients and so do not think of identifying stars with angels. This is a very instructive instance of a particular in which the Fathers were much closer to Matthew than are we. They were probably reading the text the way its author intended and its first readers understood it.

Theology

Over the past two decades I have been much occupied with the interpretation of Matt. 5–7, the Sermon on the Mount.[28] In my quest to understand this precious and difficult portion of our Bible, which ever escapes both our understanding and our practice, I have paid considerable attention to the history of its interpretation. I have accordingly reviewed the monastic interpretation of medieval Catholicism, according to which

28. See esp. my book *The Sermon on the Mount: Inspiring the Moral Imagination* (New York: Crossroad, 1999).

many of Matthew's imperatives are evangelical counsels directed firstly toward the "religious," not commandments requisite for salvation and applicable to all alike.[29] I have considered the more prosaic approach of many Anabaptists and Tolstoy, an approach which tends towards literal application: away with armies and oaths.[30] I have fretted over the now much-maligned doctrine of the two kingdoms, which divides life into two spheres, the public and the private, the sphere of Caesar and the sphere of God, with the sermon on the mount being addressed to the latter, not the former.[31] I have made myself familiar with the theory of the impossible ideal: Matthew's Jesus asks us to give what we cannot give, with the result that we fathom our own frailty and fall back upon God's grace; the Sermon on the Mount is in significant measure preparation for the gospel.[32] I have read the proponents of an ethic of intention, according to whom the Sermon on the Mount speaks to individuals about attitudes and internal dispositions: everything depends not upon the act but, as in our modern sentencing of murderers, on intentions, or the heart.[33] I have also pondered the christological interpretation of Karl Barth and Eduard Thurneysen, two men who, not without some plausibility, turned the Sermon on the Mount into a self-portrait: Jesus and Jesus alone lived his own words; the commander embodied his commandments.[34]

Missing from my brief list of interpretations of the Sermon on the Mount, because missing from my reading of the subject, is any specifically Eastern Orthodox interpretation. Some years ago this lacuna began to trouble me. Does the East have anything different or characteristic to offer on this subject? Does it tend, because like Roman Catholicism it has religious orders, to hold to something like the monastic interpretation? Or, since the Eastern Church has never failed to mingle religion and politics, has it developed something analogous to the Lutheran doctrine of the two

29. See E. Dublanchy, "Conseils évangéliques," in *Dictionnaire de théologie catholique*, vol. 3 (ed. A. Vacant, E. Mangenot, and É. Amann; Paris: Letouzey et Ané, 1938), cols. 1176–82, and Brigitta Stoll, *De Virtute in Virtutem: Zur Auslegungs- und Wirkungsgeschichte der Bergpredigt in Kommentaren, Predigten, und hagiographischer Literatur von der Merowingerzeit bis um 1200* (BGBE 30; Tübingen: Mohr-Siebeck, 1988), pp. 114–25. For my own take on this approach and its continuing relevance see my chapter "The Problem of Audience," in *Resurrecting Jesus* (London: T&T Clark, 2005), pp. 27–55.

30. See esp. Leo Tolstoy, *What I Believe* (London: Elliot Stock, 1885).

31. For Luther's own views on the matter, which are hard to pin down, see Paul Althaus, *The Ethics of Martin Luther* (Philadelphia: Fotress, 1972), esp. pp. 43–81.

32. Cf. Werner Elert, *The Christian Ethos* (Philadelphia: Muhlenberg Press, 1957), pp. 63–69, who stresses that *lex* (including the Sermon on the Mount) *semper accusat*.

33. See esp. Wilhelm Herrmann, *Die sittliche Weisungen Jesu: Ihr Mißbrauch und ihr richtiger Gebrauch* (2nd ed.; Göttingen: Vandenhoeck & Ruprecht, 1907).

34. See esp. Eduard Thurneysen, *The Sermon on the Mount* (Richmond, Va.: John Knox, 1964). Cf. herein, pp. 147–53.

kingdoms? I do not, unfortunately, have the answers to these questions. As of now, I am unaware of books or articles on the East that answer my questions.[35] Perhaps my investigative powers are feeble and such books and articles indeed exist, waiting for me to stumble upon them; or, just perhaps, there really is next to nothing on the subject. In either case my ignorance has spurred me on to look for myself; that is, I have gone to the Eastern fathers, with what I imagine to be productive results.

Perhaps the chief difficulty of the Sermon on the Mount is its seemingly impossible demands. How can Matthew's Jesus demand perfection of imperfect people in an imperfect world (5:48), people who so often must choose not the good but the lesser of two evils? Who can, with consistency and purity of heart, exorcise all anger (5:21–26) and love the enemy as does the heavenly Father (5:43–47)? Who can always turn the other cheek (5:38–42)? Who is sufficient for these things? According to Justin Martyr, the second-century Jew Trypho had this to say: "I am aware that your precepts in the so-called Gospel are so wonderful and so great, that I suspect no one can keep them; for I have carefully read them."[36] Closer to our own time, another Jew, Joseph Klausner, urged that the Sermon on the Mount presents an "extremist morality," one that "has not proved possible in practice," for it contains "too high an ideal for ordinary mankind, and even too high for the man of more than average moral caliber."[37] There are, of course, several standard responses to this objection to the Sermon on the Mount's impracticality; but in my view one helpful approach to the problem appears in the fourth-century Cappadocian Gregory of Nyssa in his understanding of Christian perfection.

Our usual ideas of perfection, so heavily influenced by Plato, tend to be static. Many, for instance, have identified Christian perfection with sinlessness, that is, a constant state marked by the absence of sin. But Gregory—here, as so often, developing Origen—held a very different notion. He rejected the Platonic idea that change is a defect and developed an innovative doctrine of perpetual progress.[38] Gregory wrote that the "one limit of perfection is the fact that it has no limit. . . . Why? Because no good has any limit. . . ."[39] Again: "One ought not to be distressed when one considers this tendency [towards mutability] in our nature; rather let us change in such a way that we may constantly evolve towards

35. The Orthodox work of Jim Forest, *Ladder of the Beatitudes* (Maryknoll, N.Y.: Orbis, 1999), is confined to 5:3–12: it fails to say much about the rest of the discourse.

36. Justin Martyr, *Dial.* 10 (PTS 47, ed. Marcovich, p. 87).

37. Joseph Klausner, *Jesus of Nazareth: His Life, Times, and Teaching* (New York: Macmillan, 1925), pp. 395, 397, 392–93 respectively.

38. See Jean Daniélou, "Introduction," in *From Glory to Glory: Texts from Gregory of Nyssa's Mystical Writings* (Crestwood, N.Y.: St. Vladimir's Seminary Press, 1979), pp. 46–71.

39. Gregory of Nyssa, *V. Mos.* 1.5 (Gregorii Nysseni Opera 7.1, ed. Musurillo, p. 3).

what is better, being transformed from glory to glory, and thus always improving and ever becoming more perfect by daily growth, and never arriving at any limit of perfection. For that perfection consists in our never stopping in our growth in good, never circumscribing our perfection by any limitation."[40] From this point of view, Jesus' difficult commands may be conceptualized as a ladder to be climbed, rung by rung, or as a challenge which, ever constant, becomes more and more effective over the course of time.

This promising interpretation, if I may defend Gregory, accords not only with the nature of many of the qualities prescribed by the Sermon on the Mount—who would say of love of neighbor, for instance: Just so much, no more?—but also with 7:13–14, where the words of Jesus are set forth as a *way*. The approach likewise harmonizes, as Gregory enjoyed observing, with Paul's discussion in Phil. 3, where the apostle calls himself "perfect" and yet declares that he has not yet obtained perfection, for that consists precisely in pressing ever onward: "Not that I have already obtained this or am already perfect" (v. 12: τετελείωμαι); "but this one thing I do, forgetting what lies behind and straining forward to what lies ahead, I press on toward the goal for the prize of the heavenly call of God in Christ Jesus. Let those of us who are perfect (v. 15: τέλειοι) be thus minded." Perhaps then it should come as no great surprise that the Matthean Jesus demands everything, up to and including the impossible, because anything less than that, anything less than the eschatological will of God, would put a limit on goodness. But there is no boundary to virtue.

One can, then, follow Gregory's lead and construe the call to moral perfection as a call to perpetual progress, and with this in mind the Sermon on the Mount's high standards are not so baffling. There are after all two sorts of impossible commands. One is utterly beyond reach. If Jesus had asked people to add a cubit to their height, then the criticism of Trypho and Klausner would be justified. But the charge to be perfect in love is not the same thing at all. While absolutely nothing can be done about one's stature, something can always be done about one's capacity to love. It is not a question of all or nothing, of either going over the speed limit or falling below the minimum speed tolerated. Like the kingdom, love may ever be pursued or sought (6:33). It can always be increased, deepened, its circumference enlarged. This explains why John Climacus could speak of love as "the progress of eternity":[41] it can never come to completion. It is no different with many of the other qualities or virtues called for by

40. Gregory of Nyssa, *Perf.* (Gregorii Nysseni Opera 8.1, ed. Jaeger et al., pp. 213–14).
41. John Climacus, *Scal.* 30 (PG 88.1160B); cf. 26 (PG 88.1068B): "Love has no boundary, and both in this age and the age to come we will never cease to advance in it."

the Sermon on the Mount. Since their measure is God, and since God is infinite in all the virtues, our progress in them, that is, our imitation of God, which 5:48 demands, must be never-ending.

I shall not continue expounding this approach to the Sermon on the Mount; I only observe that Gregory's interpretation of Christian perfection, foreshadowed by Origen and taken up by John Climacus, has given me a fresh perspective, one I have found fruitful for exegesis and valuable for life. I do not contend that this interpretation must characterize the East as a whole; nor do I even regard it as exclusively Eastern. It was, however, my reading of the Eastern fathers, especially Gregory of Nyssa, that pushed me in a new direction.

Rhetoric

I have to this point claimed that the Fathers can, in several different ways, improve our attempts to gain both the original sense of the New Testament texts and assist us in doing theology. Before concluding I should like to add that they aid us in yet another way. We all, whether preachers or theologians or devotional writers or New Testament scholars, know the value of saying the right thing in just the right way; and we are all aware that some people have had the gift of doing just that. I do not know how many times I have consulted T. W. Manson's *The Sayings of Jesus*, not so much to learn his judgment on a particular matter as to see rather how he expressed that judgment.[42] Manson had the rhetorical knack for memorable expression, which is why he has been—and still is—so often quoted.

There were those among the Fathers with a like skill. Augustine is perhaps the preeminent example. But Chrysostom belongs in his company. If one looks at my own three volumes on Matthew, one will find Chrysostom quoted more often than any other commentator, ancient or modern, including John Calvin. Chrysostom, to be sure, was a long-winded preacher who often did not know when to stop; yet equally often he was concise, elegant, and to the point.

Consider Matt. 11:25: "I thank you, Father, Lord of heaven and earth, because you have hidden these things from the wise and the intelligent and have revealed them to infants." This preface to one of the Synoptics' most valuable passages might appear, upon reflection, both odd and troubling. Does the thanksgiving really cover not only the bestowal of revelation but also its hiding? Here is Chrysostom's answer to the question: "And while his being revealed to these [the babes] was a fit matter of joy, his

42. T. W. Manson, *The Sayings of Jesus* (London: SCM, 1949).

concealment from those [the wise and understanding] was not for joy but
tears. Thus at any rate he acts, where he weeps for the city. Not therefore
because of this does he rejoice, but because what wise people knew not,
was known to these; as when Paul says, 'I thank God, that you were servants of sin, but you obeyed from the heart the form of doctrine which
was delivered to you.'"[43] These are just the right words. They could not
be bettered: a concise judgment based upon the perfect parallel from Paul
and another pertinent text from Matthew.

Let me offer one more example from the same Father. Mark 7:24–30
contains the famous episode of Jesus and the Syrophoenician woman.
In Matt. 15:21–28, however, she is called a Canaanite. Assuming that
Matthew used Mark as his source, why the difference? Various answers
can be and have been given, but perhaps most modern exegetes have
come to suppose that with the word "Canaanite" our evangelist wanted
to evoke the thought of Israel's enemies and likewise Israel's revulsion
of Gentile ways; so in context the word serves the purpose of showing
that Jesus overcame Israel's ancient prejudices. But the insight is an old
one, and again Chrysostom had it just right: "The evangelist [Matthew]
speaks *against* the woman, that he may show forth her marvelous act,
and celebrate her praise the more. For when you hear of a Canaanite
woman, you should call to mind those wicked nations who overset from
their foundations the very laws of nature. And being reminded of these,
consider also the power of Christ's advent."[44] Once more I submit that
these words could not be bettered. The commentaries should quote them,
as they should quote the Fathers regularly, because the Fathers often said
the right things in ways that have not been surpassed. They constitute a
rhetorical treasure.

————•+•————

My goal in this all-too-brief chapter has not been to exalt the past
uncritically. I am not the exegetical equivalent of a political or cultural
conservative who prefers the company of the deceased. On the contrary,
I eagerly go to the new book shelves of my library every week. I am simply urging that it is foolish to imagine that the part is somehow greater
than the whole. Current exegetical work is part of a much larger body of
literature, and why should we wish to limit the number of our teachers?
The more the better.

When we do enlarge our horizon to take in the Fathers, our respect
for them likewise enlarges. It is not just that we may find them theologi-

43. Chrysostom, *Hom. Matt.* 38.1 (PG 57.429).
44. Chrysostom, *Hom. Matt.* 52.1 (PG 58.519).

cally edifying or spiritually uplifting or homiletically useful but that their exegesis, even judged by our own very different interests and standards, sometimes hits a target that we have missed. The Fathers are of course full of bad judgments and dated opinions on all sorts of matters, and they were ignorant of all sorts of things now known, most notably perhaps the Jewish context of the New Testament writings. And of course they had prejudices we cannot tolerate.[45] But then all this will likewise be the future's verdict upon us, and we like to think that we still have some useful things to say. I submit that it is the same with the church fathers, and that sometimes we may move forward by going backwards.

45. Moreover, many of our interests were foreign to them. For example, the concern of the next two chapters herein, which have to do with larger literary structures, finds scant parallels in patristic exegesis.

PART II

Literary and Historical Studies

7

Structure, Biographical Impulse, and the *Imitatio Christi*

Modern structural analyses of Matthew tend to fall into two camps.[1] One lays chief emphasis upon the twice repeated ἀπὸ τότε ἤρξατο ὁ Ἰησοῦς (From then Jesus began) of 4:17 and 16:21, with the upshot that the Gospel falls into three large parts: 1:1–4:16; 4:17–16:20; and 16:21–28:20.[2] The other camp, with B. W. Bacon as its progenitor, regards as determinative the five-fold καὶ ἐγένετο ὅτε ἐτέλεσεν ὁ Ἰησοῦς (and it happened when Jesus had finished) in 7:28–29; 11:1; 13:53; 19:1; and 26:1. This set phrase, as we shall see, highlights the recurrent alternation between narrative and discourse.[3]

1. For helpful if dated surveys of the subject see David R. Bauer, *The Structure of Matthew's Gospel: A Study in Literary Design* (JSNTSS 31; Sheffield: Almond, 1988), pp. 21–55, and Marianne Meye Thompson, "The Structure of Matthew: An Examination of Two Approaches," in *Studia Biblica et Theologica* 12 (1982), pp. 195–238.

2. So David E. Garland, *The Intention of Matthew 23* (NovTSup 52; Leiden: Brill, 1979), pp. 13, 177–78; Edgar Krentz, "The Extent of Matthew's Prologue," *JBL* 83 (1964), pp. 401–14; Jack Dean Kingsbury, *Matthew: Structure, Christology, Kingdom* (Philadelphia: Fortress, 1975), pp. 7–25; and Russell Pregeant, *Matthew* (Chalice Commentaries for Today; St. Louis: Chalice, 2004), pp. 9–11. Cf. Ernst Lohmeyer, *Das Evangelium nach Matthäus* (ed. Werner Schmauch; KEK; Göttingen: Vandenhoeck & Ruprecht, 1956), pp. 1, 64, 264, and T. B. Slater, "Notes on Matthew's Structure," *JBL* 99 (1980), p. 436.

3. B. W. Bacon, *Studies in Matthew* (New York: Henry Holt, 1930). For a useful discussion of the issues see Kari Syreeni, *The Making of the Sermon on the Mount: A Procedural Analysis*

My sympathies lie with Bacon and his descendants. Matthew 4:17 and 16:21 just cannot, despite recurrent attempts to show otherwise, bear the literary weight that some exegetes have placed upon them. The chief defects of the tripartite scheme are these:

- ἀπὸ τότε (from then) recurs in 26:16 while ἤρξατο (began) is used of Jesus in 11:7 and 20 (the last with τότε, "then"). So the phraseology of 4:17 and 16:21, because not unique, fails to call attention to itself. Matters are otherwise with καὶ ἐγένετο ὅτε ἐτέλεσεν ὁ Ἰησοῦς. The entire phrase, as well as its components, καὶ ἐγένετο ὅτε (and it happened when) and ἐτέλεσεν (he finished), are reserved for the five-fold formula in 7:28; 11:1; 13:53; 19:1; and 26:1.
- One hesitates to see 4:17 as marking a major structural break because it is so firmly wedded to 4:12–16.[4]
- For a similar reason, one also hesitates to discern a major structural rift at 16:21. In the words of R. T. France, "A division of the gospel which does not allow these sections [16:13–20 and 21–23] to be read in direct sequence is surely not going to do justice to Matthew's dramatic purpose. In other words, while 16:21 marks the beginning of a new emphasis in Jesus' ministry, it does not mark the end even of the episode which immediately precedes it, let alone the end of a whole major section of the gospel."[5]
- Should we not expect more from a structural analysis than what amounts to the proposition that Matthew, like most books and stories, has a beginning, a middle, and an end?

It is, however, not my purpose herein to argue any further against the conclusions of others. I wish rather to introduce and defend a position of my own.

---

of *Matthew's Redactoral Activity* (Annales Academiae Scientiarum Fennicae, Dissertationes humanarum litterarum 44; Helsinki: Suomalainen Tiedeakatemia, 1987), pp. 75–87, and for additional scholars in general agreement with Bacon's division of Matthew see Kingsbury, *Matthew*, p. 3, n. 13. Bacon himself argued that a Greek fragment, which Rendell Harris dated to the second century, referred to Matthew in this manner: "Matthew curbs the audacity of the Jews, checking them in five books as it were with bridles." See Morton S. Enslin, "The Five Books of Matthew: Bacon on the Gospel of Matthew," *HTR* 24 (1931), pp. 67–69.

4. See esp. Frans Neirynck, "ΑΠΟ ΤΟΤΕ ΗΡΞΑΤΟ and the Structure of Matthew," *ETL* 64 (1988), pp. 21–59; reprinted in *Evangelica II, 1982–1991: Collected Essays* (BETL 99; Leuven: Leuven University Press/Peeters, 1991), pp. 141–82.

5. R. T. France, *Matthew: Evangelist and Teacher* (Grand Rapids: Zondervan, 1989), p. 152. See further Neirynck, "Structure."

Narrative and Discourse in Matthew

The First Gospel exhibits a striking alternation between narrative and discourse:

1–4	Narrative
5–7	Discourse
8–9	Narrative
10	Discourse
11–12	Narrative
13	Discourse
14–17	Narrative
18	Discourse
19–23	Narrative
24–25	Discourse
26–28	Narrative

That this regular alternation, which reminds one of the repeated oscillations of speech and narrative in Exodus, Leviticus, Numbers, and Deuteronomy, is an important part of Matthew's architecture is all but proven by the consistent repetition of the stereotyped formula after the five discourses:

καὶ ἐγένετο ὅτε ἐτέλεσεν ὁ Ἰησοῦς . . .
(and it happened when Jesus had finished)

7:28   . . . τοὺς λόγους τούτους
          (these words)

11:1   . . . διατάσσων τοῖς δώδεκα μαθηταῖς αὐτοῦ
          (teaching his twelve disciples)

13:53   . . . τὰς παραβολὰς ταύτας
          (these parables)

19:1   . . . τοὺς λόγους τούτους
          (these words)

26:1   . . . τοὺς λόγους τούτους
          (these words)

For Bacon, the five-fold formula was evidence that Matthew consists of five "books" that are structurally homologous to the Pentateuch. On his view, each discourse (D) belongs with a narrative (N). His first "book," for instance, consists of 3:1–4:25 (N) + 5:1–7:27 (D) whereas his fifth "book" covers 19:2–22:46 (N) + 23:1–25:46 (D). Now I need not review once again the formidable difficulties in the way of Bacon's scheme; they are well known.[6] The important point is instead another: even when rejecting the details of Bacon's outline, many have both continued to bind each discourse to a narrative and attempted to discern some common theme in the resultant union.[7] Yet once one abandons the vain attempt to construct a Matthean Pentateuch, what is the rationale for such procedure? What happens when instead one simply evaluates each narrative section and each discourse on its own terms, as a large thought unit?[8] The results, in my judgment, allow both the structure and plot of the First Gospel to emerge clearly.

Chapters 1–4 open with the title (1:1)[9] and a historical preface (1:2–17, the tripartite genealogy). Three infancy stories (1:18–25; 2:1–12; 2:13–23) follow, after which we have the section on John the Baptist (3:1–6, 7–12, 13–17) and three additional pericopae that directly prepare for the ministry (4:1–11, 12–17, 18–22). All of this material constitutes an extended introduction. It is, so to speak, all background. We learn *who* Jesus is (1:1, 2–17, 18; 2:1, 4; 3:11, 17; 4:3, 6), *where* he is from (2:6), *how* he enters the world (1:18–25), *why* he enters the world (1:21; 2:6), *when* he comes into the world (1:17; 2:1), and *what* he proclaims in public (4:17). So the scene is set for the rest of the story.[10]

The Sermon on the Mount, the first major discourse, commences with a little narrative introduction (4:23–5:2) and closes with a little narrative conclusion (7:28–8:1). The discourse proper, 5:3–7:27, is also symmetrical. Blessings open it (5:3–12); warnings close it (7:13–14, 15–23, 24–27). In between are three major sections, each one primarily a compilation of imperatives. The topics are Jesus and the law (5:17–48), Jesus and the cult

6. See esp. W. D. Davies, *The Setting of the Sermon on the Mount* (Cambridge: Cambridge University Press, 1963), pp. 14–25.

7. See, e.g., Craig L. Blomberg, *The New American Commentary*, vol. 22, *Matthew* (Nashville, Tenn.: Broadman, 1992), pp. 22–25; David Hill, *The Gospel of Matthew* (New Century Bible; London: Oliphants, 1972), pp. 44–48; Christopher R. Smith, "Literary Evidences of a Fivefold Structure in the Gospel of Matthew," *NTS* 43 (1997), pp. 540–51. Contrast Charles H. Lohr, "Oral Techniques in the Gospel of Matthew," *CBQ* 23 (1961), p. 427; but Lohr goes astray in suggesting a chiastic arrangement of the whole.

8. Cf. the outline of J. C. Fenton, *Saint Matthew* (Pelican Gospel Commentaries; Harmondsworth: Penguin, 1963), pp. 14–15.

9. On 1:1 see chapter 8 below.

10. Whereas Kingsbury urges that 1:1–4:16 is the Gospel's prologue, I would, in agreement with D. W. Gooding, "Structure littéraire de Matthieu, XIII, 53 à XVIII, 35," *RB* 85 (1978), pp. 47–59; Wilhelm Wilkens, "Die Komposition des Matthäusevangeliums," *NTS* 31 (1985), pp. 24–38; and Ulrich Luz, *Das Evangelium nach Matthäus* (4 vols.; EKK 1/1–4; Düsseldorf: Benziger, 1990–2002), 1:120–21, include 4:17–22. For while 4:17 does give us the content of Jesus' public proclamation, 4:18–22 is still more prolegomena: before the teacher teaches, he needs pupils. Cf. Richard A. Edwards, *Matthew's Story of Jesus* (Philadelphia: Fortress, 1985), p. 11: 1:1–4:22 establishes "the framework of the story."

(6:1–18), and Jesus and social issues (6:19–7:12).[11] The sermon accordingly contains the Messiah's demand for the people of God, which in context means the people of Israel.

If the Sermon on the Mount confronts us with words, Matt. 8 and 9 recount deeds. The chapters offer a snapshot of Jesus' activities within Israel, particularly his compassionate miracles. He does, to be sure, speak in this part of the gospel, but the emphasis undeniably falls upon his beneficent acts in and for the descendants of Abraham (cf. 8:16–17).

Having learned of Jesus' teaching (Matt. 5–7) and of Jesus' activities (Matt. 8–9), readers next come, in chapter 10, to Jesus' instructions for his disciples, to his hortatory descriptions of what they, as extensions of himself, must say and do. The theme of imitation is prominent. The disciples are to proclaim what Jesus proclaims (compare 10:7 with 4:17) and to do what Jesus does (compare 10:8 with chapters 8–9 and 11:2–6). The disciple is like the teacher, the servant like the master (10:24–25). Jesus is the first Christian missionary, and the disciples, in their capacity as missionaries, must enter into his work.

The chapters on the words and deeds of Jesus (Matt. 5–9) and the words and deeds of the disciples (Matt. 10) lead up to Matt. 11–12. These two chapters record primarily the response of "this generation" to John the Baptist and Jesus, to God's eschatological messenger(s), especially its reaction to τὰ ἔργα τοῦ Χριστοῦ, "the deeds of the Messiah" (11:2). This is what the material on the Baptist (11:2–6, 7–15, 16–19) is all about as well as the woes on Galilee (11:20–24) and the conflict stories in chapter 12 (1–8, 9–14, 22–37, 38–45). It all adds up to an indictment of corporate Israel: many of the people, under the sway of its hard-hearted leaders, have rejected the Messiah.[12]

Given that the eschatological expectations of Judaism envisage, and indeed have their *raison d'être* in, the salvation of God's people, the rejection recorded in chapters 11–12 poses the same grave problem as that Rom. 9–11 addresses: How can so many in Israel reject the Messiah? How can his own receive him not? Chapter 13 is the beginning of an answer. It supplies a sort of minitheodicy—not a solution to the problem of evil in general but a solution to the rejection of Jesus in particular. The chapter teaches that there can be different responses to one and the same message (13:1–23), that the devil works in human hearts (13:24–30), and that all will be well in the end (13:31–33, 36–43, 47–50). The chapter as a whole,

---

11. See chapter 10, "The Configuration of the Sermon on the Mount and Its Meaning."

12. Cf. the rubric of Robert H. Gundry, *Matthew: A Commentary on His Handbook for a Mixed Church under Persecution* (2nd ed.; Grand Rapids: Eerdmans, 1994), p. vii: "The Opposition and Persecution Incurred by Jesus and His Disciples (11:2–12:50)." On the unity of Matthew 11–12 see further Donald Verseput, *The Rejection of the Humble Messianic King* (European University Studies, Series XXIII, Theology; Frankfurt am Main: Peter Lang, 1986).

read in its larger context, grapples with the Messiah's unexpected reception, or rather lack thereof.

What follows the collection of parables? The fourth major narrative section begins in chapter 14 and ends in chapter 17. It is much less easy to outline or to summarize. But granted the truth of Markan priority and the existence of Q, Matthew, by the time he comes to 14:1, has used up most of Q, and what remains he wishes for the most to save for the discourses in 18 and 24–25. So, beginning with 14:1, it is not so easy to be creative. This is why there is a change in the compositional procedure, why Matthew, in the subsequent narrative sections, follows Mark with less deviation.

Yet all this does not eliminate a thematic approach to 14–17. The most memorable pericope is undoubtedly 16:13–20, where Jesus founds his church. The fact fits so well the larger literary context because after so many within corporate Israel have, at least for the time being, forfeited their expected role in salvation-history, an alternative institution is needed. So Jesus establishes his church. That the ecclesia is indeed the most important subject of the section appears not only from the ever-increasing focus upon the disciples as opposed to the crowds but also from Peter's being the rock upon which the church is built, because it is precisely in this section that Peter comes to the fore. Among the insertions into the Markan material are these four passages:

14:28–33	Peter walks on the water
15:15	Peter asks a question
16:13–20	Jesus blesses Peter
17:24–27	Peter asks a question and answers a question

Peter's emerging preeminence correlates with the emergence of the church.

Matthew 18, the next major discourse, confirms this. The chapter addresses issues specific to the ecclesia, to the Christian community. How often should one forgive a brother (18:21–22)? What is the procedure for excommunicating someone (18:15–20)? These and other ecclesiastical questions merit attention precisely at this point because Jesus has just established his church.

Having founded the new community and given it teaching, it remains for Jesus to go to Jerusalem. This then is the subject of the next narrative section, Matt. 19–23. The material is mostly from Mark, with the woes of 23 added.[13]

Before the passion narrative proper, however, Jesus, in chapters 24–25, speaks of the future, that is, the future of Israel and of the church. Here readers move past Matt. 26–28 into the time beyond the narrative. That the

---

13. Against the proposal, occasionally made, that 23 is a sixth major discourse see Keegan, "Introductory Formula."

discourse, which foretells judgment upon Israel and salvation through difficulty for the church, comes last makes perfect sense. Eschatology naturally belongs at the end. This is why each of Matthew's major discourses winds down with teaching on eschatology,[14] why Revelation concludes the New Testament, why the little apocalypse in *m. Sotah* 9:15 is the last chapter in its tractate, and why the final section of traditional systematic theologies concerns the last things.

Finally, and following chronological order, Matthew brings his book to a close as does Mark (and Luke and John for that matter). The passion and resurrection constitute the conclusion, to which everything before leads.[15]

The analysis just offered possesses, I should like to suggest, at least three virtues. First, it is not supposititious or so much writing upon the waters but instead falls out naturally from the alternation of narrative and discourse. Secondly, it has explanatory power, for it reveals why just about everything is exactly where it is. Why is the story of the plucking of the grain (12:1–8 = Mark 2:23–28) in the third major narrative section and not, let us say, somewhere in the second, in chapter 8 or 9? Because the controversy story belongs best in Matt. 11–12, where the issue is Israel's rejection of Jesus. Why does the missionary discourse (10:5–42; cf. Mark 6:7–13) come before the parable discourse (13:1–52; cf. Mark 4:1–34) and not, as in Mark, follow it? Because overture and rejection must precede explanation of failure. Why does the discourse in Matt. 18 trail the narrative section in chapters 14–17 and not that in chapters 8–9 or that in chapters 11–12? Because the special instruction to the church naturally follows closely the narrative section in which the church is founded.

Thirdly, the proposed outline also gives us the plot, by which I mean, in the words of Aristotle, "the arrangement of the incidents" (*Poet.* 6.6 [1450a]). If the primary structure of the Gospel is narrative // discourse // narrative // discourse, etc., the plot falls out from the major theme of each narrative section and each discourse. Pictorially, and in minimum compass:

1–4	Narrative	Introduction: main character introduced
5–7	Discourse	Jesus' demands upon Israel
8–9	Narrative	Jesus' deeds within and for Israel
10	Discourse	Ministry through others' words and deeds
11–12	Narrative	Israel's negative response
13	Discourse	Explanation of Israel's negative response
14–17	Narrative	Founding of the church
18	Discourse	Teaching for the church

14. 7:24–27; 10:41–42; 13:47–50; 18:23–35; 24:1–25:46.
15. See further chapter 11 below.

19–23	Narrative		Commencement of the passion
24–25		Discourse	The future: judgment and salvation
26–28	Narrative		Conclusion: passion and resurrection

I submit that this outline is much more helpful and informative than that which divides Matthew into three main parts.[16]

Matthew as Biography

Matthew, as we have seen, records Jesus' origins and infancy, his words and deeds, his death and resurrection, and it records these things in roughly chronological order: the birth comes before the ministry, the ministry before the death, and the death before the resurrection. For this reason, many readers of Matthew, prior to the twentieth century, and despite the book's many gaps and relative brevity, often spoke of it as a biography, a life of Jesus. Most twentieth-century scholars, however, came to reject this view on the ground that the canonical gospels are not biographical retrospectives but rather expressions and extensions of the earliest Christian proclamation.[17] Yet recently there has been another change in the minds of at least some scholars, a reversion to the older view, to the idea that the Gospels are biographies, *if* the term is used not in its modern sense but in accord with ancient usage.[18] The canonical gospels then qualify as a subtype of Graeco-Roman biography.[19]

16. I also find it more helpful than the outline suggested, on the basis of the isolation of major events, by Frank J. Matera, "The Plot of Matthew's Gospel," in *CBQ* 49 (1987), pp. 233–53. For criticism of Matera and yet another proposal for Matthew's structure see Warren Carter, "Kernels and Narrative Blocks: The Structure of Matthew's Gospel," *CBQ* 54 (1992), pp. 463–81.

17. For reviews of the discussion see Richard A. Burridge, *What Are the Gospels? A Comparison with Greco-Roman Biography* (2nd ed.; Grand Rapids: Eerdmans, 2004) (his outline of Matthew, on p. 191, is close to my own); Detlev Dormeyer, *Evangelium als literarische und theologische Gattung* (Erträge der Forschung 263; Darmstadt: Wissenschaftliche Buchgesellschaft, 1989); Detlev Dormeyer and Hubert Frankemölle, "Evangelium als literarische Gattung und als theologischer Begriff: Tendenzen und Aufgaben der Evangelienforschung im 20. Jahrhundert, mit einer Untersuchung des Markusevangeliums in seinem Verhältnis zur antiken Biographie," *ANRW* (1984), 2.25.2: 1543–1694; Hubert Frankemölle, *Evangelium, Begriff und Gattung: Ein Forschungsbericht* (2nd ed.; SBB 15; Stuttgart: Katholisches Bibelwerk, 1994); Dirk Frickenschmidt, *Evangelium als Biographie: Die vier Evangelien im Rahmen antiker Erzählkunst* (Tübingen: A. Francke, 1997); and Robert Guelich, "The Gospel Genre," in *The Gospel and the Gospels* (ed. Peter Stuhlmacher; Grand Rapids: Eerdmans, 1991), pp. 173–208.

18. For overviews of antique biography see Patricia Cox, *Biography in Late Antiquity: The Quest for the Holy Man* (Berkeley: University of California Press, 1983), and David E. Aune, "Greco-Roman Biography," in *Greco-Roman Literature and the New Testament: Selected Forms and Genres* (ed. David E. Aune; Atlanta: Scholars Press, 1988), pp. 107–26.

19. See, e.g., David E. Aune, *The New Testament in Its Literary Environment* (Philadelphia: Westminster, 1987), pp. 29–42; Burridge, *What Are the Gospels?*; Frickenschmidt, *Evangelium;*

What does one make of this recent revival of an older view? I once urged that Matthew is an omnibus of genres: apocalypse, community rule, catechism, cult aetiology, etc.[20] My contention was that Matthew, like the book of Job,[21] the Qumran Pesharim,[22] Philostratus's *Vita Apollonii*,[23] and, for a more recent analogy, Coleridge's *Biographia Literaria*, is several things at once. That is, it mixes genres. I am no longer sure that this is the correct view. Significant resemblances obtain between the First Gospel and certain Hellenistic biographies, and these may well suffice to determine classification. I am currently inclined, because of the work of Richard Burridge, to think not just that Matthew contains biographical features but that it is in fact an instance of Greco-Roman biography.[24]

Whether or not my change of opinion is justified, and however one finally formulates an answer to the question of Matthew's genre, the undisputed fact is that Matthew, despite its incompleteness as a biography in the modern sense, is the partial record of an individual's life and so biographical. This immediately raises a question. Early Christians desirous of communicating their religious convictions knew many types of literature—the sayings collection (Q, *Thomas*), the epistle (Romans, *1 Clement*), the apocalypse (Revelation, *4 Ezra*), and the community rule (1QS, the *Didache*), to name the more obvious. Matthew is none of these but rather something that looks much more biographical. Why?

Martin Hengel, *Acts and the History of Earliest Christianity* (Philadelphia: Fortress, 1980), pp. 3–34; Philip Shuler, *A Genre for the Gospels: The Biographical Character of Matthew* (Philadelphia: Fortress, 1982); Graham N. Stanton, *A Gospel for a New People: Studies in Matthew* (Louisville: Westminster/John Knox, 1993), pp. 59–71; idem, "Matthew: ΒΙΒΛΟΣ, ΕΥΑΓΓΕΛΙΟΝ, or ΒΙΟΣ?," in *The Four Gospels 1992: Festschrift Frans Neirynck* (ed. F. van Segbroeck, C. M. Tuckett, G. van Belle, and J. Verheyden; 3 vols.; BETL 100; Leuven: Leuven University Press, 1992), 2:1187–1201; Charles H. Talbert, *What Is a Gospel? The Genre of the Canonical Gospels* (Philadelphia: Fortress, 1977); idem, "Once Again: Gospel Genre," *Semeia* 43 (1988), pp. 53–73.

20. W. D. Davies and Dale C. Allison Jr., *A Critical and Exegetical Commentary on the Gospel according to St. Matthew* (3 vols.; ICC; Edinburgh: T&T Clark, 1988, 1991, 1997), 1:2–3. I was then in agreement with Robert A. Guelich, *Mark 1–8:26* (WBC 34A; Waco: Word, 1989), p. xx: "'Biographical' . . . does not necessarily imply that they [Matthew, Luke, John] belong to the literary genre biography, since biographical accounts can come in various genres, for example, in comedic or tragic dramas." I now prefer to think that Burridge, *What Are the Gospels?* p. 240, is right: each genre develops out of others and so shares features of several.

21. Cf. Roland E. Murphy, *Wisdom Literature: Job, Proverbs, Ruth, Lamentations, Ecclesiastes, and Esther* (Grand Rapids: Eerdmans, 1981), pp. 16–20.

22. See Maurya P. Horgan, *Pesharim: Qumran Interpretations of Biblical Books* (CBQMS 8; Washington, D.C.: Catholic Biblical Association of America, 1979), pp. 249–59.

23. Cf. Gerd Petzke, *Die Traditionen über Apollonius von Tyana und das Neue Testament* (SCHNT; Leiden: Brill, 1970), p. 60.

24. Burridge, *What Are the Gospels?* Cf. Craig S. Keener, *Commentary on the Gospel of Matthew* (Grand Rapids/Cambridge, U.K.: Eerdmans, 1999), pp. 16–24. Contrast Luz, *Matthäus*, 1:41–42.

It will not do to answer that our author just follows Mark. That begs the question, for is it not Matthew's choice of genre, determined by his goals for writing, that makes him imitate Mark, not vice versa? It is also inadequate to advert to the prevalence of biographies in the Graeco-Roman world, for while we now know that, by the first century, all of Judaism had been to some extent Hellenized, so that it is not surprising that a cultured Jew such as Matthew could write in Greek and adopt a Hellenistic genre, Graeco-Roman literature included many different types of writing, so the question remains, Why does Matthew write the sort of book that he does?

While fully recognizing that the Gospel has no word on the subject, so that of its author's express purpose we cannot speak, surely the specific content of Matthew's Christian faith partly explains why the First Gospel is a story about Jesus. The distinctiveness of Matthew's thinking over against that of his non-Christian Jewish contemporaries is the acceptance of Jesus as the center of his religion: it is around him as a person that his theological thinking revolves. The fact is crucial. For Matthew, revelation belongs supremely to a life. The significance of this appears when Matthew's comparatively brief Gospel is set over against the massive and highly complex literature of rabbinic Judaism in both its halakhic and haggadic forms.[25] The rabbinic sources narrate stories about rabbis but no sustained lives such as we find in the Gospel of Matthew; they issue report upon report of what Rabbi X or Rabbi Y purportedly said, but no biographies. Indeed, particular sages are only very seldom an organizing category or principle in rabbinic literature.[26] All this is simply to state the obvious, that whereas rabbinic Judaism, with its subordination of the individual to the community and its focus upon a particular book, the Torah, instead of a particular human being, produced no religious biographies,[27] the substance of Matthew's faith is neither a dogmatic system nor a legal code but a human being whose life is, in outline and in detail, uniquely significant and therefore demanding of record.[28]

No less instructive than the contrast between Matthew and the rabbinic sources is the difference between Matthew and the Dead Sea Scrolls. The importance of the so-called Teacher of Righteousness for the community that produced those scrolls is manifest. It is, however, quite difficult to say very much regarding him. Despite his far-flung significance, the sect

25. Cf. Burridge, *What Are the Gospels?* pp. 300–303.

26. Jacob Neusner, *Why No Gospels in Talmudic Judaism?* (Brown Judaic Studies 135; Atlanta: Scholars Press, 1988), shows that "the raw materials for gospels" were to hand, yet these never evolved into biographies.

27. Helpful here is Robert L. Cohn, "Sainthood on the Periphery: The Case of Judaism," in *Sainthood: Its Manifestations in World Religions* (ed. Richard Kieckhefer and George D. Bond; Berkeley, University of California Press, 1988), pp. 43–68.

28. Cf. Burridge, *What Are the Gospels?* pp. 248–50.

did not, from what we can gather, pass on many traditions about him. The reason is obvious. Although 1QpHab. 8:2–3 speaks of fidelity to the Teacher of Righteousness, that teacher just was not the center of the Essene's religion, and so his life never found its biographer. The contrast with Matthew speaks worlds. Do we not have here, if I may so put it, with only a bit of exaggeration, the difference between a theocentric faith and a christocentric faith?

Matthew inherits the words of Jesus and seeks to do justice to them. In this sense his Jesus is recognizably rabbinic: our Gospel presents the sayings of Jesus as the rabbinic texts present those of the sages. Unlike the rabbinic sources, however, Matthew combines his sources to produce a book which records not only what Jesus said but what he did. This combination of words and deeds distinguishes Matthew not only from the rabbinic corpus but also from Q and the *Gospel of Thomas*, both of which have little to say about Jesus' deeds.[29]

In Matthew's procedure one may detect several factors, the first being the Hellenistic tradition, which so stressed the need for teachers to live as they taught. Socrates was of course here the great model: his speech was as his life. But in Philo the motif is transferred to Moses.[30] And Matthew gives the palm to Jesus, who exhibits congruity between word and deed.[31] He is Torah incarnate, animate law.[32]

Another factor to which we should pay due regard is Matthew's Christocentrism, which locates revelation and salvation in a person and that person's history. The fivefold alternation of narrative and discourse, which holds together aspects of the life of Jesus that others in the early church did not so conjoin, reflects the strong conviction that there should be no isolation of word and deed because what matters is their common source, namely, Messiah Jesus. In line with this, Matthew opens his Gospel with two chapters in which Jesus neither says nor does anything at all, chapters

---

29. Maybe caution is in order. Were the compilers of Q and the *Gospel of Thomas* uninterested in what Jesus did? Or were the deeds of Jesus reported and passed down alongside Q or the *Gospel of Thomas*? To draw an analogy: one might judge, from *The Discourse of Epictetus* and the *Enchiridion*, that Arrian was interested only in Epictetus's teaching; but according to Simplicius (6th cent. CE) Arrian also wrote Epictetus's biography.

30. Philo, *Mos.* 1.29: Moses "exemplified his philosophical creed by his daily actions. His words expressed his feelings, and his actions accorded with his words, so that speech and life were in harmony, and thus through their mutual agreement were found to make melody together as on a musical instrument."

31. See further below, pp. 149–51.

32. For the concept of the king as living, incarnate law, as νόμος ἔμψυχος, see E. R. Goodenough, "The Political Philosophy of Hellenistic Kingship," in *Yale Classical Studies*, vol. 1 (ed. A. H. Harman; New Haven: Yale University Press, 1928), pp. 55–102, and for its relevance to Matthew's Jesus, Dale C. Allison Jr., *The New Moses: A Matthean Typology* (Minneapolis, Minn.: Fortress, 1993), pp. 228–30.

in which things just happen to the Messiah. Does this not betoken a fundamental interest in the person of Jesus himself?[33]

Matthew does not, however, write a story about Jesus simply because such is congruent with his christocentric theology or a Hellenistic *topos*. There are additional contributing factors. Recall, for instance, the fact, so obvious we are liable to miss it, that Jewish tradition before and after Matthew's day strongly tended to associate traditional words with specific individuals. One can of course find exceptions, the rabbinic "our rabbis taught" being a prominent example. Still, by and large the generalization holds. The pentateuchal laws are, against the facts, put on the lips of Moses. It is even more striking that Proverbs groups its wisdom sayings, whose authority could scarcely be more independent of their authorship, according to sages: "The proverbs of Solomon, son of David, king of Israel," 1:1; "The words of Agur son of Jakeh," 30:1; "The words of Lemuel," 31:1. One also thinks of the pseudepigrapha, such as *1 Enoch* and *4 Ezra*, which bring together sundry materials from divers proveniences and place them under the name of a biblical worthy, and of the canonical prophets: the prophetic oracles in the Hebrew Bible come to us not as anonymous declarations but attached to the names of prophets.

Particularly instructive in this connection is the book of Jeremiah. This complex writing gathers together prophetic words—not all of them, we may be sure, from Jeremiah—under one prophet's name. Significantly, nearly two-fifths of it are biographical (19:1–20:6; 26:1–29:32; 32:1–45:5). Part of the reason is that many of Jeremiah's oracles are highly personal and closely tied to the prophet's own historical context, for which cause acquaintance with their author and his situation illuminates their interpretation. Message and messenger are inextricably bound together. Full understanding of Jeremiah's words requires familiarity with Jeremiah's story, as Baruch, or whoever added the biographical narratives to the oracles, perceived. We accordingly have both.

The situation in Matthew is similar. Many of the sayings assigned to Jesus would be liable to grave misunderstanding or lack sense nearly altogether if they were isolated from his story. Imagine what might be the meaning, without any context, of "Let the dead bury their own dead" (8:22), or of "Go nowhere among the Gentiles" (10:5), or of "Take no gold, or silver,

---

33. A caveat: W. Eichrodt, *Theology of the Old Testament* (OTL 1; Philadelphia: Westminster, 1961), p. 228, wrote: "From the very beginnings of Israel's religion it is easier for the observer to detect the main outlines of the divine activity than those of the divine being. The latter . . . remain essentially outlines, and never undergo any more speculative or metaphysical development; but the description of the divine activity is couched in precise and concrete terms." Something very similar may be said of Matthew and Jesus. The First Gospel confronts us with the "externals" of Jesus but not his inner thoughts. The latter is a subject neither of psychological speculation nor of metaphysical development. In some matters, silence reigns.

or copper in your belts" (10:9), or of "You will not have gone through all the towns of Israel before the Son of Man comes" (10:23), or of "The blind receive their sight, the lame walk, the lepers are cleansed, the deaf hear, the dead are raised, and the poor have good news brought to them" (11:5). These sayings do not work as proverbs or general maxims. Devoid of some setting, such utterances become either meaningless or misleading. Put otherwise, much of Jesus' speech demands a narrative. The former cannot survive without the latter. As with the book of Jeremiah, content demands context.[34] Speech requires biography.

Social Crisis and Ethical Imitation

There is yet another pertinent issue in our quest for the sources of Matthew's biographical impulse. The more history one learns, the less it seems that any period, of however short or long a duration, has been free of crisis: all times are out of joint. Historical stability appears to be a fiction, for something new is always confronting the status quo, and people are always anxious about what the future holds. Nonetheless, the idea of a historical crisis is not without substance, this because some periods are indeed more racked by strife and anxiety than others. And such was the first century, at least in the cradle of Christianity, Palestine. That epoch saw Jews fight Rome and lose their temple; it witnessed the birth of the Zealots and the death of the Essenes; and it produced several lengthy apocalypses, a sure sign of profound dissatisfaction.

What does all this have to do with Matthew? Perhaps a great deal, for periods of social crisis have, historically, stimulated the production of biographies.[35] The circumstance makes sense. Social crises by definition involve conflicting claims to power, and such claims typically issue in vying appeals to the past: who is the authentic heir of our tradition? In accord with this, disputes between rival philosophical schools swelled the number of Hellenistic biographies. Who were the true followers of Plato? Was Pythagoras superior to Socrates? Was Apollonius a fraud or a great philosopher? Biography—Xenophon's *Memorabilia*, Porphyry's *Life of Pythagoras*, Philostratus's *Life of* Apollonius—answered these and other questions.

Whenever social crisis results in fragmentation, so that the questioning of previous beliefs issues in the formation of a new social unit, new norms and authorities are inevitably generated. This matters for our purposes because

---

34. One reason I regard the *Gospel of Thomas* as, in general, an inferior witness to the historical Jesus is that the tendency to universalize the application of sayings is more advanced in this document.

35. Jan Romein, *Die Biographie: Einführung in ihre Geschichte und ihre Problematik* (Bern: A. Francke, 1948), pp. 60–62, 64–67.

such norms and authorities are always most persuasively presented when embodied in examples: new fashions must first be modeled. Certainly this happened with the fifteenth-century advent of the so-called "new devotion" (*devotio moderna*). That movement, with its intense individualism, gave birth to numerous lives, including, for example, the biographical works of Thomas à Kempis. The same thing also happened at the Reformation. The break with Roman Catholicism brought many into a new world, with new standards of belief and behavior. In response, new lives appeared, lives exhibiting those new beliefs and types of behavior. The Reformation replaced the traditional catalogue of Catholic saints with its own constellation of Protestant heroes. Popular biography, especially martyrology, flourished.[36]

Something similar happened among many early Christians. The first believers, whether Jew or Gentile, had made a change of allegiance. They had come to new beliefs and new ways of behaving. They accordingly needed new models. And Jesus himself, through the promulgation of the tradition about him, became the new model par excellence. Many have insufficiently appreciated this fact,[37] in part because there has been, since Luther, a reaction against an unimaginative and literalistic *imitatio Christi* (such as that Francis of Assisi exhibited), in part because so many theologians have condemned the notion of the *mimesis* of the canonical Jesus as a purely human effort which, in the event, cannot be achieved,[38] and also in part because of anxiety to preserve Jesus' unique status as a savior whose accomplishments cannot be emulated: the Christian gospel is not moral imitation of a human hero or fine example (true enough). It is symptomatic that Albrecht Dihle could make the antithetical generalization, which I consider unjustified, that whereas in the Gospels "a human life appears as an incomparable and unrepeatable piece of history . . . in Greek biography, in contrast, a human life appears as individual realization of possibilities which an immutable nature holds in readiness for all times."[39] It is also

---

36. Jean Crespin published his *Book of Martyrs* in 1554, John Foxe his *Acts and Monuments of Matters Happening in the Church* (= *Foxe's Book of Martyrs*) in 1563. The Renaissance, with its revival of Plutarch and other ancient biographers, also of course played a very important part in the popularity of biography in the fifteenth and sixteenth centuries; but then the revival of biography during the Renaissance was itself brought on by a great crisis; cf. Romein, *Biographie*, p. 28.

37. Note, however, Clyde Weber Votaw, *The Gospels and Contemporary Biographies in the Greco-Roman World* (FBBS 21; Philadelphia: Fortress, 1970); also Aune, *Literary Environment*, p. 62, who remarks that Matthew and Luke "do not explicitly emphasize the *imitation* of Jesus," the reason being that "this use of the past was implicitly understood."

38. But this objection misses Matthew, where Jesus is an ever-abiding, helpful presence, so that the believer is never alone, and the problem of a purely human effort does not arise; cf. 18:20; 28:20.

39. Albrecht Dihle, "The Gospels and Greek Biography," in Stuhlmacher, *Gospel and the Gospels*, p. 383.

symptomatic that Charles Talbert, in his discussion of ancient biography, discerned a Type A, which he defined as a life that "function[s] simply to provide the readers a pattern to copy,"[40] and that he did not so classify any of the canonical gospels,[41] or even remark that they might function *in part* to supply such a pattern.

But Matthew, which betrays no trace of Docetism, predates Nicea and reflects a time when it was still possible to think of Jesus as a real human being and therefore as a real ethical model.[42] And our evangelist, like Paul,[43] Origen,[44] and other early Christians,[45] makes Jesus a model for emulation.[46] This is why, despite the regrettable silence of many commentators, our gospel hosts a multitude of obvious connections between Jesus' words and his deeds.[47] If Jesus indirectly exhorts others to be meek ("Blessed are the

---

40. Talbert, *Gospel*, p. 94.

41. Contrast Shuler, *Genre*, who recognizes that Matthew, like the authors of encomia, encourages readers to emulate its hero.

42. "The very existence of the gospels served as a determent to the writing of lives of other holy persons. In them was to be found the noblest example of all. At this early stage of Christian history, it would have been presumptuous to bring other persons into competition with the primal model. Only after Nicea did the need arise for other exemplars. It should be remembered that the most potent arrows in the quiver of the Arians were those passages in the gospels that spoke of Jesus' human features, his limited knowledge, his obedience to God, his growth in wisdom (improvability), his suffering. Once it was declared that the Logos was 'of one substance with the Father' (defended chiefly by appeal to the Gospel of John), a vacuum was created that could be filled with other human faces." So Robert L. Wilken, "The Lives of the Saints and the Pursuit of Virtue," in *Remembering the Christian Past* (Grand Rapids: Eerdmans, 1995), pp. 121–44, at p. 127.

43. If not in Phil. 2:5–11, then at least in Rom. 15:1–7; see Michael B. Thompson, *Clothed with Christ: The Example and Teaching of Jesus in Romans 12.1–15.13* (JSNTSS 59; Sheffield: JSOT, 1991).

44. *Prin.* 4.4.4 (TzF 24, ed. Görgemanns and Karpp, pp. 796–98): "Christ is set forth as an example to all believers. As he ever chose the good, even before he knew the evil at all and loved righteousness and hated iniquity . . . so, too, should each one of us, after a fall or an error, purify himself from stains by the example set before him, and taking a leader for the journey proceed along the steep path of virtue, so that by this means we may as far as is possible become, through our imitation of him, partakers of the divine nature, as it is written, 'Whoever says that he believes in Christ should also walk even as he walked.'" Cf. *Exh. mart.* 41–42 (GCS, ed. Koetschau, pp. 38–40).

45. Note, e.g., John 13:15, 34; 15:12; 17:16; Heb. 12:1–4; 13:12–13; 1 Pet. 2:21; 1 John 2:6; Ignatius, *Phil.* 7:2; Irenaeus, *Adv. haer.* 2.22.4 (SC 294, ed. Rousseau and Doutreleau, pp. 220–22); *Apoc. Abr.* 29:10 (presuming this to be a Christian interpolation referring to Jesus: "All will imitate him"); Clement of Alexandria, *Paed.* 1.2.2 (SC 70, ed. Marrou and Harl, p. 110). Jesus is especially a moral model in Luke-Acts; cf. Charles H. Talbert, *Learning through Suffering: The Educational Value of Suffering in the New Testament and in Its Milieu* (Zacchaeus Studies: New Testament; Collegeville, Minn.: Liturgical Press, 1991), pp. 75–90.

46. Cf. Burridge, *What Are the Gospels?* pp. 208, 304–6.

47. But note Bauer, *Structure*, pp. 57–63; John K. Riches, *Conflicting Mythologies: Identity Formation in the Gospels of Mark and Matthew* (Edinburgh: T&T Clark, 2000), p. 284; and Wayne A. Meeks, *The Moral World of the First Christians* (Philadelphia: Westminster, 1986), p. 143.

meek," 5:5; cf. 18:4), he himself is such ("I am meek and lowly of heart,"
11:29; cf. 21:5).[48] If he enjoins mercy ("Blessed are the merciful," 5:7), he
himself is merciful ("Have mercy upon us, Son of David," 9:27; cf. 15:22;
20:30).[49] If he congratulates those oppressed for God's cause ("Blessed are
those persecuted for righteousness' sake," 5:10), he himself suffers and dies
innocently ("Then he [Pilate] asked, '. . . what evil has he done?'" 27:23).
All of which is just to repeat what Origen, mixing Matthew with Luke and
Paul, perceived long ago:

> Jesus confirms all of the beatitudes he speaks in the Gospel, and he justifies his
> teaching through his own example. "Blessed are the meek" is what he says of
> himself. "Learn of me, for I am meek." "Blessed are the peacemakers." Who
> is a peacemaker like my Lord Jesus, who is our peace, who made enmity to
> cease and destroyed it in his flesh? "Blessed are they who suffer persecution for
> righteousness' sake." No one more than the Lord Jesus, who was crucified for
> our sins, endured persecution for righteousness' sake. The Lord, then, displays
> all the beatitudes as being realized in himself. Conforming to that which he
> said, "Blessed are those who weep," he himself wept over Jerusalem, to lay the
> foundation of this beatitude also.[50]

Moving beyond the Beatitudes, Jesus demands faithfulness to the law of
Moses ("Do not think that I have come to abolish the law or the prophets,"
5:17–20) and faithfully keeps that law during his ministry ("Show yourself
to the priest, and offer the gift that Moses commanded," 8:4). He recom-
mends self-denial in the face of evil ("If anyone strikes you on the right
cheek, turn the other also," 5:39) and does not resist the evils done to him
("They spat in his face and struck him; and some slapped him," 26:67;
cf. 27:30). He calls for private prayer ("Whenever you pray, go into your
room and shut the door and pray to your Father who is in secret," 6:6),
and he subsequently withdraws to a mountain to pray alone ("He went
up the mountain by himself to pray," 14:23). Jesus, moreover, advises his
followers to employ certain words in prayer ("Your will be done," 6:10),
and he uses those words in Gethsemane ("If this cannot pass unless I drink
it, your will be done," 26:42). He rejects the service of mammon ("Do not
store up for yourself treasures on earth," 6:19), and he lives without concern
for money ("The Son of Man has nowhere to lay his head," 8:20). He com-

48. Cf. Chromatius, *Tract. Matt.* (CCSL 9a, ed. Étaix and Lemarié, p. 272); Albertus Magnus,
Super Mt. cap. I–XIV ad loc. (Opera Omnia 21/1, ed. B. Schmidt, p. 107); Bauer, *Structure*, p.
61; John P. Meier, *The Vision of Matthew: Christ, Church, and Morality in the First Gospel* (New
York: Paulist, 1979), p. 129; and esp. now Deirdre J. Good, *Jesus the Meek King* (Harrisburg,
Pa.: Trinity Press International, 1999), pp. 61–93. Good refers to several others who stress Jesus'
embodiment of "meekness" as well as the spirit of the Beatitudes in general.

49. Cf. Bauer, *Structure*, pp. 61–62.

50. Origen, *Hom. Luke* 38.1–2 (SC 87, ed. Crouzel, Fournier, and Périchon, p. 443).

mands believers to carry crosses ("If any want to become my followers, let them deny themselves and take up their cross and follow me," 16:24), and he does so himself, both figuratively and literally (Pilate "handed him over to be crucified," 27:26). One could go on and on in this vein, citing instances of Jesus animating his speech. Jesus, as the author of the *Pseudo-Clementine Recognitions* put it, never "enjoins upon us anything different from what he himself practiced."[51]

Our Gospel also goes out of its way to make the twelve disciples emulate their Lord in numerous particulars. Chapter 10 alone offers the following parallels:[52]

The Disciples	Jesus
They are to heal every disease and every infirmity (10:1)	He heals every disease and every infirmity (4:23)
They are to preach that "the kingdom of heaven is at hand" (10:7)	He preaches that "the kingdom of heaven is at hand" (4:17)
They are to cast out demons (10:8)	He casts out demons (9:32–33, etc.)
They are to heal lepers (10:8)	He heals lepers (11:5)
They are to raise the dead (10:8)	He raises the dead (11:5)
They are not to go to the Samaritans but to the lost sheep of Israel (10:6)	He does not go to the Samaritans but to the lost sheep of Israel (15:24)
They will be handed over to sanhedrins (10:17)	Jesus is handed over to the Sanhedrin (26:57–68)
They will be dragged before governors (10:18)	Jesus is taken before the governor (27:1–26)
They will be called Beelzebul (10:25)	Jesus is called Beelzebul (9:34; 10:25)
The disciples will carry a cross (10:38)	Jesus is crucified (20:19; etc.)

What do such correlations imply? If the disciples imitate Jesus, the thought that others should follow their lead and do likewise lies very near to hand.[53] One can accordingly take the phrase in 28:20, τηρεῖν πάντα ὅσα ἐνετειλάμην ὑμῖν (to observe all that I have commanded you), to be all-encompassing: the reference is not to the Sermon on the Mount or even to Jesus' words but to his life in its totality. His person is, for those baptized, a command, so his followers must creatively mirror the virtues he speaks and embodies. If Jesus demands the perfect imitation of God (5:48), he himself is the perfect instance of such imitation. As Ignatius has it, "Be imitators of Jesus Christ, as he was of his Father" (*Phil.* 7:2). On the moral level at least our

51. *Ps.-Clem. Rec.* 2.28 (GCS 42, ed. Rehm, p. 68).
52. See further below, pp. 222–25; also Schuyler Brown, "The Mission to Israel in Matthew's Central Section," *ZNW* 69 (1978), pp. 78–79.
53. Cf. the formulation in 1 Cor. 11:1: "Become imitators of me as I am of Christ."

Gospel encourages its readers to identify closely with the main character, who functions, to use the words of another first-century Christian, as "the pioneer and perfecter of our faith" (Heb. 12:2).

Matthew's use of δικαιοσύνη (righteousness) reinforces the point. With the possible exception of 5:6, the word everywhere, in my judgment, indicates either God's norm for human conduct or behavior in accord with that norm.[54] Jesus, furthermore, not only demands δικαιοσύνη: he also lives it. Pilate's wife rightly calls him δίκαιος (27:19), a "just" or "righteous" man, and, according to 3:15, in submitting to baptism by John he fulfills all righteousness (πληρῶσαι πᾶσαν δικαιοσύνην). Although the meaning of this last phrase is much contested, the case that πληρῶσαι (to fulfill) has eschatological sense is convincing,[55] and δικαιοσύνη in all probability refers to the divine demand.[56] If so, Jesus is the eschatological fulfillment of the will of God, which in turn implies that his behavior, his courageous self-command that becomes humble obedience to God and leaves nothing good undone, is for Matthew programmatic and exemplary. The Son of God first does what he later asks others to do. Ulrich Luz is right: Jesus is, in 3:15, the *Urbild* and *Vorbild* of Christians.[57] I only add: he is the *Urbild* and *Vorbild* of Christians throughout the Gospel, a consistent "example of piety, righteousness, and submission."[58] If, for Aristotle, the "good man" is the "canon" (κανών) in ethics (*Eth. nic.* 3.4), in Matthew Jesus is the "canon" of Christian morality. The Messiah goes infallibly right.

Investigation of Matthew's employment of ὑποκριτής, "hypocrite," tends to the same conclusion. One of the main charges against Jesus' chief opponents, the Pharisees, is that they are "hypocrites."[59] Precisely what that means, especially the extent to which it connotes the pretense of conscious deception, has been the subject of some dispute.[60] One thing, however, is clear. Hypocrisy involves, among other things, disjunction between word and deed. This is evident in 23:2–3: "The scribes and the Pharisees sit on Moses' seat; therefore, do whatever they teach you and follow it; but do not do as they do, for they do not practice what they teach." That is, the Jewish leaders are guilty not of erroneous doctrine but of failure to live up

54. Benno Przybylski, *Righteousness in Matthew and His World of Thought* (SNTSMS 41; Cambridge: Cambridge University Press, 1980).

55. See John P. Meier, *Law and History in Matthew's Gospel* (AnBib 71; Rome: Biblical Institute, 1976), pp. 73–81. For another view see David P. Scaer, *Discourses in Matthew: Jesus Teaches the Church* (St. Louis: Concordia, 2004), pp. 245–63.

56. Cf. Przybylski, *Righteousness*, pp. 91–94.

57. Luz, *Matthäus*, 1:213.

58. The words are those of Irenaeus, *Adv. haer.* 2.22.4 (SC 294, ed. Rousseau and Doutreleau, pp. 222).

59. See 15:7; 22:18; 23:13, 14–15, 23, 25, 27, 29; cf. 23:3; also 6:2, 5, 16; 7:5. For ὑπόκρισις see 23:28.

60. See Garland, *Matthew 23*, pp. 91–123.

to their own injunctions. In other words, the ability to discern what should be done exists, but not the inclination or power to achieve it. This is why the Pharisees are the superior examples of how *not* to behave. Their words outshine their deeds, as if in illustration of La Rochefoucauld's famous dictum: *l'hypocrisie est un hommage que le vice rend à la vertu.* Matthew's Jesus, however, is the antithesis of all this. The disciples not only confront his words but study the Messiah himself. "Learn of me" (μάθετε ἀπ᾿ ἐμοῦ, 11:29) means, in effect, "Follow me" (ἀκολούθει μοι, 9:9; cf. 4:19). One learns not just with the ears but also with the feet. Education is much more than heeding an infallible wordsmith. It additionally involves the mimetic following of Jesus, who is virtue embodied.

The Moral Aims of Biography

André Maurois wrote that "biography is a type of literature which, more than any other, touches close upon morality."[61] This rings true. Prior to recent times, in which biographers have so preoccupied themselves with information, entertainment, or psychological subtleties, biography has usually, to greater or lesser degree, enshrined clear moral aims. It has operated with the premise that the best sermon is a good example. One thinks, for instance, of the proliferation of biographies among the early Puritans, with their transparent religious exhortations designed to prevent or remedy character defects, or of the "moralizing"—the word now suffers ill repute—in the at one time well-read books of Samuel Smiles, such as *Lives of the Engineers* and *Men of Invention and Industry*—the sorts of books not much written after Lytton Strachy's *Eminent Victorians* (1918). Plutarch's *Lives*[62] (which so influenced nineteenth-century English biography), Petrarch's biographies, and the Roman Catholic and Eastern Orthodox legends of the saints also come to mind. Athanasius wrote the *Life of Saint Anthony* in part to supply "an ideal pattern" for others desirous to "emulate" Anthony's resolution.[63] Many have no doubt implicitly held the opinion of Samuel Johnson: "No species of writing seems more worthy of cultivation than biography since

61. André Maurois, *Aspects of Biography* (trans. S. C. Roberts; New York: Appleton, 1929), p. 136.

62. Note esp. Plutarch, *Pericles* 2: "Virtue in action immediately takes such hold of a person that he no sooner admires a deed than he sets out to follow in the steps of the doer. Fortune we prize for the good things we may possess and enjoy from her, but virtue for the good deeds we can perform: the former we are content to receive at the hands of others, but the latter we desire others to experience from ourselves. Moral good, in a word, has a power to attract towards itself. . . . These, then, are the reasons which have impelled me to persevere in my biographical writings."

63. Athanasius, *V. Ant.* prol. (SC 400, ed. Bartelink, p. 126).

none can be more delightful or more useful, none can more certainly enchain the heart by irresistible interest, or more widely diffuse instruction of every diversity of condition."[64] Carlyle put it succinctly: "Biography is almost the one thing needful."[65]

The greatest influence upon our conduct is the conduct of others. From this undoubted truth of psychology, that we emulate what appears before us, it follows that if one wishes to shape behavior and impact morality, one will be well advised to put forward what Milton termed "the salutary influence of example": words will not suffice. One must employ sight as well as sound. That is why Sir. 44–50, Heb. 11, and *1 Clement* conjure mental visions of heroes and their exploits, and also why *m. ʾAbot* 6:6 observes that one learns Torah not just through study but also through attending to service of the sages. Smiles wrote: "Example is one of the most potent of instructors, though it teaches without a tongue. It is the practical school of mankind, working by action, which is always more forcible than words."[66] This declaration is nothing other than a wordy, Victorian version of the old, succinct Latin proverb: example is better than precept. As Seneca wrote: "The way is long if one follows precept, but short and helpful if one follows patterns" (*Ad Lucilium* 6.4).

The sentiment is of some help in understanding the First Gospel. For the evangelist's moral interest, apparent above all in the Sermon on the Mount, could not be better served than by a story in which the crucial moral imperatives are imaginatively and convincingly incarnated, which is exactly what the First Gospel supplies.[67] It, to quote Clement of Alexandria, offers two types of teaching, "that which takes the form of exhortation to obedience, and that which is presented in the form of examples."[68] When Eduard Thurneysen forwarded his christological interpretation of the Sermon on the Mount, according to which this last is a self-portrait, he was onto something.[69] Jesus, in the First Gospel, embodies his sentences; the

---

64. Samuel Johnson, in *Essays from the Rambler, Adventurer, and Idler* (ed. W. J. Bate; New Haven: Yale University Press, 1968), p. 110 (from no. 60, Saturday, 13 Oct. 1750).

65. Thomas Carlyle, *Critical and Miscellaneous Essays*, vol. 4 (London: Chapman and Hill, 1869), p. 52.

66. Samuel Smiles, *Self Help: With Illustrations of Character and Conduct* (Philadelphia, J. B. Lippincott, 1880), p. 371.

67. Against the objection, often brought against the Sermon on the Mount, that its demands cannot be lived, Matthew himself would probably have referred to Jesus' own life as proof to the contrary.

68. Clement of Alexandria, *Paed.* 1.2.2 (SC 70, ed. Marrou and Harl, pp. 110).

69. Eduard Thurneysen, *The Sermon on the Mount* (Richmond: John Knox, 1964). Thurneysen did not, however, stress Jesus' role as moral exemplar.

Lord lives as he speaks and speaks as he lives.[70] Ephraem put it this way: "What he taught us, Christ first did, and by this went before us, so that we might follow him."[71] I indeed believe that Matthew's Gospel implies what Maximus the Confessor plainly states, that "the one who loves Christ thoroughly imitates him as much as he can."[72]

---

70. Birger Gerhardsson has seen this clearly, "The Hermeneutic Program in Matthew 22:37–40," in *Jews, Greeks, and Christians: Religious Cultures in Late Antiquity* (ed. Robert Hamerton-Kelly and Robin Scroggs; SJLA 21; Leiden: Brill, 1976), pp. 145–49.

71. Ephraem, *Exp. Gos.* 62 (CSCO 29, Scriptores Armeniaci 5, ed. Egan, p. 48). Ephraem cites "blessed are the poor in spirit" (5:3) and asserts that Jesus was poor. He further quotes "Blessed are you when people revile you and utter all sorts of evil against you" (5:11) and observes that Jesus was reviled and killed.

72. Maximus the Confessor, *Caritas* 4.55 (PG 90.1060C).

8

Matthew's First Two Words

(MATT. 1:1)

The First Gospel opens with this: βίβλος γενέσεως Ἰησοῦ Χριστοῦ υἱοῦ Δαυὶδ υἱοῦ Ἀβραάμ. English Bibles have translated these eight words in various ways:

The book of the generation of Jesus Christ, the son of David, the son of Abraham (KJV, RV)

A genealogy of Jesus Christ, a descendant of David and Abraham (Twentieth Century New Testament)

The birth-roll of Jesus Christ, the son of David, the son of Abraham (Moffatt)

The book of the genealogy of Jesus Christ, the son of David, the son of Abraham (RSV)

An account of the genealogy of Jesus the Messiah, the son of David, the son of Abraham (NRSV)

This is the record of the ancestry of Jesus Christ who was the descendant of both David and Abraham (Phillips)

A table of the descent of Jesus Christ, son of David, son of Abraham (NEB)

This is the family record of Jesus Christ, who was a descendant of David, who was a descendant of Abraham (TEV)

A record of the genealogy of Jesus Christ the son of David, the son of Abraham (NIV)

This is the family tree of Jesus Christ, the Son of David, the son of Abraham (Barclay)

The book of the genealogy of Jesus Christ, the Son of David, the Son of Abraham (NKJV)[1]

These translations consistently render βίβλος γενέσεως by "genealogy" or some equivalent, such as "record of the ancestry" or "family tree." This unanimity of the English versions would seem to imply that Matt. 1:1 is a heading for the genealogy, that is, a heading for 1:2–17. When one turns to the commentaries, however, one quickly learns that there is no accord at all concerning the meaning and function of Matthew's first few words. A review of the secondary literature reveals the following:

(1) Many interpreters, observing that βίβλος γενέσεως is, in Gen. 5:1, immediately followed by a genealogy listing the descendants of Adam, understand Matt. 1:1 to introduce the genealogy only.[2]

1. For another list of English translations of Matt. 1:1 see Edgar J. Goodspeed, *Problems of New Testament Translation* (Chicago: University of Chicago Press, 1945), pp. 9–10.
2. E.g., Augustine, *C. Faust.* 2.1 (CSEL 25, ed. Zyca, pp. 253–54); John Calvin, *Commentary on a Harmony of the Evangelists, Matthew, Mark, and Luke* (3 vols.; Grand Rapids: Eerdmans, 1949), 1:88–89; Hugo Grotius, *Opera omnia theologica* (Amsterdam: Joannis Blaeu, 1679), 2.1:5; Johan Jakob Wettstein, Η ΚΑΙΝΗ ΔΙΑΘΗΚΗ: *Novum Testamentum graecum editionis receptae cum lectionibus variantibus codicum mss., editionum aliarum, versionum et patrum nec non commentario pleniore ex scriptoribus veteribus hebraeis, graecis* (2 vols.; Amsterdam: Ex Officina Dommeriana, 1751–1752), p. 225; Matthew Poole, *Annotations on the Holy Bible* (3 vols.; London: Bohn, 1846), 3:1–2; A. H. McNeile, *The Gospel according to St. Matthew* (London: Macmillan, 1915), p. 1; M.-J. Lagrange, *Évangile selon Saint Matthieu* (7th ed.; Paris: Gabalda, 1948), p. 3; Ernst Lohmeyer, *Das Evangelium nach Matthäus* (ed. W. Schmauch; KEK; Göttingen: Vandenhoeck & Ruprecht, 1958), p. 4; Josef Schmid, *Das Evangelium nach Matthäus* (RNT; Regensburg: F. Pustet, 1959), p. 35; W. Barnes Tatum, "'The Origin of Jesus Messiah' (Matt. 1:1, 18a): Matthew's Use of the Infancy Traditions," *JBL* 96 (1977), pp. 523–35; David E. Garland, *Reading Matthew: A Literary and Theological Commentary on the First Gospel* (London: SPCK, 1993), p. 14; Donald A. Hagner, *Matthew 1–13* (WBC 33a; Dallas: Word, 1993), pp. 5, 19; Wolfgang Wiefel, *Das Evangelium nach Matthäus* (Leipzig: Evangelische Verlagsanstalt, 1998), pp. 27–28.

(2) Others, noting that γένεσις appears again in Matt. 1:18 and cannot there mean "genealogy" ("birth" is the usual English translation), hold instead that the verse introduces the entirety of chapter 1.[3]

(3) Some take 1:1 to stand over the entire infancy narrative.[4] On this view, βίβλος γενέσεως κ.τ.λ. introduces 1:2–2:23.

(4) A handful of commentators consider 1:1 to be the superscription of the first main part of the gospel, this being, in their judgment, 1:1–4:16.[5]

(5) A significant number of exegetes interpret 1:1 as being in the first instance the title for the entire gospel. Jerome and Chrysostom were already of this opinion.[6] Supporters of this option typically understand βίβλος to carry its ordinary sense, namely, "book," and they take γενέσεως to mean either "history" or "story."[7] As partial

---

3. E.g., Anton Vögtle, "Die Genealogie Mt 1.2–16 und die matthäische Kindheitsgeschichte," in *Das Evangelium und die Evangelien* (Düsseldorf: Patmos, 1971), p. 73. Cf. Raymond E. Brown, *The Birth of the Messiah: A Commentary on the Infancy Narratives in the Gospels of Matthew and Luke* (new updated ed.; New York: Doubleday, 1993), p. 59: "It is unlikely that Matthew means his title to cover more than the genealogy (1:2–17), with 1:18–25 included if that section is looked on as explaining 1:16."

4. E.g., Willoughby C. Allen, *A Critical and Exegetical Commentary on the Gospel according to St. Matthew* (ICC; 3rd ed.; Edinburgh: T&T Clark, 1912), pp. 1–2; A. Plummer, *An Exegetical Commentary on the Gospel according to St. Matthew* (London: Macmillan, 1910), p. 1.

5. Edgar Krentz, "The Extent of Matthew's Prologue," *JBL* 83 (1964), pp. 409–14; J. D. Kingsbury, *Matthew: Structure, Christology, Kingdom* (Philadelphia: Fortress, 1975), pp. 7–17; David R. Bauer, *The Structure of Matthew's Gospel: A Study in Literary Design* (JSNTSS 31; Sheffield: Almond, 1988), pp. 73–77; Dirk Frickenschmidt, *Evangelium als Biographie: Die vier Evangelien im Rahmen antiker Erzählkunst* (Tübingen: A. Francke, 1997), pp. 460–64.

6. Jerome, *Comm. Matt.* ad loc. (SC 242, ed. Bonnard, p. 72); Chrysostom, *Hom. Matt.* 2.3(5) (PG 57.27).

7. Rabanus Maurus, *Comm. Matt.* ad loc. (PL 107.731D); Dionysius bar Salibi, *Expl. Evang.* ad Matt. 1:1 (CSCO 77, Scriptores Syri 33, ed. Sedlaeck and Chabot, p. 29); Albertus Magnus, *Super Mt. cap. I–XIV* ad loc. (Opera Omnia 21/1, ed. B. Schmidt, pp. 11–12); Nicolas of Lyra, *Postilla super totam Bibliam* (Strassburg, 1492), vol. 4, ad loc.; Juan Maldonatus, *Comentarii in Quatuor Evangelistas* (2 vols.; Mainz: F. Kirchhemius, 1853–1854), 1:10–11; John Gill, *Gill's Commentary* (6 vols.; Grand Rapids: Baker, 1980), 5:2; Zachary Pearce, *A Commentary with Notes on the Four Evangelists and the Acts of the Apostles* (2 vols.; London: E. Cox, 1777), 1:1; John Wesley, *Explanatory Notes upon the New Testament* (London: Epworth, 1950), p. 15; Adam Clarke, *The Holy Bible, Containing the Old and New Testaments: The New Testament*, vol. 1, *Matthew to Romans* (London: Thomas Tegg & Son, 1836), 35; T. Zahn, *Das Evangelium des Matthäus* (3rd ed.; Leipzig, 1910), pp. 39–44; Pierre Bonnard, *L'Évangile selon saint Matthieu* (CNT 1; Neuchâtel: Delachaux & Niestlé, 1963), p. 16; Paul Gaechter, *Das Matthäus Evangelium* (Innsbruck: Tyrolia, 1963), pp. 34–35; Walter Grundmann, *Das Evangelium nach Matthäus* (THKNT 1; Berlin: Evangelische Verlagsanstalt, 1968), p. 61; Hubert Frankemölle, *Jahwebund und Kirche Christi: Studien zur Form- und Traditionsgeschichte des 'Evangeliums' nach Matthäus* (NTAbh 10; Münster: Aschendorff, 1974), pp. 360–65; Francis Wright Beare, *The Gospel according to Matthew* (New York: Harper & Row, 1981), p. 64; Alexander Sand, *Das Evangelium nach Matthäus* (RNT; Regensburg: F. Pustet, 1986), pp. 39–41; Detlev Dormeyer,

justification they can appeal to several texts in the biblical tradition that begin with the word "book" (ספר/βιβλίον) + a proper name and then follow this with a genealogy.[8]

(6) According to J. C. Fenton, the various interpretations just presented are not mutually exclusive. Rather, 1:1 is "telescopic: it can be extended to include more and more of what Matthew is beginning to write about. First, it can cover *the genealogy* which immediately follows it; then, it can refer to the account of *the birth* of Jesus (the same word is translated *birth* in 1:18); thirdly, it can mean 'history,' or 'life-story'; and finally, it can refer to the whole new creation which begins at the conception of Jesus and will be completed at his second coming."[9] J.-L. Leuba has put forward a similar view.[10]

It is not my purpose herein to argue for or against any of the six interpretations just listed.[11] I should instead like to call attention to the fact that, if unacquainted with the secondary literature, average readers of one of the English versions cited above would never guess that the meaning of Matt. 1:1 is so much in dispute. They would rather just take interpretation (1) for granted. This is hardly a desirable state of affairs. With what justice do our translators ignore the rather large and august body of interpreters who have seen things differently, that is, opted for interpretation (2) or (3) or (4) or (5) or (6)? The simple fact is this: the commentators are divided because the import of the Greek is not obvious. βίβλος γενέσεως can stand as the heading for 1:2–17, for 1:2–25, for 1:2–2:23, for 1:2–4:16, or for 1:2–28:16.

"Mt 1,1 als Überschrift zur Gattung und Christologie des Matthäus-Evangelium," in *The Four Gospels 1992: Festschrift Frans Neirynck* (ed. F. van Segbroeck, C. M. Tuckett, G. van Belle, and J. Verheyden; 3 vols.; BETL 100; Leuven: Leuven University Press, 1992), 3:1361–83; M. Eugene Boring, "The Gospel of Matthew," in *The New Interpreter's Bible* (Nashville: Abingdon, 1995), 8:125–27; Moisés Mayordomo-Marín, *Den Anfang hören: Leserorientierte Evangelienexegese am Beispiel von Matthäus 1–2* (FRLANT 180; Göttingen: Vandenhoeck & Ruprecht, 1998), pp. 206–17; Ulrich Luz, *Das Evangelium nach Matthäus* (4 vols.; EKK 1/1–4; Düsseldorf: Benziger, 1990–2002), 1:177–19 (this marks a change from the first edition, in which Luz argued that 1:1 was the introduction to chapter 1). Cf. the so-called "Toledoth Jesu," תולדת ישו, one of several titles for a polemical Jewish version of the story of Jesus.

8. E.g., Tob. 1:1; Bar. 1.1; *Apoc. Abr.*, title; 2 Esd. 1:1–3; *Sepher Ha-Razim*, preface; cf. 4Q544 (4QAmram[b]) 1:1: "Copy of the book of the words of the vision of Amram, son of Qahat, son of Levi."

9. J. C. Fenton, *The Gospel of St. Matthew* (Pelican Gospel Commentaries; Harmondsworth/ Baltimore: Pelican, 1963), p. 36.

10. J.-L. Leuba, "Note exégétique sur Matthieu 1.1a," *RHPR* 22 (1942), pp. 56–61.

11. Elsewhere I have defended the sixth option: W. D. Davies and Dale C. Allison Jr., *A Critical and Exegetical Commentary on the Gospel according to St. Matthew* (3 vols.; ICC; Edinburgh: T&T Clark, 1988, 1991, 1997), 1:149–60.

The usual translations have yet another defect. Matthew's first two words, as the vast majority of interpreters now recognize, are intended to recall the Septuagint rendering of Gen. 2:4 (αὕτη ἡ βίβλος γενέσεως οὐρανοῦ καὶ γῆς [This is the book of the genesis of heaven and earth]) or 5:1 (αὕτη ἡ βίβλος γενέσεως ἀνθρώπων [This is the book of the genesis of human beings]);[12] they may also allude to the book of Genesis in its entirety, which first-century Jews already knew as Γένεσις.[13] The single English word "genealogy," or a simple equivalent, conveys none of this. Any translation must of course make interpretative choices. Greek is not English, and there is no perfect one-to-one correspondence between Greek words and phrases and English words and phrases. In the present instance, however, there is an English word whose field of meaning is not far from the field of meaning for γένεσις, a word that happily allows for the possibility of all six proposed interpretations.

The dictionaries give the English word, "genesis," the following meanings, among others: "the first book of the Pentateuch"; "coming into being"; and "mode of originating"; and its synonyms include "beginning," "birth," and "origination." What, then, would an English reader make if a translation of Matthew were to open with, "Book" or "Record" or "Account of the genesis of Jesus Christ"? The initial response would probably be puzzlement. To what exactly does "Book/Record/Account of the genesis" refer? The reader would be in precisely the same position as the exegete of the Greek (and in an altogether different place than the reader of the modern English translations of the New Testament). Upon reflection, however, such a English reader, knowing that "genesis" can mean "origination" or "mode of originating," might conclude that "Book/Record/Account of the genesis," because of its position, serves as the heading of the genealogy. Yet one could just as readily construe the words as covering 1:2–25 ("genesis" can after all mean "birth"). And if the reader understood "genesis" to mean "beginning," it would also be possible to think of 1:1 as introducing all up to either 2:23 or 4:16. One acquainted, moreover, with the New Testament idea that the advent of

12. βίβλος γενέσεως appears in the LXX only in these two places.
13. Not only do the earliest mss. of the LXX have Γένεσις (B S: Γένεσις: A: Γένεσις Κόσμου) but Justin, *Dial.* 20.1 (PTS 47, ed. Marcovich, p. 102) (ἐν τῇ βίβλῳ Γενέσεως); Origen. apud Eusebius, *HE* 6.25.2 (GCS 9.2, ed. Schwartz, p. 572); Melito of Sardis apud Eusebius, *HE* 4.26.14 (LCL, ed. Lake, p. 392); and the author of Audet's so-called "Hebrew-Aramaic List of Books of the Old Testament" (from the end of the second century CE: J.-P. Audet, "A Hebrew-Aramaic List of Books of the Old Testament in Greek Transcription," *JTS* 1 [1950], pp. 135–54) knew the book by this name. But the decisive datum comes from Philo of Alexandria, who three times refers to the first book of Moses as "Genesis": *Post.* 127; *Abr.* 1; *Aet.* 19. Indeed, in *Aet.* 19 he asserts that Moses himself gave the book its name. On additional parallels between Matt. 1 and Genesis see now Raik Heckl, "Der biblische Begründungsrahmen für die Jungfrauengeburt bei Matthäus: Zur Rezeption von Gen. 5,1–6,4 in Mt 1," *ZNW* 95 (2004), pp. 161–80.

Jesus marked a new creation[14] just might wonder whether 1:1 has some-thing to do with the Christ-event as a whole and therefore something to do with the Gospel of Matthew as a whole (cf. interpretations [5] and [6]). In addition, "Book/Record/Account of the genesis" could easily set off in the minds of the English readers—just as βίβλος γενέσεως probably set off in the minds of Matthew's first audience—the question of whether there is not some relationship to the primeval history and its themes.[15] In sum, the connotations of and the interpretative possibilities raised by the ambigu-ous phrase, "Book/Record/Account of the genesis," are almost exactly the connotations of and the interpretative possibilities raised by the disputed Greek text. For this reason, translators should consider transliterating the γενέσεως of Matt. 1:1. At the very least, if English versions continue to favor "An account of the genealogy of Jesus" or some such, they should add in the margin or in a footnote: "'Genealogy' is lit. 'genesis.'"

Ulrich Luz, in the second edition of his commentary on Matthew, has recorded a change of mind on this issue. Whereas in his first edition he translated Matthew's opening Greek by the German, "'Urkunde des Ur-sprungs' Jesu Christi, des Davidsohns, des Abrahamsohns" (The "record of the origin" of Jesus Christ, the son of David, the son of Abraham), in his latest edition he deems it wisest simply to transliterate γενέσεως: "Buch der 'Genesis' Jesu Christi, des Davidsohns, des Abrahamsohns" (Book of the "genesis" of Jesus Christ, the son of David, the son of Abraham).[16] Maybe future translators of the Bible will find the wisdom to follow Luz's lead.

---

14. Paul speaks more than once of a "new creation" (2 Cor. 5:17; Gal. 6:15), and he likens his Lord to a "last Adam" (Rom. 5:12–21; 1 Cor. 15:42–50). Note also the prologue of John's Gospel (1:1–18), which clearly opens the story of Jesus by setting it against the background of the Genesis creation story. See further Nils A. Dahl, *Jesus in the Memory of the Early Church* (Minneapolis: Augsburg, 1976), pp. 120–40.

15. Thereby perhaps implying a parallel between one beginning and another beginning, between the creation of the cosmos and Adam and Eve on the one hand and the new creation brought by the Messiah on the other. Cf. Rabanus Maurus, *Comm. Matt.* ad loc. (PL 107.731D), and Ps.-Anselm = Geoffrey Babion, *En. Matt.* ad loc. (PL 162.1227C).

16. Luz, *Matthäus*, 1:117.

9

Divorce, Celibacy, and Joseph

(MATT. 1:18–25)

Jesus, in Matt. 5:32, prohibits divorce παρεκτὸς λόγου πορνείας. In Matt. 19:9, he forbids divorce μὴ ἐπὶ πορνείᾳ. These two exception clauses,[1] which surely have the same meaning, are problematic.[2] Do they refer to incest ("except for incest")[3] or to adultery ("except for

---

1. The attempt to read παρεκτός or μὴ ἐπί as either "even in the case of" or "disregarding the case of" seems to have been abandoned; see Bruce Vawter, "Divorce and the New Testament," *CBQ* 39 (1977), pp. 528–44, and Ulrich Luz, *Das Evangelium nach Matthäus* (4 vols.; EKK 1/1–4; Düsseldorf: Benziger, 1990–2002), 1:362.

2. For a succinct survey of exegetical opinion see Raymond F. Collins, *Divorce in the New Testament* (Collegeville, Minn.: Liturgical Press, 1992), pp. 199–205.

3. See esp. Joseph A. Fitzmyer, "The Matthean Divorce Texts and Some New Palestinian Evidence," in *To Advance the Gospel: New Testament Studies* (New York: Crossroad, 1981), pp. 79–111, and Ben Witherington, "Matthew 5.32 and 19.9—Exception or Exceptional Situation?" *NTS* 31 (1985), pp. 571–76. Against this, one may observe the following: (i) Lev. 18:6–18 LXX, which contains the laws on incest, does not use πορνεία; (ii) Fitzmyer's reading would presumably be relevant for a Gentile Christian audience—incest was known in the pagan world—whereas Matthew seems written first to Jewish Christians; and (iii) an incestuous union would not, in Jewish eyes, have constituted a licit marriage, so no formal abolition of it would be required.

adultery")[4] or to something else again (maybe "except for fornication," that is, intercourse before marriage)?[5] One of the more valuable contributions to the debate has come from Markus Bockmuehl. He has demonstrated that, for many ancient Jews, divorce for adultery was not optional but closer to automatic. For the Jewish Christians of the Matthean community, then, the exception clause, which according to Bockmuehl refers to any unlawful sexual behavior within marriage, would have served as needed clarification.[6] Unfaithfulness produced a state of impurity that, as a matter of legal fact, dissolved marriage. It made "husband and wife unfit for continued conjugal union."[7] Or so, at least, runs Bockmuehl's argument.[8]

4. So Joachim Gnilka, *Das Matthäusevangelium* (2 vols.; HTKNT; Freiburg: Herders, 1986, 1988), pp. 167–69, and the majority of modern commentators. See esp. David Janzen, "The Meaning of Porneia in Matthew 5.32 and 19.9: An Approach from the Study of Ancient Near Eastern Culture," *JSNT* 80 (2000), pp. 66–80.

5. So Abel Isaksson, *Marriage and Ministry in the New Temple: A Study with Special Reference to Mt. 19.1[sic]3–12 and 1 Cor. 11.3–16* (ASNU 24; Lund: Gleerup, 1965), pp. 135–41. But the linguistic evidence for confining πορνεία to "fornication" is lacking; and it is not clear why premarital intercourse should be worse than extramarital intercourse. There is also a problem here because many scholars (rightly, I believe) think of marriage as commencing with betrothal, not cohabitation.

6. Markus Bockmuehl, "Matthew 5.32; 19.9 in the Light of Pre-rabbinic Halakhah," *NTS* 35 (1989), pp. 291–95; reprinted as "Matthew's Divorce Texts in the Light of Pre-rabbinic Jewish Law," in *Jewish Law in Gentile Churches: Halakhah and the Beginning of Christian Public Ethics* (Grand Rapids: Baker Academic, 2003), pp. 17–21. The arguments against Bockmuehl in David Instone-Brewer, *Divorce and Remarriage in the Bible: The Social and Literary Context* (Grand Rapids: Eerdmans, 1992), pp. 95–96, do not persuade. Although Instone-Brewer is right to deny a unified opinion in Judaism, the number of texts Bockmuehl cites surely reflects a widespread conviction; and the dates of Prov. 18:22 LXX ("he who keeps an adulteress . . . is ungodly"); 1QapGen 20:15 (Bockmuehl: "It would seem natural in context to read this prayer as Abraham's desperate plea for God to save his marriage at the eleventh hour," before Pharaoh goes into Sarah); *Jub.* 33:7–9 ("'I [Bilhah] am not clean for you [Jacob] since I have become polluted for you because Reuben has defiled me and lay with me at night'. . . . And then Jacob did not draw near her since Reuben had defiled her"); and Philo, *Abr.* 98 (the king of Egypt's desire to take Sarah put Abraham's marriage in danger of being destroyed: κινδυνεύσαντα διαφθαρῆναι τὸν γάμον), none of which appears in Instone-Brewer's index, show the conviction to be pre-rabbinic. Note also perhaps Isa. 50:1 and Jer. 3:7–10. Further, and long before any of those texts, Lev. 20:10 and Deut. 22:21–22, which prescribe execution for adultery, clearly presuppose that, once unfaithfulness has been established, marriage will not continue. See further now David Rothstein, "Sexual Union and Sexual Offences in Jubilees," *JSJ* 35 (2004), pp. 363–90, and Aharon Shemesh, "4Q271.3: A Key to Sectarian Matrimonial Law," *JJS* 49 (1998), pp. 244–63. They establish that some Jews regarded physical union itself as constituting matrimony, with the implication that marrying a woman who had been with another man was adultery.

7. Bockmuehl, "Divorce Texts," p. 21. Cf. the ruling in Hermas, *Mand.* 4.1.4–6.

8. Cf. Luz, *Matthäus*, 1:364, n. 48. He cites Prov. 18:22 LXX (see n. 6); *m. Sotah* 5:1 (the adulteress is "unclean"); and *b. Git.* 90b (of one who behaves improperly: "such a one it is a religious duty to divorce," for which the proof text is Deut. 24:1–2; cf. *t. Sotah* 5:9). *T. Reub.* 3:15 is also

Joseph and Divorce

There is, however, perhaps an even better argument for equating πορνεία with "adultery," or for understanding the word to include "adultery" within its range of sexual sins, and this argument comes not from extra-biblical sources but from Matthew itself. The First Gospel contains a story in which a main character decides to obtain a divorce. I refer to Joseph's predicament in 1:19–25. Here Mary becomes pregnant through the Holy Spirit, Joseph learns of her pregnancy before he is aware of its supernatural cause, and he, in response, determines to acquire a certificate of divorce.[9] Joseph seeks a divorce, even though he has not lived with Mary, because betrothal counts as marriage.[10] Yet, in the event, he does not carry through his resolution, for the angel of the Lord appears and disabuses him of his mistaken inference, namely, that his wife has been unfaithful.

Although discussions of Matt. 5:31–32 and 19:1–12 have, to the extent of my reading, paid scant or, much more often, no attention at all to 1:18–25, it is difficult to fathom why.[11] The text, in what may well be a redactional notice, plainly asserts that Joseph is "just" or "righteous" (δίκαιος). In fact, this estimation of his character is part and parcel of the sentence which informs us of Joseph's decision to divorce: "Although Joseph, her husband, was a righteous man, he was unwilling to expose her to public disgrace; and so he resolved to divorce her quietly." This prompts a question. What if the prohibitions of divorce in 5:32 and 19:9 were, as in Mark and Luke, absolute or unqualified; that is, what if these two verses seemed not to allow

---

relevant: Jacob never again slept with Bilhah after learning that she had slept with Reuben. For relevant Christian interpretations of Matt. 1 see next note.

9. For this understanding of Matthew's text see Raymond E. Brown, *The Birth of the Messiah: A Commentary on the Infancy Narratives in the Gospels of Matthew and Luke* (new updated ed.; New York: Doubleday, 1993), pp. 125–28. Cf. Justin, *Dial.* 78 (PTS 47, ed. Marcovich, p. 204: Joseph "supposed Mary to be pregnant by intercourse with a man"); *Prot. Jas.* 13–14 (Joseph asks, "Who has done this evil in my house and defiled the virgin?" and then he observes, "If I conceal her sin, I shall be found to be in opposition to the law of the Lord"); Chrysostom, *Hom. Matt.* 4:7(4) (PG 57.44: "it was not suspicion but the burden of the womb that wholly convicted her" of adultery, and "to keep her in the house seemed to be transgression of the law").

10. Cf. Gen. 19:14; Judg 14:15; 15:1; and the rabbinic texts in SB 2:393–98.

11. To the best of my recollection, the exception among the commentaries known to me is my own: W. D. Davies and Dale C. Allison Jr., *A Critical and Exegetical Commentary on the Gospel according to Saint Matthew* (3 vols.; ICC; Edinburgh: T&T Clark, 1988–1998), 1:531, 3:16; but the comments there require expansion. Bockmuehl, "Matthew's Divorce Texts," p. 20, also refers to Matt. 1:19, but only in passing. See further now Luz, *Matthäus*, 4:98, n. 51, and Janzen, "Porneia," pp. 72, 79, both citing an earlier version of the present chapter. Isaksson, *Marriage*, pp. 138–39, comprehends the relevance of 1:18–25 for interpreting the exception clauses, but his observations have been ignored, presumably because he wrongly insists on equating πορνεία with premarital unchastity. This is not the situation in Matt. 1. Having been betrothed to each other, Joseph and Mary are man and wife; see references in previous note.

one to prosecute a divorce because of unchastity within marriage? Would our gospel not then exhibit a blatant contradiction? Would we not then have a reliable narrator affirming us that Joseph, who determines to obtain a divorce on account of his wife's imagined adultery, is "righteous," a man who acts in accord with God's will as expressed in the Torah, whereas Jesus would be, to the contrary, denying the validity of Joseph's envisaged action? Although I would not go so far as to affirm with confidence that Matthew must have added the exception clauses precisely because his Gospel tells a story in which Jesus' pious father determines to obtain a divorce on the ground that his wife has been, or so he believes, unchaste,[12] I would also not rule such a possibility out of court. Maybe we have been looking for an explanation outside of the text—Matthew shared the halakhik view of the school of Shammai (so many),[13] or Matthew's brand of Judaism required divorce for adultery (so Bockmuehl), or Matthew's community had a problem with Gentile converts incestuously married (so Joseph Fitzmyer)—whereas we should have been looking for an explanation from within Matthew itself: the exception clauses allow for harmony with the conduct of the righteous Joseph in 1:18–25.

Whatever the precise redactional motivation, the important point for us is that harmony between Joseph's deed and Jesus' imperative obtains only when πορνεία is equated with or includes "adultery," for adultery is, despite some church fathers and some modern exegetes, the imagined crime of Mary. If, on the other hand, πορνεία be taken to mean "incest" or "fornication," then the contradiction observed above would remain: in 5:32 and 19:9 Jesus makes provision for a legitimate divorce, but that provision has nothing to do with the course Joseph decides to follow. I again submit that such a reading would be inconsistent with the narrator's depiction of Joseph as "just." Would Jesus' father really be so characterized if his actions so obviously contradict a ruling of Jesus?

One could just perchance exonerate a Joseph whose conduct does not accord with the Gospel's teaching on divorce by claiming that he is innocent before the fact. In other words, Mary's dismayed husband acts as he does because Jesus has not yet made his ruling; Joseph behaves according to Moses, not the eschatological will of God as the Messiah reveals it. Yet it is doubtful that the First Gospel allows any real contradiction between Moses and Jesus.[14] The rationalization, furthermore, seems gratuitous.

12. For one thing, it may be that Matthew's tradition already had added the qualification to Jesus' word on divorce.

13. See, e.g., Reinhard Neudecker, "Das 'Ehescheidungsgesetz' von Dtn 24,1–4 nach altjüdischer Auslegung. Ein Beitrag zum Verständnis der neutestamentlichen Aussagen zur Ehescheidung," *Bib* 75 (1994), pp. 350–87.

14. I find myself largely agreeing with William R. G. Loader, *Jesus' Attitude towards the Law: A Study of the Gospels* (WUNT 2/97; Tübingen: Mohr Siebeck, 1997), pp. 137–72.

Surely the designation of Joseph as "just" naturally implies that readers regard him as a model of right behavior. Surely they may assume that, as a "just" individual, Joseph does nothing to contradict the moral teaching that the First Gospel promulgates elsewhere.

Chaste Conduct in Marriage

If Matt. 1:18–25 relates itself to 5:32 and 19:9 as example to precept in the matter of divorce, it may also, I should like to suggest, be profitably connected with the word about eunuchs in 19:10–12. This last I understand to be, not a recommendation of singleness following separation,[15] but a qualified[16] defense of celibacy. Some have a calling that cancels married life.[17] My reasons for so thinking need not be rehearsed here, for the only needful point is that 19:10–12, like other passages in the Jesus tradition,[18] has an ascetic orientation. It teaches that sexual intercourse need not be a duty, that sexual abstinence will be incumbent upon some.[19]

What does this have to do with Matt. 1:18–25? The pericope concludes with this: "When Joseph awoke from sleep, he did as the angel of the Lord commanded him; he took her as his wife, but had no marital relations with her until she had borne a son; and he named him Jesus" (vv. 24–25). Discussion of these words has generally observed that they underline the literal fulfillment of the formula quotation in 1:23: "Look, the virgin shall

15. *Pace* Q. Quesnell, "'Made Themselves Eunuchs for the Kingdom of Heaven' (Mt 19.12)," *CBQ* 30 (1968), pp. 335–58.

16. Note how the qualifications are piled up: "not all," "those to whom it is given," "he who is able." Johann Albrecht Bengel, *Gnomon Novi Testament* (2 vols.; Tübingen: Ludov. Frid. Fues, 1850), 1:132–33, comments: Jesus pits his words against "the universal enunciation of his disciples."

17. Cf. Davies and Allison, *Matthew*, 3:21–26; Gnilka, *Matthäusevangelium*, 2:154–56. The most helpful treatment of Matt. 9:12 to my knowledge remains Alexander Sand, *Reich Gottes und Eheverzicht im Evangelium nach Matthäus* (SBS 109; Stuttgart: Katholisches Bibelwerk, 1983).

18. Dale C. Allison Jr., *Jesus of Nazareth: Millenarian Prophet* (Minneapolis: Fortress, 1998), pp. 272–16, and *Asceticism and the New Testament* (ed. Leif E. Vaage and Vincent L. Wimbush; New York: Routledge, 1999), esp. the articles by Anthony J. Saldarini ("Asceticism and the Gospel of Matthew," pp. 11–28) and Stephen J. Patterson ("Askesis and the Early Jesus Tradition," pp. 49–69).

19. Contrast *Ps.-Phoc.* 175–76 ("Remain not unmarried, lest you die nameless. Give nature her due; beget in your turn as you were begotten"; on this see the commentary by Pieter W. van der Horst, *The Sentences of Pseudo-Phocylides* [SVTP 4; Leiden: Brill, 1978], pp. 225–27); *m. Yebam.* 6:6 ("No man may abstain from keeping the law, 'Be fruitful and multiply' [Gen. 1:28], unless he already has children"); and *b. Yebam.* 63b ("R. Eliezer stated, 'He who does not engage in propagation of the race is as though he sheds blood'"). For additional rabbinic texts of similar import see Harvey McArthur, "Celibacy in Judaism at the Time of Christian Beginnings," *AUSS* 25 (1987), pp. 164–68.

conceive and bear a son, and they shall name him Emmanuel" (Isa. 7:14). If Joseph, after his wife's virginal conception, were to have sexual intercourse with her, she would not be a virgin when Jesus is born, so the evangelist could not then say, following Isaiah, "the virgin shall . . . bear a son."

Additional commentary upon 1:24–25, when offered, has tended to focus on what, if anything, the verses might have to do with the later notion of Mary's perpetual virginity.[20] Perhaps, however, attention should also be directed to 19:10–12, which reveals acceptance of or sympathy for an ascetic manner of life, including sexual abstinence for a religious cause. That such sympathy should appear in what most have regarded as a Jewish document is no surprise. Religious celibacy was not foreign to ancient Judaism.[21] The haggadah, in fact, made Moses himself a celibate. Already Exod. 19:15 has the lawgiver instruct the people in this fashion: "Be ready by the third day; do not go near a woman." Later tradition, which inferred that Moses must have determined to remain in a state of constant purity and so continence in order to be ever ready to receive revelation, made much of this.[22]

There were also less exalted occasions on which some ancients might have determined to break off sexual relations, and one of those was pregnancy. Largely under the influence of Stoicism, certain morally serious Greeks and Romans, and many Christians after them, came to believe that the primary purpose of sex was procreation, and that one should "never use the bodily members simply for pleasure" (Porphyry, *Ad Marc.* 35). It followed that, in general, men should refrain from "sowing seed from which they are unwilling to have any offspring" (Plutarch, *Mor.* 144B) and that, in particular, intercourse during pregnancy was "against nature," without good purpose, unseemly. Consider the following texts:

> [Sexual association with a woman] should never occur for pleasure, but only for the procreation of children. For those powers and instruments and appetites ministering to copulation were implanted in people by God, not for the sake of pleasure, but for the eternal continuation of the race. (Ps.-Ocellus Lucanus, *Univ. nat.* 4.1–2)

20. The obvious answer is that while ἕως οὖ need not entail the resumption of sexual relations (cf. the legitimate observations of Chrysostom, *Hom. Matt.* 5.5(3) [PG 57.58]), the First Evangelist nonetheless would surely not have chosen such an expression if he thought Mary "ever virgin"; cf. Luz, *Matthäus*, 1:152–53. One understands why Helvidian and Jovinian used Matt. 1:25 to argue against her perpetual virginity.

21. Allison, *Jesus of Nazareth*, pp. 188–97; McArthur, "Celibacy"; Geza Vermes, *Jesus the Jew* (London: Collins, 1973), pp. 99–102; Pieter W. van der Horst, "Celibacy in Early Judaism," *RB* 109 (2002), pp. 390–402.

22. See Philo, *Mos.* 2.68–69; the targumim on Num. 12.1–2; *Sifre Num.* § 99; ARN A 2; *b. Šabb.* 87a; *Deut. Rab.* 11.10; *Exod. Rab.* 46.3; *Cant. Rab.* 4:4; Louis Ginzberg, *The Legends of the Jews* (6 vols.; Philadelphia: Jewish Publication Society, 1909–1938), 2:316; 3:107, 258; 6:90 (with additional references). Cf. the sexual abstinence of David and his men in 1 Sam. 21:1–6.

Those who have sexual intercourse with no thought of begetting children will set themselves against the most valuable institutions of the community. (Ibid. 4.4)[23]

It is also shameful to love one's own wife overmuch. In loving his wife a wise man takes reason for his guide, not passion. He resists the assault of passions, and does not allow himself to be impetuously swept away into the marital act. Nothing is more depraved than to love one's spouse as if she were an adulteress. Those men, however, who say they couple with a woman only to beget children for the sake of the state of the human race, should at least imitate the animals, and when their wives' womb swell, they should not destroy their posterity. They should show themselves to be not suitors but husbands. (Seneca, as quoted by Jerome, *C. Jovinianum* 1.49 [PL 23.281A–B])

Men who are not wanton or immoral are bound to consider sexual intercourse justified only when it occurs in marriage and is indulged in for the purpose of begetting children, since that is lawful, but unjust and unlawful when it is mere pleasure-seeking, even in marriage. (Musonius Rufus, frag. 12 [in Stobaeus, *Anth.* 4.22.90])

Each of us thinks of the woman he has married as his wife only for the purpose of bearing children. For as the farmer casts his seed on the soil and awaits the harvest without sowing over it, so we limit the pleasure of intercourse to bearing children. (Athenagoras, *Leg.* 33.1–2 [ed. Schoedel, p. 80])

[A man's] wife, after conception, is as a sister, and is considered as if she were of the same father. (Clement of Alexandria, *Strom.* 6.12.100 [GCS 15, ed. Stählin, p. 482])[24]

Let the married men examine themselves and seek if they approach their wives for this reason alone, that they might receive children, and after conception desist. . . . Even the beasts themselves know, when they have conceived, not to further grant opportunity to their males. (Origen, *Hom. Gen.* 5.4 [SC 7 bis, ed. Doutreleau, p. 172])[25]

True marital chastity avoids intercourse with a menstruating or pregnant woman. (Augustine, *C. Julianum* 3.21[43] [PL 44.724])[26]

23. For the view from another Hellenistic Pythagorean see Ps.-Charondas, *Preambles to the Laws*, in Hölgar Thesleff, *The Pythagorean Texts of the Hellenistic Period* (Turku, Finland: Åbo Akademi, 1965).

24. Cf. Clement of Alexandria, *Paed.* 2.10.83, 91, 93, 95 (SC 108, ed. Mondésert and Marroua, pp. 164–66, 176, 178–80; 182–84); idem, *Strom.* 3.7.57–60 (GCS 15, ed. Stählin, pp. 222–24).

25. Cf. *Hom. Gen.* 5.4 (SC 7bis, ed. Doutreleau, pp. 132–34), and *Cels.* 5.42 (ed. Marcovich, p. 356). In the latter Origen praises the customs of "the Jews," who do not "have sexual intercourse without offspring."

26. Cf. *Bon. coniug.* 10(11) (CSEL 41, ed. Zycha, p. 203): "Necessary sexual intercourse for begetting is free from blame and is alone worthy of marriage. But that which goes beyond this

Had the attitude that these texts exhibit—an attitude that is at odds with modern sensibilities and so is far from the minds of contemporary readers of Matthew—entered the Judaism of Matthew's time?[27] It had indisputably entered Philo's thinking. He could speak of men who "behave unchastely, not with the wives of others, but with their own" (*Spec.* 3.9); and what he meant is clear from *Jos.* 43: "the end we seek in wedlock is not pleasure but the begetting of lawful children."[28] Obviously the pleasure of the sexual act was not, for Philo, something to be sought for its own sake. The goal was rather procreation.

But what of others? Tobit 8:7 ("I now am taking this kinswoman of mine, not because of lust, but with sincerity"); *T. Iss.* 2:3 (God "perceived that she [Rachel] wanted to lie with Jacob for the sake of children and not for sexual gratification"); and *T. Benj.* 8:2 ("the person with a mind that is pure with love does not look on a woman for the purpose of having sexual relations") reflect similar sentiments.[29] Sexual intercourse is, in these texts, for offspring, not for sensual satisfaction. And then there is Josephus. When describing the Essenes, he remarks that they, or rather one group of them, "have no intercourse with them [women] during pregnancy, thus showing that their motive in marrying is not self-gratification but the procreation of children" (Josephus, *Bell.* 2.161). On this Todd Beal, identifying the authors of the Dead Sea Scrolls as Essenes, has observed: "that the purpose of marriage" was, for members of the

---

necessarily no longer follows reason but lust." Additional relevant texts include Iamblichus, *Vit. Pyth.* 210 (cf. Stobaeus, *Ecl.* 4.37.4 = Aristoxenus, frag. 39); Lucan, *De bello civ.* 2.387–88; Dio Chrysostom, *Orat.* 7:133–37; 36; *Sentences of Sextus* 231–32 (cf. 239); Plotinus, *Enn.* 3.5.1; Justin, *1 Apol.* 29 (PTS 38, ed. Marcovich, p. 75); Ambrose, *Exp. Luke* 1.43–45 (SC 45, ed. Tissot, pp. 68–70); Cyril of Jerusalem, *Cat.* 4:25 (PG 33.488A); *b. Yebam.* 61b. Discussion in P. Veyne, "La famille et l'amour sous le Haut-Empire romain," *Annales* 33 (1978), pp. 35–63, although he may tend to overestimate the pagan sympathy for sexual abstinence. For a different evaluation see Robin Lane Fox, *Pagans and Christians* (New York: Knopf, 1987), pp. 336–74. For the belief, professed by several (but far from all) physicians, that sexual intercourse is injurious to health, see the texts and discussion in Peter Brown, *The Body and Society: Men, Women, and Sexual Renunciation in Early Christianity* (New York: Columbia, 1988), pp. 17–25; and for the medical opinion that it should be abandoned during pregnancy see Soranus, *Gyn.* 1.46, 56. According to Diogenes Laertius, *Pyth.* 9, Pythagoras taught that sex is "harmful at every season and is never good for the health."

27. I assume that a Christian Jew wrote the First Gospel and that its first audience was Jewish Christian; see Davies and Allison, *Matthew*, 1:7–58.

28. Note also Philo's comments in *Abr.* 137 (God blessed "the unions which men and women naturally make for begetting children") and *Spec.* 3.113 (some are "pleasure-lovers when they mate with their wives, not to procreate children and perpetuate the race; [then they are] like pigs and goats in quest of the enjoyment which such intercourse gives"). For discussion of Philo's views on sexual intercourse see Kathy L. Gaca, *The Making of Fornication: Eros, Ethics, and Political Reform in Greek Philosophy and Early Christianity* (Berkeley: University of California Press, 2003), pp. 190–217.

29. Trans. H. C. Kee, *OTP* 1:802–3 (alt.), 827.

Qumran sect, "procreation may be indicated by CD 7:6–7, which speaks of those who 'live in camps according to the rule of the land and take a wife and beget children' . . . Also, Josephus's statement that the Essenes have no intercourse during pregnancy . . . is entirely in harmony with the self-control commanded of the men of Qumran, who had to be at least twenty years old before they married (1QSa 1:9–10)."[30]

In addition to Josephus's generalization about one branch of the Essenes, he also, when purporting to describe the marriage laws of the Jews generally, comments that "none who has intercourse with a woman who is with child can be considered clean" (καθαρός; C. Ap. 2.202). By "clean" Josephus presumably means morally pure, as in m. Sotah 5.1, where an adulteress is "unclean" to her husband.

Also perhaps germane is Pseudo-Phocylides, a book filled with conventional wisdom. It lays down as exhortation, without any explanation, this sentence: "Do not lay your hand upon your wife when she is pregnant" (186). While some commentators take these words to refer to sexual relations with a pregnant woman, others believe that they speak against obtaining an abortion or acting violently in a way that induces a miscarriage; and, unfortunately, it seems impossible to decide who is right here: the text is too cryptic.[31] One can in any case observe that there is a much later Jewish text, b. Nid. 31a, which preserves the superstition that marital intercourse is injurious to the woman and the fetus during the first three months of pregnancy and injurious to the woman during the middle three months (although, strangely enough, these problems supposedly vanish during the third trimester).[32]

The evidence suffices to show that, both before and after Matthew's day, some ancients, including some Jews, considered intercourse during pregnancy less than seemly.[33] Now we cannot know for a fact that the author of Matthew, like Clement of Alexandria, Origen, Augustine, and so many other early Christians,[34] likewise believed that sex after concep-

---

30. Todd S. Beal, Josephus' Description of the Essenes Illustrated by the Dead Sea Scrolls (SNTMS 58; Cambridge: Cambridge University Press, 1988), p. 112.

31. See van der Horst, Pseudo-Phocylides, pp. 234–35.

32. Is this due to the influence of Greco-Roman medicine? The Hippocratic texts encourage intercourse during the ninth month as a way of preparing for birth; so Aline Rousselle, Porneia: On Desire and the Body in Antiquity (Oxford: Basil Blackwell, 1988), p. 42.

33. Cf. also Hist. Rech. 11:6–8: the Rechabites couple only once in their lives. This in turn reminds one of Sozomen, HE 7.28 (GCS 50, ed. Hansen, p. 344): Ajax of Gaza slept with his wife on only three occasions, and he had three sons to show for it.

34. The well-informed John T. Noonan Jr., in Contraception: A History of Its Treatment by the Catholic Theologians and Canonists (enlarged ed.; Cambridge: Harvard University Press,

tion was improper, a sacrifice of purpose to pleasure. But there certainly were those in the first-century Jewish world who did so think, and Matt. 1:24–25 just might be evidence that the First Evangelist shared their view. Perhaps the note that Joseph did not "know" Mary during her time with child was designed not only to make for the literal fulfillment of Isa. 7:14 but also to exhibit Joseph's exemplary behavior. If Jesus' father was not exactly a eunuch for the kingdom of heaven, he did know when to refrain from coupling with his wife. At least we may be reasonably confident that there were some early hearers of Matthew who would have found such meaning in our text, and hence in righteous Joseph an illustration of proper sexual conduct within marriage.[35]

1986), p. 78, confesses that Lactantius, *Div. inst.* 6.23 (PL 6.716A–21B), is "the only opinion I have encountered in any Christian theologian before 1500 explicitly upholding the lawfulness of intercourse in pregnancy." While this scarcely settles what Matthew may have believed, it cannot but give one some pause for reflection.

35. The interpretation I have proposed is, to the extent of my knowledge, unattested in patristic texts, this because the doctrine of Mary's perpetual virginity—which first made its appearance in the second century—rendered the thought of a temporary abstinence from sexual relations, that is, abstinence during pregnancy alone, followed by a resumption of relations with Joseph, unthinkable.

10

The Configuration of the Sermon
on the Mount and Its Meaning

Concerning the basic structure of Matthew, a topic discussed in chapter 7, consensus has escaped us. There is likewise no conformity of opinion regarding the architecture of the Sermon on the Mount, the subject of the present chapter. At the same time, my own review of recent proposals has revealed some concord amid all the unwelcome disagreement; and I should like, in the following pages, while keeping such agreement in mind, to offer my own proposals regarding the configuration of the Bible's most famous discourse. It is my conviction that the discussion has not yet run its course, that some interesting and important observations have been missed. Furthermore, the structure of Matt. 5–7 not only has hermeneutical implications but also may tell us something important about the historical setting of our gospel.

Analysis

Matthew 4:23–5:2 and 7:28–8:1. The Sermon on the Mount has a conclusion that corresponds to its introduction.[1] The following words and phrases are common to 4:23–5:2 and 7:28–8:1:

1. The same is true, albeit to much lesser extent, of the second and third discourses. διδάσκων . . . καὶ κηρύσσων (teaching . . . and preaching, 9:35) and δώδεκα μαθητάς (twelve disciples,

| 4:25 | ἠκολούθησαν αὐτῷ ὄχλοι πολλοί (great crowds followed him) |
| 8:1 | ἠκολούθησαν αὐτῷ ὄχλοι πολλοί (great crowds followed him) |

| 5:1 | τοὺς ὄχλους (the crowds) |
| 7:28 | οἱ ὄχλοι (the crowds) |

| 5:1 | τὸ ὄρος (the mountain) |
| 8:1 | τοῦ ὄρους (the mountain) |

| 5:1 | ἀνέβη (he went up) |
| 8:1 | καταβάντος (going down) |

| 5:2 | ἐδίδασκεν (he taught) |
| 7:28 | διδαχῇ αὐτοῦ (his teaching) |

In addition, "opening his mouth" (5:2) finds its counterpart in "when Jesus finished these words" (7:28).

A beginning and an end that mirror each other create an *inclusio*.[2] Standing between 4:23–5:2 and 7:28–8:1, like the books between two bookends, 5:3–7:27 is a discrete literary unit. This in turn implies that the simplest outline of the sermon is this:

4:23–5:2	Introduction
5:3–7:27	Discourse
7:28–8:1	Conclusion

Matthew 5:3–12 and 7:13–27. The nine beatitudes in 5:3–12 head the sermon.[3] Their extensive parallelism and poetic quality are harbingers of things to come:

10:1) occur at the beginning of the missionary discourse, διδάσκειν καὶ κηρύσσειν (to teach and to preach, 11:1) and δώδεκα μαθηταῖς (twelve disciples, 11:1) at its conclusion. The collection of parables in chapter 13 begins with ὁ Ἰησοῦς . . . παραβολαῖς (Jesus . . . in parables, 13:1–3) and ends with ὁ Ἰησοῦς τὰς παραβολάς ([When] Jesus [finished] the parables, 13:53).

2. For Matthew's use of *inclusio* see J. C. Fenton, "Inclusio and Chiasmus in Matthew," *Studia Evangelica* (ed. Kurt Aland et al.; TU 73; Berlin: Akademie-Verlag, 1959), pp. 174–79, and Charles H. Lohr, "Oral Techniques in the Gospel of Matthew," *CBQ* 23 (1961), pp. 408–10.

3. More than one scholar has criticized me for suggesting that, as Matt. 5:10 is redactional and redundant (cf. vv. 11–12), and as our Gospel features numerous triads, part of the evangelist's reason for adding the verse may have been a desire to reach the number nine, which is the product of 3 × 3. This suggestion, which emphatically does not imply three thematic subsections, is not far-fetched, and it certainly has ancient precedent. According to *Apophth. Patr.* (alphabetical) Epiphanius 13, the number of the beatitudes is three times the number of the Trinity: τριπλῆς δὲ Τριάδος εἰκών, ἡ τῶν μακαρισμῶν ἀρίθμησις. Cf. Severianus (Ps.-Chrysostom), *Quando ipsi sub. omn.* (ed. Hardacher, *ZKT* 31 [1907], p. 164): Ἰησοῦς δὲ ὁ κύριος ἡμῶν δίδωσιν ἐννέα

1. (5:3) μακάριοι οἱ . . . ὅτι αὐτῶν ἐστιν ἡ βασιλεία τῶν οὐρανῶν
   (Blessed are those . . . because theirs is the kingdom of heaven)
   1st clause = 26 letters; 2nd clause = 32 letters; total = 58 letters

2. (5:4) μακάριοι οἱ . . . ὅτι αὐτοί . . .
   (Blessed are those . . . because they . . .)
   1st clause = 20 letters; 2nd clause = 22 letters; total = 42 letters

3. (5:5) μακάριοι οἱ . . . ὅτι αὐτοί . . .
   (Blessed are those . . . because they . . .)
   1st clause = 16 letters; 2nd clause = 28 letters; total = 44 letters

4. (5:6) μακάριοι οἱ . . . ὅτι αὐτοί . . .
   (Blessed are those . . . because they . . .)
   1st clause = 44 letters; 2nd clause = 22 letters; total = 66 letters

5. (5:7) μακάριοι οἱ . . . ὅτι αὐτοί . . .
   (Blessed are those . . . because they . . .)
   1st clause = 19 letters; 2nd clause = 19 letters; total = 38 letters

6. (5:8) μακάριοι οἱ . . . ὅτι αὐτοί . . .
   (Blessed are those . . . because they . . .)
   1st clause = 25 letters; 2nd clause = 21 letters; total = 46 letters

7. (5:9) μακάριοι οἱ . . . ὅτι αὐτοί . . .
   (Blessed are those . . . because they . . .)
   1st clause = 21 letters; 2nd clause = 26 letters; total = 47 letters

8. (5:10) μακάριοι οἱ . . . ὅτι αὐτῶν ἐστιν ἡ βασιλεία τῶν οὐρανῶν
   (Blessed are those . . . because theirs is the kingdom of heaven)
   1st clause = 38 letters; 2nd clause = 31 letters; total = 69 letters

9. (5:11–12) μακάριοι ἐστε . . . ὅτι . . .
   (Blessed are you . . . because . . .)
   1st clause = 108 letters; 2nd clause = 71 letters; total = 179 letters

The concluding 5:11–12 should not be excluded from the total number of makarisms and joined with 5:13–16 instead of 5:3–10.[4] The beatitude does, to be sure, distinguish itself from the preceding members of the series. It is, as the letter counts indicate, much longer, it contains imperatives, and it addresses readers directly with the second person plural.[5] Verse

---

μακαρισμοὺς ἀπὸ τριπλῆς τριάδος τρίπλοκον ἐργασάμενος τῶν μακαρισμῶν τὸν στέφανον. Note also Ernst Lohmeyer, *Das Evangelium nach Matthäus* (ed. W. Schmauch; KEK; Göttingen: Vandenhoeck & Ruprecht, 1958), p. 81. But whether my speculation has any merit, it has no bearing on my larger structural proposals regarding Matt. 5–7. Criticism of one is not criticism of the other.

4. In addition to what follows see David Hellholm, "'Rejoice and Be Glad, for Your Reward is Great in Heaven': An Attempt at Solving the Structural Problem of Matt. 5:11–12," in *Festschrift Günter Wagner* (ed. Faculty of Baptist Theological Seminary, Rüschlikon, Switzerland; Bern: Peter Lang, 1994), pp. 45–86.

5. Cf. Augustine, *Serm. Dom.* 1.3.10 (CCSL 35, ed. Mutzenbecher, p. 7).

10 seems, moreover, to form an *inclusio* with verse 3—"because theirs is the kingdom of heaven" occurs in both⁶—while verses 11–12 serve as a transition from 5:3–10 to the sayings about salt and light in verses 13–16, which also feature ἐστε (you are). Yet the first eight beatitudes all begin with μακάριοι, and the appearance of this word at the beginning of 5:11 most naturally indicates continuation of the series.⁷ Beyond that, and as David Daube noticed some time ago, good precedent exists both for the last member of a series being much longer than the preceding members and for abruptly switching from one person to another, in this case from the third to the second person. Both things appear in the Bible, in Jewish prayer texts, and in English literature.⁸

The recently published 4Q525 from Qumran supplies a striking case in point. This features three short beatitudes in the form of antithetical couplets that use the third person plural. Following them is a much longer beatitude which abandons the antithetical form and which employs the third person singular:

Blessed are those who adhere to his laws,
    and do not adhere to perverted paths.
Blessed are those who rejoice in her.
    and do not explore insane paths.
Blessed are those who search for her with pure hands,
    and do not importune her with a treacherous heart

6. Although some hesitation may be in order. δικαιοσύνη appears in both vv. 6 and 10 and is not obviously part of a pattern. θεός, repeated in vv. 8 and 9, certainly is not. Even the much-remarked-upon recurrence of four words beginning with π in vv. 3–6 (πτωχοί, πενθοῦντες, πραεῖς, πεινῶντες) might be nothing more than coincidence. Who would make anything of the reiteration of m and p words in the English translations ("mourn," "meek," and "merciful" in vv. 4, 5, and 7, "poor," "pure," "peacemakers," "persecuted" in vv. 3, 8, 9, 10)? Perhaps, however, I am being too cautious here. Many now see a 4 + 4 + 1 pattern, and perhaps they are correct; see, e.g., Mark Allan Powell, "Matthew's Beatitudes: Reversals and Rewards of the Kingdom," *CBQ* 58 (1996), pp. 460–79, and Walter Petersen, *Zur Eigenart des Matthäus: Untersuchung zur Rhetorik in der Bergpredigt* (OSJCB 2; Osnabrück: Universitätsverlag, 2001), pp. 136–38.

7. Many Matthean verses both end one section and introduce another. They are doors, not walls. See Paul Gaechter, *Die literarische Kunst im Matthäus-Evangelium* (SBS 7; Stuttgart: Katholisches Bibelwerk, n.d.), pp. 54–59, and Ulrich Luz, *Das Evangelium nach Matthäus* (4 vols.; EKK 1/1–4; Düsseldorf: Benziger, 1990–2002), 1:26. 5:11–12 belongs in their company.

8. For a change in persons see Isa. 63:10–14; 4Q286 10 ii. 2–13; Sir. 47:12–23; 48:1–11; *Gos. Thom.* 68–69; *Acts Thom.* 94; Ps.-Ephraem, *Comm. res.* (ed. Phrantzoles, pp. 74–75) (the last three string together beatitudes). For examples of the climactic member of a series being longer or different see Matt. 1:2–17; Luke 6:37–38; *Acts Paul Thec.* 5–6 (beatitudes); *ARN* A 14 (the story of the death of Johanan ben Zakkai's son); *b. Pesaḥ.* 57a (woes). Discussion in David Daube, "The Last Beatitude," in *Collected Works of David Daube*, vol. 2, *New Testament Judaism* (ed. Calum Carmichael; Berkeley: Robbins Collection, 2000), pp. 321–25, and Dale C. Allison Jr., *The Jesus Tradition in Q* (Harrisburg, Pa.: Trinity Press International, 1997), pp. 96–103.

Blessed is the man who attains Wisdom,
  and walks in the law of the Most High,
  and dedicates his heart to her ways,
  and is constrained by her discipline
  and always takes pleasure in her punishments;
  and does not forsake her in the hardship of [his] wrongs,
  and in the time of anguish does not discard her,
  and does not forget her [in the days of] terror,
  and in the distress of his soul does not loathe her.
  For he always thinks of her . . .[9]

From a much later time is Ps.-Ephraem, *Beat. 55.* This collection features a series of fifty-five makarisms. As with 4Q525, the concluding member is longer than all the others, it shifts from the third person singular to the third person plural, and its character is rather different:

1. Blessed is the one who
   has become wholly free in the Lord from all earthly things of this vain life
   and loved God alone, the good and compassionate one.
2. Blessed is the one who
   has become a ploughman of the virtues
   and raised a harvest of fruits of life in the Lord,
   as a ploughed field bearing wheat.
3. Blessed is the one who
   has become a good gardener of the virtues
   and planted a spiritual vine
   and plucked grapes and filled his presses with fruits of life in the Lord.
   . . .
55. Blessed are those
   who watch according to God continually,
   for they will be overshadowed by God in the day of judgment,
   becoming sons of the bridal chamber;
   in joy and gladness they will see the bridegroom.
   But I and those like me, idle and pleasure-loving,
   will weep and lament as we watch our brothers in everlasting glory,
   while we are in torments.

(Ed. Phrantzoles, pp. 252–66)

In view of this text, 4Q525, and other parallels,[10] Matt. 5:3–12 appears to embody a conventional pattern. It seems to be a set of nine, with an irregular concluding member.

9. Florentino García Martínez, *The Dead Sea Scrolls Translated: The Qumran Texts in English* (trans. W. G. E. Watson; 2nd ed.; Grand Rapids: Eerdmans, 1996), p. 395.
10. See n. 8.

What is the chief function of Matthew's beatitudes?[11] That they implicitly contain commands is obvious. Those who take them to heart cannot but desire to become meek, to show mercy, to make peace. So 5:3–12 is imperatival; the verses commence the moral instruction of the Sermon on the Mount.[12] Yet this is not the sole or even primary *telos* of the Beatitudes in their present context. Matthew's Jesus blesses the oppressed faithful as they are now, reviled and persecuted. Setting aside momentarily the prospect of judgment, he speaks only of desired reward. He imagines eschatological good fortune and instills hope beyond the arduous present.[13] So the Beatitudes are conciliatory. Before delivering his hard imperatives, Matthew's Jesus first encourages and consoles the faithful. I like to imagine that the evangelist would have welcomed the comments of Isho'dad of Merv: Jesus, when promising rewards for multiple virtues, "offers consolation to everyone, so that although an individual be insufficient for all good works, yet he may not be deprived of them all; and that from whatever distance and by whatever way every one goes to Him, the door of the kingdom of heaven is open before him, and He does not cut off hope."[14]

If blessings precede Jesus' commands, warnings succeed them. In this way, as in so many others, Jesus is like Moses, whose teaching in Deu-

11. They do not, against Austin Farrer, *St. Matthew and St. Mark* (2nd ed.; Westminster: Dacre, 1966), pp. 160–76, and M. D. Goulder, *Midrash and Lection in Matthew: The Speaker's Lectures in Biblical Studies, 1969–71* (London: SPCK, 1974), p. 269, supply an outline of the rest of the sermon. For criticism of Goulder see Warren Carter, *What Are They Saying about Matthew's Sermon on the Mount?* (New York: Paulist, 1994), pp. 35–39. For Augustine's similar proposal see Hans Dieter Betz, *The Sermon on the Mount: A Commentary on the Sermon on the Mount, Including the Sermon on the Plain (Matthew 5:3–7:27 and Luke 6:20–49)* (Hermeneia; Minneapolis: Fortress, 1995), pp. 45–46.

12. See esp. David Hellholm, "Beatitudes and Their Illocutionary Functions," in *Ancient and Modern Perspectives on the Bible and Culture: Essays in Honor of Hans Dieter Betz* (ed. Adela Yarbro Collins; Atlanta: Scholars Press, 1998), pp. 286–344. According to Powell, "Beatitudes," the first four beatitudes promise reward for the unfortunate while the next four promise reward for the virtuous.

13. See esp. Ingo Broer, *Die Seligpreisungen der Bergpredigt: Studien zu ihrer Überlieferung und Interpretation* (BBB 61; Bonn: Peter Hanstein, 1986), and Robert Guelich, "The Matthean Beatitudes: 'Entrance Requirement' or Eschatological Blessings?" *JBL* 95 (1976), pp. 415–34.

14. Isho'dad of Merv, *Comm. Matt.* ad loc. (HSem 6, ed. Gibson, p. 58); cf. *Ps.-Clem. Rec.* 2.28 (GCS 42, ed. Rehm, pp. 68–69), where the Beatitudes inspire patience. —I am at a loss to fathom why Bernard Brandon Scott and Margaret E. Dean, "A Sound Map of the Sermon on the Mount," in *Treasures Old and New: Contributions to Matthean Scholarship* (ed. David R. Bauer and Mark Allan Powell; Atlanta: Scholars Press, 1996), p. 364, assert that my outline of the sermon "relegates the beatitudes to the function of introduction, along with the framing material in 4:23–5:2. According to this arrangement, the beatitudes all but disappear." Not only do I include 5:3–12 within the discourse proper, but an introduction can be as important as a conclusion, as the Sermon on the Mount itself illustrates, and I have never said anything to indicate otherwise.

teronomy is attended by promises and curses.[15] Matthew 7:13–14 (on the two ways), 7:15–23 (on false prophets),[16] and 7:24–27 (on hearers and doers of the word) confront the audience with strong exhortations. These underscore the importance of doing—the verb ποιεῖν, "to do," appears a full nine times in these fifteen verses[17]—the will of the Father in heaven as 5:13–7:12 has set this forth. In Luther's words, "Our dear Lord has now finished preaching. Finally He closes this sermon with several warnings, to arm us against all kinds of hindrances and offenses of both doctrine and life that we confront in the world."[18] The section looks like this:

A. The two ways (7:13–14)
    1. Exhortation (7:13)
    2. The wide gate and the easy road (7:13)
    3. The narrow gate and the hard road (7:14)
B. False prophets (7:15–23)
    1. Exhortation (7:15)
    2. The deeds of the false prophets now (7:15–20)
    3. The fate of the false prophets on judgment day (7:21–23)
C. The two builders (7:24–27)
    1. The wise builder (7:24–25)
    2. The foolish builder (7:26–27)

Each of the three subsections features striking alternatives which, unlike the introductory beatitudes, underline the possibility of eschatological failure. There are two ways, one of which leads to destruction. There are two trees, one of which is thrown into the fire. And there are two builders, one of whom loses all:

15. On the Mosaic character of so much of the Sermon see Dale C. Allison Jr., *The New Moses: A Matthean Typology* (Minneapolis: Fortress, 1993), pp. 172–207.

16. Some regard 7:15–23 not as one unit but as two, consisting of 7:15–20 and 21–23. See esp. David Hill, "False Prophets and Charismatics: Structure and Interpretation in Mt 7:15–23," *Bib* 57 (1976), pp. 327–48. Hill makes his case by arguing that v. 15 refers to Pharisees, vv. 21–23 to charismatic Christian prophets. But the endeavor to identify concrete groups behind 7:15–23 is hopeless, and both 7:15–20 and 21–23 have to do with false prophets, whoever precisely they may be for Matthew and his community. 7:15–20 opens with the admonition "Beware of false prophets," whereas 7:21–23 condemns people who have prophesied in Jesus' name and so must be false prophets. The subject does not change. Cf. Petri Luomanen, *Entering the Kingdom of Heaven: A Study of the Structure of Matthew's View of Salvation* (WUNT 2/101; Tübingen: Mohr Siebeck, 1998), p. 97–99.

17. Vv. 17 (*bis*), 18 (*bis*), 19, 21, 22, 24, 26.

18. Martin Luther, *The Sermon on the Mount and the Magnificat* (ed. J. Pelikan; St. Louis: Concordia, 1956), p. 241. Cf. the scheme in *Did.* 1:1–6:1: after a barrage of imperatives, many with parallels in Matthew's sermon, there is this: "See that no one make you err from this way of teaching, for he teaches you without God" (6:1).

7:13–14   Narrow gate and hard road
           vs.
           wide gate and easy road

           Life
           vs.
           destruction

7:15–23   Good tree and good fruit
           vs.
           bad tree and bad fruit

           Those who do the will of the Father
           vs.
           those who only say "Lord, Lord"

7:24–27   Those who hear Jesus' words and do them
           vs.
           those who hear Jesus' words and do not do them

           The wise individual who builds on rock;
           the house endures the storm
           vs.
           the foolish individual who builds on sand;
           the house falls before the storm

In short, the conclusion, which warns about eschatological loss (7:13–27), is the counterpart of the beginning, which consoles with beatitudes (5:3–12). Blessings come first, warnings last. Schematically:

5:3–12   Nine blessings
5:13–7:12   Central section of the sermon
7:13–27   Three warnings

Matthew 5:13–16. The central section of the discourse, 5:13–7:12, has its own heading. In 5:13, Jesus tells his disciples that they are to be the salt of the earth and, in 5:14–16, that they are to be the light of the world. The declarations, with their repeated, emphatic, introductory ὑμεῖς ἐστε (You are, vv. 13, 14), are quite general. Hearers do not here learn how to become salt or light. This is because 5:13–16, as a wide-ranging superscription, stands above the detailed paraenesis proper. It is a transitional passage, in which the speaker moves from the life of the blessed future, promised in 5:3–12, to the demands of life in the present, outlined in 5:17–7:12. The theme is no longer gift but task. 5:13–16 is a summation of the intended aim of the discourse, a broad characterization of those who obediently enter into 5:17–7:12.[19]

Matthew 5:17–7:12. What are the major subdivisions of 5:17–7:12, the lengthy section 5:13–16 introduces? Almost all the recent commentators recognize, first of all, that a section on the Torah spans 5:17–48. That the next major section is the "cult-didache,"[20] which instructs the faithful about almsgiving (6:1–4), prayer (6:5–15), and fasting (6:16–18), is also a near consensus. 6:19–7:12 is more problematic. Although most—including Betz and Luz—recognize it as a unified section, others—Hagner and Talbert, for instance—do not. Below I shall, concurring with the former, argue that 6:19–7:12 is structurally similar to the unified 5:21–48, and further that the chief exhortations of 6:19–7:12, which have to do with money (6:19–24) and with judging others (7:1–6), fall together under the one rubric, social relations. This leads to the following scheme:

The task of the people of God in the world (5:13–7:12)
A. Summary: salt and light (5:13–16)
B. Details: Torah, cult, social issues (5:17–7:12)
   1. Jesus and the Torah (5:17–48)
   2. The Christian cult (6:1–18)
   3. Social relations (6:19–7:12)

Matthew 5:17–48. Into the many exegetical conundrums that Matt. 5:17–48 raises I thankfully need not enter here. It is enough in these pages to call attention to two facts about its structure, the first being that the six paragraphs in 5:21–48 come after a general statement of principles, 5:17–20.[21] This prefatory passage has two functions, one negative, the other positive. Negatively, 5:17–19 is *prokatalepsis*. It anticipates an incorrect interpretation of 5:21–48, which is that Jesus' words contradict the Torah, and it states in advance the truth, which is that Jesus comes not to abolish but to fulfill the law. Positively, 5:20 announces what 5:21–48 is really all about, the greater righteousness, a righteousness that should surpass (περισσεύσῃ) that of the scribes and Pharisees. Note that 5:47,

---

19. Cf. Christoph Burchard, "The Theme of the Sermon on the Mount," in *Essays on the Love Commandment* (ed. Reginald Fuller; Philadelphia: Fortress, 1978), pp. 62–64.

20. This is the terminology of Betz, *Sermon*, pp. 330–34.

21. One may compare the structure of Lev. 18:1–24 and Sir. 3:1–9 and recall the rabbinic כלל, which is a summary rule or declaration that heads a section consisting of particular cases or instances, פרטות, as in *m. ʿEd.* 3:1; *b. Hag* 6a–b; and *b. Sot.* 37b. See further David Daube, "Principles and Cases," in *New Testament Judaism*, pp. 173–75.

at the end of the section, returns to this theme: "And if you greet your brothers only, what more (περισσόν) do you do (than others)?"

The second relevant fact about the structure of 5:17–48 is that its six misnamed "antitheses" (5:21–26, 27–30, 31–32, 33–37, 38–42, 43–48) sort themselves into two sets of three.[22] Verses 21 and 27 begin with ἠκούσατε ὅτι ἐρρέθη, verse 31 with ἐρρέθη δέ. And then comes verse 33, the opening line of the fourth unit in the series. It begins with πάλιν ἠκούσατε ὅτι ἐρρέθη. Why the adverb, which occurs nowhere else in the Sermon on the Mount? The word's presence, which in no way affects the content of the surrounding material but which does break the rhythm of chapter 5, becomes explicable only if Matthew wishes to indicate that, with verse 33, he is in some sense making Jesus start over or begin a new series. πάλιν, in other words, marks an editorial dividing line. Jesus first speaks to three issues: murder (5:21–26), adultery (5:27–30), and divorce (5:31–32). He then (πάλιν) moves on to consider three more issues: oaths (5:33–37), retaliation (5:38–42), and love (5:43–48). So the evangelist is thinking in terms of triads. Rather than there being six paragraphs detailing Jesus' relationship to Mosaic imperatives, 5:21–32 and 5:33–48 contain two sets of three.[23] As a consequence, 5:17–48 is naturally outlined in this fashion:

> Jesus and the Torah (5:17–48)
> a) General principles (5:17–20)
> b) Two triads of specific instruction (5:21–48)
>   (1) The first triad (5:21–32)
>   (a) On murder (5:21–26)
>   (b) On adultery (5:27–30)
>   (c) On divorce (5:31–32)
>   (2) The second triad (5:33–48)
>   (a) Do not swear (5:33–37)
>   (b) Turn the other cheek (5:38–42)
>   (c) Love your enemy (5:43–48)

22. A few have joined vv. 31–32 to vv. 27–30 and so have counted only five paragraphs; see, e.g., Olav Hanssen, "Zum Verständnis der Bergpredigt: Eine missionstheologische Studie zu Mt 5,17–48," in *Der Ruf Jesu und die Antwort der Gemeinde: Exegetische Untersuchungen Joachim Jeremias zum 70. Geburtstag gewidmet von seinem Schülern* (ed. Eduard Lohse with Christoph Burchard and Berndt Schaller; Göttingen: Vandenhoeck & Ruprecht, 1970), p. 103, and Scott and Dean, "Sound Map," p. 333. This overlooks the extensive parallelism between 5:31–32 and the rest of the paragraphs in 5:21–48; see below.

23. So also, among others, Betz, *Sermon*, p. 263; Gaechter, *Kunst*, pp. 18–19; Walter Grundmann, *Das Evangelium nach Matthäus* (THKNT 1; Berlin: Evangelische Verlagsanstalt, 1968), p. 163; Josef Kürzinger, "Zur Komposition der Bergpredigt nach Matthäus," *Bib* 40 (1959), pp. 572–74; and Wilhelm Michaelis, *Das Evangelium nach Matthäus* (3 vols.; Zürich: Zwingli, 1948–1949), 1:270.

It is perhaps worth remarking that the lengths of 5:21–32 and 33–48 are nearly identical. The former has 1,138 letters while the latter has 1,133. This adds to the symmetry.

Three additional observations confirm the analysis. (1) The full phrase, "You have heard that it was said to those of old," appears only in 5:21 and 5:33, in the two verses that head the two triads. (2) In 5:21–32, the threefold "But I say to you" is in each instance followed by the Greek ὅτι. This construction does not occur in 5:33–48. (3) In 5:21–32, "But I say to you" prefaces legal ordinances with πᾶς ὁ + participle introducing negative results:

5:22	Negative result: "will be liable to judgment"
5:28	Negative result: "has already committed adultery with her in his heart"
5:31–32	Negative result: "makes her to commit adultery"

In 5:33–48, ἐγὼ δὲ λέγω ὑμῖν (without ὅτι) introduces straightforward imperatives. Those imperatives are general and so invite further specification:

5:34	General rule: "Do not swear at all"
5:34–37	Specifications: not by heaven, by earth, by Jerusalem, by head
5:39	General rule: "Do not resist evil"
5:39–42	Specifications: turn cheek, give coat, go extra mile, give to those asking
5:44	General rule: "Love your enemies and pray for those who persecute you"
5:45–47	Specifications: sun rises, rain falls, tax collectors love own kind, Gentiles greet own kind

The parallels within and between these two sets of triads are represented in the table on page 184.[24]

Matthew 5:21, 27, and 31 open with citations of or allusions to biblical texts that appear in Deuteronomy, although not exclusively in Deuteronomy. Matthew 5:21 cites Deut. 5:17 (or Exod. 20:13); 5:27 cites Deut. 5:18 (or Exod. 20:14); and 5:31 refers to Deut. 24:1–4. Matthew 5:33, 38, and 43, however, open with citations of or allusions to the

24. With regard to "general + and clarifying imperatives" in 5:43–48, I accept the correction of Glen H. Stassen, "The Fourteen Triads of the Sermon on the Mount," *JBL* 122 (2003), pp. 267–308, that these are not appended illustrations but climactic "transforming initiatives."

Parallels between Two Triads in Matthew 5:21–48

First triad (5:21–32): murder // adultery // divorce	Second triad, 5:33–48: oaths // retaliation // love
	introductory πάλιν
21–26 ἠκούσατε ὅτι ἐρρέθη τοῖς ἀρχαίοις	33–37 ἠκούσατε ὅτι ἐρρέθη τοῖς ἀρχαίοις
27–30 ἠκούσατε ὅτι ἐρρέθη	38–42 ἠκούσατε ὅτι ἐρρέθη
31–32 ἐρρέθη δέ	43–48 ἠκούσατε ὅτι ἐρρέθη
21–26 οὐ + imperative from Pentateuch	33–37 imperative from Pentateuch
27–30 οὐ + imperative from Pentateuch	38–42 imperative from Pentateuch
31–32 imperative from Pentateuch	43–48 imperative from Pentateuch
21–26 ὃς δ' ἄν/ ὃς δ' ἄν/ ὃς δ' ἄν	
27–30	
31–32 ὃς ἄν/ ὃς ἐάν	
21–26 ἐγὼ δὲ λέγω ὑμῖν ὅτι	33–37 ἐγὼ δὲ λέγω ὑμῖν (no ὅτι)
27–30 ἐγὼ δὲ λέγω ὑμῖν ὅτι	38–42 ἐγὼ δὲ λέγω ὑμῖν (no ὅτι)
31–32 ἐγὼ δὲ λέγω ὑμῖν ὅτι	43–48 ἐγὼ δὲ λέγω ὑμῖν (no ὅτι)
21–26 πᾶς ὁ + participle	33–37 μή + aorist infinitive (imperative)
27–30 πᾶς ὁ + participle	38–42 μή + aorist infinitive (imperative)
31–32 πᾶς ὁ + participle	43–48 positive present imperative
21–26 negative result	33–37 general rule + clarifying imperatives
27–30 negative result	38–42 general rule + clarifying imperatives
31–32 negative result	43–48 general rule + clarifying imperatives

Old Testament that appear in, among other places, Leviticus. Matthew 5:33 summarizes Lev. 19:12 (but Num. 30:2 and Deut. 23:21 are no less relevant); 5:38 cites Lev. 24:20 (although the eye-for-eye principle also appears in Exod. 21:24 and Deut. 19:21); and 5:43 quotes Lev. 19:18. All this raises the possibility that the evangelist just may have thought of 5:21–32 as offering contrasts with laws in Deuteronomy and of 5:33–48 as offering contrasts with laws in Leviticus.[25] But given that most of the references do not belong exclusively to Deuteronomy and Leviticus, prudence suggests not pursuing this line of thought. Moreover, as no other thematic pattern explains Matthew's twin triadic sets, it seems best to surmise that we have here only a purely formal arrangement. It is probably not of hermeneutical consequence.

25. Cf. David E. Garland, *Reading Matthew: A Literary and Theological Commentary on the First Gospel* (London: SPCK, 1993), pp. 62–63: 5:21–32 deals with laws from Exodus and Deuteronomy, 5:33–48 with laws from Leviticus.

Matthew 6:1–18. The structure of this section is remarkably close to its predecessor, 5:17–48.[26] Both have general headings employing δικαιοσύνη (5:17–20; 6:1). Both expand their initial generalizations with specific examples (5:21–48; 6:2–18). Both introduce those examples with repeating formulas—"You have heard that it was said" or "It was said" in 5:21–48, "Whenever you" + verb in 6:1–18. Both feature constructions with δέ that contrast traditional teaching and practices with Jesus' alternative imperatives (5:22, 28, 32, 34, 39, 44; 6:3, 6, 17). And both repeat the emphatic λέγω ὑμῖν—ἐγὼ δὲ λέγω ὑμῖν (but I say to you) in 5:22, 28, 32, 34, 39, 44 ἀμὴν λέγω ὑμῖν (Amen I say to you) in 6:2, 5, 16. The only significant structural difference between 5:17–48 and 6:1–18 is that whereas the former has six (= 3 × 2) examples, the latter has only three:

> The Christian cult (6:1–18)
> a) General principle (6:1)
> b) A triad of specific instruction (6:2–18)
>   (1) Almsgiving (6:2–4)
>   (2) Prayer (6:5–15)
>   (3) Fasting (6:16–18)

If one takes a closer look at this section, it quickly becomes obvious that the parallelism between 6:2–4 (Do not give alms as do the "hypocrites" in the synagogues), 5–6 (Do not pray as do the "hypocrites" in the synagogues), and 16–18 (Do not fast as do the "hypocrites") is truly remarkable.[27] Each paragraph has exactly the same structure:

> 1. Declaration of subject (6:2, 5, 16)
> 2. Behavior rejected (6:2, 5, 16)
>   a. negative imperative (6:2, 5, 16)
>   b. rejected behavior (6:2, 5, 16)
>   c. improper motive (6:2, 5, 16)
>   d. present result/reward, from people (6:2, 5, 16)
> 3. Behavior approved (6:3–4, 6, 17–18)
>   a. subject restated (6:3, 6, 17)
>   b. approved behavior (6:3, 6, 17)
>   c. proper motive (6:4, 6, 18)
>   d. future result/reward, from God (6:4, 6, 18)

26. See already Erich Klostermann, "Zum Verständnis von Mt 6.2," ZNW 47 (1956), pp. 280–81.
27. In addition to what follows see Hans Dieter Betz, *Essays on the Sermon on the Mount* (Philadelphia: Fortress, 1985), pp. 56–62, and Petersen, *Eigenart*, pp. 227–32.

The repeated structure is, moreover, mirrored in the recurrent vocabulary:

6:2	ὅταν (whenever)
6:5	ὅταν (whenever)
6:16	ὅταν (whenever)

6:2	μή (not)
6:5	οὐκ (not)
6:16	μή (not)

6:2	ὥσπερ οἱ ὑποκριταί (as the hypocrites)
6:5	ὡς οἱ ὑποκριταί (as the hypocrites)
6:16	ὡς οἱ ὑποκριταί (as the hypocrites)

6:2	ὅπως δοξασθῶσιν ὑπὸ τῶν ἀνθρώπων (that they may be glorified by men)
6:5	ὅπως φανῶσιν τοῖς ἀνθρώποις (that they may be seen by men)
6:16	ὅπως φανῶσιν τοῖς ἀνθρώποις (that they may be seen by men)

6:2	ἀμὴν λέγω ὑμῖν (Amen I say to you)
6:5	ἀμὴν λέγω ὑμῖν (Amen I say to you)
6:16	ἀμὴν λέγω ὑμῖν (Amen I say to you)

6:2	ἀπέχουσιν τὸν μισθὸν αὐτῶν (they have their reward)
6:5	ἀπέχουσιν τὸν μισθὸν αὐτῶν (they have their reward)
6:16	ἀπέχουσιν τὸν μισθὸν αὐτῶν (they have their reward)

6:3	σοῦ δέ (but you) + imperative
6:6	σὺ δέ (but you) + imperative
6:17	σὺ δέ (but you) + imperative

6:4	ἐν τῷ κρυπτῷ (in secret)
6:6	τῷ πατρί σου τῷ ἐν τῷ κρυπτῷ (to your Father in secret)
6:18	τῷ πατρί σου τῷ ἐν τῷ κρυφαίῳ (by your Father in secret)

6:4	καὶ ὁ πατήρ σου (and your father)
6:6	καὶ ὁ πατήρ σου (and your father)
6:18	καὶ ὁ πατήρ σου (and your father)

6:4	ὁ βλέπων ἐν τῷ κρυπτῷ (who sees in secret)
6:6	ὁ βλέπων ἐν τῷ κρυπτῷ (who sees in secret)
6:18	ὁ βλέπων ἐν τῷ κρυφαίῳ (who sees in secret)

6:4	ἀποδώσει σοι (will reward you)
6:6	ἀποδώσει σοι (will reward you)
6:18	ἀποδώσει σοι (will reward you)

The lengths of the three sections are, further, almost identical: 6:2–4 has 292 letters; 6:5–6 has 302 letters; 6:16–18 has 297 letters.

Matthew 6:7–15. Matthew 6:7–15 interrupts all this parallelism in order to expand the teaching on prayer. Matthew's Jesus enjoins hearers not to pray as the Gentiles (6:7–8) but instead to utter the Lord's Prayer (6:9–13) and to forgive others (6:14–15).[28] The remarkable fact is that, as with the other units so far examined, this one also has triadic subunits: 6:7–8 (exhortation not to pray as do the Gentiles) + 9–13 (the Lord's Prayer) + 14–15 (forgiveness).[29] Furthermore, in Matthew, as contrasted with Luke, the Lord's Prayer consists of (1) an address (6:9b), (2) three "You" petitions (6:9c–10), and (3) three "we" petitions (6:11–13). This results in the following analysis:

On prayer (6:5–15)
    (a) How to pray: not as the "hypocrites" in the synagogues (6:5–6)
    (b) How to pray, continued (6:7–15)
        i) Not as the Gentiles (6:7–8)
        ii) The Lord's Prayer (6:9–13)
            α) The address (6:9): "Our Father who is in heaven"
            β) Three "You" petitions (6:9–10)
                (1) "Hallowed be your name"
                (2) "Your kingdom come"
                (3) "Your will be done, on earth as it is in heaven"
            γ) Three "we" petitions (6:11–13)
                (1) "Give us this day our daily bread"
                (2) "And forgive us . . . forgiven our debtors"
                (3) "And do not bring us to the time of trial"
        iii) On forgiveness (6:14–15)

Matthew 6:19–7:12. The disparity among scholars attempting to fathom the structure and theme of 6:19–7:12 is considerable. Despite this, the formal unity of the passage, that is, its identity as a separate subsection, seems probable. Matthew 6:16–18 obviously ends the section on alms-giving, prayer, and fasting, and 7:13 just as obviously introduces a new section that is all about eschatological warning. So 6:19–7:12 is clearly set off from what goes before and from what comes after. The main issue, then, is the internal division of the passage.

Some have despaired altogether of comprehending Matthew's rationale in this section. Krister Stendahl confessed that the section is impervious

---

28. On the interpretation of 6:14–15, see the unfortunately neglected article by Krister Stendahl, "Prayer and Forgiveness," *SEÅ* 22 (1957), pp. 75–86.

29. Cf. the analysis of Luz, *Matthäus*, 1:429–61.

to structural analysis: "VI 19–VII 29 offers material which has been brought together into the Sermon on the Mount by Matthew, in such a manner that we find no clue as to its arrangement."[30] Joseph Fitzmyer has similarly characterized 6:19–7:12 as "a series of loosely related sayings."[31] This, however, seems a rather desperate description. Given the undeniable care with which the evangelist has crafted his sermon through 6:18, it would indeed be erratic for him, beginning at 6:19, to assemble miscellaneous materials without imposing any thematic coherence or formal structure.[32] But we need not be nonplussed about the redactor's procedure. The structure of 6:19–7:12, while admittedly much less obvious than that of 5:17–48 or 6:1–18, discloses itself to close investigation. And, once more, symmetry and triads are the compositional keys.

Matthew 6:19–7:12 begins with an exhortation to gather treasure not on earth but in heaven (6:19–21). A parable about the eye (6:22–23) comes next. It is in turn followed by a second parable, that of the two masters (6:24). These three relatively short units all feature perfect antithetical parallelism:

| 6:19 | Do not | store up for yourselves treasures on earth, |
| 6:20 | but | store up for yourselves treasures in heaven, |

| 6:19 | | where | moth and rust | consume |
| | and | where | thieves | break in and steal |

30. Krister Stendahl, "Matthew," in *Peake's Commentary on the Bible* (ed. M. Black and H. H. Rowley; Middlesex: Nelson, 1962), p. 779. For an orientation to the problem see Betz, *Sermon*, pp. 423–28. Earlier critics sometimes argued that 6:21ff. was no original part of Jesus' own sermon; see the discussion of E. Christian Achelis, *Die Bergpredigt nach Matthäus und Lucas* (Bielefeld: Velhagen & Klasing, 1875), pp. 426–31.

31. Joseph A. Fitzmyer, *The Gospel according to Luke: Introduction, Translation, and Notes* (2 vols.; AB 28, 28A; Garden City, N.Y.: Doubleday, 1981, 1985), 1:620. Cf. Donald A. Hagner, *Matthew 1–13* (WBC 33a; Dallas, Tex.: Word Books, 1993), p. 84: 7:1–12 collects "various teachings."

32. Cf. Günther Bornkamm, "Der Aufbau der Bergpredigt," *NTS* 24 (1978), p. 425. Contrast John P. Meier, *The Vision of Matthew: Christ, Church, and Morality in the First Gospel* (New York: Paulist, 1979), p. 65, who affirms that, after 6:18, "Matthew's concern about architectonic structure in the sermon lessens." One might draw an analogy with Matthew's macro structure. The arrangement of the earlier chapters, 1–13, reflects more redactional creativity than the later chapters, 14–28. See on this esp. M. Eugene Boring, "The Convergence of Source Analysis, Social History, and Literary Structure in the Gospel of Matthew," in *Society of Biblical Literature 1994 Seminar Papers* (ed. Eugene H. Lovering Jr.; Atlanta: Scholars Press, 1994), pp. 587–611. We have seen, nonetheless, on pp. 135–42 above, that while Matthew's hand is more obvious in the ordering of chapters 1–13 than in the arrangement of 14–28, the basic scheme of alternating narrative and discourse, with each narrative and discourse having a main theme, continues to the end.

| 6:20 | | where | neither | moth nor rust | consumes |
| | and | where | | thieves do not | break in and steal |

| 6:22 | if your eye is | healthy, | your whole body will be full of light |
| 6:23 | if your eye is | unhealthy, | your whole body will be full of darkness |

| 6:24 | For | [he] either | will | hate | | the one | and love | the other |
| 6:24 | or | [he | will] | be devoted to the one | and despise | the other |

The two treasures, the two eyes, and the two masters are also thematically united. The command not to store up treasure in heaven, the admonition to possess a good eye, which means being generous,[33] and the charge to serve God, not money, all have to do with one's disposition towards what v. 24 calls "mammon."

Matthew 6:25–34, an extended section that offers encouragement by reference to the mindfulness of the Father in heaven, then comes after 6:19–24. Its chief function is clear. Although serving God at the expense of mammon might create fretfulness about what one will eat and drink and wear, Jesus assures his disciples that the heavenly Father will care for them, so they can lay aside their anxieties. The key word, which unifies the section, is the verb, μεριμνάω, "worry" (vv. 25, 27, 28, 31, 34), which three times becomes a negative imperative: "Do not worry" (vv. 25, 31, 34).

What then do we make of 7:1–12? It is the structural twin of 6:19–34. It, like 6:19–34, opens with a prohibition, "Do not judge" (7:1–2: μὴ κρίνετε; cf. 6:19–21: μὴ θησαυρίζετε). Then, continuing the theme, there is, as in 6:22–23, a parable about vision and the eye, 7:3–5: "Why do you see the splinter in your neighbor's eye, but do not notice the log in your own eye?" Next follows a second parable, that about giving holy things to dogs and casting pearls before swine (7:6; cf. 6:24). It is almost exactly the same length as 6:24,[34] and like 6:24 it is chiastic:

    a. No one can serve two masters.
       b. For either he will hate the one
          c. and will love the other,
          c. or he will be devoted to the one
       b. and will despise the other.
    a. You cannot serve God and mammon.
                  (Matt. 6:24)

33. Cf. 20:15, where an "evil eye" means a lack of generosity, and see Dale C. Allison Jr., "The Eye as a Lamp, Q 11:34–36: Finding the Sense," in *The Jesus Tradition in Q* (Harrisburg, Pa.: Trinity Press International, 1997), pp. 133–67.

34. Matt. 6:24 contains 138 letters; 7:6 has 134 letters.

a. Do not give dogs what is holy.
  b. Do not throw your pearls before swine.
  b. Lest they (the swine) trample them under foot,
a. and (lest the dogs) turn to attack you

                                  (Matt. 7:6)

Furthermore, 7:6 is based on a proverb or traditional line,[35] rejects a particular activity, and contrasts incompatibles. In 6:24 the incompatibles are God and mammon whereas in 7:6 they are "dogs" and "the holy" and "pearls" and "swine."[36] Matthew 7:1–6 is then succeeded by 7:7–11, a passage that, like 6:25–34, offers encouragement by reference to the care of the Father in heaven: "Ask and you will receive." Matthew 7:7–11 and 6:25–34 are further alike:

- Both are based on arguments from the lesser to the greater: "If God so clothes the grass of the field . . . will he not much more clothe you?" (6:30); "If you then, who are evil, know how to give good gifts to your children, how much more will your Father in heaven give good things to those who ask him?" (7:11).
- Both have been constructed around key words or exhortations that are repeated (μεριμνάω in 6:25, 27, 28, 31, and 34; αἰτέω in 7:7, 8, 9, 10, and 11; δίδωμι in 7:6, 7, 11 [bis])
- Both use two major illustrations to make their respective cases, the birds of the air and the lilies of the field in chapter 6, the son who asks his father for bread and the son who asks his father for fish in chapter 7.

35. For relevant rabbinic texts see SB 1:433, 447.

36. Interpretation is notorious, but I remain satisfied with the proposal I made in W. D. Davies and Dale C. Allison Jr., *A Critical and Exegetical Commentary on the Gospel according to Saint Matthew* (2 vols.; ICC; Edinburgh: T&T Clark, 1988–1991), 1:572–75: 7:1–5 has commanded that there be not too much severity; 7:6 follows up by saying that there should not be too much laxity; the text anticipates a problem and searches for balance. Cf. the interpretations of Johann Albrecht Bengel, *Gnomon Novi Testamenti* (2 vols.; Tübingen: Ludov. Frid. Fues, 1850), 1:61, and Georg Strecker, *The Sermon on the Mount: An Exegetical Commentary* (Nashville: Abingdon, 1988), p 147. Matt. 7:6 circumscribes the warning about judging others in 7:1–5. The latter, then, does not eliminate the use of critical faculties when it comes to sacred concerns. As 18:15–20 shows, it is sometimes necessary to deal with the faults of others. Although this interpretation remains general, and while it is possible that Matthew had something more specific in mind, the main point is clear: one must not be meekly charitable against all reason. Contrast Luz, *Matthäus*, 1:497, who proposes that, within its Matthean context, the saying means nothing; the evangelist passed on the logion only because it was in his tradition. Already John Calvin, *Commentary on a Harmony of the Evangelists, Matthew, Mark, and Luke* (3 vols.; Grand Rapids: Eerdmans, 1949), 1:227, interpreted 7:6 apart from its context, on the assumption that it was not first spoken with the materials it now stands beside.

- Both deal firstly with the vertical rather than the horizontal dimension of religion. The central issue is not ethics but one's relationship to the gift-giving Father in heaven.
- Both grow out of the immediately preceding imperatives. Those who do not store up treasure on the earth (6:19–21), who are generous with their money (6:22–23), and who serve God, not mammon (6:24), will naturally suffer anxiety about physical needs, the antidote to which is trust in the heavenly Father's care (6:25–34). And those who, although they are called not to judge others (7:1–5), must sometimes nonetheless discern and act on the difference between the unclean and the holy (7:6), should seek wisdom from God for so difficult an assignment (7:7–11).[37] Theophylact said this, regarding 7:7–8: Jesus "has, in the foregoing, commanded us to do great and difficult things. So then he shows us here how they can be accomplished, and that is through unceasing prayer."[38]
- Both use threefold repetition. If 6:25–34 is built around the thrice-repeated μὴ μεριμνᾶτε/μεριμνήσητε,[39] 7:7–11 opens with this:

> Ask, and it will be given to you;
>   seek, and you will find;
>   knock, and the door will be opened to you.
> For everyone who asks receives,
>   and everyone who seeks finds,
>   and to the one knocking, it will be opened.

- The length of the initial three units in 6:19–24 (464 letters) is not far from the length of the three initial units in 7:1–6 (483 letters).

37. Cf. James 1:5. 7:7–11, if related to its context, cannot be about prayer in general but must concern prayer for discernment in particular; see Charles H. Talbert, *Reading the Sermon on the Mount* (Columbia, S.C.: University of South Carolina Press, 2004), pp. 132–35. He writes: "Reading verses 7–11 in context results in seeing the pericope as an enablement of verse 6. If one needs to discern what is appropriate judging and discerning, ask God for wisdom and God will provide it." Cf. 18:15–20, where the instructions on excommunication are accompanied by the assurance of divine help via the presence of the risen Jesus. So far from 7:6 being without meaning in its present context (so Luz), it qualifies 7:1–5 (see n. 36) and is itself in turn the immediate setting for 7:7–11.

38. Theophylact, *Comm. Matt.* ad loc. (PG 123.212C).

39. Cf. the analysis of Talbert, *Sermon*, p. 126:
    6:25–30 Prohibition (v. 25a): "Do not be anxious"
                Four reasons (vv. 25b–30)
    6:31–33 Prohibition (v. 31): "Do not be anxious"
                Two reasons (v. 32)
    6:34   Prohibition (v. 34a): "Do not be anxious"
                Two reasons (vv. 34b, c)

The structure of 6:19–7:12 appears, then, to be as follows:

Instruction

6:19–21	Prohibition	7:1–2	Prohibition
6:22–23	Parable: eye and sight	7:3–5	Parable: eye and sight
6:24	Parable: incompatibles	7:6	Parable: incompatibles

Encouragement

6:25–34	Heavenly Father's care (a minori ad maius)	7:7–11	Heavenly Father's care (a minori ad maius)

7:12 The Golden Rule, forming an inclusio with 5:17–20

As with 5:21–48 and 6:1–18, the structural parallels between 6:19–34 and 7:1–11 are reflected in common vocabulary, although the correlations are much less extensive:[40]

- Exhortations in 6:19–21 and 7:1–2

  6:19 μή (not) + second person plural present imperative
  7:1   μή (not) + second person plural present imperative

- Parables on eye and sight in 6:22–23 and 7:3–5

  6:22–23 ὁ ὀφθαλμός (the eye)
           ὁ ὀφθαλμός σου (your eye).
           ὁ ὀφθαλμός σου (your eye)
  7:3–5   τῷ ὀφθαλμῷ (the eye)
           τοῦ ὀφθαλμοῦ σου (your eye)
           τῷ ὀφθαλμῷ σου (your eye)

- The heavenly Father's care of those who seek him, 6:25–34 and 7:7–11

  6:27 τίς ... ἐξ ὑμῶν (which of you?)
  7:9   τίς ... ἐξ ὑμῶν (which of you?)

  6:30 εἰ ... πολλῷ μᾶλλον (if ... how much more?)
  7:11 εἰ ... πόσῳ μᾶλλον (if ... how much more?)

---

40. They are nonetheless sufficient to falsify the assertion of Scott and Dean, "Sound Map," p. 363, that the latter part of chapter 6 and the first part of chapter 7 do not "share significant phonetic/syntactical qualities."

| 6:32 | ὁ πατὴρ ὑμῶν ὁ οὐράνιος (your heavenly Father) |
| 7:11 | ὁ πατὴρ ὑμῶν ὁ ἐν τοῖς οὐρανοῖς (your Father in heaven) |

| 6:32 | οἶδεν (he knows—of divine knowledge) |
| 7:11 | οἴδατε (you know—of human and divine knowledge) |

| 6:32–33 | ἐπιζητοῦσιν . . . ζητεῖτε (they seek . . . you seek) |
| 7:7–8 | ζητεῖτε . . . ὁ ζητῶν (you seek . . . the one seeking)[41] |

Three further comments on 6:19–34 and 7:1–12 are in order.

1. 6:19–7:12, on my proposed analysis, contains two triadic units, 6:19–24 and 7:1–6. In this it resembles 5:17–48, where the six so-called antitheses are actually two sets of three. Thus, the first and third major sections of 5:17–7:12 are structurally similar. To this extent at least, those who have offered chiastic analyses of the Sermon on the Mount, such as Luz and Daniel Patte, have not built upon sand.[42]

> Matt. 5:17–48, two triads
> 5:21–26 + 27–30 + 31–32
> 5:33–37 + 38–42 + 43–48
> Matt. 6:1–18, one triad
> 6:2–4 + 5–15 + 16–18
> Matt. 6:19–7:12, two triads
> 6:19–21 + 22–23 + 24
> 7:1–2 + 3–5 + 6

2. Beyond the formal parallelism, what unites 6:19–34 and 7:1–12? The former, whose major theme is, What should I do with and about wealth? and the latter, whose first issue is, What should be my attitude toward my neighbor? are about life in the temporal "secular" world. This means that 6:19–7:12 deals with what may be called "social issues."[43] The ap-

41. I cannot here enter into debate with Stassen, "Fourteen Triads," pp. 297–300, who accepts my proposal of parallelism between 6:19–34 and 7:1–12 but seeks to modify it. I simply record my judgment that (i) there is no real correlation between 7:12 and 6:34; (ii) 6:34 is not missing from my scheme; its absence from the chart in my article is a typo; (iii) although Strasson's scheme—"Traditional righteousness" + "Vicious cycle plus judgment" + "Transforming initiative"—does work remarkably well for much of the Sermon on the Mount and is a contribution to interpretation, it does not work for all of it, especially for 6:19–7:12.

42. Luz, *Matthäus*, 1:254; Daniel Patte, *The Gospel according to Matthew: A Structural Commentary on Matthew's Faith* (Philadelphia: Fortress, 1987), pp. 62–65. For critical commentary see Carter, *Sermon*, pp. 39–42.

43. Betz, *Sermon*, p. 423, prefers: "the conduct of daily life." Although A. Tholuck, *Commentary on the Sermon on the Mount* (Edinburgh: T&T Clark, 1874), pp. 395–96, gives 7:1–12

propriateness of this is evident. Having received instruction in 5:17–48 on the Torah and in 6:1–18 on the cult, disciples next learn, in 6:19–7:12, how to behave in the world at large. The Sermon on the Mount seeks to cover a wide swath of religion and life.

3. The Golden Rule sums up in one sentence the right conduct toward others and therefore appropriately closes 6:19–7:12, a section that concerns social behavior. But 7:12 is not simply the conclusion of 6:19–7:12 or of 7:1–11. It rather brings to a climax the entire central section of the Sermon the Mount, 5:17–7:11. The verse should therefore be printed, as it sometimes has been, as a separate paragraph. Mention of "the law and the prophets" takes the reader back to 5:17 and creates an *inclusio*, between which Matthew has set forth Jesus' relationship to the Torah, given rules for the new cult, and offered instruction and encouragement for life in the world. "Whatever you wish that people do to you, do so to them" is, in nice rabbinic fashion, a general rule that is not only the quintessence of the law and the prophets but also the quintessence of the Sermon on the Mount and so the quintessence of Jesus' moral teaching.[44] John Gill, representing a host of exegetes, wrote: "These words are the epilogue, or conclusion of our Lord's discourse; the sum of what he had delivered in the two preceding chapters . . . is contained in these words; for they not only respect the exhortation about judging and reproving; but every duty respecting our neighbour; it is a summary of the whole."[45]

Gill's reading is consistent with the rest of Matthew. In 22:34–40, for instance, the evangelist has Jesus declare that the first commandment is to love God and that a second is "like it," that is, of equal importance, namely, to love one's neighbor. Here too the command to love is that upon which "depend all the law and the prophets." Similarly, at the end of the list of commandments required for entering into life, Matthew adds this: "You shall love your neighbor as yourself" (19:16–30; contrast Mark 10:17–31). And in 5:43–48, Matthew chooses to save until the end, as the last of his paragraphs on the Torah, the command to love one's enemy. It

---

the title "Sundry Admonitions," he nonetheless thinks of these verses as "a final summary of one's duties towards one's neighbour."

44. On the *inclusio* that 5:17 and 7:12 create see esp. Kari Syreeni, *The Making of the Sermon on the Mount: A Procedural Analysis of Matthew's Redactoral Activity* (AASF, Dissertationes Humanarum Litterarum 44; Helsinki: Suomalainen Tiedeakatemia, 1987), pp. 173–78. Within the context of the First Gospel, the Golden Rule is not a principle from which all of the law's commands can be deduced, nor is it the hermeneutical key to interpreting the law or for determining the validity of different commandments; it is instead simply the most basic or important demand of the law, a demand that in no way replaces Torah but instead states its true end. See D. J. Moo, "Jesus and the Authority of the Mosaic Law," *JSNT* 20 (1984), pp. 6–11. Note 23:23: some commandments are more weighty than others, but this should not lead to neglect of the lighter commandments.

45. John Gill, *Gill's Commentary* (6 vols.; Grand Rapids: Baker, 1980), 5:57.

is, accordingly, the climactic paragraph, and it issues in the exhortation to be perfect, that is, to be catholic in doing good, as the heavenly Father is perfect. There can be no doubt, then, concerning the preeminence that the demand to love one's neighbor holds in Matthew; and since, as Augustine observed, the Golden Rule is really just another way of delivering that demand,[46] it scarcely surprises to find it at the conclusion of Matt. 5:17–7:12, the epitome of Jesus' moral instruction.[47]

Outline of Results

The discussion to this point produces the following outline of the Sermon on the Mount:

I. Introduction: the crowds on the mountain (4:23–5:1)
II. Nine beatitudes for the people of God (5:3–12)
III. The task of the people of God in the world (5:13–7:12)
   A. Summary statement: salt and light (5:13–16)
   B. The three pillars (5:17–7:12)
      1. Jesus and the Torah (5:17–48)
         a) General principles (5:17–20)
         b) Two triads of specific instruction (5:21–48)
            (1) The first triad (5:21–32)
               (a) On murder (5:21–26)
               (b) On adultery (5:27–30)
               (c) On divorce (5:31–32)
            (2) The second triad (5:33–48)
               (a) Do not swear (5:33–37)
               (b) Turn the other cheek (5:38–42)
               (c) Love your enemy (5:43–48)
      2. The Christian cult (6:1–18)
         a) General principle (6:1)
         b) A triad of specific instruction (6:2–18)
            (1) Almsgiving (6:2–4)
            (2) Prayer (6:5–15)
               (a) How to pray: not as the "hypocrites" in the synagogue (6:5–6)
               (b) How to pray, continued (6:7–15)

---

46. Augustine, *Serm. Dom.* 2.22.75 (CCSL 35, ed. Mutzenbecher, p. 173).

47. I use the word "epitome" with hesitation, because Betz, *Sermon*, passim, has contended that the Sermon on the Mount was formulated for Jewish Christians as an epitome or systematic statement of the teaching of Jesus. For criticism see my review in *JBL* 117 (1998), pp. 136–38. In my judgment, the sermon is, for Matthew, the quintessence of Jesus' moral demand, not an epitome of his teaching in general.

   i) Not as the Gentiles (6:7–8)
   ii) The Lord's Prayer (6:9–13)[48]
    α) The address (6:9)
    β) Three "You" petitions (6:9–10)
    γ) Three "we" petitions (6:11–13)
   iii) On forgiveness (6:14–15)
  (3) Fasting (6:16–18)
 3. Social issues (6:19–7:12)
  a) God and mammon (6:19–34)
   (1) A triad on true treasure (6:19–24)
    (a) Prohibition: "Do not store up treasure on earth" (6:19–21)
    (b) Parable on vision: the good eye (6:22–23)
    (c) Parable about incompatibles: God and mammon (6:24)
   (2) Encouragement: "Do not be anxious" (6:25–34)
  b) Regarding one's neighbor (7:1–11)
   (1) A triad on attitude toward others (7:1–6)
    (a) Prohibition: "Do not judge" (7:1–2)
    (b) Parable on vision: the log in one's eye (7:3–5)
    (c) Parable about incompatibles: pearls and swine (7:6)
   (2) Encouragement: "Ask, seek, knock" (7:7–11)
  c) Concluding statement: the Golden Rule = the law and the prophets (7:12)
IV. Three warnings: the prospect of eschatological judgment (7:13–27)
 A. The two ways (7:13–14)
 B. "Beware of false prophets" (7:15–23)
 C. The two builders (7:24–27)
V. Conclusion: the crowds and the mountain (7:28–8:1)

Further Observations

With the foregoing outline in place, several general observations about the structure of the Sermon on the Mount become possible.

48. While the Lord's Prayer is at the center of Matt. 5–7, and while this may the result of planning, Bornkamm ("Bergpredigt"), Grundmann (*Matthäus*, pp. 204–6), and Guelich (*Sermon*, pp. 323–25) have not demonstrated that the Lord's Prayer contains the organizing principles for any part of Matt. 5–7. See my critical comments on Bornkamm in "The Structure of the Sermon on the Mount," *JBL* 106 (1987), pp. 424–29. There is also no reason, *pace* Augustine, *Serm. Dom.* 2.11.38 (CCEL 25, ed. Mutzenbecher, pp. 128–29), to correlate the individual petitions of the Lord's Prayer with the various beatitudes.

Consolation amid moral demands. The parallel sections on God the Father's care in 6:25–34 and 7:7–11 distinguish themselves from the rest of the Sermon on the Mount. After the Beatitudes, uncompromising demands constantly bombard the disciples. Respite comes only in two places, in 6:25–34 and in 7:7–11. Admittedly, even in 6:25–34 and 7:7–11 there are imperatives. But μὴ μεριμνᾶτε really means, as the context establishes, "You need not worry at all." Similarly, αἰτεῖτε does not hang heavy upon the readers' shoulders; instead it introduces good news: "It will be given to you." 6:25–34 and 7:7–11 proffer encouragement and so serve to ease the burden of the Sermon on the Mount. They inform disciples that, as they seek to live Jesus' well-nigh impossible demands, their prayers will be answered, their needs supplied.

Matthew contains one other paragraph whose function is similar to that of 6:25–34 and 7:7–11. These words are in the middle of the missionary discourse in chapter 10:

> So have no fear of them, for nothing is covered up that will not be uncovered, and nothing secret that will not become known. What I say to you in the dark, tell in the light; and what you hear whispered, proclaim from the housetops. Do not fear those who kill the body but cannot kill the soul; rather fear him who can destroy both soul and body in hell. Are not two sparrows sold for a penny? Yet not one of them will fall to the ground apart from your Father. And even the hairs of your head are all counted. So do not be afraid; you are of more value than many sparrows. (10:26–31)

This unit comes after two paragraphs, 10:16–23 and 24–25, which describe the persecution and difficult fate of Christian missionaries, and it obviously aims to console. The prospect of suffering is tempered by words about the Father's care. The key is the imperative, "Do not be afraid." Like the "Do not be anxious" of 6:25–34, which is a way of saying, "There is no need to be anxious," it really means, "There is no need to fear." Also like the "Do not be anxious" of 6:25–34, it is repeated thrice, at the beginning, middle, and end of the paragraph.[49] The argument, moreover, is again *a minori ad maius*: "You are of more value than many sparrows" (10:31; cf. 6:26, 30; 7:11). Perhaps it also bears remarking that the sparrows of 10:26–31 recall the birds of 6:25–34. In any event, 10:26–31 provides another example of the type of argument and arrangement found in 6:25–34 and 7:7–11.

A context of grace. One may, if one has not read carefully, think of Matt. 5–7 as unremitting in its requirements. Does it do anything more than make demands? And does it offer any hints as to how one is to accomplish what one is supposed to do? Is the Sermon not advice without help?

---

49. Cf. Dominique Hermant, *Matthieu: Un écrivain? Les cinq discours du premier Evangile, un corpus organisé* (Lyon: Profac, 1999), pp. 32–33.

Such a view fails to understand aright four different portions of the discourse—4:23–5:2; 5:3–12; 6:25–34; and 7:7–11. I have just urged that these last two passages speak the language of grace: the God who demands is at the same time the Father who from day to day is with and for his children. He is a giver of gifts and supplies their every need. I should now like to consider the other two passages.

Matthew 4:23–5:2 introduces the sermon. It relates that the disciples are not the only ones to hear Jesus. So do the crowds (cf. 7:28–29). What crowds? *Those who have already been healed by Jesus.*

> Jesus went throughout Galilee, teaching in their synagogues and proclaiming the good news of the kingdom and curing every disease and every sickness among the people. So his fame spread throughout all Syria, and they brought to him all the sick, those who were afflicted with various diseases and pains, demoniacs, epileptics, and paralytics, and he cured them. And great crowds followed him. (4:23–25)

Before the crowds hear the Messiah's word they are the object of his compassion and healing. Having done nothing, nothing at all, they are benefited. So grace comes before task, succor before demand, healing before imperative. The first act of the Messiah is not the imposition of his commandments but the giving of himself. Today's command presupposes yesterday's gift.

The same conclusion lies near to hand in the Beatitudes, 5:3–12, which promise that the congregation of the righteous will inherit the earth (5:5), see God (5:8), and receive grand reward (5:12). Human effort can obtain none of these things. If they are ever to be gained at all, it will only be because they have been given. The Beatitudes, then, depict the future as a gift. As William Manson had it, "As the forefront position of the Beatitudes indicates, it is in grace that the Christian revelation begins, and it is on grace that it rests. . . . God wills that the kingdom of heaven and its righteousness shall be given to men, and he accomplishes this purpose."[50]

The Sermon on the Mount sets forth God's grace in the past (4:23–5:2), in the present (6:25–34; 7:7–11), and in the future (5:3–12); and this circumstance is the theological context for 5:13–7:12. Amos Wilder was justified in writing that Matt. 5–7 offers "not so much ethics of obedience as ethics of grace."[51]

Triadic Structure in the Sermon on the Mount. The most obvious structural fact about the Sermon on the Mount is that its building blocks come in threes. There are three major topics: Torah (5:17–48), the Christian cult

50. William Manson, *Jesus the Messiah: The Synoptic Tradition of the Revelation of God in Christ: With Special Reference to Form Criticism* (London: Hodder & Stoughton, 1943), p. 80.
51. Amos N. Wilder, *Eschatology and Ethics in the Teaching of Jesus* (rev. ed.; New York: Harper & Brothers, 1950), p. 113.

(6:1–18), and social issues (6:19–7:12). Each section treating these topics displays in its turn threefold structures. There are six (= 2 × 3) paragraphs on Jesus and the Torah. Alms, prayer, and fasting are the three chief topics of 6:1–18, the "cult-didache." And, in 6:19–7:12, there are two very similar triadic sections (6:19–21 + 22–23 + 24 and 7:1–2 + 3–5 + 6), to which are appended in each case words of theological encouragement (6:25–34 and 7:7–11). The sermon, in addition, winds up with three warnings, 7:13–14, 15–23, and 24–27. (The structure is evident in the figure on page 200.)

One might be tempted to dismiss this symmetry and these triads as artificial, the product of exegetical ingenuity rather than evangelistic planning. But human beings have often used the number three to arrange both oral and written materials. Whatever the precise reasons, which surely have much to do with both memory and aesthetics, examples of triads within triads, as well as matching panels of triads, abound. Clearly they appeal to the human mind. One recalls the structure of "Goldilocks and the Three Bears," which from one point of view is rather like the Sermon on the Mount.[52] (See the figure on page 201.)

One could offer comparable analyses of "The Three Little Pigs" or "The Three Billy Goats Gruff," noting the extensive parallelism and the multiple triads (which is why so many of us can without difficulty carry in our heads the essentials of these stories). But the phenomenon is scarcely confined to fairy tales. Moving from the juvenile to the philosophic, chapters 7, 8, and 9 of *The Celestial Hierarchy* of Ps.-Dionysius divide the angelic realm into (1) seraphim, cherubim, and thrones, (2) dominions, powers, and authorities, and (3) principalities, archangels, and angels. Gregory Palamas's *Triads in Defense of the Holy Hesychasts* consists of three books, each one addressing three topics. Immanuel Kant, in *The Critique of Pure Reason*, analyses the logical function of the understanding in judgments in terms of four triads while his four categories of the so-called pure understanding are also triadic.

But what about triads in Matthew's more immediate environment?[53] The Jesus tradition was, at its inception, oral.[54] It is, accordingly, full of mne-

---

52. I have consulted the version of Joseph Jacobs, *English Fairy Tales* (London: David Nutt, 1890), in which Goldilocks is "the little old woman."

53. For helpful observations on Greco-Roman and Jewish literature see Gerhard Delling, τρεῖς, *TWNT* 8 (1972), pp. 216–25. On biblical literature see esp. Karl-Martin Beyse, "Das Geheimnis der Drei: Die Dreizahl in den Erzählungen des Alten und Neuen Testaments," in *Nach den Anfängen Fragen: Herrn Prof. Dr. theol. Gerhard Dautzenberg zum 60. Geburtstag am 30. Januar 1994* (ed. Cornelius Mayer, Karlheinz Müller, and Gerhard Schmalenberg; Giessen: Fachbereichs Evangelische Theologie und Katholische Theologie und deren Didaktik, 1994), pp. 95–105. The *Didache*, which is in so many ways close to Matthew, likes explicit threes: "pour water three times on the head" during baptism (7:3); pray the Lord's prayer three times (8:3); watch for the three eschatological signs (16:6–8).

54. Here we can learn from James D. G. Dunn, *Christianity in the Making*, vol. 1, *Jesus Remembered* (Grand Rapids: Eerdmans, 2003); note also his smaller work, *A New Perspective on Jesus: What the Quest for the Historical Jesus Missed* (Grand Rapids: Baker Academic, 2005).

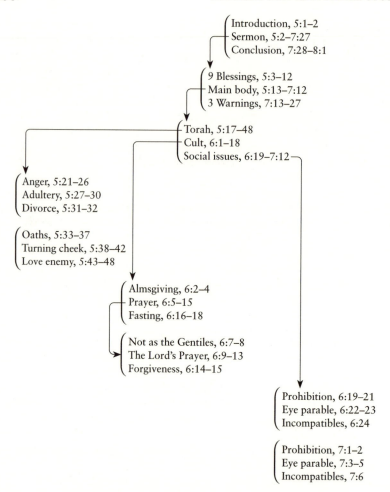

monic devices, including threes.[55] In Mark's passion narrative we find three prayers of Jesus in Gethsemane with three disciples present (14:32–42), three words of the high priest (14:55–65), three denials of Peter (14:66–72; cf. v. 30), three incidents of mockery (14:65; 15:16–20, 29–32), three crosses on Golgotha (15:27), and three scenes with women witnessing the crucifixion, the burial, and the resurrection (15:40–41, 47; 16:1–8; cf. 1 Cor. 15:3–4).[56]

55. Cf. Rudolf Bultmann, *History of the Synoptic Tradition* (new rev. ed.; New York: Harper & Row, 1963), pp. 191, 314, and Dunn, *New Perspective*, pp. 115–18.

56. For further discussion of triads in Mark see P. Mourlon Beernaert, "Structure littéraire et lecture théologique de Marc 14, 17–52," in *L'Évangile selon Marc: Tradition et redaction* (rev. ed.; ed. M. Sabbe; BETL 34; Leuven: Leuven University Press, 1988), pp. 241–68, and Franz Neirynck, *Evangelica: Gospel Studies—Études: Collected Essays* (BETL 60; Leuven: Leuven University Press, 1982), pp. 546–61.

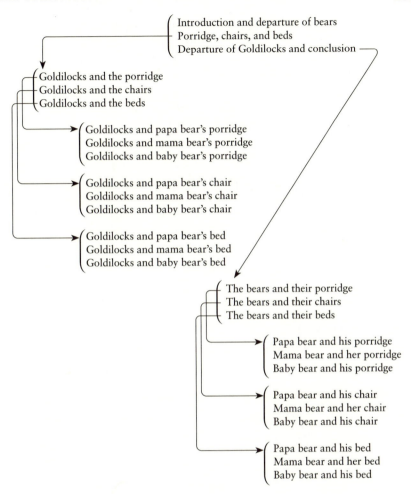

Many of the parables, as Craig Blomberg has demonstrated, feature three major characters and three major points. And, as Leslie Mitton observed several decades ago, even the logia often show triadic patterns.[57]

57. Craig L. Blomberg, *Interpreting the Parables* (Downers Grove, Ill.: InterVarsity, 1990), pp. 171–253. Recall, e.g., the father and two sons of Matt. 21:28–32, the three sorts of failed seed in Mark 4:3–9, the priest, Levite, and Samaritan in Luke 10:29–37, the father and two sons of Luke 15:11–32, and the rich man and Lazarus and Abraham in Luke 16:19–31. Triads also appear in rabbinic parables; see, e.g., *Mek.* on Exod.13:1; on Exod.17:14; and *t. Sotah* 15:7.

For the logia, see C. Leslie Mitton, "Threefoldness in the Teaching of Jesus," *ExpT* 75 (1964), pp. 228–30. Here are three examples from Q, three from Mark, three from M, and three from L: Luke 11:9 = Matt. 7:7 (Q: ask, seek, knock); Luke 12:24 = Matt. 6:26 (Q: the birds neither sow nor reap nor gather into barns); Luke 12:29 = Matt. 6:31 (Q: "What are we to eat, or: What are we to drink? or: What are we to wear?"); Mark 6:4 ("except in his own country, and among his own

The existence of such triads means that Matthew had plenty of precedent in the Jesus tradition itself for grouping material into threes. But the even more weighty observation, for our immediate purposes, is that Matthew's own editorial work outside of the sermon displays an affection for triads. Just as the author of Revelation was taken with sevens, so Matthew was taken with threes. Here are some of the more obvious examples, all of them unique to the First Gospel:[58]

Larger triadic structures

- Matt. 1:2–17 divides the ancestry of Jesus into three sets of fourteen: "So all the generations from Abraham to David are fourteen generations; and from David to the deportation to Babylon, fourteen generations; and from the deportation to Babylon to the Messiah, fourteen generations" (1:17).
- Matt. 1:18–2:23 narrates three angelic appearances to Joseph, each with a similar organization:

1. Note of circumstance

1:20	genitive absolute
2:13	genitive absolute
2:19	genitive absolute

2. Appearance of the angel of the Lord in a dream

1:20	ἰδοὺ	ἄγγελος	κυρίου		κατ' ὄναρ ἐφάνη	αὐτῷ
		λέγων				
2:13	ἰδοὺ	ἄγγελος	κυρίου φαίνεται	κατ' ὄναρ		τῷ Ἰωσὴφ
		λέγων				

---

kin, and in his own house"); 9:43–47 (cutting off hand, cutting off foot, plucking out eye); 13:9 (the disciples will be hauled before councils, synagogues, and governors); Matt. 19:12 (three types of eunuchs); 23:8–9 (imperative not to call another "rabbi," "father," or "instructor"); 25:14–30 (three different servants entrusted with money); Luke 7:44–46 ("You gave me no water for my feet, but she has bathed my feet . . . You gave me no kiss, but from the time I came in she has not stopped kissing my feet. You did not anoint my head with oil, but she has anointed my feet with ointment"); 10:19 (authority to tread upon serpents, scorpions, and the power of the enemy); 14:18–20 (three excuses for not attending dinner: "The first said. . . . Another said. . . . Another said . . .").

58. In addition to what follows see Davies and Allison, *Matthew*, 1:62, 71, 86–87 (although I no longer agree with all said there). Others recognizing Matthew's fondness for triads include Willoughby C. Allen, *A Critical and Exegetical Commentary on the Gospel according to St. Matthew* (3rd ed.; ICC; Edinburgh: T&T Clark, 1912), pp. lxv, 26, 81–86, 257–58; Gaechter, *Kunst*, pp. 18–22; Kürzinger, "Komposition"; Luz, *Matthäus*, 1:27–28; James Moffatt, *An Introduction to the Literature of the New Testament* (3rd rev. ed.; Edinburgh: T&T Clark, 1918), p. 257; and Wesley G. Olmstead, *Matthew's Trilogy of Parables: The Nation, the Nations and the Reader in Matthew 21.28–22.14* (SNTSMS 127; Cambridge: Cambridge University Press, 2003), pp. 33–39.

2:19–20 ἰδοῦ ἄγγελος κυρίου φαίνεται κατ' ὄναρ τῷ Ἰωσὴφ
... λέγων

3. Command of the angel to Joseph
1:20 παραλαβεῖν Μαρίαν
2:13 ἐγερθεὶς παράλαβε τὸ παιδίον καὶ τὴν μητέρα αὐτοῦ καί
2:20 ἐγερθεὶς παράλαβε τὸ παιδίον καὶ τὴν μητέρα αὐτοῦ καί

4. Explanation of command
1:20 introductory γάρ
2:13 introductory γάρ
2:20 introductory γάρ

5. Joseph rises and obediently responds
1:24–25 ἐγερθείς (Joseph's action matches the angel's command)
2:14–15 ἐγερθείς (Joseph's action matches the angel's command)
2:21 ἐγερθείς (Joseph's action matches the angel's command)

- Matt. 8:1–9:34, the narrative section that follows the Sermon on the Mount, contains three sets of three:[59]

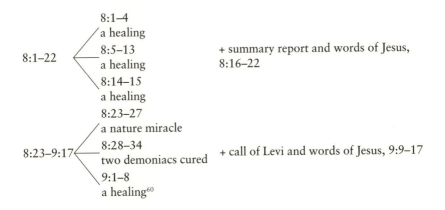

8:1–22
8:1–4
a healing
8:5–13
a healing
8:14–15
a healing

+ summary report and words of Jesus, 8:16–22

8:23–9:17
8:23–27
a nature miracle
8:28–34
two demoniacs cured
9:1–8
a healing[60]

+ call of Levi and words of Jesus, 9:9–17

59. So already W. C. Allen, "Two Critical Studies in St. Matthew's Gospel," *ExpT* 11 (1900), pp. 279–85; cf. Gaechter, *Kunst*, pp. 20–21. There are, to be precise, ten *miracles* in Matt. 8–9. But as the two miracles in 9:18–26 are part of one indissoluble unit, there are only nine miracle *stories*; cf. John P. Meier, *Matthew* (NTM 3; Wilmington, Del.: Michael Glazier, 1980), pp. 79–80, and Michaelis, *Matthäus*, 2:1, 16.

60. The miracles in the central section, 8:23–9:17, take place either on the sea or on the sea shore. This further binds them together and serves to divide 8:1–9:38 into three parts.

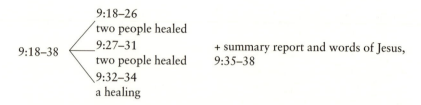

9:18–38
9:18–26
two people healed
9:27–31   + summary report and words of Jesus,
two people healed   9:35–38
9:32–34
a healing

- Matt. 13:24–33 contains three parables of growth with closely related introductions:

  13:24   ἄλλην παραβολήν (another parable)
          + αὐτοῖς (to them)
              + ὡμοιώθη ἡ βασιλεία τῶν οὐρανῶν
                (the kingdom of heaven is like)
              + dative
  13:31   ἄλλην παραβολήν (another parable)
          + αὐτοῖς (to them)
              + ὁμοία ἐστὶν ἡ βασιλεία τῶν οὐρανῶν
                (the kingdom of heaven is like)
              + dative
  13:33   ἄλλην παραβολήν (another parable)
          + αὐτοῖς (to them)
              + ὁμοία ἐστὶν ἡ βασιλεία τῶν οὐρανῶν
                (the kingdom of heaven is like)
              + dative

- 13:44–50 features three more parables. These also have similar introductions that clearly mark them off as a triadic series:

  13:44   ὁμοία ἐστὶν ἡ βασιλεία τῶν οὐρανῶν
          (the kingdom of heaven is like)
          + dative
  13:45   πάλιν ὁμοία ἐστὶν ἡ βασιλεία τῶν οὐρανῶν
          (again, the kingdom of heaven is like)
          + dative
  13:47   πάλιν ὁμοία ἐστὶν ἡ βασιλεία τῶν οὐρανῶν
          (again, the kingdom of heaven is like)
          + dative

- Matt. 21:28–22:14 brings together three parables, each with a polemical edge. Following the first parable, ἄλλην παραβολὴν ἀκούσατε (Hear another parable) introduces the second, and καὶ ἀποκριθεὶς ὁ

Ἰησοῦς πάλιν εἶπεν ἐν παραβολαῖς αὐτοῖς λέγων (And answering Jesus spoke again to them in parables, saying) introduces the third.[61]

- The story of the Roman guard at Jesus' tomb unfolds in three stages: the assignment in 27:62–66, the failure in 28:4, and the rationalization in 28:11–15.

Smaller triadic structures

- Matt. 1:1, the title, contains three names: Jesus, David, Abraham (no parallel)
- Matt. 2:11 tells of magi offering three gifts, gold, frankincense, and myrrh (no parallel)
- Matt. 4:23 characterizes Jesus' ministry as teaching, preaching, and healing (contrast Mark 1:39)
- Matt. 5:22 condemns three sins having to do with anger and insults (no parallel)
- Matt. 6:31 counters three questions that express anxiety (contrast Luke 12:29)
- Matt. 11:5 groups Jesus' miracles into three sets of two (contrast Luke 7:22)
- Matt. 15:21–27 has three pleas for help, with "Lord" repeated three times (contrast Mark 7:24–30)
- Matt. 16:24–28 offers three explanatory γάρ (for) clauses (contrast Mark 8:34–38)
- Matt. 17:25 has Jesus ask three questions of Peter (no parallel)
- Matt. 20:19 lists three punishments: "mocked and flogged and crucified" (contrast Mark 10:34)
- Matt. 22:37 speaks of loving God with heart, soul, and mind (contrast Mark 12:30; Luke 10:27)
- Matt. 23:23 makes justice, mercy, and faith the weightier matters of the law (contrast Luke 11:42)
- Matt. 23:34 refers to "prophets and wise men and scribes" (contrast Luke 11:49)

These samples remove all doubt about Matthew's proclivity for arranging his materials, on both larger and smaller scales, into threes.

---

61. On the unity and interpretation of this parabolic triad see now Olmstead, *Trilogy of Parables*, pp. 39–46, and passim.

The Setting of the Sermon on the Mount

What, if anything, does the structure of Matt. 5–7 tell us about the *Sitz im Leben* or setting of the First Gospel? We have already seen that triads, in and of themselves, do not demand any special background. They appear in *The Critique of Pure Reason* as well as in "Goldilocks and the Three Bears," in Mark and Q as well as in Matthew. There are, however, reasons for giving this matter some further thought.

The first chapter of *Mishnah ʾAbot*, which purports to hand down general maxims from the great teachers of days gone by, features a number of summarizing triads. Here is a sample:[62]

> Moses received the Law from Sinai and committed it to Joshua, and Joshua to the elders, and the elders to the prophets, and the prophets committed it to the men of the Great Synagogue. They said three things:
>
> > Be deliberate in judgment,
> > > raise up many disciples,
> > > > and make a fence around the Law.
> > > > > (1:1)

> Simeon the Just was one of the survivors of the Great Synagogue. He used to say:
>
> > Upon three things the world stands:
> > > upon Torah,
> > > > upon temple service,
> > > > > and upon deeds of loving-kindness.
> > > > > > (1:2)

> Jose b. Joezer of Zeredah said:
>
> > Let your house be a meeting-house for the Sages
> > > and sit amid the dust of their feet
> > > > and drink in their words with thirst.
> > > > > (1:4)

> Joshua b. Perahyah said:
>
> > Provide yourself with a teacher
> > > and get for yourself a fellow[-disciple];
> > > > and when you judge anyone incline the balance in his favor.
> > > > > (1:6)

---

62. For the triadic form of so much of *ʾAbot*, see the translation of J. Neusner, *Torah from Our Sages: Pirke Abot: A New American Translation and Explanation* (Chappaqua, N.Y.: Rossel Books, 1984), pp. 23–24, 28–32, 39–44, 71–79, 99, 112–14, 136–41.

Nittai the Arbelite said:

> Keep yourself far from an evil neighbor
>> and consort not with the wicked
>>> and lose not belief in retribution.

(1:7)

Shemaiah said:

> Love labor
>> and hate mastery
>>> and seek not acquaintance with the ruling power.

(1:10)

Shammai said:

> Make the [study of the] Law a fixed habit;
>> say little and do much,
>>> and receive all people with a cheerful countenance.

(1:15)

Simeon . . . said:

> All my days have I grown up among the Sages, and
> I have found naught better for a man than silence;
>> and expounding [the Law] is not the chief thing but rather doing [it];
>> and the one who multiplies words occasions sin.

(1:17)

Rabban Simeon b. Gamaliel said:

> Upon three things the world stands:
> upon truth,
>> upon judgment,
>>> and upon peace,
> as it is written, "Execute the judgment of truth and peace."

(1:18)

To judge from these quotations, rabbinic tradition, at least by the time of the *Mishnah*, remembered many of the olden masters for having uttered three words or three phrases or three short sentences.[63] In fact, every say-

---

63. It is easy to find additional triads in rabbinic literature; see, e.g., *m. ʾAbot* 4:13 (three crowns); *Sifre* Deut. 357 (three stages in the lives of important people); *ARN* A 4 (three ways people differ from one another), 22 (three sorts of craftsmen); 22 (three questions); *ARN* B 43 (three companies of the just); *b. Ber.* 5a (three things God gave to Israel), 7a (three things Moses asked of God), *b. Hag.* 5b (three sorts of people God weeps over every day); *b. B. Mes.*

ing in *Abot* 1, with the possible exception of 1:9, seems to be triadic.[64] This anthology of threes is akin to *m. ʿEd.* 2:4–8; *ARN* B 31, 45, 46, 47, 48; *b. Ber.* 54b–54a; and *b. Pesaḥ.* 113a–b, all of which also collect triads or sayings having to do with three things. The boundaries of the anthology are indicated both by the traditional chapter division as well as by the repetition, in 1:2 and 18, of על שלשה דברים העולם קים/עומד (Upon three things the world stands). This forms an *inclusio*.

One of the more discussed maxims of *m. ʾAbot* 1 was the second, attributed to Simeon the Just, a teacher of the Maccabean period.[65] He purportedly made the world stand upon Torah, upon temple service, and upon deeds of loving-kindness (1:2). Some time ago, my late teacher, W. D. Davies, urged that the potential implications of this for Matthew are large. Simeon's succinct summary of the three things that matter most correlates with the fundamental structure of the Sermon on the Mount "in a roughly parallel triadic way. In v. 17–48 we find the Torah of Jesus set forth; in vi. 1–18 the true עבודה or worship, and in vi. 19–vii.12 what corresponds to גמילות חסדים, the culmination, in vii. 12, expressing the true piety or obedience in terms of the Golden Rule. On these three elements is the house of the new Israel to be built."[66] The correspondence is indeed striking. Matthew 5–7 concerns itself foremost with three subjects very closely related to the three items upon which, according to *m. ʾAbot* 1:2, the world stands, and it treats them in the same order. Simeon refers to Torah while Jesus, as the new Moses, interprets and adds to Torah (5:17–48). Simeon refers to temple service while Jesus promulgates directives for the Christian cult (6:1–18; cf. *Pirqe R. El.* 16, where the middle member of Simeon's triad is equated with prayer). And Simeon refers to deeds of loving-kindness while Jesus enjoins generosity and combats judging one's neighbor, who should be treated according to the Golden Rule (6:19–7:12). Davies decided that the Sermon on the Mount is a

---

58b (three sorts of people in hell); *b. Mak.* 23b (three enactments of the tribunal below approved by the tribunal above); *b. Pesaḥ.* 113a–b (three sorts that inherit the world to come); *b. Roš. Haš.* 16b (three classes of people at the last judgment); *b. Šabb.* 62b (three things that bring one to poverty); *b. Yebam.* 79a (three characteristics of Israel). For the examples from the *Babylonian Talmud* I am indebted to Paul Isaac Hershon, *A Talmudic Miscellany, or, A Thousand and One Extracts from the Talmud, the Midrashim, and the Kabbalah* (London: Trübner, 1880), pp. 36–67.

64. Cf. Neusner, *Torah*, p. 35: "While nearly everyone else in our well-crafted chapter says three things, Hillel says a great many. The pattern normally followed is to have sayings set up in triplets of clauses closely related but distinct in counsel. . . . Instead, Hillel is given a triplet of three full sayings."

65. *ARN* A 4; *ARN* B 5, 31; *y. Taʿan.* 4:2; *y. Meg.* 3:6; *Pirqe R. El.* 16; and *Pesiq. Rab.* 5:3 also cite the saying; *ARN* B 53 and *Pirqe R. El.* 12 allude to it; and *m. ʾAbot* 1:18 and *ARN* A 4 reinterpret it (see n. 80).

66. Davies, *Setting*, pp. 305–7 (quotation from p. 307).

Christian version of or alternative to Simeon's three pillars. His argument persuaded T. W. Manson.[67] Eugene Boring has also gone along.[68] What should we think?

While we cannot here exit the realm of speculation, Davies' thesis stands a very good chance of being correct. The reasons for so thinking are multiple, and Davies failed to summon all of them. I should like to finish this chapter, then, by bolstering his case.

Summing up Torah. Various authorities, in *b. Mak.* 24a–24b, reduce the 611 commandments of the Torah to eleven, then to six, then to three, then to two, and then to one, and Jewish literature contains additional attempts to summarize Torah succinctly or to state in a maxim what matters most.[69] Matthew's Gospel shows us that its author was keenly interested in this sort of exercise. The Golden Rule in 7:12 presents itself as a summary of the law and the prophets (contrast Luke 6:31). In 19:18–19, the commandments required for entering into life are condensed to the second half of the Decalogue plus Leviticus 19:18 (cf. Mark 10:19). In 22:34–40, Jesus is happy to answer the question, "Which commandment in the law is the greatest?" He responds by juxtaposing the Shema and Lev. 19:18, just as he does in Mark 12:28–34. Matthew alone, however, has his Lord add: "On these two commandments hang all the law and the prophets." Furthermore, Matthew 23:23 reveals that the evangelist was acquainted with the tradition of summarizing one's religious or moral duty in a triad: "You . . . have neglected the weightier matters of the law: justice and mercy and faith."[70]

By prefacing 5:21–7:11 with a statement about the law and the prophets and then following it with a generalization about the same, Matthew shows

67. T. W. Manson, *Ethics and the Gospel* (New York: Scribner, 1961), pp. 52–53, offers in passing an analysis like that of Davies, based, I have been told, upon conversations with the latter before his *Setting of the Sermon on the Mount* appeared in print.

68. M. Eugene Boring, "The Gospel of Matthew," in *The New Interpreter's Bible* (Nashville: Abingdon, 1995), 8:172. P. F. Ellis, *Matthew: His Mind and His Message* (Collegeville, Minn.: Liturgical Press, 1974), p. 37, also endorsed Davies' argument, as I did earlier; see Davies and Allison, *Matthew*, 1:70–71.

69. Cf. Philo, *Decal.* 18–19 (the Decalogue summarizes the law); *Sifra* on Lev. 19.18 ("You will love your neighbor as yourself" is, for Akiba, "the greatest principle in the Law" whereas Ben Azzai thinks this honor goes to Gen. 5:1); *b. Ber.* 63a (Bar Kappara said, "Upon what short text do all the essential principles of the Torah depend? 'In all your ways acknowledge Him and He will direct your paths'"); *b. Šabb.* 31a ("A certain heathen came before Shammai and said to him, 'Make me a proselyte, on condition that you teach me the whole Torah while I stand on one foot.' Thereupon he repulsed him with the builder's cubit which was in his hand. When he went before Hillel, he said to him, 'What is hateful to you, do not do to your neighbor. That is the whole Torah, while the rest is commentary. Go and learn it'").

70. Contrast Luke 11:42, which mentions only justice and love. Although *The Critical Edition of Q: Synopsis, Including the Gospels of Matthew and Luke, Mark and Thomas* (ed. James M. Robinson, Paul Hoffmann, and John S. Kloppenborg; Leuven: Peeters, 2000), p. 266, reckons Matthew here nearer to Q, Matthew's proclivity for the triad casts reasonable doubt upon this verdict.

us, as we have seen, that he conceives of the Sermon on the Mount itself as a sort of summing up, as Jesus' take on the law and the prophets. In other words, the sermon relates itself to the ancient attempts to offer a précis of what matters most.

Matthew and scribal tradition. Ernst von Dobschütz, in a famous article, observed that Matthew delights in detailed parallelism, in remarkable and sometimes tedious repetition, as well as in numerical schemes, and that all of this makes him resemble the rabbis.[71] Furthermore, von Dobschütz added that Billerbeck's rabbinic commentary on the New Testament cites more comparative material for Matthew than for the other Gospels, that the evangelist's fondness for referring to God as the "Father in heaven" has its match in the rabbinic corpus, and that the exception clauses added to the rulings on divorce in 5:32 and 19:9 recall the teaching of the School of Shammai on that subject. From all this, von Dobschütz inferred that Matthew was close to the rabbis, that he was indeed a "converted rabbi."

Despite the avalanche of Matthean studies since 1928, some of which have gone so far as to contend that Matthew was a Gentile Christian,[72] my judgment is that, while we cannot show that Matthew was a "converted rabbi," we do know that he was a Jew; and the evangelist's stylistic proclivities do put him closer to the rabbis than to any other group known to us. The recent study of Lawrence Wills brings confirmation.[73] Calling attention to Matthew's compositional habit of reformulating sayings to create precise antithetical parallelism,[74] Wills observes that examples of such perfect parallelism elsewhere occur only occasionally. The one exception is *Mishnah ʾAbot* (the source of Simeon's triad). This contains numerous instances of precise antithetical parallelism, as in 3:9:

מתקימת	חכמתו			מחכמתו	מרבין	שמעשיו	כל	
מתקימת	חכמתו	אין		ממעשיו	מרבין	שחכמתו	וכל	

71. Ernst von Dobschütz, "Matthäus als Rabbi und Katechet," *ZNW* 27 (1928), pp. 338–48; translated into English as "Matthew as Rabbi and Catechist," in *The Interpretation of Matthew* (ed. Graham Stanton; Philadelphia: Fortress, 1983), pp. 19–29.

72. See Davies and Allison, *Matthew*, 1:7–58, with refutation.

73. Lawrence M. Wills, "Scribal Methods in Matthew and Mishnah Abot," *CBQ* 63 (2001), pp. 258–64. Also pertinent is Craig A. Evans, "Targumizing Tendencies in Matthean Redaction," in *When Judaism and Christianity Began: Essays in Memory of Anthony J. Saldarini* (ed. Alan J. Avery-Peck, Daniel Harrington, and Jacob Neusner; 2 vols.; SuppJSJ 85; Leiden: Brill, 2004), 1:93–116. Evans shows that several Matthean characteristics align the book with the targum on Isaiah.

74. E.g., 6:14–15 (no parallel), 19–20 (contrast Luke 12:33–34), 22–23 (contrast Luke 11:34–36); 7:13–14 (contrast Luke 13:23–24); 10:32–33 (contrast Mark 8:38; Luke 12:8–9); 12:35 (contrast Luke 6:45); 16:19 (no parallel); 25:31–46 (no parallel).

Everyone whose deeds are more than his wisdom, his wisdom endures.
And everyone whose wisdom is more than his deeds, his wisdom does not
endure.

Wills counts twelve clear instances of this sort of parallelism in *'Abot*.[75]
His reasonable conclusion is that, given the good evidence for Matthew
having been some sort of professional scribe,[76] "the evangelist probably
learned a scribal tradition—including the use of precise antithetical parallelism—from teachers similar to those in *Abot*."[77] This supposition more
than accords with Davies' suggestion that the Sermon on the Mount
reflects a tradition preserved in *'Abot*.

The destruction of the temple. Most modern scholars have dated Matthew to the 80s or 90s of the first century, and Davies urged that, during
this time, some Jewish teachers were discussing and reinterpreting Rabbi
Simeon's famous three pillars. The cause of this was the destruction of the
temple in Jerusalem. This disaster made the middle member of Simeon's
triad problematic and compelled revision. How can the world rest upon
the Jerusalem cult if the temple has ceased to be?

The lengthy commentary in *ARN* B 5–8 leaves no doubt that Simeon's
three pillars became at some point the subject of much discussion and
reinterpretation. Furthermore, *ARN* A 4 (cf. B 8), as part of a commentary
on Simeon's famous maxim, has the following story. When he heard Rabbi
Joshua cry out, "Woe unto us, that this, [the temple,] the place where the
iniquities of Israel were atoned for, is laid waste," Rabbi Johanan ben
Zakkai responded, "My son, be not grieved: we have another atonement
as effective as this. And what is it? It is deeds of loving-kindness, as it is
said, 'For I desire mercy and not sacrifice'" (Hos. 6:6). In this tale, the
third of Simeon's pillars does duty for the second. The temple cult, being
no more, has surrendered its place to acts of mercy.[78]

ARN A 4 (cf. B 6) also contains, in the following, fictitious dialogue
between Vespasian, the Roman conqueror of Jerusalem, and Johanan
ben Zakkai, another interpretation of Simeon's maxim. "Are you Rab-

---

75. 1:3; 2:9; 3:2, 3, 5, 10 (*bis*), 11; 4:6, 9, 11a, 20. There are also nine examples of less
precise parallelism: 2:4; 3:17; 4:5, 11; 5:16, 17, 18, 19 (*bis*).

76. See 13:52 and David E. Orton, *The Understanding Scribe: Matthew and the Apocalyptic
Ideal* (JSNTSS 25; Sheffield: Sheffield Academic Press, 1989), although I query Orton's tendency
to set apocalyptic over against Pharisaism.

77. Wills, "Scribal Methods," p. 257.

78. According to Jacob Neusner, *Development of a Legend: Studies on the Traditions Concerning Yohanan ben Zakkai* (SPB 16; Leiden: Brill, 1970), pp. 114–15, we cannot with any
confidence date the dialogue in *ARN* 4. Despite his uncertainties about the story in *ARN* 4,
Neusner does seem to affirm, in *Judaism in the Beginning of Christianity* (Philadelphia: Fortress,
1984), pp. 95–97, that Johanan, after the destruction of Jerusalem in 70 CE, occupied himself
with reinterpreting Simeon's pillars.

ban Johanan ben Zakkai?" Vespasian inquired. "Tell me, what may I give to you?" "I ask nothing of you," Rabban Johanan replied, "except Jamnia, where I might go and teach my disciples and there establish a [house of] prayer and perform all the commandments." Here Johanan asks for three things. He seeks a place in which it is possible (1) to study Torah, (2) to offer prayer, and (3) to perform all the commandments. Once more one detects the influence of the three great pillars, and again they have undergone revision.[79] Torah has become the study of Torah. The temple cult has become prayer. And deeds of loving-kindness have become obedience to all of the commandments.

If we can indeed believe the sources when they report, what otherwise seems almost unavoidable, that the destruction of the temple constrained teachers to reformulate traditional convictions about the most important matters, then we have here a close parallel to Davies' evaluation of Matthew 5–7. The evangelist, by making Jesus' teaching about Torah, the cult, and social issues the sum of the law and the prophets, would be doing something analogous to what other Jewish thinkers—in particular, according to rabbinic sources, Johanan ben Zakkai—were doing after the temple fell.[80]

Matthew and Johanan ben Zakkai. Beginning, to my knowledge, with von Dobschütz, several scholars have observed some intriguing—Luz calls them "astonishing"[81]—connections not just between Matthew and rabbinic traditions in general but between Matthew and traditions about Johanan ben Zakkai in particular:

- Matthew's distinctive version of the parable of a king inviting people to a royal wedding feast (22:1–14; cf. Luke 14:16–24) has its closest parallel in a parable that *b. Šabb.* 153 attributes to Johanan ben Zakkai.[82]

79. Cf. Judah Goldin, "The Three Pillars of Simeon the Righteous," *PAAJR* 27 (1958), pp. 51–52.

80. For a reinterpretation of Simeon's statement from a later time see *m. ʾAbot* 1:18, with the comments of Jacob Neusner, *The Rabbinic Traditions about the Pharisees before 70* (3 vols.; Leiden: Brill, 1971), 1:18, and Benedict Viviano, *Study as Worship: Aboth and the New Testament* (SJLA 26; Leiden: Brill, 1978), pp. 30–31.

81. Luz, *Matthäus*, 1:98 ("erstaunlich").

82. "This may be compared to a king who summoned his servants to a banquet without appointing a time. The wise ones adorned themselves and sat at the door of the palace, 'for,' they said, 'is anything lacking in a royal palace?' The fools went about their work, saying, 'can there be a banquet without preparations?' Suddenly the king desired the presence of his servants: the wise entered adorned, while the fools entered soiled. The king rejoiced at the wise but was angry with the fools. 'Those who adorned themselves for the banquet,' ordered he, 'let them sit, eat, and drink. But those who did not adorn themselves for the banquet, let them stand and watch'"; cf. *Eccl. Rab.* on 9:8. B. W. Bacon, *Studies in Matthew* (New York: Henry Holt, 1930), pp. 72–73, was much impressed by this parallel and used it to support von Dobschütz's conjecture of a link between Matthew and Johanan ben Zakkai.

- The only scripture Matthew formally cites more than once is Hos. 6:6 ("I desire mercy, not sacrifice"). Jesus quotes it in Matt. 9:13 and 12:7, both times without synoptic parallel. The New Testament does not otherwise refer to Hos. 6:6. *ARN* 4, however, as we have seen, makes Hosea's declaration central to Johanan ben Zakkai's post-70 program.

- Although the author of Matthew was Jewish, he was open to the Gentile Christian mission (cf. 28:16–20).[83] Similarly, the traditions about Johanan make him friendly toward non-Jews: *b. Ber.* 17a; *b. B. Bat.* 10b; *Deut. Rab.* 7:7.

- Whereas Matthew's intense eschatological expectation is patent, the traditions about the death of Johanan focus on judgment and even mention the two ways, which Matt. 7:13–14 stresses; see *b. Ber.* 28b; *ARN* A 25; and *y. ʾAbod. Zar.* 3:1. The two ways also appear on Jonathan's lips in *m. ʾAbot* 2:9.

- On the assumption that the "righteous" of Matt. 25:31–46 include non-Christians who have cared for "the least of these,"[84] so that salvation is possible for those outside the church, a good parallel appears in the thought of Johanan in *b. B. Bat.* 10b, where he teaches that "charity makes atonement for the heathen."

- Instead of "kingdom of God," which he uses rarely, Matthew, alone of New Testament writers, prefers "kingdom of heaven," which he uses often. Although the Hebrew equivalent, מלכות שמים, is popular in rabbinic literature, Johanan ben Zakkai is the earliest sage to whom it is attributed; see *y. Qidd.* 1:2.

- If Matt. 15:11, without abolishing Torah observance, makes defilement a matter of the heart and so of ethics rather than a matter of externals, Johanan ben Zakkai does something similar in *Num. Rab.* 19:8: defilement does not inhere in objects but is a matter of divine intent and human disposition (cf. *Pesiq. R. El.* 40b).

To these intriguing similarities one may add that *m. ʾAbot* 2:9, which tells about the students of Johanan, displays repeated antithetical parallelism, and further that *m. ʾAbot* 2:10, which transmits teaching from Johanan's students, reverts to the triadic pattern of chapter 1: "They [the disciples of Johanan] said three things. . . ." Five examples follow.

---

83. Although I agree with him about much, David C. Sim, *The Gospel of Matthew and Christian Judaism: The History and Social Setting of the Matthean Community* (Studies in the New Testament and Its World; Edinburgh: T&T Clark, 1998), has, in my judgment, gone too far in downplaying Matthew's hospitality to Gentiles.

84. See esp. Arland J. Hultgren, *The Parables of Jesus: A Commentary* (Grand Rapids: Eerdmans, 2000), pp. 309–27.

So two of Matthew's chief compositional techniques are associated with traditions about the school of Johanan.

One must be careful not to infer too much from parallels such as these. They certainly do not, let us say, require that Matthew studied under Johanan. Still, taken in conjunction with the other observations we have made, they do intrigue. Johanan, according to *ARN* 4, involved himself in reinterpreting Simeon the Just's three pillars; and Matthew, according to Davies, set about to do something similar. So when we find a number of notable parallels between Matthew and Johanan, the proposed interpretation of the Sermon on the Mount gains some credence.

Deeds of loving-kindness. Charles Talbert has criticized Davies' thesis in part because "6:19–7:12 is not about deeds of loving-kindness."[85] Davies did not, however, contend that the three major topics of Matthew's sermon and the three pillars of Simeon correspond perfectly. Matthew's sermon is not, on the hypothesis being considered, a simple restatement of Simeon's triad but a reinterpretation of it. One might as well argue that Simeon b. Gamaliel's triad in *m. ʾAbot* 1:18 is unrelated to Simeon the Just's triad in *m. ʾAbot* 1:2 because their content differs; but the latter clearly rewrites the former.[86] Beyond this, one may query Talbert's assertion that "6:19–7:12 is not about deeds of loving-kindness." (1) If 6:19–24 is about money, *t. Peʾah* 4:19 teaches that גמילות חסדים include what one does with money (cf. *b. Sukk.* 49a). (2) The traditional Jewish understanding of "deeds of lovingkindness," according to Maimonides, includes "interpersonal relationships,"[87] which is certainly the topic of 7:1–6. (3) Matthew 7:7–11 concerns prayer, and tradition has Johanan ben Zakkai making prayer one aspect of גמילות חסדים. (4) According to Pinchas Peli, "there are many examples in talmudic literature from which it seems that the term gemilut hasadim is especially associated with certain deeds which have the common characteristic of mutual responsibility, whose essence is embodied in the maxim 'do, that it should be done to you.'" This certainly calls to mind Matt. 7:12: "Do to others as you would have them do to you."[88] On the whole, then, 6:19–7:12 corresponds remarkably well to rabbinic understandings of גמילות חסדים.

Hosea 6:6. It is, finally, precisely Hos. 6:6 that Johanan, in *ARN* 4, uses to revise Simeon's triad, and Hos. 6:6 is the one Old Testament text that Matthew's Gospel, as noted, formally cites more than once. This could be coincidence. But it is equally consistent with the supposition that Matthew was familiar with Jews who, after 70, called upon Hos. 6:6

85. Talbert, *Sermon*, p. 23. Cf. Betz, *Sermon*, p. 423.
86. See n. 80.
87. Maimonides, *Commentary on the Mishnah* ad *Peʾah* 1:1.
88. Pinchas H. Peli, "The Havurot That Were in Jerusalem," *HUCA* 55 (1984), p. 68.

when discussing what matters most, and that the evangelist joined their discussion in his own fashion. If so, then the Sermon on the Mount is, in fact, a Christian response to Simeon's three pillars and so a presentation of the most important human responsibilities.

Interpreters of Matthew have, from early times, sensed the Jewish character of the Gospel. Papias, according to Eusebius (*HE* 3.39.14–16 [SC 31, ed. Bardy, p. 157]), claimed that the book was written in "the Hebrew dialect." Whatever the origin of that intriguing tradition, subsequent interpreters found it believable, and the older commentaries are full of remarks on Matthew's Jewish orientation. According to the *Opus Imperfectum*, the author of our Gospel wrote in order to edify Jews (PG 56:613), and Theophylact believed that he wrote for Christian Jews (*Comm. Matt.* prol. [PG 123:145C]).

The modern commentaries are here not so much different from their ancient predecessors. Most contemporary exegetes—although admittedly not all—have surmised that the author of Matthew, whatever his name, must have been a Jew. Their judgment is no longer based upon ecclesiastical tradition but rather upon analysis of the text itself, its language and themes. Now it is my conviction that, in this particular matter, the majority is correct, and I offer the present chapter as yet one more reason for so thinking. If I am right about the links between the Sermon on the Mount and Simeon's triadic summary of what matters most, our author's Jewishness does not show itself only in his vocabulary and his theology. His expert, first-hand acquaintance with Judaism and his engagement with its theological traditions disclose themselves also in the very structuring of his materials.

11

Foreshadowing the Passion

Although many have quoted, with approval or qualified approval, Martin Kähler's appraisal of Mark as a passion narrative with an extended introduction,[1] fewer have spoken of Matthew in these terms.[2] There are at least two reasons for this. The first is that Matthew's passion narrative occupies a proportionately smaller amount of space. Whereas Mark 14, 15, and 16 are three chapters in a book of 16 chapters, Matt. 26, 27, and 28 are three chapters in a book of 28. A second reason for not transferring Kähler's characterization of Mark to Matthew is that the latter contains much more teaching on subjects not directly related to Jesus' suffering and death. One need recall only the lengthy Sermon on the Mount and the community discourse in chapter 18.

The two facts just referred to do not, nonetheless, negate a third, which is that the passion and resurrection do indeed constitute the climax of Matthew's story. In many ways the entire narrative leans forward, so to speak, to its end, so that the reader of Matt. 1–25 is never far from thinking of the ensuing chapters, 26–28. Already in chapter 1, for instance, the prophecy that Jesus "will save his people from their sins" (1:21), although unelaborated, moves one to think of his salvific death

1. See M. Kähler, *The So-called Historical Jesus and the Historic Biblical Christ* (Fortress Texts in Modern Theology; Philadelphia: Fortress, 1964), p. 80, n. 11.
2. Cf. Kähler, *Jesus,* p. 80, n. 11: "the situation is the same [in Matthew] as in Mark" only "if one subtracts the infancy narratives" and several chapters of discourse material.

on behalf of others (20:28; 26:28). And in chapter 2, the chief priests and scribes of the people conspire with the secular authority to kill "the king of the Jews," so that the end is foreshadowed in the beginning.[3] The conflict stories later on, especially in chapter 12, supply additional preparation for the passion: the growing strife between Jesus and the Jewish leaders inexorably leads to the trial, which in turn issues in the appearance before Pilate and Jesus' execution.[4] Then again there are the passion predictions, both explicit and implicit.[5] These regularly move the reader from present narrative time to future narrative time, to the trial and crucifixion in chapters 26–27. Throughout Matthew, then, the end, so often foreshadowed and prophesied, is like the Jesus of John's Gospel: it draws all to itself.

Nothing said thus far is anything other than obvious. There are, however, or so at least I shall now argue, a handful of texts that more subtly anticipate the Messiah's betrayal and burial and events in between (26:47–27:66). In particular, 5:38–42; 10:17–23; 14:1–12; 17:1–8; and 20:20–23 contain language otherwise associated with the passion of Jesus. I believe that, although the vast majority of commentators, ancient and modern, are typically and altogether silent about the fact,[6] these five passages constitute a collectivity. Their joint shadow falls forward, to the crucifixion, while its shadow falls back upon them. Put otherwise, all five paragraphs interact with the end of the story and thereby augment the meaning of the whole.

This is a study of internal references; I shall be relating Matthew to Matthew. The Gospel, on my reading, anticipates being heard and re-heard, and so anticipates an audience that will accordingly appreciate its intratextuality, its allusions to itself. That such informed hearers are the

3. This correlation belongs to a larger pattern; additional parallels between Matthew 1–2 and 26–28 include: salvation for Gentiles: 1:3, 5, 6; 2:1–12 // 27:54; 28:19; appearance of angel: 1:20; 2:13, 19 // 28:5; angelic message, "Do not fear": 1:20 // 28:5; Jesus as abiding divine presence: 1:23 // 28:20; gathering of chief priests and scribes: 2:4 // 26:57; 27:41; "seeing . . . they worshiped": 2:11 // 28:17; warning in a dream: 2:12, 22 // 27:19; plot to kill Jesus: 2:13–18 // 26:1–5; Jesus going to Galilee: 2:22 // 28:7, 10, 16. For discussion of some of these and further suggestions see Hubert Frankemölle, *Jahwebund und Kirche Christi: Studien zur Form- und Traditionsgeschichte des "Evangeliums" nach Matthäus* (NTAbh 10; Münster: Aschendorff, 1974), pp. 321–25.

4. See John Paul Heil, *The Death and Resurrection of Jesus: A Narrative-Critical Reading of Matthew 26–28* (Minneapolis: Fortress, 1991), pp. 16–17, and Jack Dean Kingsbury, "The Developing Conflict between Jesus and the Jewish Leaders in Matthew's Gospel," *CBQ* 49 (1987), pp. 57–73.

5. 9:15; 12:40; 16:21–23; 17:12, 22–23; 20:17–19, 22–23, 28; 21:38–39; 26:2.

6. It is symptomatic that Heil, *Death and Resurrection*, pp. 7–20, in a section entitled "The Previous Narrative Prepares for Matthew 26–28," discusses none of these passages except 14:1–12.

implied hearers of Matthew I believe to be the case, although I shall not pursue the evidence here.[7] I can observe, however, that when one comes to the end, one is asked to start over, for the imperative to do "all that I have commanded you" (28:20) means to do "all that I have commanded you in the previous chapters." In this way the crowning imperative at the end requires that one continually engage the text. And that demands recurrent hearing.

Although this is not an exercise in redaction criticism, I believe that Matthew's Gospel is what it is because of its author's intentions, some of which may be highlighted by paying special heed to Matthew's revisions of Mark.[8] I shall, then, at least in the footnotes, observe that all of the allusions I propose are stronger in Matthew than in the parallel synoptic segments. In each instance, it appears, redactional activity has produced or enhanced the allusion.

Turning the Other Cheek

In his fifth demonstration of the general statement in 5:17–20, which declares that he has come not to abolish the law and the prophets but to fulfill them, Matthew's Jesus exhorts his listeners to abandon the principle of an eye for an eye and so to eschew violence. Several arresting illustrations follow: "Do not resist (ἀντιστῆναι) an evildoer. But if anyone strikes (ῥαπίζει) you on the right cheek (σιαγόνα), turn (στρέψον) the other also; and if anyone wants to sue (κριθῆναι) you and take your coat, give your cloak (ἱμάτιον) as well. . . . Give (δός) to everyone who begs from you, and do not refuse (ἀποστραφῇς) anyone who wants to borrow from you" (5:39–42). These several imperatives share, as a handful of exegetes over the centuries have observed, significant vocabulary with Isa. 50:6–9 LXX.[9] The following words are common to both passages:

7. Obviously I do not construe the implied reader or hearer as a first-time reader or hearer. For the argument that at least the implied reader of Mark is a rereader expected to be alert to subtle clues see Elizabeth Struthers Malbon, "Echoes and Foreshadowings in Mark 4–8: Reading and Rereading," *JBL* 112 (1993), pp. 211–30. Also helpful here is Ulrich Luz, *Das Evangelium nach Matthäus* (4 vols.; EKK 1/1–4; Düsseldorf: Benziger, 1990–2002), 1:42–44. Much of what I have elsewhere argued for the audience of Q holds, *mutatis mutandis*, for Matthew; see Dale C. Allison Jr., *The Intertextual Jesus: Scripture in Q* (Harrisburg, Pa.: Trinity Press International, 2000), pp. 1–24.

8. On the possibility and utility of seeking authorial intentions see Dale C. Allison Jr., *The New Moses: A Matthean Typology* (Edinburgh: T&T Clark, 1993), pp. 1–8.

9. Cf. Albertus Magnus, *Super Mt. cap. I–XIV* ad loc. (Opera Omnia 21/1, ed. B. Schmidt, p. 155); John Trapp, *A Commentary upon the Old and New Testaments* (ed. W. Webser; 5 vols.; 2nd ed.; London: Richard D. Dickinson, 1865), 5:77; Matthew Poole, *Annotations on the Holy Bible* (3 vols.; London: Henry G. Bohn, 1846), 3:25; William Manson, *Jesus*

Word	Matthew	Isaiah
ἀνθίστημι	5:38: ἀντιστῆναι	50:8: ἀντιστήτω
σιαγών	5:39: σιαγόνα	50:6: σιαγόνας
ῥαπίζω/ῥάπισμα	5:39: ῥαπίζει	50:6: ῥαπίσματα
κρίνω	5:40: κριθῆναι	50:8: κρινόμενος
ἱμάτιον	5:40: ἱμάτιον	50:9: ἱμάτιον
δίδωμι	5:42: δός	50:6: δέδωκα
ἀποστρέφω	5:42: ἀποστραφῆς	50:6: ἀπέστρεψα

When one takes into account the thematic parallels—both Matt. 5:38–42 and Isa. 50:4–11 depict the unjust treatment of an innocent individual, and both use the terminology of the law court[10]—it becomes difficult to credit chance. Matthew's text borrows from the third servant song.[11]

How do these echoes from Isa. 50:4–9 work on informed hearers? They do more than just inject a vague scriptural aura. Rather, we come to the truth when we observe that the passion narrative again alludes to Isa. 50:6, in 26:67 ("Then they spat [ἐνέπτυσαν] in his face and struck him; and some slapped [ἐράπισαν] him") and in 27:30 ("They spat [ἐμπτύσαντες] on him, and took the reed and struck him on the head").[12] So the scrip-

the Messiah: The Synoptic Tradition of the Revelation of God in Christ: With Special Reference to Form-Criticism (London: Hodder & Stoughton Ltd., 1943), pp. 30–32; Robert H. Gundry, The Use of the Old Testament in St. Matthew's Gospel: With Special Reference to the Messianic Hope (NovTSup 18; Leiden: Brill, 1967), pp. 72–73; Werner Grimm, Weil Ich Dich Liebe: Die Verkündigung und Deuterojesaja (ANTJ; Bern: Herbert Lang, 1976), pp. 183–86; Ulrich Luck, Das Evangelium nach Matthäus (ZBK; Zürich: Theologischer Verlag, 1993), p. 76 .

10. Isa. 50:6–9 LXX reads: "I gave (δέδωκα) my back to scourges, my cheeks (σιαγόνας) to slaps (ῥαπίσματα), and I did not turn away (ἀπέστρεψα) my face from the shame of spitting. . . . Who is the one who goes to court against (κρινόμενος) me? Let that one stand up against me (ἀντιστήτω). . . . You will wax old as a garment (ἱμάτιον)."

11. When one turns to the parallel in Luke 6:29–30, only three of the seven words common to Matthew and Isaiah appear there: σιαγών, ἱμάτιον, δίδωμι. How should we explain this? Three arguments direct us to Matthew's redactional activity. (i) It is more likely that someone assimilated a Gospel text to a famous biblical passage than that obvious assimilation to that passage decreased with time or that Luke erased it. (ii) Elsewhere, in 26:67, the First Evangelist alludes to Isa. 50:6; see the following note. (iii) Matthew's tendency to rewrite passages with the vocabulary of a particular Jewish scripture is demonstrable. For an example from the beginning of the Gospel see Matt. 2:19–21, which rewrites Exod. 4:19–20, and the comments of W. D. Davies and Dale C. Allison Jr., A Critical and Exegetical Commentary on the Gospel according to Saint Matthew (2 vols.; ICC; Edinburgh: T&T Clark, 1988–91), 1:271. For an example from the end of the Gospel see Matt. 28:16–20, which draws upon Deut. 31:14–15, 23 and Josh. 1:1–9, and the analysis of W. D. Davies and Dale C. Allison Jr., "Matt. 28:16–20: Texts behind the Text," RHPR 72 (1992), pp. 89–98.

12. Isa. 50:6 LXX uses both ἔμπτυσμα and ῥαπίσματα; cf. Justin Martyr, 1 Apol. 38 (PTS 38, ed. Marcovich, p. 86); Irenaeus, Adv. haer. 4.33.12 (Fontes Christiani 8/4, ed. Brox, p. 270);

tural text associated with turning the other cheek is also associated with the passion of Jesus. Furthermore, of the seven words common to Matt. 5:38–42 and Isa. 50:4–9, two appear again in the passion narrative: ῥαπίζω (26:67) and ἱμάτιον (27:31, 35). Indeed, ῥαπίζω appears precisely twice in the First Gospel, in 5:39 and 26:67, and in both places an innocent person is struck, just as, in 5:40 and 27:31 and 35, an innocent person's clothes are taken. The confluence of words, themes, and images is arresting. Matthew 5:38–42 potentially superimposes three images: those of the suffering Christian, the suffering Jesus, and Isaiah's suffering servant. Informed hearers of 5:38–42 may, then, recall not only Isa. 50:4–9 but also, as did Augustine, Ephraem, and Matthew Henry, the suffering and example of Jesus.[13]

Further stimulus to do this comes from another word that appears in Matt. 5:38–42. Jesus commands, in verse 41, "If anyone forces (ἀγγαρεύσει) you to go one mile, go also the second mile."[14] The Greek verb behind the English "forces" is ἀγγαρεύω, a word weakly attested in early Christian literature but occurring a second time in the First Gospel, in 27:32: "As they went out, they came upon a man from Cyrene named Simon; they compelled (ἠγγάρευσαν) this man to carry his cross."

Commentators sometimes cite 27:32 as clarification for 5:41. According to Daniel Harrington: "[5:41] refers to the legal right of Roman soldiers to press civilians into service. For example, Simon of Cyrene is pressed into service to carry the beam of Jesus' cross."[15] Eduard Schweizer says the same thing: "The term translated as 'force' is a technical word for requisitioning by civil or military authorities, and is applied in 27:32 to Simon from Cyrene, who is forced by the Romans to carry Jesus' cross to the place of execution. As in that case, individuals probably demanded such services often, even contrary to precise legalities."[16]

Jerome, *Comm. Matt.* ad loc. (SC 259, ed. Bonnard, p. 286); Ps.-Epiphanius, *Testim.* 48.3 (Texts and Translations 4, Early Christian Literature Series 1, ed.. Hotchkiss, p. 48); Isidore of Seville, *Fide cath. ex vet.* 13 (PLSuppl. 4.1832); Sedulius Scotus, *Comm. Matt.* ad loc. (ed. Löfstedt, p. 590); Gundry, *Old Testament*, p. 61; Davies and Allison, *Matthew*, 3:604. In *Gos. Pet.* 3:9, the mocking even more clearly alludes to Isa. 50:6: ἐμάστιζον, σιαγόνας, and ἐράπισαν all have parallels in Isa. 50:6 LXX.

13. Augustine, *Serm. Dom.* 1.19.58 (CCSL 35, ed. Mutzenbecher, pp. 68–69); idem, *Mend.* 15(27) (CSEL 41, ed. Zycha, p. 447); Ephraem, *Comm. Diat.* 6:13 (SC 121, ed. Leloir, p. 129: Jesus exemplifies turning the other cheek when he himself is later struck on the cheek); Matthew Henry, *Commentary on the Whole Bible*, vol. 5, *Matthew to John* (New York: Fleming H. Revell, n.d.), ad 5:41 (he refers to "Christ's example" in this connection).

14. There is no Lukan parallel.

15. Daniel J. Harrington, *The Gospel of Matthew* (Sacra Pagina 1; Collegeville, Minn.: Liturgical Press, 1992), p. 89.

16. Eduard Schweizer, *The Good News according to Matthew* (Atlanta: John Knox, 1975), p. 130.

Robert Gundry finds a more organic connection: "ἀγγαρεύσει probably anticipates the story of Simon of Cyrene, whom Roman soldiers requisitioned to carry Jesus' cross."[17] In other words, the ἀγγαρεύσει of 5:41 foreshadows the ἠγγάρευσαν of 27:32, so that Jesus' own fate displays his own imperative.

The intratextual relationship between 5:41 and 27:32 is like that between 5:38–42 and the passion narrative as a whole: the one illustrates the other. If Jesus speaks of eschewing violence and of not resisting evil, of being slapped, of having one's clothes taken, and of being compelled to serve the Romans, the conclusion to his own life makes his words concrete. He eschews violence (26:51–54). He does not resist evil (26:36–56; 27:12–14). He is struck and does not strike back (26:67). His garments are taken (27:28, 35). And one requisitioned by Roman order carries his cross (27:32). In short, he is "the first to fulfill the precepts which he taught."[18]

All this comports with two themes that run throughout Matthew, the first being the congruence between Jesus' words and deeds, between his speech and his action, the second being his status as moral exemplar, which requires an "imitation" of Christ.[19] The allusions to the passion narrative in 5:38–42 serve both Christology and moral exhortation.

The Afflictions of Missionaries

Matthew 10:17–23 paints a very bleak picture of what awaits the Christian missionary:

> Beware of them, for they will hand you over (παραδώσουσιν) to councils (συνέδρια) and flog (μαστιγώσουσιν) you in their synagogues; and you will

---

17. Robert H. Gundry, *Matthew: A Commentary on His Handbook for a Mixed Church under Persecution* (2nd ed.; Grand Rapids: Eerdmans, 1994), p. 94. Cf. Paschasius Radbertus, *Exp. Matt. Libri XII* ad 5:41 (CCCM 56, ed. Paulus, p. 349).

18. Augustine, *Serm. Dom.* 1.19.58 (CCSL 35, ed. Mutzenbecher, p. 68).

19. In addition to chapter 7 above, pp. 135–55, see David R. Bauer, *The Structure of Matthew's Gospel: A Study in Literary Design* (JSNTSS 31; Sheffield: Almond, 1988), pp. 57–63; Georg Strecker, *Der Weg der Gerechtigkeit: Untersuchung zur Theologie des Matthäus* (3rd ed.; Göttingen: Vandenhoeck & Ruprecht, 1971), pp. 177–84 (arguing, among other things, that 26:54 illustrates 5:39–42); and David B. Howell, *Matthew's Inclusive Story* (JSNTSS 42; Sheffield: JSOT, 1990), pp. 251–59. Heil, *Death and Resurrection*, p. 110, also rightly sees that one of the major imperatives implicit in the passion narrative is emulation of "the inspiring model of Jesus as the innocently suffering just one, who, in complete trust in God, patiently endures rejection and death." Cf. his p. 88, and see further Frank J. Matera, *Passion Narratives and Gospel Theologies: Interpreting the Synoptics through Their Passion Stories* (New York: Paulist, 1986), pp. 142–48.

be dragged (ἀχθήσεσθε) before governors (ἡγεμόνας) and kings because of me, as a testimony before them and the Gentiles. When they hand you over (παραδῶσιν), do not worry about how you are to speak or what you are to say; for what you are to say will be given to you at that time; for it is not you who speak, but the Spirit of your Father speaking through you. Brother will betray (παραδώσει) brother to death, and a father his child, and children will rise against parents and have them put to death (θανατώσουσιν); and you will be hated by all because of my name. But the one who endures to the end will be saved. When they persecute you in one town, flee to the next; for truly I tell you, you will not have gone through all the towns of Israel before the Son of Man comes.

This paragraph, according to F. W. Beare, reflects "conditions which did not exist in the lifetime of Jesus for his followers, and must be seen rather as bearing upon the mission of those early years of the church."[20] Without debating what might or might not go back to the pre-Easter period, 10:17–23 is not, as it currently stands in our Gospel, unrelated to subsequent events. It rather anticipates those events, for the prophesied misfortune of the missionary mirrors the coming fate of Jesus.[21] He, like them, is "handed over" (παραδίδοται, 26:45; etc.; cf. 10:17, 19, 21).[22] He, like them, appears before a sanhedrin (συνέδριον, 26:59; cf. 10:17).[23] He, like them, is whipped (μαστιγῶσαι, 20:19; cf. 10:17).[24] He, like them, is led (ἀπήγαγον; cf. 10:18) before the governor (ἡγεμών, 27:1–2, 11–26; cf. 10:18).[25] He, like them, bears testimony before government officials (26:57–68; 27:11–26; cf. 10:18–20). He, like them, is betrayed by a member of the group closest to him (26:14–16, 20–25, 47–56; cf. 10:21). And he, like them, falls victim to a plot of his en-

20. F. W. Beare, *The Gospel according to Matthew* (San Francisco: Harper & Row, 1981), p. 241.

21. In addition to what follows see chapter 7, pp. 151–53 above.

22. Matthew "utilizes this verb [παραδίδωμι] almost exclusively for John the Baptist, Jesus and the disciples of Jesus, and in so doing, lines up his ecclesiology with his Christology"; so Scot McKnight, "New Shepherds for Israel: An Historical and Critical Study of Matthew 9:35–11:1" (PhD diss., University of Nottingham, 1986), p. 242.

23. συνέδριον appears only three times in Matthew: 5:22; 10:17; 26:59.

24. 10:17; 20:19; and 23:34 contain the only Matthean uses of μαστιγόω. Mark 13:9, the Markan parallel to Matt. 10:17, has δέρω. According to Gundry, *Matthew*, p. 192, in both 10:17 and 23:34 "Matthew uses whipping to portray persecution of the disciples in terms of Jesus' suffering."

25. ἡγεμών in Matthew: 2:6; 10:18; 27:2, 11, 14, 15, 21, 27; 28:14 (the last eight belong to the passion narrative). Heil, *Death and Resurrection*, p. 67, observes this: "That Jesus has been led before a 'governor' (*hēgemoni*) establishes him as a paradigm for his disciples (and readers), whom he warned of the same fate." Cf. Leopold Sabourin, *The Gospel according to St. Matthew* (2 vols.; Bombay: St. Paul's Press, 1982), 2:532.

emies, who wish to kill him (ὅπως . . . θανατώσωσιν, 26:59; θανατῶσαι, 27:1; cf. 10:21).[26]

Informed hearers of 10:17–23 may espy some or all of these parallels not only because the notion of Jesus Christ as model missionary permeates chapter 10 as a whole[27] but also because the immediate sequel, 10:24–25, explicitly sets the mistreatment of Jesus beside the mistreatment of the disciples: "A disciple is not above the teacher, nor a slave above the master; it is enough for the disciple to be like the teacher, and the slave to be like the master. . . . If they have called the master of the house Beelzebul, how much more will they malign those of his household."[28] Here, in the words of Theophylact, Jesus teaches his disciples "to endure insults. For if I, your teacher and master, have endured them, how much more so should you, my disciples and servants."[29]

Joachim Gnilka is correct: the verses to which 10:23–24 are annexed speak of flight, persecution, hatred, betrayal, and killing, which things also characterize the passion of Jesus; so when evil befalls those faithfully committed to him, they may take heart, knowing that nothing less happened to him.[30] In other words, what we discover in 10:17–23 is what we have already found in 5:38–42: Jesus, smitten in his passion, is the exemplar of suffering discipleship.[31] Put another way, 10:17–23 is a prophecy of Jesus' passion which, in the language of Col. 1:24, the

26. θανατόω: Matt. 10:21; 26:59; 27:1. The disciples are also like Jesus in having the Spirit come upon them; see 3:16 and 10:19–20.

27. See Davies and Allison, *Matthew*, 2:197; Luz, *Matthäus*, 2:155; McKnight, "New Shepherds," pp. 377–80.

28. The parallel in Luke 6:40 is very different; Matthew has heightened the correlation between master and disciple.

29. Theophylact, *Comm. Matt.* ad 10:24–25 (PG 123.241B). Cf. Chrysostom, *Hom. Matt.* 34.1 (PG 57.399): "It is enough for your encouragement that even I, who am your master and lord, shared in the same reproach that you suffer."

30. Joachim Gnilka, *Das Matthäusevangelium* (2 vols.; HTKNT 1/1–2; Freiburg: Herder, 1986–1988), 1:380. Warren Carter, *Matthew and the Margins: A Sociopolitical and Religious Reading* (Maryknoll, N.Y.: Orbis, 2000), pp. 236–39, also does justice to this theme, as does Bauer, *Structure*, pp. 59–60. Cf. also Luck, *Matthäus*, p. 129, and Erasmo Leiva-Merikakis, *Fire of Mercy, Heart of the Word: Meditations on the Gospel according to Saint Matthew* (San Francisco: Ignatius, 1996), 1:557: "Persecution is prophesied here, not in broad, general terms, but very specifically, and we are struck by the similarity of the specific trials the disciples can expect and those the Lord himself endured during the passion. In fact, we may interpret this passage not only as Jesus' prophecy of what his followers would have to endure . . . but also as one of the prophecies of *his own* Passion." On p. 559 Leiva-Merikakis adds: "Jesus' prophecy for his disciples must first be realized in himself."

31. Cf. Hilary, *Comm. Matt.* ad loc. (SC 254, ed. Doignon, p. 234): "Knowledge of future things leads to acquiring great patience, especially if our own will has been molded by another's example" (*exemplo*).

disciples will later fill up or complete.[32] Matthew, like Paul, teaches that "we suffer with him" (Rom. 8:17).[33]

The Martyrdom of John the Baptist

Matthew 4:17, which recounts the first public words of Jesus in Matthew, introduces and summarizes his proclamation this way: "From that time, Jesus began to preach and to say, 'Repent, for the kingdom of heaven is at hand.'" John the Baptist says exactly the same thing in 3:2, which introduces and summarizes his proclamation.[34] This establishes a parallelism that recurs elsewhere: throughout Matthew John is like Jesus and Jesus is like John.[35] If John rebukes the Pharisees and Sadducees, calling them a "brood of vipers" (3:7), Jesus denounces the scribes and Pharisees with the same damning expression (12:34; 23:33). If John warns that "every tree that does not bear fruit is cut down and thrown into the fire" (3:10), Jesus says exactly the same thing in the Sermon on the Mount (7:19). If John is a prophet and more than a prophet (11:9; 14:5; 21:26), the same holds for Jesus (12:41; 13:57; 21:11, 46). If John acts with the authority of heaven, it is no different with Jesus (21:23–32). And if "this generation" rejects John with the assertion that he has a demon (11:18), it likewise rejects Jesus with a closely related accusation: "he casts out demons by the prince of demons" (12:24).

Then there is 14:1–12, where Herod Antipas calls for the head of John the Baptist. Although this colorful tale distinguishes itself from the rest of

32. One might resist my conclusion by offering that (i) with the exception of the enigmatic v. 23, Matt. 10:17–23 is largely a transposition of Mark 13:9–13 and (ii) the links observed between Jesus and his disciples also appear in Mark, Matthew's source, from which one might infer that we have here simply to do with a Markan scheme that Matthew may or may not have consciously adopted. Against this, however, (i) the presence of a theme in Mark scarcely entails Matthew's inability to observe this theme, transmit it in his Gospel, and expect his audience to find it there; (ii) one of the verbal links between 10:17–23 and Jesus' fate appears only in Matthew: μαστιγόω is redactional (see n. 24); (iii) Matthew trails 10:17–23 with 10:24–25, which makes the imitation of Christ explicit. So the correlation between 10:17–23 and the passion is more than a leftover from Mark.

33. Cf. also Phil. 3:10 ("the sharing of his sufferings"); 1 Pet. 2:21 ("Christ also suffered for you, leaving you an example"); 4:1 ("Since . . . Christ suffered in the flesh, arm yourselves also with the same intention"), 13 ("sharing Christ's sufferings").

34. There is no close synoptic parallel to Matt. 3:2.

35. See further Janice Capel Anderson, *Matthew's Narrative Web: Over, and Over, and Over Again* (JSNTSS 91; Sheffield: JSOT, 1994), pp. 86–90, 172–74, and John P. Meier, "John the Baptist in Matthew's Gospel," *JBL* 99 (1980), pp. 383–405. The former characterizes John as "foreshadower" as well as forerunner and observes that the episodes associated with him form a "second story" that mirrors the main story about Jesus.

Matthew by being about someone other than Jesus, it is hardly unrelated to the rest of the narrative. As Theophylact rightly wrote, "In what has gone before, Matthew has not given an account of John, as it was his intent to write only about Christ. Nor would he have mentioned it now if it did not relate to Christ."[36] In line with this, the forerunner's demise is, not unlike the story of the wicked tenants in 21:33–44, a christological parable. The martyrdom, which opens with Herod's peculiar identification of the living Jesus with the dead John (14:1–2) and so presupposes significant likeness between the two figures, is told in such a way as to anticipate Jesus' cruel fate:

John	Jesus
Herod the tetrarch is responsible for John's death	Pilate the governor is responsible for Jesus' death
John is seized (κρατέω, 14:3)	Jesus is seized (κρατέω, 21:46; 26:4, 48, 50, 55, 57)
John is bound (δέω, 14:3)	Jesus is bound (δέω, 27:2)
Herod fears the crowds because they think John a prophet (ἐφοβήθη τὸν ὄχλον, ὅτι ὡς προφήτην αὐτὸν εἶχον, 14:5)	The chief priests and Pharisees fear the crowds because they think Jesus a prophet (21:46): ἐφοβήθησαν τοὺς ὄχλους, ἐπεὶ εἰς προφήτην αὐτὸν εἶχον
Herod is asked by another to execute John and is grieved to do so (14:6–11)	Pilate is asked by others to execute Jesus and is reluctant to do so (27:11–26)
John is buried by his disciples (14:12)[37]	Jesus is buried by a disciple (27:57–61)

Matthew 14:1–12 belongs in the company of the other passages we have already investigated. Like 5:38–42 and 10:17–23, it presages the end of the story. John's execution resembles, down to details, the execution of Jesus. 14:1–12 is like precognition: it enables us to sense the future.

The Transfigured Jesus

When Jesus takes Peter and James and John to a high mountain, a series of peculiar events transpire (17:1–8). Jesus' face shines as the sun; his garments become white as light. Moses and Elijah appear. Peter unaccountably offers in response to build three tents; a voice

---

36. Theophylact, *Comm. Matt.* ad loc. (PG 123.293D–296A).

37. Cf. the comments on 14:12 of Trapp, *Commentary*, 5:188 ("A pious and courteous office, such as Joseph of Arimathea boldly performed to Christ") and John Gill, *Gill's Commentary* (6 vols.; Grand Rapids: Baker, 1980), 5:133 (John's disciples asked for the body of John "as Joseph [of Arimathea] did to Pilate").

from a shining cloud says, "This is my Son, the Beloved; with him I am well pleased; listen to him!" Reacting to all this, the disciples fall on their faces and fear exceedingly (v. 6: ἐφοβήθησαν σφόδρα). It is this last circumstance, the fear of the disciples, to which I wish initially to call attention.

The phrase ἐφοβήθησαν σφόδρα occurs only one other place in the First Gospel, in 27:54. The context is the crucifixion: "Now when the centurion and those with him, who were keeping watch over Jesus, saw the earthquake and what took place, they feared exceedingly (ἐφοβήθησαν σφόδρα) and said, 'Truly this man was God's Son.'"[38] I should like to raise the possibility that we have here the same phenomenon that we have already seen in 5:38–42; 10:17–23; and 14:1–12. Common vocabulary—here a verb of perception + ἐφοβήθησαν σφόδρα—may nudge informed listeners to reflect upon one scene in the light of another.[39]

My reason for so thinking is that although the shared phrase, ἐφοβήθησαν σφόδρα, is not much in itself, several further details are common to 17:1–8 and the account of the crucifixion: the number six ("after six days," 17:1; "from the sixth hour," 27:45), the presence of three named onlookers (17:1, three male disciples: Peter, James, and John; 27:55–56, three female disciples: Mary Magdalene, Mary the mother of James and Joseph, and the mother of the sons of Zebedee), and the confession of Jesus as God's "Son" (17:5; 27:54; cf. 27:40, 43).

These shared features, moreover, arouse attention because they exist in the midst of several striking contrasts. In 17:1–8, Jesus initiates the action (17:1, "Jesus took with him Peter and James and John") while in 27:27–56 he is passive (27:31, "and they led him away"; the verb παραλαμβάνω is common to 17:1 and 27:27). In 17:1–8, Jesus ascends

38. In Matt. 17:6, the phrase is redactional; cf. Mark 9:6: ἔκφοβοι γὰρ ἐγένοντο. σφόδρα occurs in Matthew seven times; in Mark once; in Luke once. A verb of perception + φοβέομαι has no parallel in 9:8; 17:6; and 27:54.

39. I am encouraged in this conviction by an additional difference between Matt. 27:54 and Mark 15:39. Whereas Mark mentions the centurion only (15:39), Matthew refers to the centurion "and those with him" (27:54). Why the introduction of additional observers? Commentators are not very persuasive in returning an answer. The two explanations most often met with are these: (i) "the confession of the centurion and his men that the crucified Jesus is Son of God foreshadows the conversion of Gentiles to Christ" (Nils Alstrup Dahl, *Jesus in the Memory of the Early Church: Essays* [Minneapolis: Augsburg, 1976], p. 49), and (ii) "the miraculous signs that were taking place are explicitly confirmed as the direct manifestation of God" (Donald J. Verseput, "The 'Son of God' Title in Matthew's Gospel," *NTS* 33 [1987], p. 548). But why these things would not hold true if the confession were made by one person alone is not indicated—although one could appeal, I suppose, to the Torah's requirement of two or more witnesses. I submit that the explanation perhaps is rather this, that without the plural subject there would be no exact correlation between 17:6 and 27:54. It is only Matthew's plural subject ("the centurion and those with him") that permits the use of ἐφοβήθησαν σφόδρα, with the verb in the plural.

a mountain (17:1) and in 27:27–56 he is raised on a cross (27:35). In 17:1–8, readers behold a private epiphany (17:1, κατ' ἰδίαν) whereas in 27:27–56 they recall a public spectacle (27:39 refers to "those who passed by"). In 17:1–8, light floods the scene (v. 2, "he was transfigured before them, and his face shone like the sun, and his clothes became dazzling white") whereas in 27:27–56 darkness descends (v. 45, "darkness came over all the land"). In 17:1–8, Jesus' garments (ἱμάτια) become luminous (17:2), and in 27:27–56 his garments (ἱμάτια) are stripped from him and given to others (27:28, 31, 35). In 17:1–8, Jesus is honored and glorified, but in 27:27–56 he is humiliated and shamed. In 17:1–8, Elijah appears (17:3), and in 27:27–56 Elijah fails to appear (27:46–50). In 17:1–8, Jesus is flanked by two famous saints who converse with him (17:3), and in 27:27–56 he is flanked by two nameless criminals who revile him (27:38).[40] In 17:1–8, God confesses Jesus (17:5, "This is my Son, the Beloved; with him I am well pleased; listen to him!") while in 27:27–56 God seemingly abandons Jesus (27:46, "My God, my God, why have you forsaken me?"). And whereas, in 17:1–8, disciples fall before Jesus out of reverence (17:6, ἔπεσαν ἐπὶ πρόσωπον αὐτῶν), in 27:27–56 unbelieving soldiers fall before Jesus in order to mock him (27:29, γονυπετήσαντες). All this may be seen at a glance:

The Transfiguration (Matt. 17:1–8)	The Crucifixion (Matt. 27:27–56)
Similarities	
"After six days" (17:1)	"From the sixth hour" (27:45)
Three named onlookers (17:1)	Three named onlookers (27:55–56)
Jesus is God's "Son" (17:5)	Jesus is God's "Son"
"They feared exceedingly" (17:6)	"They feared exceedingly" (27:54)
Contrasts	
Jesus takes others (17:1)	Jesus is taken by others (27:27)
Elevation on mountain (17:1)	Elevation on cross (27:35)
Private epiphany (17:1)	Public spectacle (27:39)
Light (17:2)	Darkness (27:45)

40. Cf. Robert H. Smith, *Matthew* (ACNT; Minneapolis: Augsburg, 1989), p. 209: "Here Jesus is with Moses and Elijah; at the crucifixion he will be flanked not by two honored ancients but by two contemporary criminals (27:38). Where does Jesus really belong? In both places! The point of the transfiguration is that the downward way of Jesus is not only deep darkness but astonishing light." Note also Joseph S. Exell, *The Biblical Illustrator, St. Luke*, vol. 2 (New York: Fleming H. Revell, n.d.), pp. 160–61, who attributes these words to a certain T. S. Evans: "Myriads of angels . . . behold Him between two saints transfigured, whom afterwards they beheld in horror between two thieves disfigured."

The Transfiguration (Matt. 17:1–8)	The Crucifixion (Matt. 27:27–56)
Garments illumined (17:2)	Garments stripped off (27:28, 35)
Jesus is glorified (17:2–6)	Jesus is shamed (27:27–31)
Elijah appears (17:3)	Elijah does not appear (27:45–50)
Two saints beside Jesus (17:3)	Two criminals beside Jesus (27:38)
God confesses Jesus (17:5)	God abandons Jesus (27:46)
Reverent prostration (17:6)	Mocking prostration (27:29)

Between 17:1–8 and 27:27–56 there is a curious confluence of similar motifs and contrasting images. Taken together, they turn the transfiguration into a potentially allusive pattern.[41]

Putting 17:1–8 and 27:27–56 together creates pictorial antithetical parallelism, something like a diptych in which the two plates have similar outlines but different colors. If one scene were sketched on a transparency and placed over the other, many of its lines would disappear.[42] My proposal is that, whether Matthew's tradition produced them through design[43] or, as I am inclined to imagine, happy coincidence begot most of them, informed readers of Matthew are encouraged to observe the correlations.[44]

41. I first observed this, without having run across any exegetical precedent, in Davies and Allison, *Matthew*, 2:706–7. I am happy to see that David E. Garland, *Reading Matthew: A Literary and Theological Commentary on the First Gospel* (London: SPCK, 1993), pp. 183–84, has seconded my reading. Thomas G. Long, *Matthew* (Westminster Bible Companion; Louisville: Westminster John Knox, 1997), p. 194, in turn cites Garland and writes that "several students of the Gospel of Matthew have pointed to the contrasting parallels between Matthew's description of the transfiguration and the account of the crucifixion." Long then goes on to cite many of the parallels to which I have called attention.

42. Many traditional artistic representations of the transfiguration and crucifixion have similar basic patterns: Jesus is raised in the middle, with two men on either side of him, one slightly below him on his right, one slightly below him on his left; and at the bottom are three onlookers, side by side.

43. The potential allusion could be ancient if, as a few have suggested, the transfiguration was joined to a pre-Markan passion narrative; see, e.g., Rudolf Pesch, *Das Markusevangelium* (2 vols.; HTKNT 2/1–2; Freiburg: Herder, 1976–77), 2:69, and C. Grappe, "Mt 16.18–19 et le récit de la passion," *RHPR* 72 (1992), pp. 33–40. But of this I am doubtful.

44. It is perhaps worth remarking that Luke, in his account of the transfiguration (9:28–36), makes the crucifixion the topic of conversation between Jesus and the ancient worthies. In this way he links the two events. Ecclesiastical exegetes have done something similar when they have understood the transfiguration to be preparation for the passion: without memory of the glorified Jesus, the disciples would have become too dispirited, or even have been unable to endure the later scandal of Jesus' execution by crucifixion; so Jerome, *Comm. Matt.* ad loc. (SC 259, ed. Bonnard, pp. 26, 28); Ps.-Jerome, *Comm. Mark* ad 9:1 (CCSL 82, ed. Cahill, p. 40); Leo the Great, *Tract.* 51.3 (CCSL 138A, ed. Chavasse, pp. 298–99); etc.

The literary intertwining of 17:1–8 and 27:27–56 does not generate one obvious lesson or meaning. The juxtaposition is rather an opportunity for reflection. Matthew's Jesus is a figure of humility and glory, defeat and victory. He is the crucified Son of Man and the Son of Man triumphant, the mocked criminal and the exalted Lord. This paradoxical Christology, which conveys so much pathos and fills the narrative, is pictorially illustrated in starkest fashion by the association of 17:1–8 and 27:27–56. It is one and the same Jesus who is transfigured by light and wrapped in a supernatural darkness, who is glorified by God and abandoned by God, who is exalted and humiliated, honored and shamed. Why these things should be so is a puzzle thrown up by the Gospel as a whole, which, however, returns no obvious or straightforward answer. But the text does inevitably pose the question and, at the very least, it instills in readers the idea that one is faced here with a great religious paradox or mystery. In accord with God's hidden but sovereign will, the Messiah lives the extremes of human fate, the polarities of possible experience. He becomes a coincidence of opposites. Exaltation to eschatological glory as God's Son and the degradation of crucifixion strangely become, in Jesus, the two complementary halves of the same divine purpose.

False Ambition and True Service

In 20:20–23, the mother of the sons of Zebedee prostrates herself before Jesus and asks him to command "that these two sons of mine will sit, one at your right hand and one at your left, in your kingdom" (v. 21). In response, Jesus addresses not the mother but the brothers and declares: "You do not know what you are asking. Are you able to drink the cup that I am about to drink?" When they confidently affirm, "We are able," Jesus solemnly tells them that they will indeed drink his cup but that to sit on his right and left is not his to give.

This exchange brings two future events, the kingdom of God and Jesus' passion, into close association. The implied lesson is that the way to the one is the way to the other, that entrance into the kingdom cannot come without first drinking the cup of suffering and judgment. Tribulation precedes glory. Death comes before resurrection.

With this in mind, one wonders about the request in verse 21 to sit on Jesus' right and left (εἷς ἐκ δεξιῶν σου καὶ εἷς ἐξ εὐωνύμων σου) and the reference back to this in 20:23 (ἐκ δεξιῶν μου καὶ ἐξ εὐωνύμων). Both closely resemble 27:38, which depicts two unnamed criminals hanging on crosses to the left and right of Jesus:

Matt. 20:21	εἷς	ἐκ δεξιῶν σου	καὶ εἷς	ἐξ εὐωνύμων σου
Matt. 20:23		ἐκ δεξιῶν μου	καὶ	ἐξ εὐωνύμων
Matt. 27:38	εἷς	ἐκ δεξιῶν	καὶ εἷς	ἐξ εὐωνύμων[45]

In this day of verbal inflation and rapid reading, perhaps we are apt to pass off such parallelism as due to a stylistic preference for which, as with taste, there is no accounting. This is probably, however, an error, an act of underinterpretation, a withholding from the text of what is its due. Informed readers of 20:20–28 can simultaneously think about 27:38 and so place side by side in the imagination two analogous yet very different scenes, two scenes with similar form but dissimilar content.[46] On the one hand, there is the image of a glorified Jesus enthroned in Jerusalem in his kingdom, with two honored disciples sitting at his right and left.[47] On the other hand, there is the image of a crucified Jesus hanging from a cross outside Jerusalem, with two miserable criminals on either side.

45. The three corresponding clauses in Mark, which even include two different words for "left," are further apart:

Mark 10:37	εἷς σου	ἐκ δεξιῶν	καὶ εἷς	ἐξ ἀριστερῶν
Mark 10:40		ἐκ δεξιῶν μου	ἤ	ἐξ εὐωνύμων
Mark 15:27	ἕνα	ἐκ δεξιῶν	καὶ ἕνα	ἐξ εὐωνύμων αὐτοῦ

It is Matthew's redactional work, then, that has given us three nearly identical phrases.

46. I first made this suggestion, without citing any forerunner, in an earlier version of the present chapter (CBQ 56 [1993], pp. 701–14) and then repeated myself in Davies and Allison, Matthew, 3:88, 101. Independently and simultaneously the same interpretation showed up in Douglas R. A. Hare, Matthew (Interpretation; Louisville: John Knox, 1993), p. 320: "The two brigands on Jesus' left and right constitute the king's retinue! They are perhaps presented as caricatures of James and John, who requested these positions of honor, assuring Jesus of their willingness to share his cup but who instead of dying with him forsook him and fled (20:20–23; 26:56)." Cf. also Robert H. Gundry, Mark: A Commentary on His Apology for the Cross (Grand Rapids: Eerdmans, 1993), p. 577 on Mark 10:37 ("their asking to be seated, as they say, 'one on your right and one on your left in your glory' [cf. Matt. 19:28 par. Luke 22:28–30] shows ignorance of the necessity that they take up their crosses and follow Jesus [see 8:34–38 and cf. the irony that two bandits, 'one on (his) right and one on his left,' will be crucified rather than seated in glory with him [15:27]"). Later is Craig S. Keener, Commentary on the Gospel of Matthew (Grand Rapids: Eerdmans, 1999), p. 681: "The 'robbers' on either side, one on the left and one on the right (27:38; cf. Jn 19:18), could recall the promise to those enthroned on either side of Jesus (20:23)"; cf. his remark on 20:23: "it is possible that Jesus points cryptically to a different throne than the disciples envision: if Jesus was to be enthroned on a cross, the place reserved for those on either side of that throne was for two robbers (27:38)" (p. 486). Luz, Matthäus, 4:321, commenting on 27:38, now offers a similar observation, as does Carter, Matthew and the Margins, p. 532: "James and John sought to be on Jesus' left and right in 20:21–22, and assured him that they could drink his cup of suffering. But they did not have this sort of scene in mind and fled (26:56)." Frederick Dale Bruner, Matthew: A Commentary (2 vols.; rev. ed.; Grand Rapids: Eerdmans, 2004), 2:328, endorses the reading in my commentary on Matthew.

47. For kings flanked on right and left note 1 Kings 22:19 and Matt. 25:31.

Bringing the two images together engenders irony, for while the two sons have the first scene in mind, Jesus is contemplating the second. The irony, in turn, serves the main point of the passage, which is the priority of suffering for Christian discipleship. As Acts 14:22 has it, "through many tribulations we must enter into the kingdom of God."

Beyond the common (εἷς) ἐκ δεξιῶν . . . καὶ (εἷς) ἐξ εὐωνύμων, several additional features may send readers of 20:20–28 ahead to the passion narrative.

1. Matthew 20:20–28 immediately follows a passion prediction (20:17–19), it contains a symbolic prophecy of Jesus' suffering ("the cup that I am about to drink"; cf. 26:39), and it ends with the crucial, pregnant assertion that the Son of Man came not to be served but to serve "and to give his life as a ransom for many" (v. 28). From beginning to end, then, the passage envisages the upcoming sacrificial death. The context of 20:21 and 23 coheres, accordingly, with the proposal that in those two verses there is an ironic allusion to the crucifixion.

2. When the mother of the sons of Zebedee, in 20:20–28, envisages her sons at the right and left of Jesus, she is clearly imagining a scene of enthronement. This matters because, in Matthew, the crucifixion is a mock coronation. The Roman soldiers dress Jesus in a scarlet robe, place a crown of thorns on his head, and put a bogus scepter in his hand. They then cry out, "Hail, king of the Jews" (27:27–31). And when they finally raise him up on his cross, they put a placard over his head: "This is Jesus, the King of the Jews" (27:37). So the earthly Jesus does become king; he does get enthroned. But he is no potentate. He rules from a cross instead of a throne. He is not served but serves, by giving his life as a ransom for many. So, in 20:20–23, James and John and their mother have everything backwards. While they, like Jesus, have an enthronement in mind, mother and sons anticipate eschatological triumph in the kingdom of God whereas Jesus foresees himself mocked as king and tortured on a cross.

3. The mother of the sons of Zebedee appears only twice in the First Gospel, in 20:20–28 and in 27:55–56 ("Many women were also there, looking on from a distance; they had followed Jesus from Galilee and had provided for him. Among them were Mary Magdalene, and Mary the mother of James and Joseph, and the mother of the sons of Zebedee"). If, in the former pericope, she imagines her two sons at the right and left of a powerful and glorified Jesus, in the latter pericope her eyes behold two criminals on the right and left of a tormented and shamed Jesus. Her presence, then, joins the two scenes and so contributes irony to each.[48]

---

48. She does not appear in the Markan parallel to Matt. 27:55–56. In 27:56, she replaces Mark's Salome (15:40). Her presence both in 20:20–23 and the crucifixion is, then, Matthew's doing.

Intra-Matthean Allusion

Matthew 5:38–42; 10:17–23; 14:1–12; 17:1–8; and 20:20–23 display a recurrent rhetorical strategy: each borrows language from the subsequent passion narrative. The result is that the five texts are potentially allusive. For informed hearers, they allow the merging of events and the seeing of two things at once—5:38–42 and the passion, 10:17–23 and the passion, 14:1–12 and the passion, 17:1–8 and the passion, and 20:20–23 and the passion.

In denying that Matthew, with its infancy narrative and several long discourses, is "a passion narrative with an extended introduction," Kähler underestimated the breadth of material directly associated with the passion. In addition to passion predictions and the developing plot, the First Gospel moves towards its end via *scenes of anticipation*, scenes that foreshadow the end of Jesus.[49] The persecution of the infant Jesus in chapter 2, the exhortations not to resist evil in chapter 5, the prophecies of persecution in chapter 10, the death of John the Baptist in chapter 14, the transfiguration in chapter 17, and the encounter of Jesus with the sons of Zebedee and their mother in chapter 20 all relate themselves to the end of the Gospel. They prepare for it, and it retrospectively explicates them. So there are numerous points at which Matthew's Gospel, before the Jewish leaders set their plot to arrest Jesus in motion (26:3–5), moves thoughts to the crucifixion:

Explicit predictions: 16:21–23; 17:12, 22–23; 20:17–19, 28; 26:2

Implicit predictions: 9:15; 12:40; 20:22–23; 21:38–39

Growing conflict: 9:1–13, 32–34; 12:1–14, 22–45; 15:1–14; 16:1–12; 19:1–12; 21:12–17, 23–46; 22:15–46

Scenes of anticipation: 2:1–23; 4:12; 5:38–42; 10:17–23; 14:1–12; 17:1–8; 20:20–28

Although the fact has often not received due recognition, the interaction of the passion complex with chapters 1–25 is one of the main features of the book. Matthew's story constantly carries hearers forward to its conclusion.

And yet many of the links between 26:47–27:56 and the texts examined herein go unnoticed in the commentaries. One reason for this lies in

49. On the phenomenon of anticipation in Matthew in general see Anderson, *Web*, pp. 152–72, and Charles H. Lohr, "Oral Techniques in the Gospel of Matthew," *CBQ* 23 (1961), pp. 411–14.

the nature of allusions. They are, by definition, quiescent, and—this is what gives them their rhetorical power—they function without explicit authorial prompting.[50] Allusions demand both imagination and prior knowledge of an absent text. It is up to the reader, attending to common words, themes, and images, to divine connections and pull together separated passages. To quote Blake: "The wisest of the Ancients consider'd what is not too Explicit as the fittest for Instruction, because it rouzes the faculties to act."[51]

Another and more important reason for the relative silence of at least modern scholarship is a habit. The historical-critical method has trained us to relate the First Gospel to texts other than itself. We are quite used to looking for allusions, even very subtle allusions, but almost always to things outside Matthew—to the Septuagint, for example, or perhaps to the historical situation of the author. But this must not lead us to forget that Matthew's author almost certainly composed his Gospel with some sort of liturgical or catechetical end in view, which means that he created a work designed to be read and heard again and again. Surely, then, he anticipated listeners who would appreciate intratextual allusions, who could connect similar phrases and like images, who could move from 5:38–42; 10:17–23; 14:1–12; 17:1–8; and 20:20–23 to the passion of Jesus and back again. Our evangelist did not write for bad or casual readers but instead for good and attentive listeners. What Robert Alter has written about the Hebrew Bible, that its ancient audiences were "accustomed to retain minute textual details,"[52] is equally true, I submit, of Matthew's Gospel.

There is no consensus regarding the central theological theme of Matthew. For Jack Dean Kingsbury, the book is dominated by the title "Son of God" and all that it connotes.[53] R. H. Fuller rather supposes that the First Gospel is concerned primarily not with Christology but with eccle-

50. On this see further Dale C. Allison Jr., *The Jesus Tradition in Q* (Harrisburg, Pa.: Trinity Press International, 1997), pp. 117–19.

51. William Blake, Letter to Dr. Tusler, 23 August, 1799; see Geoffrey Keynes, *The Letters of William Blake, with Related Documents* (3rd ed.; Oxford: Clarendon, 1980), p. 8. Blake instances not only Homer and Plato but two biblical worthies—Moses and Solomon.

52. Robert Alter, *The World of Biblical Literature* (New York: Harper Collins, 1992), p. 113.

53. Jack Dean Kingsbury, *Matthew: Structure, Christology, Kingdom* (Philadelphia: Fortress, 1975). Kingsbury writes on p. 53 that "1.23 is Matthew's 'thumbnail definition' of the predication Son of God, and . . . his entire Gospel may be seen as an attempt to elaborate on the implications of this passage and others that are similar to it, e.g., 14:27; 18:20; 28:20."

siology[54] while R. T. France offers that "the essential key to Matthew's theology is that in Jesus all God's purposes have come to fulfillment."[55] Scot McKnight has made another suggestion. On his view, Matthew features four "major themes": Christology, the kingdom of heaven, salvation history, discipleship.[56]

I refrain in this place from entering into detailed review of any of these proposals. I wish only to observe that they all suffer the disadvantage of not explicitly referring to the death of Jesus. How can this be correct? Jesus' demise dominates the plot, it is referred to often, both directly and indirectly, it is foreshadowed in divers ways, and, alongside the resurrection, it concludes the book. It is, accordingly, never far from the consciousness of the careful listener. One might, then, propose another theme as the center of Matthean thought: Jesus died and rose, or (as France might put it) he died and rose to bring God's purposes to fulfillment.

One is more than uncertain, however, that our Gospel is ruled by one controlling idea, or that its thought is focused in a point of singularity. Our book's author was probably much more like Shakespeare, whom Coleridge dubbed "myriad-minded," than he was like Heraclitus, whose fragments can be organized around one great theme (everlasting fire). McKnight is wise to affirm that the First Gospel rests upon several foundation stones. If that is indeed the case, however, surely one should add to his list of major themes what amounts to a restatement of the Pauline *kerygma*: Christ died and rose according to the Scriptures.

---

54. R. H. Fuller and Pheme Perkins, *Who Is This Christ?* (Philadelphia: Fortress, 1983), p. 91: "Neither Matthew nor Luke is concerned primarily with christology. Matthew, responding to the situation created by Jamnia, seeks to present the church, over against the synagogue, as the true Israel of God, living under the Torah as expounded by Jesus."

55. R. T. France, *Matthew* (Tyndale NT Commentaries; Leicester: InterVarsity, 1985), p. 38. Cf. Frankemölle, *Jahwebund*, passim.

56. Scot McKnight, "Matthew, Gospel of," *Dictionary of Jesus and the Gospels* (ed. Joel B. Green, Scot McKnight, and I. Howard Marshall; Downers Grove, Ill.: InterVarsity, 1992), p. 532.

12

Deconstructing Matthew

The Gospel of Matthew often seems to speak against itself. Its Jesus can say one thing and then do another, as when he forbids demeaning another as a "fool" (5:22) and then himself upbraids the scribes and Pharisees as "fools" (23:17). He can also offer instruction in one place that does not obviously accord with what he teaches elsewhere. Having endorsed Torah in 5:17–20, in 12:1–8 he seems to break the Sabbath without much regret. Jesus can even bestow upon words and phrases contradictory meanings. If, in 13:37–43, the "sons of the kingdom" are the righteous who will shine like the sun, in 8:12 the "sons of the kingdom" are thrown into the outer darkness, where there will be weeping and gnashing of teeth.

Such inconcinnities, which have often puzzled interpreters, raise some hard hermeneutical questions. Do most or all such tensions have source-critical solutions? Does redaction criticism have any explanation for Matthew's failure to expunge obvious discord? Should interpreters give our evangelist the benefit of the doubt and seek, whenever possible, to harmonize Matthew with itself, or does honesty require recognition that the Gospel is, in some significant ways, not consistently coherent?

I should like, in the next few pages, to make a start toward answering these questions regarding the matter of Matthew's lack of perspicuity.[1] My

---

1. For earlier treatments of the problem see David E. Garland, *The Intention of Matthew 23* (NovTSup 52; Leiden: Brill, 1979), pp. 52–55; Kenzo Tagawa, "People and Community

goal is twofold: (1) to offer a rough typology of the responses of exegetes to the problem and (2) to evaluate, if all too briefly, those strategies. To begin with, I list some of the contradictions most often alleged:

Tension between Jesus' Words and Deeds

- "If you are angry with a brother, you will be liable to judgment" (5:22) seems problematic because Jesus is undeniably angry when, in chapter 21, he turns over tables in the temple as well as when, in chapter 23, he publicly castigates the scribes and Pharisees.

- "If you insult [literally: 'say "Raka,"' a term of abuse] a brother, you will be liable to the council; and if you say, 'You fool' (μωρέ), you will be liable to the Gehenna of fire" (5:22) appears to stand in tension with chapter 23 in its entirety, for there Jesus insults his opponents again and again. In verse 17 he even calls them "fools" (μωροί).

- "Love your enemies and pray for those who persecute you" (5:44) moves one to wonder why, throughout Matthew, Jesus does nothing but attack his enemies. He makes no move toward reconciliation but instead reprimands them and calls down divine judgment. One understands the commentary of the Jewish scholar G. C. Montefiore: "What one would have wished to find in the life-story of Jesus would be one single incident in which Jesus actually performed a loving deed to one of his Rabbinic antagonists or enemies. That would have been worth all the injunctions of the Sermon on the Mount about the love of enemies put together. . . . But no such deed is ascribed to Jesus in the Gospels. Toward his enemies, towards those who did not believe in him, whether individuals, groups, or cities (Matt. xi.20–24), only denunciation and bitter words!"[2]

- Jesus, in 5:17–19, denies that he has come "to abolish the law or the prophets," to which he adds, "Whoever breaks one of the least of these commandments and teaches others to do the same, will be called least in the kingdom of heaven." Many find this incongruent with 12:1–8, where Jesus seems to disregard Torah when he defends plucking grain on the Sabbath, observing among other things that "something greater than the temple is here." Some also find 5:17–19 out of accord with 12:9–14, where Jesus heals on the Sabbath.

---

in the Gospel of Matthew," *NTS* 16 (1970), pp. 149–62; and C. F. D. Moule, "St. Matthew's Gospel: Some Neglected Features," in *Studia Evangelica*, vol. 2 (ed. Frank L. Cross; TU 87; Berlin: Akademie-Verlag, 1964), pp. 91–99.

2. G. C. Montefiore, *Rabbinic Literature and Gospel Teachings* (London: Macmillan & Co., 1930), p. 104.

- Jesus endorses the Decalogue's imperative to honor one's parents and criticizes others for not doing this (15:4–6; 19:17–19). Yet he tells a would-be follower, who simply wants to bury his father, "Follow me, and let the dead bury their own dead" (8:21–22). In 12:46–49, when he learns that his mother and siblings seek him, Jesus asks, "Who is my mother, and who are my brothers?" He then points to his disciples and says, "Here are my mother and my brothers! For whoever does the will of my Father in heaven is my brother and sister and mother'" (12:46–50). Is this an illustration of honoring parents?

Tensions Internal to Jesus' Teachings

- Jesus refers to Gentiles (ἐθνικοί, ἔθνη) in a disparaging manner in 5:47; 6:7, 32; and 18:17. In 10:5–6 he orders his missionaries, "Go nowhere among the Gentiles, and enter no town of the Samaritans, but go rather to the lost sheep of the house of Israel." Then, in 15:24, he says, "I was sent only to the lost sheep of the house of Israel." And yet the risen Jesus, at the end of the Gospel, instructs his disciples to "go . . . and make disciples of all nations" (28:19). The textual tension is even greater when one takes into account the naming of four Gentile women in the genealogy, the worshiping Gentile magi in chapter 2, the quotation in 4:14–16 of Isa. 9:1–2, which mentions "Galilee of the Gentiles," and the use in 12:17–21 of Isa. 42:1–4, which ends with "and in his name the Gentiles will hope."
- Although Jesus vigorously endorses the law, down to its jots and tittles (5:17–19), he forbids oaths in 5:33–37, although the Torah makes provision for them. Theophylact, *Comm. Matt.* ad loc. (PG 123:199B), was reduced to this: At the time of Moses, "it was not evil to swear. But after Christ, it is evil." Many other exegetes have thought that 5:38–42, which speaks against the principle of "eye for eye," also erases Torah.
- Jesus plainly teaches, in 5:43–48, that God loves everybody, even the wicked; and yet again and again in our Gospel God consigns the wicked to hell (13:42; 22:13; 24:51; etc.).[3]
- If, in 6:17–18, Jesus delivers guidance for fasting, in 9:15 he denies that his followers can fast while the bridegroom is with them.
- Jesus warns: "'Take heed and beware of the leaven of the Pharisees and Sadducees. . . .' Then they understood that he had not told them

---

3. On the history of this perceived tension see Dale C. Allison Jr., "The Problem of Gehenna," in *Resurrecting Jesus* (London: T&T Clark, 2005), pp. 56–100.

to beware of the leaven of bread, but of the teaching of the Pharisees and Sadducees" (16:6, 12, RSV). This unqualified warning not to heed the teaching of the Jewish leaders seems flatly contradicted by what Jesus says later: "The scribes and the Pharisees sit on Moses' seat; therefore, do whatever they teach you and follow it; but do not do as they do, for they do not practice what they teach" (23:2–3). Exegetes have long scratched their heads and exercised their ingenuity over this one.

• If the Son of Man is Lord of the Sabbath, and if certain contingencies override the Sabbath (12:1–8, 9–14), then why should the disciples worry whether their eschatological flight might be on a Sabbath (24:20)? If they can, on account of hunger, loosen observance on one occasion, why can they not, for similar exigencies, loosen observance on another?

Different Uses by Jesus of the Same Word or Phrase

• 13:38 identifies "the sons of the kingdom" as the good seed of the parable in 13:24–30 and promises them eschatological reward. 8:12 identifies "the sons of the kingdom" with those who will be cast into Gehenna at the last judgment.

• If Matthew's Jesus often uses the word δίκαιος (righteous) of those who do God's will (1:19; 5:45; 10:41; 13:17, 43, 49; 23:28, 29, 35; 25:37, 46; 27:4, 19), in 9:13 he proclaims, to the contrary, "I did not come to call the righteous (δικαίους) but sinners."

Of these various incongruities, the last two occasion the least comment. We scarcely expect authors to use words or phrases in one way only. Although Χριστός is a messianic title in Rom. 9:5, elsewhere in Romans it is a proper name. And whatever precisely γένεσις may mean in Matt. 1:1 (βίβλος γενέσεως Ἰησοῦ Χριστοῦ; see chapter 8), it must have a different meaning in 1:18 (τοῦ δὲ Ἰησοῦ Χριστοῦ ἡ γένεσις οὕτως ἦν, usually translated as "The birth of Jesus Christ took place this way" or some such). It is, moreover, natural enough to surmise that, in Matt. 8:12, where "the sons of the kingdom" are cast out, and in 9:13, where Jesus does not come for the "righteous," terms that usually have positive connotations instead convey irony: those who should be in, or who think themselves in, are actually out. The world is upside down.

What, however, should we make of the other disagreements? Those between word and deed are especially challenging because Matthew, as we have seen in earlier chapters, is much concerned to correlate Jesus' actions with his imperatives. If, for example, Jesus praises the meek and the merciful and the oppressed, the narrative goes out of its way to show us that he himself is all three. Matters seem all the worse because, for the evangelist, hypocrisy, the disjunction between speech and behavior, is the sin Jesus denounces most. Surely he himself must be free of such. Is there not a real puzzle here?

My observation has been that there are roughly five ways of responding to these questions and to the apparent contradictions in Matthew, and I should now like to review them in turn.

Denying contradictions. One can, for theological reasons, affirm that appearances are deceiving and deny that any of the observed contradictions are in fact contradictions. This has been the traditional strategy of ecclesiastical interpreters. Most of them, because of their presuppositions about the Bible, have not discerned the relevant problems or have preferred to resolve them as quickly as possible.

Many Christians have admittedly been able to tolerate outright contradictions between the two Testaments. Marcion, the Orthodox defenders of icons, and pacifistic Anabaptists, in different ways, all argued for nontrivial discontinuity between the new revelation and the old revelation. Some ecclesiastical commentators also frankly recognized that the Gospels do not always agree exactly on what happened.[4] But that a particular book might truly oppose itself is, to my knowledge, a relatively recent thought. So traditional commentators, when mindful of the tension between, let us say, Matthew's final pericope (28:16–20) and Jesus' order not to go among Samaritans or Gentiles (10:5–6), automatically assumed that their job was to explain away that tension. Some asserted that 10:5–6 is not about literal Samaritans or Gentiles. Jesus is rather saying, Do not practice pagan ways. Others, more credibly, understood Jesus to be saying only: Israel must come first, but this does not, in the end, exclude Gentiles.[5]

Again, when older commentators came to 23:2–3, where Jesus says, "The scribes and the Pharisees sit on Moses' seat; therefore, do whatever they teach

---

4. E.g., Origen, *Comm. John* 10:14, 19–20 (SC 120, ed. Blanc, pp. 390, 395: the Gospels at points "contradict the order of history," so that "their truth is not to be found in the material letter. . . . From the point of view of history, they sometimes changed things in favor of serving their spiritual aims, so as to speak of a thing which happened in one place as though it had happened in another. . . . The spiritual truth was often preserved in the material falsehood"); Dionysius bar Salibi, *Expl. Evang.* Introduction 38 (CSCO 77, Scriptores Syri 33, ed. Sedlaeck and Chabot, p. 21: Matthew and Mark do not follow chronological order, as do Luke and John, but gather into one place words said on several occasions); Juan Maldonatus, *Comentarii in Quatuor Evangelistas* (2 vols.; Mainz: F. Kirchhemius 1853–1854), 1:107 ("We must not search too insistently for consecutive order in the writings of the evangelists, for they did not intend to set things down in the order in which they were done or said by Christ. This is particularly clear in his discourses, in which they neither report all that he said, nor quote him in the order in which he spoke, being satisfied to cite the principal elements of his teaching").

5. Texts and discussion in T. W. Manson, *Only to the House of Israel? Jesus and the Non-Jews* (FBBS 9; Philadelphia: Fortress, 1964), pp. 1–4.

you," they hurriedly, despite the seemingly emphatic πάντα ὅσα (all things whatsoever), informed readers that Jesus just cannot mean what he says. John Gill wrote: "This must be restrained to things that were agreeable to the chair of Moses, in which they sat, to the law of Moses, which they read and explained, to other parts of scripture and truth in general; for otherwise many of their glosses and traditions were repugnant to the law, and ought not to be observed, as appears from ch. v and ch. xv. 6."[6] There could not be, for Gill, any real inconsistency here or elsewhere in Matthew.

Contradictions and tradition history. Many modern scholars, uninhibited by some of the older theological assumptions, have, to the contrary, not hesitated to find contradictions in Matthew. They have indeed often welcomed them as an aid in reconstructing the development of the Jesus tradition. Joachim Jeremias, for example, persuaded himself that our Gospel displays an "unconcerned juxtaposition of conflicting traditions,"[7] and he could assert that Matt. 10:5–6 conflicts with the evangelist's own universalism, as this comes to expression in 28:16–20. This enabled Jeremias to argue that while the conclusion of Matthew, which welcomes Gentiles, is a Christian innovation, 10:5–6, which confines missionary work to Israel, can go back to Jesus.[8] Here Matthean inconsistency abets the quest for the historical Jesus.

Jeremias's conviction, that Matthew is not always coherent, shows up in many books and articles from the twentieth century, especially the first half. Georg Strecker, to illustrate, found Matt. 23:2–3 meaningless in its present context. He inferred that the evangelist took it over from his tradition without alteration. On Strecker's view, it is a remnant, devoid of present textual sense. Although it is evidence for the belief and practice of a contributor to Matthew's tradition, it is not evidence for Matthew's own point of view.[9] For Strecker, as for F. W. Beare, the evangelist is "unwilling to subtract" from his tradition "materials which he has received, even though they are essentially incompatible with his own understanding of Jesus and the gospel."[10]

6. John Gill, *Gill's Commentary* (6 vols.; Grand Rapids: Baker, 1980), 5:217.

7. Joachim Jeremias, *New Testament Theology: The Proclamation of Jesus* (New York: Scribner, 1971), p. 307, n. 1.

8. Joachim Jeremias, *Jesus' Promise to the Nations* (Philadelphia: Fortress, 1982), pp. 20–25, 34–35.

9. See, e.g., Georg Strecker, *Der Weg der Gerechtigkeit: Untersuchung zur Theologie des Matthäus* (3rd ed.; Göttingen: Vandenhoeck & Ruprecht, 1971), p. 16. Cf. Moule, "Neglected Features," pp. 96–97.

10. Francis Wright Beare, "The Sayings of Jesus in the Gospel according to St. Matthew," in *Studia Evangelica*, vol. 4 (ed. F. L. Cross; TU 102; Berlin: Akademie-Verlag, 1968), pp. 152–53. Cf. Werner Georg Kümmel, *Introduction to the New Testament* (rev. ed.; Nashville: Abingdon, 1973), pp. 116–17: "the evangelist could not carry out" his "objective free from contradictions."

Hans Dieter Betz, in his commentary on the Sermon on the Mount, has continued the convention of hunting for contradictions in order to differentiate the Matthean from the pre-Matthean. He has urged, for example, that the entirety of the sermon must have come to Matthew pretty much as it is because it exhibits tensions with the remainder of the Gospel. Matthew 5–7, according to Betz, opposes the Gentile mission, does not have a "higher Christology," and makes no allusion to Jesus' salvific death and his resurrection, all themes foundational for Matthew.[11]

Betz even contends that the pre-Matthean sermon itself was inconsistent. He discovers "some tensions between the Lord's Prayer and the SM as a whole." He agrees with those commentators who find it "hard to reconcile" the secret piety of 6:1–18 with the use of good deeds for missionary work (5:13–16). And he thinks that "a contradiction seems to exist between a theology of God's hiddenness (6:1–6, 16–18) and another theology emphasizing God's manifest activity in creation (5:45; 6:25–34; 7:11, 24–27)." Betz accordingly affirms that the compiler of the sermon "did not care to harmonize" sources but instead showed "a considerable degree of tolerance for diversity."[12]

Betz is akin to those students of Q who have argued that it, too, was not a homogenous whole but rather contained conflicting traditions. James Robinson, for example, has espied a contrast in the reconstructed Q between what he calls the "judgmentalism" of a later redactional layer and the more generous spirit of earlier materials.[13] "Those parts of Q that have, over the years, been recognized as the archaic collections, seem to have been ignored by the redactor, where God passing judgment has replaced God taking pity on sinners!"[14] For Robinson, the friction between judgment and mercy marks a difference between Jesus and his interpreters. This analysis, like that of Betz, means that Matthew is sometimes inconsistent because his sources were inconsistent.

Although the particular arguments of Robinson and Betz may leave us unpersuaded, we should not in principle reject what they are doing. That Matthew is an author does not mean that he is not also a tradent; and, despite his omnipresent and creative editorial hand, tradition does sometimes show itself to be such. Consider 12:31–32: "People will be

11. Hans Dieter Betz, *The Sermon on the Mount: A Commentary on the Sermon on the Mount, Including the Sermon on the Plain (Matthew 5:3–7:27 and Luke 6:20–49)* (Hermeneia; Minneapolis: Fortress, 1995), pp. 44, 145, 147, 153, 160, 320, 566–67.

12. Betz, *Sermon*, pp. 391, 347, 343, and 339 respectively.

13. James M. Robinson, "The Critical Edition of Q and the Study of Jesus," in *The Sayings Source Q and the Historical Jesus* (ed. A. Lindemann; BETL 158; Leuven: Leuven University Press, 2001), pp. 27–52.

14. Robinson, "Critical Edition," p. 40.

forgiven for every sin and blasphemy, but blasphemy against the Spirit will not be forgiven. Whoever speaks a word against the Son of Man will be forgiven, but whoever speaks against the Holy Spirit will not be forgiven, either in this age or in the age to come." The distinction between speaking against the Son of Man and speaking against the Spirit does not hold up because Jesus is the bearer of the Spirit (3:16; 12:18, 28); so to speak against the one is to speak against the other. How then do we explain 12:31–32? My guess is that it may be an example of a saying whose Greek form, with "Son of Man" used as a title for Jesus, misrepresents the Aramaic original, with "son of man" meaning just "a human being." Whether that is so or not, Matthew here fails to make good sense; and, apart from a source-critical solution, no plausible explanation is in sight. One would very much like to know what Matthew himself would say about this.

If a few pieces of Matthew's jigsaw puzzle do not seem to fit, some others go together but only with a bit of force.[15] Matthew 10:5–6, where Jesus prohibits missionaries from going to Gentiles, does not really contradict 28:16–20, where he sends missionaries into the world. Those recent commentators who hold that Matthew's Gospel sees things like Rom. 1:16 are probably right: the gospel goes first to the Jew, then to the Greek. This also resolves the tension between the instructions on fasting in 6:17–18 and the denial of fasting in 9:15. Surely readers are expected to put the latter in the pre-Easter period, the former in the post-Easter period.

There is about all this, nonetheless, a bit of clumsiness. Given how Matthew ends his Gospel, it is hard to imagine that he created 10:5–6 *ex nihilo*. It seems more likely that the saying, which reappears in 15:24, came to him from his Jewish-Christian tradition. He was able to reproduce it, and indeed to emphasize it, because he interpreted it in terms of salvation-history: although the Messiah at first restricted himself to the lost sheep of the house of Israel, he later sent missionaries into all the world. While there is no contradiction, surely the harmony is an imposition, a theological reconciliation of different traditions from different times and places.

Finding coherence. Despite Matthew's debt to sometimes disparate traditions, I adopted, when writing my commentary on Matthew, the dominant conviction of the guild today, which is that we should, whenever possible, seek coherence in the First Gospel. This view has come into its own ever since literary criticism became as popular as redaction

---

15. The situation is not, however, so desperate that anyone has followed E. L. Abel, "Who Wrote Matthew?" *NTS* 17 (1970/1971), pp. 138–52, who contended that our Gospel passed through the hands of two editors with two different theologies.

criticism. The last few decades have seen a sort of reversion to the older theological view, which always found harmony. Let me offer two illustrations. The first comes from recent treatments of 23:2–3, the saying about the Pharisees in the seat of Moses. Few are any longer content to avow that these verses are simply unassimilated tradition, an erratic boulder on Matthew's textual landscape. According to John Meier, 23:2–3 is like 10:5–6: it holds only for the pre-Easter period.[16] According to Doug Hare, the verses are a way of establishing "the level of accountability to which the Pharisaic teachers must be held. They were granted responsibility for leading Israel at the dawn of the messianic age, and they failed."[17] According to Mark Allan Powell, believers do not have copies of the Torah, so they have to learn Moses from the synagogue (v. 2); but they should heed Moses without adopting the interpretations of the scribes and Pharisees (v. 3).[18] Despite their different interpretations, Meier, Hare, and Power all seek to harmonize 23:2–3 with the rest of Matthew, where Jesus attacks the teaching of the scribes and Pharisees. This typifies the present interpretive mood.

A second notable illustration of the contemporary desire to find consistency in Matthew is the work of David Sim.[19] Although there is nothing unusual in his associating Matthew with a Jewish Christian community, he is in smaller company in arguing that this community "was critical of the surrounding Gentile society and adopted a policy of avoiding and shunning it."[20] How then does Sim interpret the passages that others have called upon to show that Matthew favored, without hesitation, the Gentile mission? Sim argues, among other things, that the four women in the genealogy need not be there only or primarily because they are Gentiles, and that the concluding commission, "Go into all the world . . . and make disciples of all nations" (28:16–20), does not say anything about the Matthean community's own participation in the Gentile mission. In this way, Matthew's character as a Jewish-Christian document becomes reason to offer new readings of texts that others have understood as pro-Gentile. Matthew is rendered consistent, in this case consistently less pro-Gentile.

16. John P. Meier, *Law and History in Matthew's Gospel* (AnBib 71; Rome: Biblical Institute, 1976), p. 199.

17. Douglas R. A. Hare, *Matthew* (IBC; Louisville: John Knox, 1993), p. 265.

18. Mark Allan Powell, "Do and Keep What Moses Says (Matthew 23:2–7)," *JBL* 114 (1995), pp. 419–35.

19. David C. Sim, *The Gospel of Matthew and Christian Judaism: The History and Social Setting of the Matthean Community* (Edinburgh: T&T Clark, 1998); idem, "The Gospel of Matthew and the Gentiles," *JSNT* 57 (1995), pp. 19–48.

20. Sim, "Gentiles," p. 39.

Whatever one makes of Sim's particular conclusions, there is much to be said for his general presupposition, which is that Matthew's Gospel, the product of a man with a theological agenda, is likely to be, if not perfectly coherent, then at least more coherent than less coherent. The Gospel is something other than a bundle of contradictions. Regarding, for instance, its view of the law, many today now recognize that it is not so difficult to take 5:17–20 at face value because so many passages once roundly thought to contradict Torah just do not do so.[21] Many of us no longer perceive tensions where others before us saw them. Furthermore, we can, with the help of redaction criticism, espy Matthew making his text more consistent. His decision to excise Mark's editorial comment in 7:19, that Jesus "declared all food clean," is in line with the program 5:17–20 announces. One beholds the same striving for consistency in other places. Surely it is not coincidence, given Jesus' condemnation of anger in 5:21–26, that Matthew fails to reproduce the remark of Mark 3:5, that Jesus looked around "with anger," or (if it stood in his copy of Mark) that he omits the notice of Mark 1:41, that Jesus was "moved with anger." On the assumption of Markan priority, our evangelist rewrites his source so that his Gospel no longer says, in so many words, Jesus was angry. One understands why Robert Gundry could write: "Matthew was neither a dim-witted tailor who, contrary to Deuteronomy 22:11, sewed together a literary garment of wool and linen without knowing the difference between his material, nor a modern churchman who saw contradictions in the tradition that came to him but deliberately included everything so that ecumenicity might swallow up theology, lumps and all."[22]

Moral dilemmas. This, however, is not the end of the matter. Consider again the disavowal of anger and its relationship to the rest of the Gospel. While Matthew successfully avoids remarking upon Jesus' anger, it remains impossible to envisage Jesus turning over tables in the temple or condemning the scribes and Pharisees apart from upset and anger. Similarly, while exegetes have all too often read Paul and their own interests into Matthew and so have found conflict with Torah where no such conflict exists, there remain places where Jesus, despite the expectation that 5:17–20 establishes, fails to mind Moses. He clearly fails on a couple of occasions to honor father and mother, and he transgresses the Sabbath law in 12:1–8. So questions remain.

Were we to call up Matthew's ghost, as Saul called up Samuel, and were we to confront him about the conflicts just indicated, I doubt that

---

21. See William R. G. Loader, *Jesus' Attitude towards the Law: A Study of the Gospels* (WUNT 2/97; Tübingen: Mohr Siebeck, 1997), pp. 137–72.

22. Robert H. Gundry, *Matthew: A Commentary on His Handbook for a Mixed Church under Persecution* (2nd ed.; Grand Rapids: Eerdmans, 1994), pp. 454–55.

he would be much troubled. My own guess is that he would observe the obvious, which is that sometimes there are competing moral imperatives. His Jewish tradition knew all too well that commandments can conflict with each other and that to break the Torah is not to abolish it. The Hasidim did not do away with the Sabbath when they went to war on Saturday. Nor were their actions intended in any way to nullify the authority of the Torah or to lessen the sanctity of the Sabbath. They rather faced a moral dilemma: Do we sin by breaking the Sabbath, or do we sin by letting the nation perish? They chose the lesser of two evils, breaking the Sabbath, in order to obtain the greater of two goods, the life of the nation. This was not lawlessness but the subordination of one imperative to another. Later on, in a less anxious setting, the rabbis debated at leisure the tensions between the various commandments and which have priority over which.[23] What do you do, for example, when your father implores you to behave in a way that desecrates the Sabbath? Do you disobey your father, or do you dishonor the Sabbath (*b. Yebam.* 5b)? And do you circumcise a male infant on the eighth day if that day is the Sabbath? Which commandment should you break (*m. Šabb.* 18:3; 19:1–3)? Sometimes imperatives just cannot be harmonized.

Matthew presumably knew all this as well as the rabbis, which may well explain why he tolerated some of the contradictions we have observed. His Jesus upholds the law, and the Sabbath, as part of the law, is not abrogated. Certainly Jesus nowhere says, Who cares about the Sabbath? He nonetheless breaks the Sabbath if doing so restores a broken body or feeds the hungry. These merciful acts are clearly also imperatives and plainly take priority over Sabbath observance. Again, parents should be honored, as the Decalogue enjoins and as Jesus reiterates; but if showing such honor hinders hearkening the call to discipleship, then it must slide (12:1–14). Salvation prevails over the Sabbath; discipleship outweighs filial obligation. Sometimes one command must decrease while another must increase.

Matthew may have thought about the dilemma of anger in similar terms. The ban on anger belongs to the larger Matthean narrative, so although 5:21–26 demands self-control and kindness in word and deed, the instances in which Jesus becomes angry can be understood as qualifying that imperative, as proving that, in extreme situations, it can be trumped. Surely Matthew, as a student of the Jewish Bible, believed that prophets must occasionally speak the harsh truth and display the divine

---

23. For the problem of master vs. parents see Gerald J. Bildstein, "Master and Parent: Comparative Aspects of a Dual Loyalty (Mishnah Baba Meziah 2:11 and Mark 3:31–35)," in *The Mishnah in Contemporary Perspective* (ed. Alan J. Avery-Peck and Jacob Neusner; HO 1/65; Leiden: Brill, 2002), pp. 255–66.

indignation; and he may also have believed that this sometimes dire necessity may temporarily displace some less urgent obligation, in this case
the embargo on anger.

Might Matthew have understood Jesus' treatment of the scribes and
Pharisees in the same light? Hans Windisch wrote: "The violent invectives
in ch. 23, including such terms of abuse as 'hypocrites,' 'fools,' 'blind,'
'serpents' and 'brood of vipers,' issue from the agitated soul of a violently
indignant prophet whose words are to be measured with another measure
than those of an ordinary man. The anger against hypocrisy, corruption,
and neglect of the most important duties that is here expressed is something other than the anger that is the result of a lack of self-control, love,
and understanding."[24] If there is an obligation to love everyone, surely
there is likewise for Matthew an obligation to save others. Perhaps this
is why his Jesus can hurl polemic against those who lead others to hell
(23:13–15). Whether this thought satisfies us, it may very well have satisfied the evangelist.

Point of view. Matthew's ghost, I suggest, would be able to understand
and field many and perhaps most of our queries about his apparent
inconsistencies. I even imagine he might be pretty sophisticated about
competing moral imperatives. On one final matter, however, he would
likely be nonplussed.

Many modern readers sense a conflict between the affirmation that
God is a loving and universally compassionate Father (5:43–48) and the
repeated threat that certain unfortunates will go, or rather will be sent by
this same Father, to unending torment. Indeed, Matthew, whose Gospel
has more to say about hell than the other canonical gospels, has sometimes gotten much of the blame for Christianity's emphasis upon hell,
usually as part of attempts to detach Jesus from the difficult doctrine.[25]
Other modern critics have spread the blame, implicating also a secondary stage of Q, or positing, more generally, a post-Easter reversion to the
apocalyptic ideas of John the Baptist.

Whatever the justice in these reconstructions, Matthew, understandably enough, did not share the modern aversion to hell. He was educated
into the first-century Jewish and Christian traditions, in both of which
the God of love is equally the God of judgment. Surely, then, if he could
talk with us, the evangelist would be unsympathetic with our contemporary queasiness about transcendent wrath and punishment. There is no

24. Cf. Hans Windisch, *The Meaning of the Sermon on the Mount* (Philadelphia: Westminster, 1951), p. 103.

25. E.g., Lily Dougall and Cyril W. Emmet, *The Lord of Thought: A Study of the Problems
Which Confronted Jesus Christ and the Solution He Offered* (London: SCM, 1922), and Percy
Dearmer, *The Legend of Hell: An Examination of the Idea of Everlasting Punishment, with a
Chapter on Apocalyptic* (London: Cassell & Co., 1929).

indication from first-century Jewish or Christian texts that anybody back then perceived divine love and judgment as necessary antitheses. Even in Marcion's theology, the good God does not prevent sinners from falling into the fire of this world's creator.[26]

From one point of view, I think that we too should reject setting up love and judgment as antagonists. When scholars pit these two themes against each other and then attribute them to different sources or to different communities or to different individuals, we should refuse assent. Some early Christians, including Matthew, did freely add sayings about judgment and hell to the Jesus tradition, but judgment and hell were there from the beginning. The contradiction, if that is what one wishes to call it, between the God of love and the God of wrath goes back to the beginning, to Jesus himself, and beyond him to the Jewish theology in which he was raised.[27]

From another point of view, I am a modern person whose religious sentiments leave him nonplussed as to how anyone could reconcile the image of a God who loves all with the image of a God who sends some to Gehenna forever. Yet I recognize that the difficulty is in the eye of the beholder; it belongs to my time and to my place and to my theology, not to Matthew's time or place or theology. Put otherwise, there is, from the Gospel's point of view, no theological contradiction in its portrait of God. To judge otherwise is, I believe, to be unimaginative and anachronistic, to fault an ancient for not being modern. One can of course choose at this point to disagree with Matthew and so deconstruct his Gospel. But such an exercise goes well beyond the competence of the historian and the literary critic and lands one in the realm of theology, which becomes another subject.

26. Adolf von Harnack, *Marcion: The Gospel of the Alien God* (Durham, N.C.: Labyrinth, 1990), pp. 90–91.

27. See Allison, "The Problem of Gehenna."

13

Slaughtered Infants

When King Baldad, in *T. Job* 37:3–4, asks the afflicted Job, who has been sitting on a dung heap for twenty years, "Who destroyed your goods or inflicted upon you these plagues?" the innocent and wise victim answers, without qualification, "God." This verdict has its antecedents in the Hebrew Scriptures, whose authors did not balk at the notion that evil as well as good can come from God:[1]

> See now that I, even I, am he; there is no god beside me. I kill and I make alive; I wound and I heal; and no one can deliver from my hand. (Deut. 32:39; cf. 1 Sam. 2:6–7)

> The LORD has put a lying spirit in the mouth of all these your prophets; the LORD has decreed disaster for you. (1 Kings 22:23; cf. 2 Chron. 18:21–22)

> Shall we receive the good at the hand of God, and not receive the bad? (Job 2:10)

> I form light and create darkness, I make weal and create woe; I the LORD do all these things. (Isa. 45:7)

1. But for caution regarding the apparent meaning of the following texts in their original literary contexts see Fredrik Lindström, *God and the Origin of Evil: A Contextual Analysis of Alleged Monistic Evidence in the Old Testament* (ConB OT 21; Lund: CWK Gleerup, 1983).

I have watched over them to pluck up and break down, to overthrow, destroy, and bring evil. (Jer. 31:28)

Is it not from the mouth of the Most High that good and bad come? (Lam. 3:38)

I gave them statutes that were not good and ordinances by which they could not live. I defiled them through their very gifts . . . in order that I might horrify them. (Ezek. 20:25–26)

Is a trumpet blown in a city, and the people are not afraid? Does disaster [evil] befall a city, unless the LORD has done it? (Amos 3:6)[2]

Separating God from Evil

Despite passages such as these, there was a tendency in some postexilic circles—a tendency with two very different outcomes in Marcion and Augustine—to dissociate God from all evil. Many came to doubt instinctively that the Almighty makes woe as well as weal, that evil as well as good comes from God's mouth. Already 1 Chron. 21:1 transfers to Satan an act perhaps thought unworthy of the deity even though 2 Sam. 24:1 makes God the instigator.[3] In like manner, *Jub*. 17:16, in the teeth of Gen. 22:2, where God orders Abraham to sacrifice Isaac, makes the slaughter of a child Mastema's idea. The sentiment behind these revisionist narratives is related to what Philo says in *Det*. 122: "For Moses does not, as some impious people do, say that God is the author of ills. No, he says that 'our own hands' cause them."[4] Similar sentiments appear in

2. Also relevant is Exod.11:10 ("the Lord hardened Pharaoh's heart"; cf. Rom. 9:18; 11:8, 10) and those texts in which God tempts human beings: Gen. 22:1; Exod.16:4; 20:20; Deut. 13:3; Ps. 26:2; Jth. 8:25; Wisd. 3:5; 4Q378 frag. 6 ii; 4QMysteries[a] frag. 3a ii–b 14. Recall also 1QS 3:25 (God "created the spirits of Light and Darkness") and the rabbinic texts according to which "God created the evil inclination" (יצר הרע, *b. B. Bat*. 16a) and implanted it in human hearts; see Frank Chamberlin Porter, "The Yeçer Hara: A Study in the Jewish Doctrine of Sin," in *Biblical and Semitic Studies: Critical and Historical Essays by the Members of the Semitic and Biblical Faculty of Yale University* (New York: Scribner, 1902), pp. 93–156.

3. On the problem of the Chronicler's motivation here see C. Breytenbach and P. L. Day, "Satan," in *DDD*, pp. 729–30. One might find a similar phenomenon in Job if one were to follow the critics who have judged the parts concerning Satan in the prologue (1:6–12; 2:1–7) to be secondary.

4. Cf. Philo, *Conf*. 161 ("There are many who, wishing to shirk all charges to which they are liable and claiming to escape the penalties of their misdeeds, ascribe the guilty responsibility, which really belongs to themselves, to God, who is the cause of nothing evil, but of all that is good"); idem, *Fuga* 79–80 ("It is not right to say that any secret wrongs committed with secret hostility . . . are done as God ordains; they are done as we ordain"); and *Opif*. 75 ("When man orders his course aright, when his thoughts and deeds are blameless, God the universal ruler may

the New Testament, in James 1:13 ("No one, when tempted, should say 'I am being tempted by God.' For God cannot be tempted by evil and he himself tempts no one") and 1 John 2:16 ("For all that is in the world—the desire of the flesh, the desire of the eyes, the pride in riches—comes not from the Father but from the world").

By the turn of the era, many Jews, under the influence of Hellenistic thought, had come to understand the traditional motif of God's goodness[5] to require God's isolation from evil of any sort. The following texts, which constitute a collective antithesis to the Jewish texts just quoted above, illustrate an important strand of Greco-Roman theology:

[Zeus:] My word, how mortals take the gods to task! / All their afflictions come from us, we hear. / And what of their own failings? Greed and folly / double the suffering in the lot of man. (Homer, *Od.* 1:32–34)[6]

Of the good things God and no other must be described as the cause, but of the evil things we must look for many different causes, only not God. (Plato, *Rep.* 379C)

To call God a cause of evil to anyone, being good himself, is a falsehood to be fought tooth and nail. (Ibid. 380B)

No destiny shall cast lots for you, but you shall all choose your own destiny. . . . The blame is for the chooser; God is blameless. (Ibid. 617E)

The divine and blessed being has no trouble himself and brings no trouble to others. (Epicurus, in Oecumenius, *Cath. ep.* ad Jas. 1:13 [PG 119.464A])

[The reason that governs the universe] has no malice, nor does it do evil to anything, nor is anything harmed by it. (Marcus Aurelius, *Med.* 6.1.1)

Consider God the cause of all you do well. God is not the cause of evil. (Sextus, *Sent.* 113–14)

Consider nothing that is evil as belonging to God. (Ibid. 440)

---

be owned as their source; while others from the number of his subordinates are held responsible for thoughts and deeds of a contrary sort, for it could not be that the Father should be the cause of an evil thing to his offspring").

5. See 1 Chron. 16:34; Ps. 145:9; Philo, *Decal.* 176; Mark 10:18; *m. Ber.* 9:2; etc.

6. *Homer: The Odyssey* (trans. R. Fitzgerald; Garden City, N.Y.: Doubleday, 1961), p. 14. Cf. Euripides, *Tr.* 914–1032: Helen's attempt to blame the gods for everything is followed by Hecabe's extended rebuttal.

Do not think that God caused the terrible things that have befallen you. For God is completely free of evil. For he who orders others to flee evil would never cause evil to someone. (Ps.-Libanius, *Ep. char.* 78)

The drift of these texts is plain, and given the hellenization of early Judaism, one is hardly astonished at the eventual unease of many Jews, although certainly not all, with the old thought that God dispatches evil as well as good.

The evangelist Matthew shared their unease. This follows from examination of his so-called formula quotations. A full ten times Matthew's narrative stops in order to offer editorial commentary drawn from the Old Testament (1:22–23; 2:15, 17–18, 23; 4:14–16; 8:17; 12:17–21; 13:35; 21:5; 27:9–10). The formula introducing each formal citation is this: "in order to fulfill the word (of the Lord) through the prophet saying":

> ἵνα/ὅπως (τότε: 2:17; 27:9)
>> + πληρωθῇ (ἐπληρώθη: 2:17; 27:9)
>>> + τὸ ῥηθέν
>>>> + (ὑπὸ κυρίου: 1:22; 2:15)
>>>>> + διά
>>>>>> + (Ἰερεμίου: 2:17; 27:9; Ἠσαΐου: 4:14; 8:17; 12:17)
>>>>>>> + τοῦ προφήτου (τῶν προφητῶν: 2:23)
>>>>>>>> + λέγοντος (lacking: 2:23)
>>>>>>>>> + biblical quotation

For our purposes the significant variation occurs in 2:17 and 27:9. In these two places we see Matthew wanting to distance his good God from evil in the world. When he introduces the scriptural proof texts for the slaughter of the infants in Bethlehem and for the tragedy of Judas's betrayal and suicide, he uses the temporal τότε (then) instead of the purposive ἵνα (in order that) or ὅπως (so that). The dual deviation from the usual form betrays a theological conviction. For in both places the subject is tragic death, and the evangelist, by replacing ἵνα or ὅπως with τότε, refrains from directly attributing such tragedy—as opposed to what he elsewhere clearly understands as the just punishment of the wicked[7]—to the hand of God.[8] Culpability, in Matt. 2 and 27, lies, it

7. See 7:21–23; 10:33; 11:20–24; 12:32; 13:36–43; 25:31–46; etc. Whatever we ourselves may think of the matter, Matthew seems to believe that the punishment of the wicked will be good, not evil.

8. Cf. M. Eugene Boring, "The Gospel of Matthew," in *The New Interpreter's Bible* (Nashville: Abingdon, 1995), 8:500; Ulrich Luz, *Das Evangelium nach Matthäus* (4 vols.; EKK 1/1–4; Düsseldorf: Benziger, 1990–2002), 1:185; 4:240; Paul Schanz, *Die Composition des Matthäus-*

appears, with Herod, who takes the lives of others, and with Judas, who takes his own life. Our Gospel, then, implicitly draws a distinction between what God foresees, permissively wills, and records in Scripture on the one hand, and what God actively wills and ensures will come to pass on the other. Matthew's God is the good father who gives good gifts to his children (7:7–11), not a transmoral being who determined, from the foundation of the world, that infants should be slaughtered and that Jesus' betrayer should take his own life, and then caused those events to be written down before the fact, after which he brought it all to pass. In short, 2:17 and 27:9 belong with those postexilic texts that refrain from making God do evil things.

The Problem of Evil

If one declines to ascribe evil to the deity, the confounding question arises, Where then does evil come from, and how can our good God permit it?[9] This is of course the theistic problem of evil, which philosophers and theologians continue to discuss because they have never successfully solved it: all the theological artillery brought to bear upon the quandary has left it standing.[10] Now our Gospel is no philosophical treatise, and nowhere does it explicitly treat this vexing question. One need not, however, be a philosopher to sense the problem of evil. Nor does it take a philosopher to conjure possible answers. Matthew's Gospel is proof enough, even though it concerns itself with the suffering of the righteous in particular, not with the suffering of the world in general. If one reads through it carefully while keeping the issue of theodicy in mind, several well-known strategies become apparent. More specifically, and as the following pages document, Matthew deploys variations of at least five common responses to the problem of evil.

The devil and evil spirits. It is inevitable, if one believes in malicious spirits, to think of them as the cause of many unfortunate circumstances. The New Testament, following Jewish precedent, offers plenty of evidence. Luke 13:16, for instance, attributes a woman's physical deformity to

---

Evangeliums (Tübingen: Ludwig Friedrich Fues, 1877), p. 111; George M. Soares Prabhu, *The Formula Quotations in the Infancy Narrative of Matthew* (AnBib 63; Rome: Biblical Institute, 1976), pp. 50–51; etc.

9. For a survey of Jewish responses from near Matthew's time see Alden Lloyd Thompson, *Responsibility for Evil in the Theodicy of IV Ezra* (SBLDS 29; Missoula, Mont.: Scholars Press, 1977), pp. 20–66.

10. For a helpful and sobering survey of the most recent discussion see Derk Pereboom, "The Problem of Evil," in *The Blackwell Guide to the Philosophy of Religion* (ed. William E. Mann; Malden, Mass.: Blackwell, 2005), pp. 148–70.

Satan's mischief: "And ought not this woman, a daughter of Abraham whom Satan bound for eighteen long years, be set free from this bondage on the sabbath day?"[11] Paul, in 2 Cor. 12:7, characterizes the thorn in his flesh as "a messenger of Satan to torment me." Whatever the nature of that "thorn," the apostle personifies its cause as an evil spirit.

Matthew likewise thinks of the devil and his minions when he thinks of evil. Documentation hardly seems necessary. The presupposition of Jesus' many exorcisms is that Satan and demons are the immediate causes of various illnesses.[12] Wicked spirits are also sources of temptation to disobey God[13]—so much so that, in Jesus' model prayer, the final Greek words may mean, "Deliver us from the evil one."[14] Everywhere Matthew assumes that evils assault human beings because invisible powers, full of malice, oppress the human race.

The evangelist's most obvious use of the devil (about whom he offers no theoretical reflection) as an explanatory category occurs in chapter 13, which brings together several parables. The collection immediately follows the large narrative section in chapters 11–12 and should be interpreted accordingly. Those chapters record Israel's response to what Jesus has said (chapters 5–7), to what he has done (chapters 8–9), and to what his disciples, in imitation of him, have said and done (chapter 10). Most of that response is negative: there is much unbelief. This is the setting for chapter 13, which is largely an attempt, reminiscent of Rom. 9–11, to explain why the Messiah has, against all scripturally based expectation, met such a poor, even hostile reception. How can it be that people have deemed him to be a glutton and a drunkard (11:16–19), have accused him of breaking Torah (12:1–14), have attributed his deeds to the devil (12:22–32)?

An answer of sorts appears in the parable of the weeds (13:24–30), which is missing from the other canonical gospels. I need not quote it nor its interpretation in full (13:31–43), only observe that, according to 13:38–39, "the weeds are the children of the evil one, and the enemy who sowed them is the devil." Here the dilemma of a rejected Messiah is partly explained by the devil. He shares responsibility for the apparent failure of God's word. We have here the same appeal as in 2 Cor. 4:4: "In their case the god of this world has blinded the minds of the unbelievers, to

11. Cf. Acts 10:38: "God anointed Jesus of Nazareth with the Holy Spirit and with power . . . he went about doing good and healing all who were oppressed by the devil, for God was with him."

12. Matt. 4:24; 8:16, 28–34; 9:32–33; 10:8; 17:14–20.

13. Matt. 4:1–11; cf. 1 Cor. 7:5; 1 Thess. 3:5; Rev. 2:10.

14. ῥῦσαι ἡμᾶς ἀπὸ τοῦ πονηροῦ. Whether this refers to "the evil one" (so Eastern church tradition) or to "evil" in general (so most Western church tradition, with Tertullian, Calvin, and Reformed commentators, including Barth, being exceptions) is impossible to decide.

keep them from seeing the light of the gospel of the glory of Christ, who is the image of God." The devil explains why some people have missed the truth; that is, he is a source of epistemological as well as physiological calamity.[15] One recalls Rev. 12:9, where the "ancient serpent, who is called the devil and Satan," is "the deceiver of the whole world."

Matthew 13:24–30 and 36–43 are not the only verses in which Matthew calls upon the devil to explain the world's unbelief and hostility. In the parable of the sower (13:3–8) and its interpretation (13:18–23), there are four paradigmatic responses to Jesus (cf. Mark 4:3–9, 13–20). When the sower sows the word, some understand (vv. 8, 23). Others lose out because of the cares of the world and the lure of wealth (vv. 7, 22). Still others believe but fail to endure (vv. 5–6, 20–21). And then there are those who never understand at all, the reason being that the devil interferes with their perception: "When anyone hears the word of the kingdom and does not understand it, the evil one comes and snatches away what is sown in the heart; this is what was sown on the path" (v. 19, commenting on v. 4). On the hypothesis of Markan priority, Matthew has added "and does not understand it" (contrast Mark 4:15). This underlines that the devil is an epistemological problem; his activity explains why some fail to see the truth.

Free will. Matthew, however, is too sophisticated to have nothing more to say about sin and suffering than that the devil is behind much of both. We see this above all in the parable of the sower (13:3–8). Like the parable of the weeds, it too wrestles with the circumstance, peculiar because against all Jewish expectation, that the Messiah encounters not enthusiastic welcome but rampant opposition. In attacking the problem, 13:3–8 + 18–23 assigns some role, as just observed, to the devil. But the parable does not content itself with that: the devil is not the sole source of human failure. Whereas he blinds some, others stumble because of the cares of the world, or because of wealth and various troubles (13:20–22). Our parable says, in effect, Do not blame Jesus for the mixed response to his message. Think rather that his gospel does not compel belief or force people to do the right thing against their wills. Opportunity does not guarantee response; proclamation does not abolish sin.

That individuals are free to accept or reject what they hear is the main message of Matt. 13:1–23, which in effect offers something like the free-will defense for the problem of evil. The root of Israel's trouble lies not with God but instead with people who are free to harden their hearts. Confronted with the choice between good and evil is "the conscience

---

15. Cf. also *T. Jud.* 19:4 ("the prince of error blinded me"); *T. Sim.* 2:7 ("the prince of error blinded my mind"); Acts 26:18 ("to open their eyes so that they may turn from darkness to light and from the power of Satan to God").

of the mind which inclines as it will" (*T. Jud.* 20:1–2). In other words, Matthew 13:3–8 + 18–23 appeals to human decision and so emphasizes the mystery of human responsibility. The verses assume that "our works are in the choosing and power of our souls, to do right and wrong in the works of our hand" (*Ps. Sol.* 9:4); they imply that "lawlessness was not sent upon the earth; but men created it by themselves" (*1 En.* 98:4);[16] or, as *2 Bar.* 54:19 so memorably puts it: "Each of us has become our own Adam." From one point of view, the parable of the sower complements what Philo says in *Deus* 47: "The human being, possessed of a spontaneous and self-determined will, whose activities for the most part rest on deliberate choice, is with reason blamed for what he does wrong with intent."[17]

Eschatological vindication. But the devil and free will are not enough for Matthew. He shares the eschatological faith of many ancient Jews, a faith that was a way of maintaining belief in God's goodness and justice despite the agonies and unfairness of this world, a way of believing "that even a mortal life of disprivilege can have meaning and value."[18] The Beatitudes in 5:3–12, for example, do not bless disciples because of their present circumstances. The followers of Jesus are rather, as the future tenses reveal, blessed because of what awaits them after death or in the future messianic kingdom. This is not common sense or wisdom born of experience—that the meek will inherit the earth is, apart from divine intervention turning the world upside down, utter nonsense—but an eschatological assurance that posits God doing the unprecedented: evil will come to an end in the kingdom of God.

In so far as the promises connected with the kingdom bring consolation, they serve as a practical theodicy. Although the Beatitudes hardly explain evil or human suffering, they do lessen anguish and doubt by putting misfortune into perspective. This happens through an exercise of the imagination. Matt. 5:3–12 avows that all is not what it seems to be. Only the future will make amends and bring to light the true condition of the world and those in it. So the Beatitudes offer reprieve by generating hope and eclipsing the present. This is the eschatological solution to

16. Cf. *1 En.* 98:5 (Gk.): "Neither was lawlessness given from above but because of transgression." For comment see George W. E. Nickelsburg, *1 Enoch 1: A Commentary on the Book of 1 Enoch, Chapters 1–36; 81–108* (Hermeneia; Minneapolis: Fortress, 2001), pp. 476–77.

17. Cf. Philo, *Fuga* 79–80 ("The treasuries of evil things are in ourselves; with God are those of good things only"); *Dec.* 142(28) (while passions "seem to be involuntary, an extraneous visitation, an assault from outside, desire alone originates with ourselves and is voluntary"); and Chrysostom, *Hom. Matt.* 59.3 (PG 58.576: "From where do evils come? From willing and not willing. But the very thing of our willing and not willing, from where is it? From ourselves").

18. Byron R. McCane, *Roll Back the Stone: Death and Burial in the World of Jesus* (Harrisburg, Pa.: Trinity Press International, 2003), p. 137.

the problem of evil, according to which it is the final outcome that will determine the meaning of what has gone before, the issue of things that will put all in perspective, the conclusion that will tell the whole story.

The eschatological response to evil is particularly prominent in Matt. 10:26–31. This views the present moment as nothing more than a point on the great time line of history, a point traversed on the way to the end: "Nothing is covered up that will not be uncovered" (10:26). From this follows the imperative, "Do not fear those who kill the body but cannot kill the soul; rather fear him who can destroy both soul and body in Gehenna." One should not pass judgment on either God or the meaning of the current situation without taking into account the eschatological future. The present may have an air of finality, above all when, as happens not only to the infants of Bethlehem but to Jesus himself, innocents die at the hands of evildoers. But the present is always being swallowed up by the future, and someday all presents will be caught up in the eternal kingdom of God. The fate of Jesus himself is the great proleptic illustration, because in his own person the eschatological pattern of tribulation followed by vindication manifests itself.

Human ignorance. Eschatology, however, still leaves acute questions. Why, for instance, should there be evil in the first place? And why does Providence remain so tardy in exorcizing it forever? Matthew, moreover, enlarges the difficulties by reproducing, in 10:29 and 31, a saying shared with Luke 12:6–7: "Are not two sparrows sold for a penny? Yet not one of them will fall to the ground apart from your Father.[19] . . . So do not be afraid; you are of more value than many sparrows" (10:29–31).[20] These words intend to offer, by means of an argument *a fortiori*, consolation: God is sovereign, so whatever happens must somehow accord with God's will. This disallows the false supposition that God's will belongs only to the future, as 10:26–28[21] taken alone might be wrongly taken to imply. The heavenly Father is not just the guarantor of the fantastic dream that is the eschatological future but also the sovereign Lord of the present age of ills. And yet this bold assertion of God's sovereignty seems not just to fly in the face of human experience but also to contradict the immediate literary context, where the sparrow falls (v. 29) and the innocent mis-

---

19. ἄνευ τοῦ πατρὸς ὑμῶν means, as the RSV translates, "without your Father's will." Cf. the addition of *voluntate* in Irenaeus, *Adv. haer.* 2.26.2 (SC 294, ed. Rousseau and Doutreleau, p. 260), and of τῆς βουλῆς in *Ps.-Clem. Hom.* 12.31 (GCS 42, ed. Rehm, p. 190).

20. The reference to "many sparrows" is odd. One expects something like "you are of much more value than sparrows." Julius Wellhausen, *Das Evangelium Matthaei* (Berlin: Georg Reimer, 1904), p. 49, argued for a mistranslation from the Aramaic: סגיא could have been taken either with sparrows ("many sparrows") or with the verb ("you are of much more value").

21. "Nothing is hidden that will not be uncovered"; "fear him who can destroy both body and soul in Gehenna."

sionary is martyred (v. 28). How can our text affirm that God's will is done even now? The answer lies in 10:30: "And even the hairs of your head are all counted."[22]

The commentators historically show great partiality to the notion that this verse affirms God's providential care.[23] This defective interpretation, at least in the modern literature, typically compares the promise, found more than once in both Testaments and applied to various individuals, that God will not permit a single hair of their heads to fall to the ground.[24] This conventional promise, however, invariably (1) concerns "a" hair or "one" hair and (2) asserts that no harm will come to it. Neither element appears in Matt. 10:30, which is about hairs (in the plural: τρίχες) being counted (ἠριθμημέναι), not being cared for or rescued.[25] Whereas, moreover, the declaration that God will not allow a single hair to suffer harm is a pledge of deliverance from physical evil, with which one may compare Dan. 3:27 ("the hair of their heads was not singed"), our saying can mean nothing of the sort. Disciples do not, in Matt. 10:26–31, escape danger.[26]

What then can Matt. 10:30 mean? Exegetes have gone astray by reading verse 30 as though it were just a poetic variant of verse 29 ("Are

22. What follows draws upon my discussion *The Jesus Tradition in Q* (Harrisburg, Pa.: Trinity Press International, 1997), pp. 168–75. For similar conclusions see also now Warren Carter, *Matthew and the Margins: A Sociopolitical and Religious Reading* (Maryknoll, N.Y.: Orbis, 2000), p. 241; Larry Chouinard, *The College Press NIV Commentary: Matthew* (Joplin, Mo.: College Press, 1997), p. 194; and David E. Garland, *Reading Matthew: A Literary and Theological Commentary on the First Gospel* (London: SPCK, 1993), pp. 117–18.

23. Cf. Novatian, *Trin.* 8.6(43) (Fuentes Patrísticas 8, ed. Granado, pp. 108–110); Matthew Poole, *Annotations on the Holy Bible* (3 vols.; London: Henry G. Bohn, 1846), 3:46; Luz, *Matthäus*, 2:128; A. H. McNeile, *The Gospel according to St. Matthew* (London: Macmillan, 1915), p. 146; John P. Meier, *Matthew* (NTM 3; Wilmington, Del.: Michael Glazier, 1980), p. 112; etc.

24. See 1 Sam. 14:45; 2 Sam. 14:11; 1 Kings 1:52; Luke 21:18; Acts 27:34. These texts, which are in the margin of the Nestle-Aland editions of the Greek New Testament, appear to be missing from the pre-Reformation commentaries, including the great intertextual commentary of Albert the Great. They are also not yet in Grotius.

25. Cf. Dieter Zeller, *Die weisheitlichen Mahnsprüche bei den Synoptikern* (FzB 17; Würzburg: Echter, 1977), p. 100, n. 340, who also recognizes that 1 Sam. 14:45 and its relatives can have little to do with Matt. 10:30. It is not even clear, one should perhaps add, that Matt. 10:30 is especially true of the saints, as though God might not know the number of hairs on the heads of others. But Origen, *Prin.* 4.3.12 (TzF 24, ed. Marcovich, p. 768), and many after him have confined the application to a special class of people. Origen, *Herac.* 22 (SC 67, ed. Scherer, p. 98), even speaks in this connection of spiritual Nazarites.

26. This is why Tertullian, *Res.* 35 (ed. Evans, p. 98), can use Matt. 10:30 to argue for the resurrection of the dead: hairs will not be lost ultimately because God will return them at the consummation. For later discussions of this implausible interpretation see Jerome, *Comm. Matt.* ad loc. (SC 259, ed. Bonnard, p. 206), and Paschasius Radbertus, *Exp. Matt. Libri XII* ad loc. (CCCM 56, ed. Paulus, pp. 608–9).

not two sparrows sold for a penny? Yet not one of them will fall to the ground apart from your Father"). Verse 29 is about God's will, verse 30 about God's knowledge. πᾶσαι ἠριθμημέναι εἰσίν is, as has always been recognized, a divine passive: "(your hairs) are all counted (by God)."[27] The verse then refers to hairs in a way reminiscent of other texts that refer to the stars[28] or to the sands of the sea,[29] namely, in order to stress God's knowledge or human ignorance.[30] As I read the facts, then, two sets of comparative texts are relevant: those in which the hairs on a human head, like the stars and the sands of the sea, represent an overwhelmingly large number, usually beyond human reckoning,[31] and those in which God can count what human beings cannot count.[32] Particularly interesting for

27. Cf. *Ps.-Clem. Hom.* 12.31 (GCS 42, ed. Rehm, p. 190: "numbered by God"); Tertullian, *Scorp.* 9 (CSEL 20, ed. Reifferscheid and Wissowa, p. 164: "the number of our hairs has been recorded before him"); Origen, *C. Cels.* 8.70 (ed. Marcovich, p. 587: "numbered by him"); Chrysostom, *Hom. Matt.* 34.2 (PG 58.401: "God numbers the hairs"); Theodoret of Cyrus, *Cant.* (PG 81.172C: "the hairs have been numbered by the Father"); Theophylact, *Hom. Matt.* ad loc. (PG 123.243A: "our hairs are numbered by him").

28. Gen. 15:5 (cf. *T. Abr.* Rec. Lng. 1:5; 4:11; 8:5); *1 En.* 93:14; Philo, *Her.* 88; Josephus, *Ant.* 4.116; *Apoc. Abr.* 20:2–3; *Gk. Apoc. Ezra* 2:32; etc. Cf. Ps. 147:4, which Origen, *Hom. Num.* 1.1.4 (SC 415, ed. Doutreleau, pp. 34–36), links to Matt. 10:30: only God "determines the number of the stars."

29. For "the sands of the sea" as representing a multitude beyond human counting see Gen. 22:17; 32:12; 41:49; Josh. 11:4; 2 Sam. 17:11; Isa. 10:22; Jer. 33:22; Hos. 1:10; Sir. 1:2; Rev. 20:8; *T. Abr.* Rec. Lng. 1:5; 4:11; 8:5; *Gk. Apoc. Ezra* 3:2; etc.

30. Cf. the discussions in Irenaeus, *Adv. haer.* 2.26.2 and 2.28.9 (SC 294, ed. Rousseau and Doutreleau, pp. 258–60, 290), where Matt. 10:30 is appropriately used to put human beings in their place by illustrating the difference between what God knows and what human beings know.

31. E.g., Ps. 40:12; 69:4; Irenaeus, *Adv. haer.* 2.28.9 (SC 294, ed. Rousseau and Doutreleau, p. 290: let "Valentinus or Ptolemaeus or Basilides or any other of those who maintain that they have searched out the deep things of God" first demonstrate that he has knowledge about this easier-to-understand world, including "the number of hairs on his own head"); Eusebius, *Comm. Ps.* (PG 23.961C: "as hairs uncountable"); Gregory of Nyssa, *Adv. Apol.* (Opera 3.2, ed. Mueller, p. 142: counting one's hairs passes a person's knowledge); idem, *Infant.* (Opera 3.2, ed. Hörner, p. 68.23: "as numerous perhaps as the hairs on the head"). Note also that in Matt. 5:36, a reference to human hair underlines human inability.

32. In addition to the texts cited in notes 28–31 see Job 38:37 ("Who has the wisdom to number the clouds?"); *4 Ezra* 4:7 ("How many dwellings are in the heart of the sea, or how many streams are at the source of the deep, or how many streams are above the firmament?"); 5:36–37 ("Count up for me those who have not yet come, and gather for me the scattered raindrops . . . and then I will explain to you the travail that you ask to understand"); *Gk. Apoc. Ezra* 4:2–4 ("And God said, 'Count the flowers of the earth. If you can count them you also will be able to argue the case with me.' And the prophet said, 'Lord, I cannot count them—I bear human flesh.'"); *Apoc. Sedr.* 8:7 ("Since heaven and earth were created how many trees have been made in the world, and how many shall fall and how many shall be made, and how many leaves do they have?"); 8:8 ("Since I [God] made the sea how many waves have billowed, and how many have rolled slightly, and how many will arise, and how many winds blow near the shore of the sea?"); 8:9 ("Since the creation of the world . . . how many drops have fallen upon

comparison is *Apoc. Sedr.* 8:6: "Since I created everything, how many people have been born, and how many have died and how many shall die, and how many hairs do they have?"

In Job 38:37; *4 Ezra* 4:7; and *Apoc. Sedr.* 8:6–9, notices of God's ability to count what human beings cannot number appear in contexts concerned with the suffering of the righteous. This is altogether natural. The stumbling block set by innocent affliction and by the superfluity of the world's ills has no rational solution, and it may cause one to doubt God's goodness, power, or even existence. One response, however, is to affirm that human understanding has definite limits and that God and the world are truly mysterious. On the face of it, a loving and just Providence seems to have abdicated when the saints are compassed about by unmerited woe. But, as the angel of *4 Ezra* 4:10–11 declares, "You cannot understand the things with which you have grown up; how then can your mind comprehend the way of the Most High?" Human ignorance before the mystery of God invites a discreet and humble silence. "My thoughts are not your thoughts" (Isa. 55:8).

Seen in this light, Matt. 10:30 is not a bogus promise of some kind of protection or care but is instead a compressed attempt to offer consolation by intimating that human reason has its limits. The saying reminds readers that, while the misfortune of the disciples may make no sense, especially when, as in Matt. 10:29, God's providential will is affirmed, comfort may nonetheless be found in this, that God knows what human beings do not know. If one cannot even know the number of concrete hairs on one's own mundane head, then, arguing from the lesser to the greater, maybe evil too is beyond our comprehension. Afflictions may abscond with rhyme and reason, but human rhyme and reason cannot assess everything. Matthew, in its intellectual modesty before the mystery of suffering, has in it a bit of the book of Job. Like John 9:2–3, where John's Jesus refuses to attribute blindness to this or that sin, it does not pretend to know everything.

Theological ignorance comes to the fore two other places in Matthew. Both have to do with the limitations of Jesus himself. First, in 24:36, Jesus declares that, regarding the time of the end, only the Father knows. The Son, like the angels, does not know. This profession of eschatological agnosticism has nothing to do with suffering or persecution. Its purpose is rather to summon vigilance: one must be prepared for what may occur

---

the world and how many shall fall?"); *b. Sanh.* 39a ("Some say the Emperor spoke thus to him [Rabban Gamaliel]: 'The number of the stars is known to me.' Thereupon Rabban Gamaliel asked him, 'How many molars and (other) teeth have you?' Putting his hand in his mouth, he began to count them. Said he to him: 'You know not what is in your mouth and yet wouldst know what is in heaven!'"). Cf. *2 Bar.* 21:8: only God "causes the rain to fall on earth with a specific number of raindrops."

at any time. There is, however, a second place where Jesus does not know everything, and the occasion is his martyrdom, which in Matthew foreshadows the martyrdom of others.[33] When Jesus comes to his end, he cries out to the inscrutable divine silence the opening words of Ps. 22: "My God, my God, why have you forsaken me?" (27:46). Christian sensibility has sometimes been reluctant to characterize this line as a shout of dereliction. Some have suggested that citation of the first verse of Ps. 22 implies the content of the following verses; and as Ps. 22 moves from complaint to faith and praise, Jesus' words imply the same.[34] This interpretation, however, blunts the force of our verse, which is the culmination of a Matthean theme. Jesus' own family abandons him (13:54–58). Then his disciples abandon him (26:56, 69–75). Then the crowds abandon him (27:15–26). The climax of this progressive desertion is the experience, following three hours of supernatural darkness and divine silence, of felt abandonment by God, who is here no longer addressed as "Father." Now Jesus is clearly not repudiating God, who is still "my God." Certainly the soldiers who soon confess him to be God's Son have witnessed no such repudiation. But Jesus does scream out his pain in a circumstance, unprecedented in the narrative, in which God unaccountably does not seem to be God. In the depths of his torture, the Son loses intimacy with his Father in heaven; he cannot find the meaning of things. Evil has overcome his understanding. There is no sense to be had.

Given the parallels between Jesus and his disciples, which extend to the suffering of both, one may, if so inclined, generalize from Jesus' collapse: if even the Son has trouble interpreting what is happening to him, then surely others who have the same trouble need not find it ultimately debilitating. Beyond that, Jesus' inability, if only for a time, to make theological sense of his suffering and apparent failure, is followed by God's vindication of him. It follows that God's present inscrutability does not entail an unhappy conclusion.

Christological suffering. There is, I venture to suggest, one final way that Matthew's text attempts to come to terms with evil.[35] Like the appeals to eschatology and human ignorance, it is not rational but existential; that is, it comforts without explaining.

Matthew's Gospel portrays God's Son as a righteous and presumably sinless[36] individual who nonetheless suffers an assortment of miseries. He

---

33. For the parallels between the fate of Jesus and the fate of his disciples see pp. 222–25.

34. For a fascinating review of the history of interpretation see Luz, *Matthäus*, 4:335–42.

35. Perhaps I should note in passing that Matthew nowhere places blame for evil on Adam and Eve (contrast *4 Ezra* 7:48: "O Adam, what have you done? For though it was you who sinned, the fall was not yours alone, but ours also who are your descendants") or on the watchers of Gen. 6:1–4 (see esp. *1 En.* 1–36; 2 Pet. 2:4; Jude 6).

36. See the commentaries on 3:14–15.

has no place to lay his head (8:20). People maliciously revile him, unjustly accusing him of abandoning Moses to join Satan (10:25; 12:1–14, 24). Jesus is a lonely man whose closest friends, his surrogate family, do not understand him (16:5–12, 22–23; 26:51–54). When he asks some of them to keep him company in his darkest hour, they first fall asleep and then run away (26:36–46, 56). One of the twelve betrays him to sword-wielding enemies (26:47–56). Criminous authorities charge him with blasphemy, slap him, bind him, and hand him over to the pagan governor (26:57–68; 27:1–2). Roman soldiers mock, torture, and crucify him (27:27–44). He ends his life, to all appearances, a failure (27:46).

Jesus is literally sympathetic; that is, he suffers along with others. His identity as God's beloved Son (3:17; 11:25–30; 17:5) does not render him immune from agony or despair. He is, on the contrary, especially subject to misfortune and pain: in Matthew's story, Jesus suffers far more than anyone else. The savior is the innocent victim writ large. Now for those who believe in him, there is surely something reassuring in this. One recalls Heb. 4:14–15 and 5:8, where Jesus learns through suffering and so can sympathize with human weakness.[37] Suffering shared is more easily endured. And as in Hebrews, so in Matthew: the principle has become christological. It is not just that one does not suffer alone, but precisely that one suffers in the company of Jesus, God's Son.[38] This must mean that the divinity does not remain aloof from suffering, for God knows the Son (11:27) and the Son knows suffering. If the Son is a person of sorrows, acquainted with grief, his Father must be likewise beset by grief and sorrow. This does not, to be sure, do anything to unravel the mystery of iniquity. It does, however, put God on the side of the hapless Rachel weeping for her children,[39] and on the side of disciples tossed grievously to and fro by persecution. And perhaps that thought matters far more than any rational apologetic.[40]

37. I do not detect anywhere in Matthew, however, any educative theodicy; contrast Heb. 12:3–13 and Jas. 1:2–4. For this idea before Irenaeus see Barry D. Smith, *Paul's Seven Explanations of the Suffering of the Righteous* (Studies in Biblical Literature; New York: Peter Lang, 2002), pp. 157–74.

38. Cf. also Rom. 8:17: "we suffer with him."

39. I like the comment of Johann Albrecht Bengel, *Gnomon Novi Testamenti* (2 vols.; Tübingen: Ludov. Frid. Fues, 1850), on the ἠκούσθη (was heard) of Matt. 2:18: "So that it reached the Lord."

40. For a modern theological treatment that often brings out what is implicit in the Synoptics see Jürgen Moltmann, *The Crucified God: The Cross of Christ as the Foundation and Criticism of Christian Theology* (New York: Harper & Row, 1974).

Index of Names

Scripture Index